COMANCHE JACK STILWELL

COMANCHE
JACK STILWELL

ARMY SCOUT
AND PLAINSMAN

Clint E. Chambers
and
Paul H. Carlson

UNIVERSITY OF OKLAHOMA PRESS : NORMAN

This book is published with the generous assistance of
The Kerr Foundation, Inc.

Library of Congress Cataloging-in-Publication Data

Names: Chambers, Clint E., 1932– author. | Carlson, Paul Howard, author.
Title: Comanche Jack Stilwell : army scout and plainsman / Clint E. Chambers and
Paul H. Carlson.
Description: Norman : University of Oklahoma Press, [2019] | Includes bibliographical
references and index.
Identifiers: LCCN 2018038435 | ISBN 978-0-8061-6278-2 (pbk. ; alk. paper)
Subjects: LCSH: Stiwell, Jack, 1850–1903. | Scouts (Reconnaissance)—West (U.S.)—
Biography. | United States. Army—Biography. | Indians of North America—Wars—
1866–1895. | United States marshals—West (U.S.)—Biography. | Peace officers—West
(U.S.)—Biography. | Frontier and pioneer life—West (U.S.)
Classification: LCC F594.S84 C47 2019 | DDC 363.2092 [B] —dc23
LC record available at https://lccn.loc.gov/2018038435

The paper in this book meets the guidelines for permanence and durability of the Committee
on Production Guidelines for Book Longevity of the Council on Library Resources, Inc. ∞

This book is for our wives and lifelong partners,
Siva Chambers and Ellen Carlson,
whose perseverance, cooperation,
and encouragement have been unstinting.

CONTENTS

ILLUSTRATIONS

Figures

Maps

PREFACE

Simpson Everett "Jack" Stilwell is best remembered—when remembered at all—for his successful efforts in slipping through Indian lines on foot to get help for some fifty frontiersmen under siege in September 1868 at Beecher Island, in what is now far eastern Colorado. A scout for the U.S. Army, Stilwell was barely eighteen years old at the time. Part of a Kansas volunteer unit pursuing Indian warriors along the Arikaree Fork of the Republican River in northeastern Colorado, Stilwell and Pierre Trudeau, an older scout, stole away to find relief. The men traveled at night and hid during the day until they reached the help they sought at Fort Wallace in far western Kansas. The event was characteristic of Stilwell's courage and persistence.

Stilwell, however, was much more than a daring army scout. He worked as a Santa Fe teamster, a cowboy, a police officer, an unwilling hangman, a deputy federal marshal, a U.S. commissioner, a lawyer, a judge, and a commercial strawberry grower. In many ways he was a common man just trying to make a living. In other ways he was extraordinary: highly respected, courageous, independent, resourceful, intelligent, and fiercely loyal. But he died before his fifty-third birthday, physically broken by years spent in the saddle and exposure to winter's snow and freezing rain and summer's hot, unrelenting sun.

The primary aim of this book is to chart Stilwell's diverse career and bring the scattered experiences of his short life together in a readable, straightforward biography. However, he wrote little until near the end of his life, and few of his personal letters have been preserved. He left no journal, diary, or memoir.

He wrote no military reports. But through army records, census rolls, court testimony, and commentaries in newspapers and magazines by those who knew Stilwell, such as William F. "Buffalo Bill" Cody, we have been allowed some room for a balanced assessment.

A more personal reason for the book lies in family history: Jack Stilwell was the uncle of Daniel Clinton Cooley, the grandfather of author Clint Chambers. In the 1930s young Clint spent summer months on his grandfather's farm along the 98th meridian northwest of Chickasha, Oklahoma. In the evenings Grandfather Cooley sat on the farmhouse's front porch and told stories of his boyhood in Indian and Oklahoma Territories.

Many of the lively tales revolved around Cooley's uncle, Jack Stilwell, who often stopped by the family farm of his younger sister, Elizabeth Ann "Lizzy" Stilwell Cooley, near Dibble, west of Purcell, Oklahoma. One such story told how Jack made a wintertime visit when he was a deputy U.S. marshal patrolling Oklahoma Territory. Stilwell rode up on a large gray horse; he wore tall boots, a full-length buffalo coat, and a wide-brimmed hat; and he carried a Winchester rifle and a Colt revolver. After dinner that evening, Jack went to bed and slept nearly twenty-four hours, during which young Daniel Cooley and his brother Cliff fought to see who would feed, water, and care for Jack's big horse.

In the 1930s such oral tradition surrounding his colorful ancestor fired young Clint's imagination. As an adult, Clint, intent on finding the "real" Jack Stilwell, determined to track down every story he could. Such passion led him and his family into libraries, museums, archives, and government repositories from coast to coast. Nonetheless, the book is more than one man's tireless quest. Indeed, it is the product of a long collaboration between an Air Force surgeon and a university professor who were drawn together by their mutual interest in Native American studies and western history. For more than twenty years—across coffee tables, in college classrooms, and at historical association meetings—the authors chatted about Jack Stilwell and deliberated about his place in the history of the Great Plains and the American West. These discussions led, in part, to this book.

Many people have contributed to the creation of this work. At Texas Tech University's fine Southwest Collection/Special Collections Library, several friends and professional colleagues were generous with their aid, especially Tai Kreidler. Tai offered unstinting, prompt, and valued assistance with archival documents and photo collections. This group also includes Randy Vance and his staff in the collection's reading and research room, plus Jennifer Spurrier, Fredonia Paschal, Lynn Whitfield, and Connie Aquilar. Monte Monroe, the Southwest Collection archivist, provided major assistance. As editor of the *West Texas Historical Association Year Book* (now the *West Texas Historical Review*), Monte provided information and helped with proper citation forms. He also participated in many Stilwell discussions and offered ideas for additional research and review.

In Canyon, Texas, at the Panhandle Plains Historical Museum and Archives, Betty Bustos and Cesa Espinoza were similarly helpful. At the Fort Sill Museum in Oklahoma, Towana D. Spivey and Judy Crowder provided welcome assistance, as did Ramon Powers, Leslie Cade, and Katy Matthews at the Kansas Historical Society. Likewise, we received aid from Bill Welge, Kay Zahrai, and Delbert Amen at the Oklahoma Historical Society; from John R. Lovette, Bradford S. Koplowitz, Laura Carter, and Suzanne Schrems at the Western History Collection in the University of Oklahoma Library; from Mary L. Bond at the Oklahoma Collection in the University of Central Oklahoma Library; and from Maxine Kreutziger at the Kansas East Commission on Archives and History at Baker University.

At the National Archives in Washington, D.C., William E. Lind, Michael E. Pilgrim, William R. Ellis, Ann Cummings, DeAnne Blanton, Richard Fusik, Gary L. Morgan, Sue McDonough, and Robert W. Coren always provided apt and efficient help. At the National Archives Southwest Region in Fort Worth, Rodney Kraica and Margaret Hacker were also courteous and helpful.

Archivists and historians at several regional historical societies and research centers provided valuable information. They include Jennie Cook, Carmela Conning, Judy Davis, and Altamae Markham at the Park County Historical Society Archives in Cody, Wyoming; Elizabeth M. Holmes and Deb Adams at the Buffalo Bill Historical Center; Nancy Bartoo at the Historical Society of Western Pennsylvania in Pittsburg; Lori Davisson and Kim Frontz at the Arizona Historical Society; Ann K. Sindelar at the Western Reserve Historical Society in Cleveland; Mildred Wines at the Clay County Historical Society in Texas; and Leo Oliva at the Santa Fe Trail Association in Larned, Kansas. We got support from Laura A. Foster and Mark Vanbenschoten at the Frederic Remington Art Museum in Ogdensburg, New York; from Carolyn Barker, Joann Nitzel, and Jean Kyle at the Canadian County Genealogical Society in Oklahoma; from George Elmore at the Fort Larned National Historic Site; and most particularly from Mary L. Williams and Donna G. Smith at the Fort Davis National Historic Site in Texas.

Roy B. Young, Orvel Criqui, Mike Day, and Jim Dietrich shared their research with us. Susan Cooley Gabel and Monnette Dupue (Stilwell-Cooley family genealogists) were very helpful. Others who proved invaluable in our work included

Katherine Kelly and William Chalfant in Kansas; Thelma Love, John Stahl, and
Carrie Broyles in Oklahoma; Allen Best in New York; and David Murrah, James
Matthews, Kenneth Davis, and Jack Becker in Texas. Anonymous reviewers
improved the manuscript and strengthened our prose style, and Kent Calder
and the editorial team at the University of Oklahoma Press were extraordinary
and efficient with their help. To all of the above we are most grateful, as we are
to those whose names we inadvertently missed but who also provided ideas,
information, or assistance—although we alone accept responsibility for any
errors or faulty interpretations that may exist.

Most of all we are indebted to our wives, Siva Chambers and Ellen Carlson,
whose self-sacrifice during our research and writing proved enormously beneficial
and reassuring. They are good companions for traveling life's highways.

COMANCHE JACK STILWELL

Chapter 1

FAMILY BACKGROUND AND YOUTH

S impson Everett "Jack" Stilwell (1850–1903) was born into a family of sol-diers. "Starting with the founder of the family in [America], Lieut. Nicholas Stillwell," wrote John Stilwell in 1929, "and appearing in every generation of his descendants, there has occurred a striking love of military life."[1] Accordingly, Jack became a scout for the U.S. Army and served on the Great Plains and in the Southwest during the late nineteenth century. Tough and resourceful yet modest and reserved, he spoke Spanish and Numic (the Comanche language), understood the Plains Indian sign language, and knew thoroughly the topography and environment of the central and southern Great Plains.

Stilwell scouted for George Armstrong Custer during the famous winter campaign of 1868–69, and he knew well several of the leading military officers and entrepreneurs in the nineteenth-century American West. In his later years, he became a friend and aide to William F. "Buffalo Bill" Cody, and moved to northwestern Wyoming at Cody's urging. There he turned to farming and with his employees successfully raised large crops of strawberries. He married late in life and had no children.

The Stilwell family in America can trace their beginning to Nicholas Stillwell, who in 1638 emigrated from Dorking Parish near Guilford, Surrey County, England. After a brief stay in Virginia, in 1639 Nicholas and his family moved north to New Amsterdam (present-day New York City), which then was still part of the Dutch colony of New Netherlands. He established a tobacco plantation on Manhattan Island and purchased a house and lot on Beaver Street. Four years later he moved the family across the Hudson River to Gravesend (present-day Brooklyn) on Long Island. The little village in southwestern Kings County, settled by a number of English families, was something of a frontier community.[2]

Not long after he relocated, a local uprising led by a band of Lenape warriors caused Gravesend's temporary abandonment. Although Lieutenant Stilwell organized efforts to defend the community, many of the Anglo settlers fled across the Hudson River to New Amsterdam; shortly thereafter he left, too. Most of the evacuees returned within a week. Uprising averted, Stillwell returned to Gravesend, where he bought and sold land and in the 1650s served as a magistrate.

When a fleet of four English frigates sailed into the Hudson River in 1664 carrying troops intent on taking over the Dutch colony, Nicholas Stillwell stood among the very few Englishmen in New Netherlands who defended wooden-legged Peter Stuyvesant, the governor. Historian Teunis Bergem wrote that Stillwell "is entitled to credit for never swerving from his allegiance to the Dutch government, which is more than can be said of many of his English neighbors." The neighbors, Bergem wrote, consisted of "traitors to the colony to which they fled from persecution," and they had shifted their allegiance to England on "the first favorable opportunity."[3] Despite Stillwell's support, Stuyvesant capitulated to the English in 1664, and New Amsterdam was renamed New York. Years later, Nicholas moved to Dover on Staten Island, where he died in 1671.

Nicholas Stillwell's second son, also named Nicholas, was born in England in 1636 and came to America with his father and other members of the family. From 1643 he lived at Gravesend with his father, and like most immigrants in America, the younger Nicholas became a farmer. He also served as a justice of the peace, as a member of the Colonial Assembly for Kings County, and in 1689 at age fifty-three he became captain of Gravesend's militia. Four years later, as captain of a Kings County contingent of fifty men, he participated in an expedition against French soldiers and Indian warriors in New York during King William's War (1689–97), the first of the four great wars for empire between England and France. Nicholas married Catherine Morgan of Gravesend in 1671, and after her death he marred Elizabeth Corwin (or Cornell) in 1703.[4]

In 1685, just before the start of King William's War, Elias Stillwell was born. The fourth son of the younger Nicholas Stillwell, Elias grew up amid the war and its unsettled aftermath. As was often the case in the seventeenth and eighteenth centuries, he married young and more than once—three times in his case: Ann

Burbank of Staten Island (about 1706), Deborah Martling (1726), and Helen Van Name (1730). Like others in the large Stillwell family, Elias also moved his place of residence. He grew up on Staten Island, lived and farmed there, and married each of his wives there.[5] With his third wife, Helen Van Name, Elias left New York to settle in New Jersey. His sons Elias Jr., Richard, and Jeremiah moved to Pennsylvania.

In addition to military leanings, Stilwell family members enjoyed a restless character. Drawn by new opportunities or driven by a spirit of adventure, Stilwells shifted their place of residence with frequency and apparent ease, sometimes moving north or south—but most often west. Accordingly, Jeremiah Stillwell (Elias's fifth son) set out for fresh territory and new opportunities. He moved with his brothers (Elias Jr. and Richard) and others in the family to eastern Pennsylvania. Later Jeremiah moved to Virginia, where he married Rachel Reynolds, an Irish woman, at Fairfax, about fifteen miles southwest of present-day Washington, D.C. The couple relocated to Berkeley County (in what is now West Virginia) in 1775. By that time Jeremiah had become a minister in the Methodist Episcopal Church. The Virginia census of 1787 shows Jeremiah still in Berkeley County, but shortly afterward he and his family moved south and west, making their way through Virginia, North Carolina, Tennessee, and Kentucky. The family eventually settled in a place called Clark's Grant in southern Indiana.

Jeremiah and Rachel had several children, including Margaret, Charles, Thomas, Jacob, and Joseph Everett Stilwell, Jack Stilwell's grandfather (who dropped an *l* from the family name). Joseph was born in Virginia in 1788 and followed the family as it wandered westward. He and his brother Thomas settled in Lincoln County, Tennessee, and there about 1815 Joseph married Elizabeth Old.

In the early 1820s families from coastal states such as Virginia and the Carolinas and from mideastern states such as Tennessee began settling on American Indian lands in northern Alabama. The Stilwells joined the migration when Joseph and Thomas moved their families to Madison County, Alabama. Thomas had followed his father's vocation and became a Methodist minister—a circuit rider in his case. He rode for the Shoal Circuit.[6] Joseph became an election supervisor in 1824 for Hillsborough Township in the northwestern part of the county. The 1830 census shows both Joseph and Thomas, with their families, still living in Madison County.[7]

By 1833, however, both families had relocated to Brownstown Township in Jackson County, Indiana. One wonders if their move north of the Ohio River represents disapproval of slavery in Alabama or a desire to be closer to their brother, Charles Stilwell, and sister, Margaret Stilwell Tanner, who some year previous had moved to Indiana with their restless father, Jeremiah.

In north Brownstown Township, Joseph Everett Stilwell settled on a farm where he and his wife Elizabeth supported ten people.[8] Joseph, like his father and brother, became active in the local Methodist Church. He and Elizabeth established themselves as prominent members of a little church group that met at a place then called Pleasant Grove. At first they assembled weekly in someone's home, but eventually several area families, including the Stilwells, built an eighty-by-forty-foot building for their worship services. Pleasant Grove and Lanning Campground, which was nearby, became places to hold "camp meetings . . . where thousands of people would gather, and many souls were saved."[9] The Stilwells participated in the religious furor, or "camp meeting" phenomenon, part of the Great Awakening that swept the country in the 1840s.

Joseph and Elizabeth raised several sons, including Jacob Lurton (Jack's uncle) and William Henry, Jack's father. The couple's first son, Jacob Lurton, married Rhonda Shepard at Vallonia in Jackson County, Indiana, in 1846. Jacob operated a small farm in the area, and by 1850 he and Rhonda, age twenty-three, had three children. In the mid-1850s they relocated to Dallas County, Texas, where they lived for several years as Jacob farmed and raised a few cattle. Life in that slave-owning state, however, became increasingly difficult for these abolitionists, and they sometimes struggled with their proslavery neighbors.[10]

Jack's father, William Henry Stilwell, was born in Alabama about 1823 before the family's move north to Indiana. On October 3, 1849, he married Charlotte B. Winfrey (born ca. 1833) of Pleasant Run Township in Lawrence County, Indiana, which borders Jackson County on the west. The 1850 census for Lawrence County shows an entry for Wiley Winfrey, age sixty-five (born in Tennessee), and his wife Eleanor, age sixty-one (born in Maryland). They may have been Charlotte's grandparents.[11]

In characteristic Stilwell family tradition, William Henry and Charlotte moved west. In 1850 they lived in Iowa City, Iowa. Census reports for 1850 prove revealing. They suggest that on June 1 the Stilwell household included William Henry, age twenty-seven, a carpenter, born in Alabama; his wife, Charlotte, age seventeen; and Rachael L. Winfrey, age five, a young sister of Charlotte's. Simpson Everett Stilwell was born on August 18, 1850, at least two months after the census takers filed their report. Thus his name does not appear in the 1850 census for Iowa's Johnson County. Ten years later, the 1860 census for Douglas County, Kansas, gives Jack's birth year as 1850 and lists his birthplace as Iowa City.[12]

Despite the census reports, some confusion remains about Stilwell's birthplace. In his testimony for *United States vs. the State of Texas* at El Reno, Oklahoma Territory, on March 30, 1894, Jack testified that he was born on the frontier of Missouri and Kansas. "I was born right on the line," he said. "I think about fifty yards in Kansas, but it was before the lines were well defined." He emphasized, "I was born in the un-organized territory of Kansas."[13]

Three years later Jack changed his mind about his place of birth. In a deposition given to H. M. Burfield, special examiner for the commissioner of pensions, on August 19, 1897, at Anadarko (the site of the Kiowa, Comanche, and Apache reservation agency in Oklahoma Territory), he said, "I am the son of Wm. H. and Charlotte B. Stilwell, born in Iowa City, Iowa, August 18, 1850."[14] This statement seems to confirm the 1860 Douglas County, Kansas, census records.

In 1852, when Jack (called "Everett" by family members) was two years old, his mother Charlotte suffered a debilitating blow to her head. Apparently, while assisting her carpenter husband, Charlotte received a sharp blow on the head when a large board struck her. The injury did not affect her mind, but it impacted her sense of hearing. Without modern medicine to aid her recovery, Charlotte suffered a loss of balance as a result of the hearing impairment. Her niece, Lottie M. Williams, stated in 1897 that "as is frequently noticed in people who are deaf," who "both look and act differently from people whose sense of hearing is not impaired," so Charlotte showed that "some great affliction had left its mark upon her in its own indescribable manner."[15]

In the 1850s William Stilwell moved often, probably seeking construction jobs and related work. Besides Charlotte and her young sister Rachael Winfrey, the family included sons Jack and Frank (born in 1855). From Iowa they traveled south into Missouri, where son Howard was born in 1856. Not long after Howard's birth they moved to a region near the Missouri-Kansas border, onto Indian lands opened for settlement by the Kansas-Nebraska Act, passed by congress in 1854. This monumental measure was designed—for thorny and sensitive political reasons—to keep equal the number of slave and free states admitted to the Union while allowing settlement in western regions of the country. Kansas Territory was intended to one day become a slave state, while Nebraska would be a free state.

The move to eastern Kansas (made sometime in 1856 or shortly afterward) remains something of an enigma.[16] Previously, the Stilwell family had left pro-slavery Alabama for Free-Soil land on the Indiana frontier. As an adult William Henry had moved with Charlotte—also from a Free-Soil state—and little Rachael to Free-Soil Iowa; after Jack and Frank were born they relocated south into Missouri, nominally a slave state but one with strong abolitionist biases.

Kansas Territory was a different matter. After passage of the Kansas-Nebraska Act, a bitter and violent rivalry developed in Kansas, a conflict often referred to as "Bleeding Kansas." The provisions of the act allowed the people of the two territories to hold special elections to determine the eventual status of slavery. Presumably, Kansas (west of slave-state Missouri) would support slavery, and Nebraska (west of Free-Soil Iowa) would become a non-slave state. Nebraska's status was not in doubt.

In Kansas, however, both slavery supporters from southern states and anti-slavery people from northern states settled the territory. Most people moved to Kansas for economic reasons, but their plans may have been influenced by the desire to vote "free" or "slave" on the day set for voting and thus determine the status of the new state. Granted, William Henry was looking for work, and with the population near Westport (now part of Kansas City) along the Missouri River increasing, opportunities improved. His northern, Free-Soil background and his presumably antislavery bias also played a small role in the move.[17]

Still, little evidence connects Jack Stilwell's parents to the slavery issue in Kansas. As outlined above, the family moved often. Jack and Frank, for instance, were born in Iowa; Howard was born in Missouri; and in 1858 Charlotte gave birth to their fourth son, Millard, back in Iowa. In fact, in his search for work William Stilwell might have gone to the Kansas Indian agency for Sac and Fox people located in Osage and Franklin Counties. A 1902 Wyoming newspaper said as much: "From earliest youth [Jack] Stilwell's life was cast in the environment of Indians. His father was an Indian agent in Iowa and brought a large band of Sacs and Fox Indians to Kansas."[18]

No mention of William Stilwell being an Indian agent in the 1850s exists in letters received from the Sac and Fox agency in the records of the Office of Indian Affairs. William may have tried to find work there. In any case, he passed through Douglas County, Kansas, prior to or during the mid-1850s when Kansas Territory was opened to settlement. Indeed, on July 20, 1855, Stilwell used the Preemption Law of 1841 to acquire a northwest quarter section (S4, T15, R20) located in southern Douglas County.[19] The property, 160 acres in Calhoun Township (present-day Palmyra Township) contained rich soil and spread over unbroken rangeland near the Santa Fe Trail.

The date of the Stilwell family's move to the land in Kansas remains uncertain. Some claimants came to Kansas Territory, staked claims, did some work to "improve" the claim, and then left temporarily. Such may have been the case for the Stilwells. The local township census gives 1857 as the year they arrived and claimed the land, but voter registration records suggest 1858.[20] The latter records show the Stilwells in the area with a total of six people in the household, five males—William Henry, Everett (Jack), Frank, Howard, and Millard—and one female, Charlotte. Charlotte's sister Rachael was no longer with the family.[21]

One-quarter mile east of the Stilwell farm stood the town of Palmyra, founded in 1855 and organized in 1857. Palmyra sat on the natural divide between the drainage areas of the Kansas River at Lawrence and the Marais des Cygnes River at Ottawa. The Santa Fe Trail followed the rise to avoid having to cross streams and rivers with wagon trains; another benefit was a vigorous and constantly active spring at Palmyra that provided first fresh water for freighters and their animals heading southwest after leaving Westport, about thirty miles distant. The spring may have been the chief reason for Palmyra's existence.

At the large well, trail bosses and freighters traveling in either direction on the route stopped to rest and refresh their animals. Teamsters watered their livestock, cleaned their personal laundry, and cooked their meals. Palmyra provided freighters the manpower and equipment needed to repair harnesses, gear, and wagons. The town grew to include a harness shop, wagon repair shop, blacksmith shop, hotel, tavern, lawyer's office, drugstore, dry goods store, grocery, post office, two doctors, and a subscription school.[22]

Palmyra got its name, appropriately enough, from an ancient Syrian city built around a desert oasis on an important trade route linking the Roman and Persian Empires. The leaders of the new town sought more for their little village than serving overland traders, and in 1858 they organized a town company that purchased a section (640 acres) of land south of town and donated it to the Kansas Educational Association for the establishment of a college. Shortly after Palmyra's founding, additional land on the south side of the busy little town became Baldwin City, and in 1863 Palmyra and its neighbor merged as Baldwin City.[23]

Prairie City sprang up near Baldwin City and Palmyra, emerging out of a difference of opinion between William Graham and Henry Barricklow of Palmyra. The disagreement, coming as early as Palmyra's founding in 1855, caused Graham and his associates L. F. Green, James Lane, and Salmon S. Prouty to relocate about two miles southwest of Palmyra and form their own community. Lane was a leader in the Free-State movement in Kansas, and Prouty was the founder and publisher of the Prairie City newspaper, the *Freeman's Champion,* which began publishing in 1855. The two men dominated the rival community. The Stilwell farm lay about one mile north of Prairie City.

More important for young Jack Stilwell, in 1856 the Protestant Episcopal Church in Prairie City founded the Heber Institute, a school for boys. Two years later education leaders in the Presbyterian Church also created a high school for boys, called Prairie City Institute. By the end of 1858 both schools had failed, leading H. J. Canniff to organize Prairie City School District No. 1. It used the same building the failed institutes had occupied.

Jack attended school there. On June 19, 1859, Horace Greeley, noted lecturer and editor of the *New York Tribune,* spoke in the building at a Republican political party gathering of some four hundred people and made his famous statement, "Go west young man and grow up with the country." Jack, who did not hear the speech, nonetheless took the admonition seriously.

Even before Baldwin City's merger with Palmyra, its citizens began construction of Baker University in 1857. The first building, a three-story stone structure, stood on College Grove Street across from Eden Park.[24] Most rock for the building "came from the south side of a hill on property owned by Henry Barricklow." Some of the stone came from the Stilwell farm.[25] Lack of funds in early 1858 forced temporary abandonment of the project, but Baker officials found alternate quarters for classes and student housing. Then, before the year was out, settlers from miles around donated their time and labor to help finish construction. The building, "Old Castle," as it became known, housed both the university and a preparatory department.

While that activity occurred, William and Charlotte Stilwell bought and sold land and town lots. Real estate records reveal that William tried to sell the southern half of his preempted quarter section to Calvin Smith in July of 1858, but the transaction failed and William retained the land.[26] A year later William and Charlotte purchased a quarter section of land that had been preempted by Banks and Bathney Hall. Ten days later they sold the same quarter section back to Bathney. Apparently, William, trying to help Bathney, became something of a straw man to get Banks Hall's name off the deed.[27]

In August 1860 William bought a lot in Palmyra from A. Jackson Banks for $70. Two months later he sold the lot to Chloe Brown for $80. Then, in October 1861, he and Charlotte bought a lot in Baldwin City for $400.[28] In 1860 authorities valued William and Charlotte's real estate at $1,200, and the couple possessed personal property estimated at $200. They were financially comfortable, but not prosperous.[29] Meanwhile, their family continued to grow. In 1860 Charlotte gave birth to the family's first girl, named Clara May, whom Jack called Clara.

In the midst of the land speculation, Jacob and Rhonda Stilwell, Jack's uncle and aunt, left Texas with their three children to relocate in a Free-Soil section of Kansas. By early 1861 they had moved to Douglas County, where on April 16 they purchased for $1,000 eighty acres (a half quarter section) of land from William. The property represented the northern half of William's original quarter section preemption claim. They also bought a lot on G (Grove) Street in Baldwin City for $200.[30] That same day, April 16, for $1,000 William bought eighty acres across the road from the original claim. A year later he sold the farm to Louis Green. He then bought five acres of land from John Simmons. He paid $70 for the little plot located about one and one-half miles northeast of Palmyra–Baldwin City.[31]

Amid all the relocating, moving, and shifting of residences, young Jack Stilwell found school a bit unsettling. Indeed, one wonders how much schooling he received. If he started school at age six, he attended classes in Missouri. If his family moved to its original Kansas claim in 1857, Jack went to school either in Prairie City, south of the home place, or in Palmyra, to the east of it. Because 1860 census returns show the Stilwell family with a Prairie City post office address, Jack also attended Public School District No. 1. Later, after the Palmyra–Baldwin City merger in 1863, Jack enrolled at the preparatory school associated with Baker University.

No definitive record of Jack Stilwell as a student at Baker exists. However, the Baker University catalogues show that a C. A. Stilwell of Baldwin City attended Baker during the winter of 1862–63. However, there was no C. A. Stilwell in either William's or Jacob's family, who were the only Stilwells in the area. It is possible that a mistake in transcription was made when the recording teacher heard the initials S. E. (Simpson Everett) as C. A. Two of Jack's cousins, Phoebe and William, Jacob's children, attended Baker during the same 1862–63 term. The following two winters saw Phoebe and William enrolled at Baker preparatory, but not Jack. His entry in the *Dictionary of American Biography* states that Jack left school at age thirteen.[32]

Jack dropped out of school in part because serious marital problems roiled the Stilwell household. William Henry (forty years old in 1863 and now a farmer) and Charlotte (five years younger) separated. Their difficulties started around 1860 when William on multiple occasions committed adultery with Mary Brady, a twenty-something woman from Pennsylvania who lived with the family.[33] The

Stilwell farm with its little house and large family included three adults and five children: Jack, Frank, Howard, Millard, and Clara May. Charlotte discovered the affair, and she was not happy, of course, but a temporary reconciliation must have taken place: Charlotte again became pregnant and in 1861 gave birth to Elizabeth Ann (Lizzie). At some point Charlotte became aware that William also engaged in nefarious activities with Jane Grace of Kansas and Jennie Pike of Iowa.[34]

Charlotte said no more, and William left. "My father and mother separated in the spring of 1863," Jack reported years later. Charlotte sought a divorce. Her petition read, in part: since "July 1860 William Stilwell had neglected his wife and his children by being absent from home and neglecting to provide for his family." The petition accused William of adultery between 1860 and 1863 with the three women: Brady, Grace, and Pike.[35] Besides adultery and neglect of family, Charlotte accused her husband of cruel, vulgar, and harsh treatment toward her.

"At the time," said Jack, "there were myself, Frank C., Howard C., Millard O., Clara [May] and Lizzie [Elizabeth Ann]." He also reported that when his parents separated, his father moved to Savannah, Missouri. From there he went to Saint Joseph. Jack said that after the split "my mother had Frank and Clara and Lizzie with her. Howard, Millard and I were with father" and Mrs. Pike.[36]

Thirteen-years old and bitter, removed from school and from association with his mother, brother, and baby sisters, Jack became angry. William took Jack and his brothers with him to Missouri, where they lived with him and Mrs. Pike, whom the boys did not like. She represented, in their opinion, an important reason for their family's breakup. And she was not their mother.

His father, Jack noted, "married Mrs. Jennie Pike or Brenner at Marysville," Missouri, around May 1863. "I was not present," he added. "My understanding is that no divorce had yet been granted my mother when he married Mrs. Pike." Years later he reported, "I have heard from a reliable source that my mother secured a divorce from my father in Lawrence, Douglas [County, Kansas], I think about Sept. 1863."[37]

Douglas County Court records show that Charlotte filed for a divorce in May 1863, but three months later a fire destroyed the records. She refiled appropriate documents on May 12, 1865, and officials recorded them a second time. With the divorce Charlotte restored her maiden name, Winfrey, and received custody of Frank, Clara May, and Elizabeth Ann. As alimony Charlotte got three cows, two yearling calves, one yearling colt, the farm implements, household and kitchen furniture, and beds and bedding. Her real estate included the original preemption quarter section near Baldwin City, less the eighty acres that her brother-in-law Jacob and his wife Rhonda owned. She also received five acres northeast of Baldwin City.

Fortunately, Jacob Stilwell and his family remained in Baldwin City, and their presence afforded Charlotte and her children some security. In addition, Charlotte's property was protected by Section 6 of the Kansas Constitution. It guaranteed rights to women in acquiring and possessing property—real, personal, and mixed—separate and apart from their husbands, and it also provided for equal rights in the possession of their children. Because William had left the region, the court awarded Charlotte all real and personal property the couple had acquired.

Shortly after the separation and well before the divorce proceedings had begun, thirteen-year-old Jack Stilwell left his new home in Saint Joseph. The family breakup, his father's involvement with Jenny Pike, his withdrawal from school, and his new life away from his mother and younger siblings led to Jack's adventures with Santa Fe freighters. A family story, however apocryphal, passed from one generation to the next, suggests that as a boy, Jack went one day to the famous and often-busy Palmyra "Santa Fe Well" for water. When he failed to return home, family members sent to look for him discovered only empty buckets by the big spring.[38]

Many years later, Jack admitted that he ran away from his new home in Saint Joseph, leaving behind his father, his "stepmother" Jenny Pike, and two younger brothers: Howard, age seven, and Millard, about five. With the Civil War raging in the East, Free-Soil and slavery advocates fighting in Kansas, and his family in terrible disarray, young Jack Stilwell headed for Kansas City and there joined a wagon train bound for Santa Fe.[39] Overland freighting soon acquainted Stilwell with the Southwest—its land and topography, its people and languages, its customs and traditions. And it prepared him to enter, as had many of his Stilwell ancestors, a military life and a tradition of public service.

CHAPTER 2

ON THE SANTA FE TRAIL

J ack Stilwell left home in 1863 when he was thirteen years old and found work on the Santa Fe Trail. Hired by freighters, he traveled back and forth between Santa Fe and Kansas City over the next three and a half years. He spent winters in New Mexico, where he learned Spanish, hunted bison and pronghorn antelope, helped open new trail routes, and acquired a thorough knowledge of the southern plains territory. As difficult as the enterprise often was, Jack nonetheless enjoyed his labor with overland freighters.

Opened officially in 1821, the Santa Fe Trail saw freighters, adventurers, traders, soldiers, and hunters follow the route over the next four decades. The overland freighters who hired Stilwell carried their trade goods, market supplies, specie, and other items by wagon and pack animals across rivers, over sometimes barren land, and through or around mountains. They also drove horses, mules, oxen, and cattle along the trail. Manufactured goods of all kinds, including ready-made clothes, cloth, and Yankee gimcracks (items of small value) were freighted west to Santa Fe, where they were traded for animal hides and robes, gold and silver, coarse blankets, and mules, which were hauled back east.[1]

When Stilwell joined the Santa Fe traders in the spring of 1863, wagon freighting on the trail was in gradual decline, but shipping remained busy, even as the Civil War raged. The famous trail began in Missouri at either Franklin, Independence, Westport Landing, or Kansas City. About thirty miles west of Kansas City, it passed Stilwell's hometowns of Palmyra and Baldwin City, crossed the Neosho River, and continued southwestward through Council Grove and

Diamond Springs. The route struck the Arkansas River at its great bend, near a belt of sand hills close to Pawnee Rock, a sandstone pinnacle on which traders carved their names. From this point, the trail followed the Arkansas westward, passing by the future site of Fort Dodge (established in 1865). About forty miles southwest of Dodge, the route divided at a place called Cimarron Crossing, some four hundred miles from its origin.

Traders who used pack animals to haul their goods usually continued up the north bank of the Arkansas River toward the Rocky Mountains, following what became known as the Mountain Route. In the 1830s and the decades following, caravans stopped at Bent's Fort, established in 1833 just north of the river in what is now southeastern Colorado. From Bent's Fort some traders followed the Arkansas a few miles farther west before turning southwest into the mountains and crossing the upper Rio Grande. From there they traveled south to Taos, where their trail ended. Others turned southwest after leaving Bent's Fort. They then crossed over Raton Pass and headed south down a trail that skirted east of the Sangre de Cristo Mountains. This route took them to the village of Las Vegas and on to Santa Fe.

Freighters using wagons usually took a southerly route called the Cimarron Cutoff. They splashed across the half-mile-wide, quicksand-filled Arkansas, always a difficult task, and pushed southwestward through a fifty-mile stretch of barren land absent of water but filled with alkaline dust—the dreaded Cimarron Desert—until they struck the upper Cimarron River and its Cimarron Spring, located in what is now far southwest Kansas. From there they followed the Cimarron upstream and crossed over to the upper North Canadian River in far northeast New Mexico. After crossing that stream, they pushed southwest to the upper Canadian River near modern-day Springer in Colfax County; from there traders turned south to Las Vegas and the main road to Santa Fe.

Freighters following the Cimarron Route used Murphy wagons. The huge, cumbersome vehicles stood three feet wide and up to sixteen feet long; the rear wheels reached five feet tall. Over each blue wagon box, freighters stretched a white canvas cover to protect the three-ton load of goods beneath it. Ten or twelve paired mules or three or four yokes of oxen pulled each wagon. In 1831 a caravan of one hundred wagons and two hundred men made the journey to Santa Fe, meeting on the way Mexican caravans heading east.[2]

As a boy Jack Stilwell saw plenty of the mule- and ox-drawn wagons moving west toward Santa Fe or east toward Kansas City.[3] Often he lingered at the Palmyra well and listened to teamsters' tales of Santa Fe and their adventures on the long trip—some 1,200 miles—to New Mexico or back.[4] And, then, suddenly, the thirteen-year-old became an overland freighter. "In 1863," he stated years later, "I went out to New Mexico from Kansas City over the Arkansas [River] route to a point above [future] Ft. Dodge." From there, he crossed the river and "took what was known as the Cimarron Route which went past Wagon Mound to Las Vegas being the first town we struck." He "made several trips from New Mexico to Kansas City and Leavenworth," he reported. While passing through Baldwin City during those trips, usually two each season, Stilwell visited, or at least saw, his mother, although he spent only a little time with her. He grew up on the trail.[5]

Nearly thirty years later, Stilwell could still accurately describe several significant points of reference on the trail. In noting such markers, he always started from Santa Fe—a New Mexican point of view—rather than from Independence or Kansas City. He described the Cimarron Cutoff route as leaving Santa Fe, running through Apache Canyon, skirting the old ruins of a church, and continuing southeastward past San Jose and San Miguel before turning north to Tocolote. From there, he said, the trail pointed straight east a few miles to Las Vegas, where it turned northeast to La Junta and on to Wagon Mound (known by New Mexicans as Santa Clara) and the Canadian River (called the Rio Colorado by New Mexicans). After crossing the Canadian, the trail followed the river east and then northeast to Cienega del Burro, Carrizo, and the Cimarron River. The trail, he said, then moved over the Jornada Seco or "Sixty-Mile Dry Road"—the Cimarron Desert—to the Arkansas River about forty miles above Fort Dodge, where it connected with the main route to Kansas City.[6]

Stilwell also described the Mountain Route from a Santa Fe perspective. It followed the same path as the Cimarron Route to Las Vegas and La Junta. There, he said, it diverged from the dry route by turning north toward the upper Cimarron River before climbing through Raton Pass (Dick Wootton Pass, as he called it) to Trinidad, Colorado, and thence westward overland along the Purgatoire River to Las Animas on the Arkansas River. It followed the Arkansas downriver and joined the Cimarron Route at Cimarron Crossing.[7]

Stilwell's duties varied with each caravan and grew in importance as he gained experience. For a while he herded auxiliary livestock such as horses, mules, and oxen. He also worked as a bullwhacker, an employee who walked beside the oxen to crack a whip near their ears to keep them moving. On occasion he drove wagons, but more often, as he gained experience, he served as a scout and guide. Whatever his responsibilities, having grown up on a farm, he knew how to handle livestock, and he made a rapid transition to his teamster-related duties.[8]

In the Independence and Kansas City area, working on the Santa Fe Trail held a fascination for many young men. Like many other teenagers, Stilwell, a runaway with seemingly nowhere else to go, had taken to freighting partly for adventure and partly to escape an unsatisfactory home life. Writing in a Santa Fe Trail publication, Donald R. Hale claims that "wagon masters as a rule hired farm boys as teamsters. These boys had worked with breaking [young oxen] to work." He notes that a "large wagon train consisted of a wagon master, his assistant, the teamsters . . . , a man to look after extra cattle, and two or three extra men as reserve to take the place of any man who dropped out." Young employees such as Stilwell usually received wages of a dollar a day and expenses—whatever they may have been.[9]

Stilwell joined the overland trade in 1863 in the midst of the Civil War, when business on the Santa Fe Trail had entered a period of decline. Commerce on the trail always included years when the amount and value of goods carried along the route varied, but activity between its southwestern and northeastern termini had generally trended upward until the late 1850s. Santa Fe, located in a colorful, alien land, seemed exotic and intriguing with dramatic foreign appeal, at least until the U.S.-Mexican War in 1848, when New Mexico was ceded to the United States. Consequently, plenty of traders, adventurers, and interested travelers used the trail, as did soldiers of the U.S. Army. Many travelers—"argonauts," some were called—followed the well-marked route in the early 1850s while making their way to goldfields in California.[10]

By the early 1860s when Stilwell became a freighter, traffic on the trail, while not what it once had been, was still robust. In 1863, Stilwell's first year on the trail, G. M. Simcock, a merchant in Council Grove, kept a register of activity along the route. He recorded 3,000 wagons, 618 horses, 20,812 oxen, 8,046 mules, and 98 carriages that passed through town in one year. He also noted that 3,072 freighters and their employees transported some 15 thousand tons of freight with an estimated value of $40 million along the trail that year. In October, Charles G. Parker and Company drove 500 head of cattle through town on their way to New Mexico.[11]

Jack Stilwell saw plenty of activity that would have impressed a young man. Traders, teamsters, cowboys, adventurers, soldiers, and Civil War deserters streamed through Council Grove. Saloons and dance halls attracted some passers-by, while others remained quietly around campfires with pipe and tobacco, telling tales and exchanging stories. Stilwell listened to the yarns and over the years became a great storyteller himself. But there was not always peace. Fights broke out and shootings occurred. Men died or suffered injuries that forced them out of the Santa Fe trade.

The Civil War in Kansas also brought danger to the trail. On May 4, 1863, just a couple of months after Stilwell passed through Council Grove the first time, Dick Yeager, a former Santa Fe freighter turned proslavery irregular, camped with his band of guerrillas near town. His plan was to attack and destroy the important stopping point. Malcolm Conn, a Council Grove merchant who had known Yeager when he was a freighter, went to the guerrilla camp and persuaded Yeager not to attack the little community. Conn's friendship saved the town. Yeager and his band instead raided Howell's stage station at Diamond Springs (southwest of Council Grove in present-day Morris County). They killed Howell and badly wounded his wife, thus bringing the Civil War to the Santa Fe Trail.[12]

In 1863, when Stilwell left for Santa Fe, Kansas remained divided between pro- and antislavery factions, even after Kansas had entered the Union in January 1861. Indeed, partisans fought one another in something of a war within a war. Two of the larger groups included the Kansas Free-State party and proslavery bushwhackers from Missouri. The groups had been in conflict since 1854, when federal law opened Kansas Territory to settlement. Their struggles were characterized by a series of political conventions, elections, raids, massacres, pitched battles, and atrocities.

One of the worst raids occurred in August 1863, when William Clarke Quantrill, a Missouri-based, proslavery guerrilla leader with 450 men, invaded and sacked Lawrence, Kansas, a Free-Soil town. Quantrill's bushwhackers dispersed through the village to loot, plunder, and murder. They destroyed the town's business center and burned many homes. Perhaps 150 people died in the attack. After they left Lawrence, Quantrill and his raiders rode south, passed near the Stilwell farm, and from there turned southeast toward Missouri. A few men from the ravaged town followed Quantrill and his men but dared not intercept them.[13]

The sacking of Lawrence called for a Union response. Four days after the raid, Gen. Thomas Ewing, who commanded federal troops in the area, took action. From his headquarters in Kansas City, Ewing issued General Order No. 11, which called on people living in Jackson, Cass, and Bates Counties in Missouri to leave the area unless they were willing to take an oath of allegiance to the Union. If and when they refused, federal military personnel enforced the order. The directive proved effective. It suppressed bushwhacker support among the population and forced many proslavery people to move westward, deeper into Kansas and away from the Missouri border. After General Order No. 11, the bushwhackers made no more significant raids into Kansas.[14]

These events, along with the advent of railroads across Missouri and into eastern Kansas, moved the eastern end of the Santa Fe Trail steadily westward.

Baldwin City, Council Grove, and some other eastern trail towns were no longer the draw they once were. Trail activity leveled off and business declined. Stagecoach company officials in Council Grove could not fill enough local seats to remain profitable. After the Civil War the trail's main route moved north to pass through Junction City, located at the confluence of the Republican and Smoky Hill Rivers in Geary County. Council Grove suffered the loss of several businesses that had supplied wagon trains. A few Santa Fe–bound caravans continued to run through the community for a while longer, but trade was coming to an end.[15]

Even as freighting through war-torn areas became dangerous, more significant modifications occurred when railroads moved west. On September 7, 1863, one hundred workmen arrived at Wyandotte, Kansas, just west of the Missouri state line, to clear a right-of-way westward along the north bank of the Kansas River for the impending construction of a railroad.[16]

Traveler Joseph Pratt Allyn made note of the work. Railroad workers had graded two miles of what he called the "Pacific railroad's" right-of-way southwestward beyond Fort Leavenworth, located north of Kansas City. By heading west from the military post to Leavenworth City, a new village, Allyn avoided Kansas City with its Bleeding Kansas struggles. From Leavenworth he trekked west on a military road to Fort Riley, established in 1853 and located on a bluff overlooking the spot where the Republican and Smoky Hill Rivers join to become the Kansas River. From Fort Riley he traveled southwest to catch the Santa Fe Trail at Fort Larned, located on the Pawnee River just upstream from the Arkansas in south-central Kansas. The fort had been established in 1859 to guard the trail.[17]

It was during such trail adjustments that Stilwell joined the Santa Fe trade. He grew physically strong, becoming robust and resilient. He also matured quickly and soon became the de facto head of his Stilwell family. A family story, current through several generations, suggests that Jack would suddenly appear at his old farmstead near the Santa Fe Trail. His mother would see him in the distance and get ready to receive him, but oftentimes Jack would disappear. The sight of his mother healthy at home and the knowledge that his uncle Jacob lived nearby for her protection reassured Stilwell that his mother and his siblings Frank, Clara May, and Elizabeth Ann remained safe. Howard and Millard, as noted, lived with his father and Jenny Pike in Missouri, where in May 1863 William and Jenny had married.[18]

Just over a year after that marriage, family connections underwent another transformation. The Union army drafted Jack's father in the fall of 1864. William Henry Stilwell, forty-one, became a private in Company B, Eighteenth Missouri

Infantry, and received orders to head for Georgia. His unit joined Maj. Gen. William T. Sherman's army in Savannah late in 1864 while it rested in the beautiful port city after having cut its destructive way through Georgia from Atlanta to the coast.[19]

After a month-long rest, the army, now with William Henry's Eighteenth Missouri attached, moved north through the Carolinas, continuing its demoralizing practices of burning and destruction. During those cold winter months of 1865, the elder Stilwell waded through swamps, slept without a tent, endured pitiable food and bad water, and suffered long, grueling marches. For a forty-one-year-old private, it proved a brutal experience. William Henry contracted chronic diarrhea, stomach problems, rheumatism, and "derangement" of the nervous system. Although not hospitalized, he spent many evenings in camp, where the regimental surgeon treated his maladies as best he could.[20]

While his father marched with Sherman's army, Jack, when he heard the news, hurried to Missouri. Determined to locate Howard, age eight, and Millard, six, he rode to the Stilwell-Pike home in Saint Joseph, and there collected—"rescued," in his words—the boys. He took them and a few of their personal possessions by stagecoach south toward home. Jenny Pike offered no resistance to the Santa Fe Trail–hardened fourteen-year-old. In Baldwin City, Howard and Millard rejoined their mother, their brother Frank, and their sisters. Jack's father, some eleven hundred miles away and sick, did not act in response.[21]

Although the war soon ended, Jack's father made no serious effort to regain his sons. He could not. On April 26, 1865, some seventeen days after Lee surrendered to Grant at Appomattox Courthouse, Sherman accepted the submission of Gen. Joseph E. Johnston and his Confederate troops—or what was left of them—at Bennett Place near Durham Station, North Carolina. After the surrender, William Henry's unit moved overland to Washington, D.C., and went into camp. Here commanders excused the now-debilitated Missouri private from duty. A couple of months later, on July 18, 1865, while he was in Louisville, Kentucky, the army discharged him and he headed home to Saint Joseph.[22]

The war changed William Henry Stilwell. It appears he suffered some kind of post-traumatic disorder. The war-time experiences compounded mental and emotional stresses already present in him, but no extant records indicate troubling concerns in the Stilwell family's health history. In the aftermath of Charlotte's 1852 hearing loss and unsteady motor functions afterward, an unhappy home life developed, and clearly William Henry's extramarital liaisons suggest something unstable in his immediate family. In any case, after he returned from the Civil

War, he was no longer a man of sturdy mind and steady conscience. Indeed, William Henry embarrassed his family, especially Jack. Even late in his life, Jack was "very sensitive" about his parents' divorce and his father's situation after the war. He said he was "dreading to reveal the skeleton in the family closet," knowing it would cast his father in a decidedly unfavorable light.[23]

In the war's immediate aftermath, Jack stayed with overland freighting. He passed winter months (1863–64 and 1865–66) in New Mexico Territory at Fort Sumner, Las Vegas, Taos, and Fort Bascom. He hunted bison in the Texas Panhandle. He attended parties, participated in dances and fandangos, and met several women—girls—his own age. "I have been to Santa Fe several times," he said. "I speak the 'Mexican' language." Some of the freighters, wagon masters, and teamsters wintered in New Mexico on a regular basis and had New Mexican wives and families who taught Jack to speak Spanish.[24]

During Stilwell's time in eastern New Mexico, much of the territory underwent significant changes. Prior to Jack's arrival, Union forces had defeated Confederate troops at Glorieta Pass and had driven them back to Texas. Yet the federal government also had to deal with growing conflicts between Nuevo Mexicanos and Indians. Mescalero Apaches, Comanches, and Navajos took advantage of the lack of soldiers at frontier forts to expand their raids.[25]

To deal with its "Indian problem" in the Southwest, Congress agreed to establish a large reservation at Fort Sumner on the Pecos River in New Mexico Territory—the Bosque Redondo Reservation. Brig. Gen. James H. Carleton, commander of the military Department of New Mexico, with the support of Territorial governor Henry Connelly, approached the "problem" with dispatch. First, he sent troops under army scout and guide Col. Kit Carson to subdue the Mescalero Apaches and force them onto Bosque Redondo. The task was completed by March 1863—shortly before Stilwell became a Santa Fe teamster.[26]

In addition to overseeing Bosque Redondo Reservation and attending to other duties in the territory, General Carleton needed to provide protection for nonreservation people. He established Fort Bascom in 1863 to serve as a barrier to Comanche-Kiowa raids against ranchers and farmers in the area and to help prevent their forays along the Rio Grande. Situated on the Canadian River in present-day San Miguel County, the post also became an important resting stop for overland caravans supplying the Bosque Redondo Reservation. In addition, Fort Bascom helped monitor the movements of Comancheros (traders) and *ciboleros* (bison hunters) as they moved between their villages and the Llano Estacado of eastern New Mexico and West Texas.[27]

Drawn from the pueblos and villages along the Rio Grande and Pecos Rivers, Comancheros moved east with wagons loaded with craft goods, tools, implements, nonperishable foodstuffs, and guns and ammunition to trade with Comanches and Kiowas at favored sites on the Llano Estacado or in the canyons on the eastern edge of the high tableland. Some Comancheros met Indians along the Canadian River, and some traveled as far east as the confluence of Duck Creek and the Brazos River in present Kent County, Texas. The ciboleros, often with their families, traveled to the Llano flatlands to secure bison meat to supplement their winter stores. Officers at Fort Bascom kept tabs on both the hunters and the Comanchero-Indian trade.[28]

In the summer and fall of 1863, General Carleton sent Colonel Carson on another mission, this time against the Navajos. Carson's methods were brutal and destructive (destroying animals and crops, for example), but from the government's point of view they were effective. Faced with starvation and death, many Navajos in 1864 surrendered to Carson and submitted to relocation. Thus began what became known as the Long Walk across New Mexico from the Navajos' homeland in eastern Arizona Territory and western New Mexico Territory. Soldiers force-marched most Navajos to Bosque Redondo, a distance of about three hundred hot and grueling miles.[29]

The Mescaleros at Bosque Redondo escaped not long after their enemy, the Navajos, arrived; by 1868 some eight thousand Navajos lived at the reservation. Part of Carleton's plan for the Navajos' resettlement included their growing crops to feed themselves, but scant rainfall and barren soil undercut that notion. Instead, the reservation depended on New Mexican contractors, overland freighters, and American teamsters to haul supplies from the states. In the first half of 1864, supplies flooded into Bosque Redondo and Fort Sumner. The activity created a great boon to area businesses.[30]

Historian Gerald Thompson describes some of that business. Ceran St. Vrain, part owner of Bent's Fort, "delivered 19,800 pounds of wheat meal and 57,500 pounds of flour" to Bosque Redondo. Thompson also notes that Andres Dold, a Las Vegas contractor, sent "wagons carrying 20,500 pounds of flour, 14,757 pounds of wheat, and 68,872 pounds of corn"; James Hunter and his partner Charles W. Kitchen "delivered 500 head of cattle . . . [and] 228,159 pounds of corn" to the isolated reservation.[31]

Around that same time, Ike Foster, a teamster who worked for Kitchen, opened a new road to Bosque Redondo. In 1864 he guided a wagon train loaded with corn from the Fort Dodge area on the Arkansas River southwest through the Texas

Panhandle to Fort Bascom and then south to Fort Sumner. According to Charles Raber, who operated a freighting business out of Kansas City, the Texas Panhandle route Foster blazed cut two hundred miles off the route to New Mexico.[32]

Raber determined to use the route. In late March 1864 he and his men started with several wagons from Las Vegas for the states. Under contract with the government, they went first to Fort Sumner to unload supplies. Then, with empty wagons, they headed north to Fort Bascom. From there Raber cut northeast "across country until [he] struck the Arkansas River." The route, he said, "was at this time only an Indian Trail. If [Foster] could take a loaded train and break the way," he reasoned, "I could surely follow with empty wagons. It was more dangerous than the Cimarron route as it passed through the very heart of Indian country. I got through all right and met no Indians."[33]

Some of Jack Stilwell's most important work as a Santa Fe teamster related to moving goods through the Texas Panhandle to the Bosque Redondo Reservation. Two short-lived routes of the Santa Fe Trail, the Palo Duro Route and the Crooked Creek Route (collectively known as the Panhandle branches), passed through the rolling tableland. He made several trips over both branches.[34]

The Crooked Creek Route, as described by Stilwell, left Santa Fe along the familiar road to Las Vegas. From there it struck south to Anton Chico and then turned east to Gallenas Spring and Fort Bascom. From that busy little post it followed the south bank of the Canadian River to a place called Atascosa in what is today Oldham County, Texas. Here the trail crossed to the north side of the river and continued downstream through the Texas Panhandle, staying parallel to the river but bearing a little to the north to a creek on which stood the partially destroyed trading post of Adobe Walls, an abandoned post that had been established in the 1830s. The route veered slightly northeast from there, striking upper Wolf Creek and then cutting north to the Beaver River. From there it continued northeast to the Cimarron River and thence to Crooked Creek and finally to the Arkansas River below modern-day Fort Dodge. It joined the main Santa Fe Trail after crossing to the north side of the Arkansas.

The Palo Duro branch started at Fort Bascom and then tracked east and a bit north to cross to the north side of the Canadian River. From there it angled northeast to strike the head of Palo Duro Creek; that branch followed the creek to its junction with the Beaver River and followed the Beaver east until it joined with the Crooked Creek trail. The two Panhandle branches of the larger trail remained active for only a few years. Indeed, maps of the National Historic Santa Fe Trail show only the Cimarron and Mountain divisions of the trail. But the little-know southern wings proved useful so long as the Bosque Redondo Reservation and Fort Bascom remained open.[35]

Travel on the Panhandle routes was not always safe. Comanches, Kiowas, Southern Cheyennes, and Araphos saw the Texas Panhandle as their hunting preserve, and they resisted encroachment in the area. To halt ongoing attacks on the trail, General Carleton ordered Colonel Carson into the field to subdue a large group of Indians, this time the Comanches and Kiowas. In November 1864 Carson led some three hundred regular and volunteer soldiers eastward from Fort Bascom, following the Canadian River into the Texas Panhandle. Carson's command struck a Kiowa village, where they engaged a large party of Kiowas and Comanches; the Indians drove the troops to retreat to Adobe Walls, where they took shelter. A major battle ensued, and eventually the Indians forced Carson's outnumbered command to retreat to Fort Bascom.[36]

The debacle of the First Battle of Adobe Walls led Carlton to assign military escorts to all wagon trains traversing the Santa Fe Trail from Fort Sumner and Bosque Redondo to Fort Larned, Kansas. Accordingly, on March 15, 1865, he wrote Maj. Edward Bergmann, the Fort Bascom commander, telling him to inform "Comanche chiefs that they will send runners to warn the Indians that if they attack our trains either upon the Palo Duro [Panhandle], the Cimarron or the Raton Mountain Route, we will put men enough into the field against them to destroy them. Tell them . . . we do not propose to have our train stopped or our people murdered with impunity. If they keep off the road we shall not harm them."[37]

General Carleton also wrote to Andres Dold of Las Vegas. Dold remained under contract to deliver one million pounds of corn to Bosque Rondo, through multiple purchases to be made in the states and delivered in three shipments: 500,000 pounds in May, 250,000 pounds in June, and 250,000 pounds in July.[38] Carlton's letter promised that an escort would be provided. Accordingly, Capt. Charles Deus and his men of Company M, First New Mexico Volunteer Cavalry, escorted Dold's wagon train via the Panhandle Route to Fort Larned. Three months later, Deus and Company M returned to Fort Bascom.[39]

In April 1865 Carleton wrote to Major Bergmann at Fort Bascom regarding another wagon train going over the Panhandle Route. "I wish you would keep me advised of the visits of any Indians off the plains at your post," he suggested, and tell me "not only of the disposition of the Indians towards the people traveling with the trains" but also "the summer haunts of the families" of the Kiowas and Comanches. Carleton also noted that some ox-drawn trains "will assemble near your post to go in by the [Panhandle] Route. They cannot keep up with the mule trains going by the Cimarron Route without losing their stock. The trains, numbering sixty wagons or more, will be near your post in ten or twelve days." He wanted Bergmann to send troopers "to escort these trains to Fort Larned." Most of these wagon train bosses belonged to freighting and merchant families of the town of Las Vegas and San Miguel County.[40]

The Panhandle Route was indeed busy in the spring of 1865. A soldier using the pen name "Bascom" wrote a letter to the *Santa Fe New Mexican* newspaper, published May 6, 1865, that commented on the general state of quietness that prevailed but noted that the "topic of greatest interest has been the arrival and departure of [wagon] trains for the States. The preparations of the escort, their arms, equipment and supplies, the hurry of officers, the bustle of men, the packing up of clothing and storing away of articles for the road, and the sudden inunda-tion of humanity from the trains" added out-of-the-ordinary excitement to the garrison. He noted that during the previous week "seventy-one wagons arrived and camped about a mile from the post."[41]

Then "Bascom" described the Panhandle Route, the trail on which Jack Stilwell often worked. "I am informed," he wrote, that the "route is spoken of by those acquainted with it, as being supplied with water, wood, grass and the only obstacle to prevent its being a constantly traveled route is the proximity to those Indians which have been committing outrages upon freighters and have been a terror and scourge of trains."[42] The letter writer noted that the government planned additional security: "Greater safety may be expected from the strong escorts . . . being sent with those trains which go this route. Most of those which have already passed are from San Miguel del Bado" in San Miguel County (where Fort Bascom stood) and Mora County. An escort, he said, of forty-five men "will proceed to Fort Larned. The wagons escorted will number in all to about one hundred and fifty."[43] By that time fifteen-year-old Jack Stilwell had gained enough knowledge and experience to act as a guide for the train. Stilwell understood the need for escorts. "My acquaintance and knowledge of these different routes was gained from traveling them," he said in 1897. As teamsters, he indicated, "it was perfectly natural we discussed every route as to which was better, shorter, and more convenient but above all, the safest from Indians."[44]

Mamie Aguirre, wife of Pedro Aguirre, one of the first large-scale Mexican contractors on the Santa Fe Trail, also spoke about safety concerns for those traversing the Texas Panhandle. In March 1866 she reported, "We again made preparations for a return trip across the plains to Westport." Leaving from Las Cruces, the party had "an ambulance and a baggage wagon and two riding horses." The freighters took along "four other large wagons filled with harnesses for two trains that would be bought when we reached our destination. Loose mules were driven by herders." Aguirre's train went by way of Tularosa and Fort Stanton in the mountains of modern-day Lincoln County and then to Fort Sumner. They traveled fast. Aguirre wrote, "We were just forty days from Las Cruces to Westport. We were in Comanche country . . . [and] as the Comanches were then at war with the whites we were in some danger, but we were not molested at all. We crossed the Arkansas River [near] Fort Dodge."[45]

But heavy freight travel on the southern route (or routes) through the Texas Panhandle lasted only a few years. Bosque Redondo Reservation served neither the Mescaleros nor the Navajos well. Because the environment made it nearly impossible to grow crops on the reservation, too much idleness, too much hunger, and too many deaths occurred. It remained a barren place. Angry and miserable in the ill-chosen location for their internment, the Navajos never settled at Bosque Redondo, a place distant from their familiar heartland. Yearly crop failures meant the great expense of purchasing and transporting food from the states had no foreseeable end, and the Indians' situation suggested the reservation did not work.

In 1868 Gen. William T. Sherman and Col. Samuel F. Tappen visited the reservation, determined it was a failure, and ordered it closed. The Navajo people made the return Long Walk to their homeland in northwestern New Mexico and northeastern Arizona. Closing Bosco Redondo eliminated the need for great wagon loads of supplies, and Fort Bascom's usefulness declined with the drop in freight traffic. Although the fort served the army well during Gen. Philip Sheridan's campaign against southern Plains Indians in the winter of 1868–69, it was closed as a permanent military post in 1870. Even so, troops occupied it every summer for the next four years, and it housed forces engaged in the Red River War in the Texas Panhandle during the fall and winter of 1874–75.[46]

In addition to affording Stilwell deep familiarity with the terrain and trails of the Southwest, his time in New Mexico acquainted him with both Hispanic and Anglo bison hunters in the Panhandle, and he learned to hunt buffalo from them—a skill he would call upon later. "In the winter time," he said, "we used to come down on cibolero buffalo hunts, down the Canadian River and in on the head of Wolf [Creek] and through that country over the Beaver to the Cimarron River north of there so I became familiar with the country."[47] The wagon trains on which he worked in 1864 and 1865 moved through the very heart of bison grazing territory, and during the mid-1860s millions of the magnificent animals still roamed the Texas Panhandle country.

Bison hunting for sport or larder was a dangerous undertaking. Ciboleros often came with their entire families to hunt bison on the flat, high tableland of the Llano Estacado. Although they carried guns and bows and arrows, they usually hunted with spears, and the activity often was as much a sport as it was an effort to procure meat.[48] A *corrido,* or Mexican folksong, describes the death of Manuel Maes, a young New Mexican cibolero. According to the corrido, Maes died in 1863 during a typical New Mexican bison hunt. The lyrics suggest that upon spotting a herd of bison, the young man gave chase. As he galloped to the side of a fat cow, his horse shied away. Maes lost his balance, and in doing so the lance spun around and its metal point impaled him, resulting in his death. His fellow hunters left him in an unmarked grave on the Llano Estacado, but his memory is preserved in the ballad.[49]

Following the Civil War and about the time Stilwell left overland freighting, the arrival of the railroad shifted the eastern terminus of the Santa Fe Trail west to Junction City in present Geary County, Kansas. Indian raids, still a concern on routes through the Texas Panhandle, occurred less frequently to the north. Railroads had also begun to usurp the wagon freight business. As the Kansas Pacific Railroad lay tracks westward, the trail's eastern terminus moved with it. By 1871 the terminus had moved to Kit Carson, in far eastern Colorado Territory.[50]

Such adjustments were not unexpected. Throughout its history the Santa Fe Trail remained in flux, shifting according to existing circumstances. Stilwell himself saw many changes—on both the eastern and western ends of the trail. Despite the advent of the locomotive, parts of the Santa Fe Trail continued to operate for several years. The Texas Panhandle routes south from Dodge remained convenient and frequently traveled, although no longer by the great wagon trains that had followed the routes in the 1860s. Buffalo hunters in the 1870s and cattlemen in the 1880s used them as part of a developing wagon-road economy in the Dodge City–Panhandle region until railroads made them unnecessary.[51]

Jack Stilwell gained an intimate knowledge of the southern Great Plains on the Santa Fe Trail from 1863 to 1867. This experience and his practical understanding of the region's geography and Indian inhabitants proved imperative for his next endeavor—guiding army units in the field. Thus, in June 1867, at Fort Dodge, Kansas, Stilwell left Santa Fe freighting to become a scout for the U.S. Army.[52]

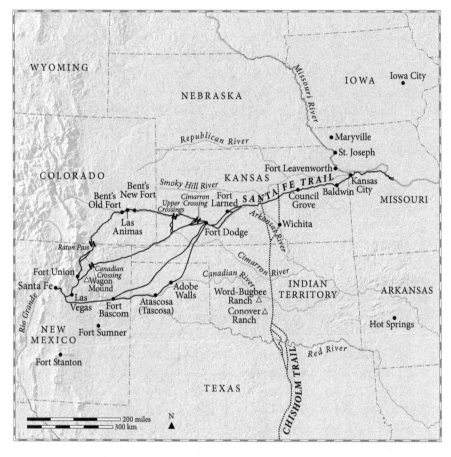

The Santa Fe Trail, cowboy workplaces, and other sites. *Map by Carol Zuber-Mallison.*

CHAPTER 3

SCOUTING FOR THE
ARMY IN KANSAS

Military scouts served as the eyes and ears of the U.S. Army in the West. Hired by army quartermasters, scouts were civilians who acted as guides, hunters, couriers, interpreters, intelligence officers, and diplomats. The work was often difficult and hazardous. George Armstrong Custer described such work as "congenial employment, most often leading to a terrible death."[1] Custer had an abiding respect for the counsel of his scouts (except, perhaps, that of his scouts in June 1876). He also respected their privacy. "Who they are," he wrote, "whence they come or whither they go, their names even, except such as they choose to adopt or which may be given to them, are all questions which none but they can answer."[2]

During a campaign or maneuver, army scouts chose the route to travel, selected river crossing points, picked campsites, and bagged fresh game to feed the troops. They served as couriers who traveled alone at night and hid during the day. Elizabeth Custer wrote: "I would far rather go into battle with inspiration of the trumpet call and clash of arms than go off alone and take my life in my hands as did the scouts."[3] Whether accompanying a small unit scouting in the field or stationed with a larger unit at a military post, scouts and guides proved essential.

Stilwell's experiences on the Santa Fe Trail served him well as an army scout in Kansas and the West. During the years when he made yearly and sometimes twice yearly trips between Kansas City or Fort Leavenworth and New Mexico Territory, Indian attacks on wagon trains were common occurrences, frequent enough that freighters had to assemble at least twenty wagons and thirty men before proceeding over the trail from Fort Larned to Fort Union (established in 1851 in the Mora Valley, not far south of Wagon Mound). In addition to providing escorts for wagon trains, the army often accompanied overland stages as they passed through "Indian country" south and west of Fort Larned. As an overland freighter Stilwell learned how to defend himself, developing a sense of self-reliance and initiative far beyond his years. Wagon masters and other trail hands came to regard him not as a boy but as a young man.

In early 1867 Fort Dodge teemed with civilian employees and army personnel who were constructing permanent stone buildings. During the winter of 1866–67 workmen quarried stone for the next summer's construction at a site about twelve miles from the post. Many of the civilian workers built dugouts along the Arkansas River to serve as temporary living quarters.[4] Passing by Fort Dodge in March 1867, Stilwell saw an opportunity for construction work and applied for and received employment. The quartermaster's Report of Persons and Articles Employed and Hired at Fort Dodge shows that he signed on a laborer on March 21, earning wages of thirty-five dollars a month. Either he joined the approximately 120 men toiling at the quarry, or he worked at a lime kiln nearby. Like most other laborers he lived in a dugout along the Arkansas doing work with little opportunity for advancement.[5]

Stilwell's fortune soon changed. On June 12 a band of warriors under Kiowa leader Satanta (White Bear), a brilliant orator and natural showman, had succeeded in running off a Seventh Cavalry horse herd that grazed east of Fort Dodge. Consequently, post troopers needed fresh mounts. Indian attacks also meant additional military personnel were needed to protect civilian employees at the quarry and kiln. Likewise, teamsters transporting stone from the quarry to the post required military escorts. On the Santa Fe Trail, mail coaches and government and commercial wagon trains traveling between Fort Larned in the east and Fort Lyon, Colorado Territory, in the west had to be provided escorts.[6]

The post commander at Fort Dodge, Maj. Henry Douglass, U.S. Third Infantry, had infantrymen, but he needed cavalry troops and more horses to respond adequately to highly mobile Indian raiders. In the meantime, until mounted troopers arrived, he loaded infantrymen into wagons and sent them into action. Douglass also needed scouts. Thus, after Indian attacks at Cimarron Crossing west of Fort Dodge in June, the quartermaster hired three new scouts: William "Apache Bill" Semans signed up on June 17, and a day later he was joined by

William Staley and Jack Stilwell. They received wages of one hundred dollars per month, a significant increase over stoneworkers' pay.[7] Semans became chief of scouts at the post, and Stilwell served under him, as did Staley, interpreter Fredrick F. Jones, and guide John H. Adkins. Semans took orders from Major Douglass, and all scouts, including the interpreter and guide, reported to Semans with orders to follow his instructions.[8]

In a letter dated June 18, 1867, Douglass described the situation in the Fort Dodge area to his superiors in the Department of Missouri. He wrote that two days earlier "a band of seventy Indians attacked the stage station at Cimarron Crossing and at the same time attacked a portion of the train of Mr. Charles G. Parker, going to the States, which was crossing the Arkansas River at the same point." Douglass noted, "The country in this vicinity is alive with Indians, who operate in bands numbering from fifty to one hundred and sometimes two hundred. The Kiowas have proved false to their professions of friendship and depredations hitherto committed on the road and other side of the river [are] traceable to them."[9]

Furthermore, Douglass indicated, Satanta "himself led his band across the river the night previous to his descent on the cavalry herd four miles below this point. . . . Cavalry can find plenty of work to do in this country, operating from this point as a center. . . . I would submit these facts for the consideration of the commanding general and would respectfully suggest that a competent force of cavalry be sent to operate in this section of the Country." Douglass concluded by calling attention to the attack on Parker's wagon train, stating, "Lieutenant Henry M. J. Karples and forty men of the 37th Infantry were sent in wagons to the Cimarron Crossing after the attack on the stage station. Of three Americans on guard at Charles Parkers' train two were killed and one escaped by swimming the Arkansas River."[10]

The Kansas frontier in the summer of 1867 was ablaze with tensions between whites and Indians, due in part to troops under the command of Gen. Winfield Scott Hancock burning a deserted Cheyenne village in April, an incident that inflamed the Plains tribes. July 1867 saw frequent strikes. Indians—perhaps Kiowas—attacked a train of ten government freight wagons on the Santa Fe Trail fifteen miles below the Cimarron Crossing. Twenty men on the train defended their position and wagons against a large, but undetermined, number of Indians. Scouts on patrol in the area, including Stilwell, heard the shooting and signaled Fort Dodge soldiers of the fight. In response Lt. Stanley A. Brown loaded thirty infantrymen into wagons to aid the government train. The freighters had fought bravely, but two of the young teamsters had died before soldiers arrived. Indian casualties were unknown.[11]

On July 18 Indians struck a ranch at Cimarron Crossing and fired on several hay cutters. Two of the cutters died, and one received a deep wound. Detachments of the Thirty-Seventh Infantry participated in several such skirmishes at Cimarron Crossing or nearby, and as a scout for the wagon-transported regiment, Stilwell participated in many of them. As a mounted scout he usually rode out to the front and side of the troopers' wagons, locating trails to follow and searching out campsites.[12]

Indians were not the only hazard at Cimarron Crossing that summer. Asiatic cholera also killed soldiers, government employees, Santa Fe traders, and emigrants. Partly as a result, in mid-July military officials at Fort Dodge hired three more scouts: J. H. Roberts, J. L. Bridges, and J. K. Nichalson. These hirings prompted Stilwell to leave the scouting service. To save money the quartermaster planned to cut the sixteen-year-old's wages by more than two-thirds, and Jack did not want to risk his life for thirty dollars per month, the wage offered to Nichalson.[13] However, he did not have to wait long for new employment. His knowledge of the country around Fort Dodge and along the Santa Fe Trail and his Indian-fighting experience served him well. He became a guide with the Eighteenth Kansas Volunteer Cavalry, a unit created in response to problems along the route of the railroad then being built across the state.

On June 24 Gov. Samuel J. Crawford of Kansas received a letter from John D. Perry, president of the Union Pacific, Eastern Division (soon to be renamed the Kansas Pacific), stating that three of his workmen had been killed and scalped at the end of the line near Fort Hays. Indians had driven hundreds of Perry's workmen to shelters, the letter stated, and he suggested that unarmed men should not be expected to expose themselves to the attacks.[14] Perry's complaints—added to cries for intervention from settlers, stage companies, and freighters on the Smoky Hill Route—spurred Crawford to form the volunteer regiment. The troopers, he reasoned, would supplement federal troops already guarding railroad workers. Before proceeding, however, Crawford contacted Edward M. Stanton, the secretary of war. Stanton forwarded the letter of request to General Grant, who referred it to General Sherman, commanding the Department of Missouri. Sherman, under political and military pressure, consented to the volunteer force.[15]

Sixty young volunteers headed for Lawrence to join others there for passage by rail to Fort Harker. Located on the Smoky Hill River in Ellsworth County, the post was founded in 1867 to replace nearby Fort Ellsworth. Such central

Kansas posts (including, east to west, Fort Riley, Fort Harker, Fort Hays, and Fort Wallace) were designed as major installations to guard stage lines, keep tabs on Indian raiders in the area, protect freighters and travelers headed west on the Smoky Hill Route to the goldfields and mining camps of Colorado, and shield construction workers on the Union Pacific.[16]

Among the passengers on the train out of Lawrence was Welsh journalist Henry M. Stanley, who later explored much of central Africa looking for the missionary Dr. David Livingstone. Stanley, who had served on both sides during the American Civil War, wrote about the Kansas volunteers. The boys were rowdy, he said, and reminded him of inmates of an insane asylum. They had "Indians on the brain," he noted. "The boys were going to hunt scalps and make knickknacks out of Indian skulls. They hallooed and yelled at everything from a telegraph post to a little calf and waved goodbye to an old cow who threatened them with her head and horns."[17]

The volunteers arrived at Fort Harker about midnight on July 10 and immediately began to have second thoughts about their decision to enlist. Fort Harker, a half-mile from the railroad, was bleak, dismal, and forlorn. No one greeted the new troops. A typical Great Plains storm rolled through central Kansas: thunder, lightning, hail, and rain. An Indian scare sent two brave volunteers into the late-night darkness in search of the intruders, but they ran into a telegraph pole. One trooper sustained a contusion over the eye and the other had the breath knocked out of him and fell into a pool of water. Upon recovery, the two of them rejoined their compatriots and all made their way through the rain and wind to the unit's camp. There they got hot coffee and hard crackers. Feeling better, the volunteers sang gleeful songs into the early morning hours. Four days later, July 15, 1867, officials mustered the Eighteenth Kansas Volunteer Calvary, four companies strong, into U.S. service.[18]

Trouble followed forthwith. The day the unit mustered into service, several men contracted Asiatic cholera. Deaths occurred in the ranks on July 15, 16, and 17. To escape the malady Maj. Horace L. Moore, commander of the Eighteenth Kansas, immediately marched his men from Harker southwest to Fort Larned. There a regimental surgeon, a commissioned officer, and several enlisted men died of cholera. The command moved upstream along the Arkansas River to Fort Dodge, arriving there on August 7. The next day they marched north to Fort Hays, recently reestablished near Big Creek on the Smoky Hill River in Ellis County. Major Moore had good reason to leave Fort Dodge quickly. Cholera had been rampant at the post in July, and by early August health issues remained troublesome. From mid-July to the end of the month, for example, forty-nine civilian and government employees suffered from cholera attacks, and of those, twenty-five died.[19]

Stilwell joined the volunteer regiment as a scout and guide at Fort Dodge and accompanied the Eighteenth as it left the post. En route to Fort Hays, Moore's command followed a trail that later became known as the Fort Hays–Fort Dodge Road. The officer responsible for the military action in Kansas, Gen. Winfield Scott Hancock—a tall, robust, hard-charging officer (called "Hancock the Superb" during the Civil War)—had recommended the route earlier in the year, for it provided water at such creeks as North Pawnee, Walnut, and Big Timbers, as well as the Smoky Hill River. About a hundred miles long, the road afforded excellent grass, good running water, and at convenient intervals plenty of wood.

At Walnut Creek a trooper belonging to Company C developed cholera. As the Eighteenth broke camp early the next morning, the young private died. Volunteers dug a grave, wrapped a blanket around the dead soldier, and buried him on the banks of the creek. No further losses from cholera occurred. Stilwell avoided the dreaded sickness. As a scout and guide he was often alone on the plains, searching for campsites and hunting to supplement regular rations. In addition, he rode far out on the expedition's flanks to check for Indian activities, note them, and report possible concerns back to Major Moore. In the saddle constantly and thus away from afflicted areas, he experienced fewer contacts with the disease than did the troopers.[20]

Stilwell and the Eighteenth Kansas arrived at Fort Hays on August 12. At that post Stilwell met another scout, twenty-three-year-old Allison John "A. J." Pliley. Born in Ohio in 1844, Pliley had moved with his family to Topeka, Kansas, by 1858. In 1862 and 1863 he accompanied wagon trains to Denver. After his stint with the freighters, he enlisted as a private with the Fifteenth Kansas Cavalry and rose to the rank of second lieutenant before he resigned in 1866. He tried to settle down and study law in Topeka, but he preferred the adventure of scouting on the western plains. He knew the country around Fort Hays well, especially the Smoky Hill Route, the shortest trail, as well as the fastest and most direct, from Missouri to Denver. Pliley and Stilwell became friends.[21]

On the very day of their arrival at Fort Hays, Stilwell, Pliley, and men of the Eighteenth Kansas went into action. Their combat became part of Hancock's War, a series of soldier-Indian engagements in Kansas during the spring, summer, and fall of 1867. In late March Hancock had marched west from Fort Riley with a large force of infantry and cavalry, seeking council with the Indians at Fort

Larned. Perceiving aggression in Hancock's show of force, the Cheyennes, fearing another Chivington–Sand Creek Massacre, abandoned their village, including tipis and supplies, along Pawnee Fork north of Larned. Hancock ordered the village and all its supplies and equipment burned. In response, Cheyennes and other Indians struck back.[22]

Ordered to run down small parties of Indians seen north of Fort Hays, the Eighteenth moved out. One group included Company B, captained by Edgar A. Barker, and Company C, headed by Capt. George B. Jenness. The volunteer companies joined Capt. George A. Armes, Company F, Tenth Cavalry, one of the Buffalo Soldier units created after the Civil War. Armes had served as a volunteer in the Civil War, but his recent military successes had assured him a commission in the regular army. A political and controversial officer, Armes suffered through nine courts-martial during his military career. Stilwell scouted for the Armes detachment, which with the two companies of Kansas volunteers headed north, marched to the Saline River, and then turned west.[23]

Maj. Horace Moore led a second battalion of the Eighteenth Kansas, including Company A under Capt. Henry C. Lindsey and Company D, headed by Capt. David L. Payne. On August 14 they met Captain Armes and his group. After the meeting Moore's command marched to the northwest, and the Armes battalion moved northeast. They planned to unite again on the Solomon River. The two columns did not reconnect. Having failed to meet Moore's battalion, Captain Armes turned back to the southwest and soon found a large Indian trail running northwest. Here, somewhere in present-day Graham County, Kansas, he handed command to Captain Barker and with a few men returned to Fort Hays for additional supplies. At the post he secured five wagons of food and forage and a twenty-five-man escort. On the way to rejoin his unit, Armes met Maj. Joel Elliott with a detachment of the Seventh Calvary. Like Armes, Elliott was looking for Indians and gave the impression that he would meet Armes on August 19 on the Republican River, about one hundred miles to the northwest. After the chance encounter, Armes and his little resupply troop rejoined the command he had left with Barker.[24]

Now, Stilwell learned—again—that military operations do not always work out as planned. As historian Wilbur S. Nye writes, in northwestern Kansas "small battalions of inexperienced cavalry led by young officers having slightly more service than their men were riding in different directions" without central coordination. A large number of Indian warriors were in the area. For army personnel in western Kansas, the situation "was asking for trouble."[25]

Traveling at night and resting in the shelter of ravines during the day, Captain Armes with his Buffalo Soldiers, Major Barker with his detachment, and Lt. John W. Price with the supply wagons headed for the upper North Fork of the Solomon River. They reached the river somewhere in modern-day Sheridan County, Kansas, on the morning of August 20. They crossed there and marched north about ten miles to Prairie Dog Creek. Here Armes ordered Lieutenant Price and sixty-five men of the Eighteenth Volunteer Cavalry to establish a temporary camp and guard the supply wagons. Armes and the others continued northwest toward the Republican River and the rendezvous, now overdue, with Major Elliott's troopers.[26]

Then, on August 20, two developments steered them toward battle. First, Armes ordered Captain Jenness and men from two companies to check a distant fire seen on the night of the nineteenth. They found only a burning log left by Indians. While returning to the main command, however, Jenness and his men got lost and spent the night on the empty plains. Second, late in the day on August 20 but while the column was still in the breaks of Prairie Dog Creek, head scout A. J. Pliley spotted Indian signal arrows fired about two miles ahead of the column, and he reported the signals to Armes. After breakfast the next morning, Armes pushed his column north out of the creek bottom and toward Pliley's sighting—an Indian camp. But late in the afternoon of August 21, as Armes moved toward the location, about two hundred Indian warriors turned the tables on the cavalry and attacked. Armes and his men dismounted (Stilwell among them), took shelter in a nearby ravine, and mounted a defense.[27]

Meanwhile Captain Jenness, he of the burning-log battalion, determined to find the supply wagons at Lieutenant Price's Prairie Dog Creek camp. Upon reaching some breaks along the creek, however, he met two messengers from Fort Hays, scout Pliley, and several guards and stragglers from Armes's column. The little group, now with Jenness commanding and Pliley guiding them, changed course and headed for the main command under Captain Armes. While doing so, Jenness and the others met a small knot of cavalrymen moving away from Armes's main column, which remained pinned down behind Indian attackers.[28]

Jenness wanted to send his combined troop, about thirty men in all, through the Indian lines to the main command. Pliley objected, suggesting the faster Indian ponies could easily outrun the hard-worked cavalry horses and turn the battle into individual combat that would favor the enemy. Jenness accepted the scout's advice. Then, with the warriors now heading his way, he ordered his troopers to dismount and form a defensive square around the horses. That maneuver, plus rapid fire from the soldiers' carbines, broke the Indian charge.

Nonetheless the detachment suffered heavy casualties: one man was killed and fourteen were wounded, including both Jenness and Pliley.[29] Still hoping to join the main column, Jenness moved the defensive square north toward Captain Armes's position. Upon seeing the large band of Indians surrounding Armes's command and with his own men under pressure, Jenness decided to return to the supply train and Lieutenant Price at the camp on Prairie Dog Creek. The plan did not work, but Pliley, knowing the great value Indians placed on horses, advised Jenness to turn all but two of their mounts free. Seeing the loose horses, the Indians broke off their vigil and pursued the animals, thus leaving the battlefield. The two horses Jenness retained carried the most severely wounded men into a ravine where everyone rested overnight.[30]

The next morning Pliley, sporting two wounds in his left calf, rode one of the horses for help and found the camp along Prairie Dog Creek. He asked for assistance to rescue Jenness and his wounded men, but Price, still in charge of the camp, refused because he was short of troopers guarding the supply wagons. Captain Armes then arrived at the camp with the main column. When Pliley asked him for help, Armes, like Price, refused to send aid to Jenness. Acting on his own authority, Captain Barker took a small force, including Stilwell, who had been pinned down with Armes, and rode to Jenness's rescue. They soon reached the wounded troopers and brought them back to the camp.[31] With the entire command still surrounded by Cheyenne warriors, Armes decided to move his troops south toward the Solomon River and Fort Hays. Fighting continued off and on through most of the day of August 22. Finally, after nightfall, the warriors withdrew, allowing Armes and his troopers to make their retreat.[32]

Although the soldiers fought well, the little operation was a failure. On August 24 Captain Armes submitted his report on the battle to Capt. Henry C. Corbin, post commander at Fort Hays. Rather than admit defeat, he suggested that the failure of Major Moore of the Eighteenth Kansas and Major Elliott of the Seventh Cavalry to meet with him as agreed led to his unit being surrounded and placed on the defense. In closing his report Armes wrote: "It gives me great pleasure to recommend the favorable notice of the Commanding General the following Officers, Guides and Enlisted men who, by their cool determination and examples of courage and perseverance under dangers most trying, contributed so greatly to the salvation of the command." After listing the officers, he made note of two scouts, including A. J. Pliley.[33]

Armes did not mention Stilwell, who was on the quartermaster roll at Fort Dodge. There was no mention of him at Fort Hays in 1867 in the National Archives

Index to Scouts, which lists the post quartermasters who paid the civilian scouts. Because Stilwell was attached to the Eighteenth Kansas Volunteers, the regular army quartermaster at Fort Hays would feel no obligation, without orders, to place him on the rolls and pay him. Such must explain Stilwell's name not being on the roll, for on September 23 Major Moore sent vouchers for the payment of two scouts who had been on expeditions with the Eighteenth Kansas Volunteer Calvary. One of them was Stilwell.[34]

In contrast to Captain Armes's statements, reports written by Major Moore and Major Elliott stated that the command suffered defeat at the hands of Indians.[35] Moreover, Armes had suggested the fighting occurred along Beaver Creek rather than Prairie Dog Creek. By situating the skirmish near the place where on June 29 Lt. Lyman Kidder's little force of the Second U.S. Cavalry had been destroyed by Cheyennes and Lakotas, Armes may have been angling to get credit for avenging the Kidder massacre. In his book *Ups and Downs of an Army Officer* (1900), he named it the Battle of Beaver Creek; George B. Jenness and Henderson L. Burgess did so as well in their articles written for the *Kansas Historical Collections* (1905 and 1913). Nonetheless, the correct location for the fight was along Prairie Dog Creek.[36]

On August 24, 1867, the same day that Captain Armes made his report, Major Moore and a detachment of 125 men of the Eighteenth Kansas, including Jack Stilwell, left Fort Hays. The command marched west up Big Creek before going into camp, and the next morning they moved north to the Saline River, where the Eighteenth joined Major Elliott and a company of the Seventh Cavalry. Together the units rode northwest to the South Fork of the Solomon and then to Prairie Dog Creek and Captain Armes's battle site. From there they continued twenty-five miles north to Beaver Creek but found no Indians. Major Elliott then scouted west and south toward Fort Wallace, in what is now Wallace County, and Major Moore returned to Fort Hays. In essence the Prairie Dog Creek fight was over.[37]

The Eighteenth Kansas remained in the field into the fall of 1867. On September 17, for example, Major Moore escorted Governor Crawford to the end of the Union Pacific rail line. A second detachment looked for Cheyenne and Arapahoe camps south of the Smoky Hill River, and Captain Jenness and a larger detachment, to which Stilwell was assigned, again patrolled toward the Saline River north and west of Fort Hays.[38] In the middle of September, Jenness's detachment moved to a railroad construction camp and spent the night in a deep ravine nearby. The next morning Jenness sent out two scouts, one of whom was Stilwell, in separate directions. The scout sent west discovered nothing. The other scout, Stilwell, sent northwest, returned to report a party of twelve Indians about four miles distant. Jenness and his detachment headed that direction, but the Indians escaped and moved out of sight. The detachment returned to Fort Hays.[39]

Clearly, in his role as army scout Stilwell had a busy summer as part of the larger operation called Hancock's War. He had guided the movements of infantry soldiers who traveled in wagons. He had fought Kiowas along the Arkansas River near Fort Dodge and at Cimarron Crossing. And he had served as one of several guides with Capt. George Armes and his Buffalo Soldiers in the fight at Prairie Dog Creek. Amidst of an outbreak of Asiatic cholera, he had succeeded in avoiding the disease by remaining in the field, often alone.

By mid-September 1867 Congress and the eastern press had judged General Hancock's war on the Plains Indians something of a disaster (an expensive one at that), and the federal government conceived a substantially new Indian policy. Federal peace commissioners—military officers, federal legislators, Indian agents, and prominent citizens—planned to meet with Indian representatives on the Great Plains: one council to be held in the north and one in the south. On the southern plains, the commissioners would meet with leaders of the Arapahos, Comanches, Cheyennes, and Kiowas at an old Indian campground along Medicine Lodge Creek, near Fort Larned.[40]

Accordingly, on September 21 Maj. Horace Moore rode with Jack Stilwell and the Eighteenth Kansas from Fort Hays to Fort Larned, arriving there two days later. The old Santa Fe Trail post had become a central link in the chain of frontier defenses, and authorities had assigned the Eighteenth to help prepare for what they expected to be a huge conference to take place during the full moon in October. Peace commissioners, military personnel, newspapermen and other civilians, and Indians were to gather, and from the government's point of view the non-Indians needed to be protected as they rode toward Fort Larned and the meeting at Medicine Lodge. Apparently the Indians would have to provide for their own safety.[41]

President Andrew Johnson appointed Commissioner of Indian Affairs Nathaniel G. Taylor to head the Indian Peace Commission, as it was called. Retired general William S. Harney, whom Indians called "Mad Bear," was the senior military member of the commission, and he assumed the duties of protecting its members and other non-Indian people who were en route to the meeting ground. At Harney's disposal were Companies G and M of the Seventh Calvary, totaling 160 men, and a Gatling gun detachment under the command of Maj. Joel Elliott of the Seventh. At Fort Larned the Eighteenth Kansas waited in the wings.[42]

George Brown, one of the newspapermen, noticed that civilian scouts, including Jack Stilwell, worked with the army escorting the peace commissioners. The scouts rode out ahead of the main body of troops until they vanished from sight across the rolling plains. Throughout the day they returned, conferred with the officers, and then rode out again in front and to the side of the commissioners' wagon train. Aware of General Sherman's dislike of reporters and the damage that negative press could wreak, General Harney made a good impression on all the newsmen, including Henry M. Stanley.[43]

To help feed people of the four Indian tribal groups gathered at Medicine Lodge Creek, the Interior Department sent food supplies through its Indian bureau. The goods were moved by rail to Fort Harker, where teamsters transferred them to army wagons or rigs hired by the peace commission. Freighters hauled the supplies to Fort Larned, where they were stored to await transport to Medicine Lodge.

Thomas Murphy, an Indian agent, led a group of men who handled distribution of the food at Medicine Lodge. As groups of Indians arrived at the campground, Murphy's men distributed food under the direction of David A. Butterfield, a trader, freighter, and stage line operator. Some confusion developed. In the past the army had supplied food to the Indians, but now the Interior Department was taking responsibility. Compounding the confusion, General Sherman sent orders to officers at Fort Larned not to issue additional rations until the peace commission arrived. Sherman's directive meant that Butterfield had no food for five thousand hungry Indians. In response, one of the commissioners, John B. Sanborn, rode ahead to Fort Larned, met with Murphy, and solved the problem. Before the remaining peace commissioners arrived at Fort Larned, teamsters from the post drove a wagon train of supplies to Medicine Lodge Creek. Other supply trains followed.[44]

Indeed, the army needed multiple wagon trains to feed the many men, women, and children at the Medicine Lodge camp. The Eighteenth Kanas played a leading role in escorting the supply trains. Henderson L. Burgess of Company D wrote: "The last service rendered in October and the early part of November 1867 was in guarding trains of provisions, arms, and ammunition together with four hundred head of native cattle, sent by the government to the peace council at Medicine Lodge."[45]

While some men of the Eighteenth Kansas delivered food and other supplies to Medicine Lodge, Major Moore took a detachment to reconnoiter the country near Fort Dodge and along the Santa Fe Trail. On October 13 Capt. David Payne and Company D left Fort Dodge to escort a wagonload of rations being sent to Moore's command near a place called Nine Mile Ridge, on the Santa Fe Trail between Cimarron Crossing and Buff Ranch. Payne and his company returned the next day.[46] On October 15 Payne rode west again, this time with a detachment of Companies A and B. For the next two weeks, Moore, Payne, and the Eighteenth Kansas provided escorts to government trains on the Santa Fe Trail. On October 31 Major Moore and his command rode back to Fort Dodge, and four days later, on November 3, they headed north to Fort Harker, where on the fifteenth of the month they mustered out of service.[47]

During four months of service the battalion had marched 2,200 miles, engaged in several fights and skirmishes with various Plains Indian tribes, escorted trains of supply wagons, and patrolled a large portion of northwestern Kansas for the U.S. Army. Undoubtedly the young would-be soldiers Henry Stanley had viewed with contempt on the train to Fort Harker had changed. Now a Kansas newspaper paid tribute to the Eighteenth and the dangerous work its men had performed for the people of Kansas, commending especially the sacrifices its soldiers made for the security of others. The paper praised Major Moore and honored the officers and men who, it noted, had fulfilled their duty faithfully.[48]

After the council at Medicine Lodge, in mid-November Jack Stilwell boarded the train at Fort Harker with members of the Eighteenth Kansas and traveled with them to Lawrence. Near the end of the year he went to Baldwin City and his Uncle Jacob's home to visit his family, only to discover that his mother and sisters, Clara and Elizabeth, had moved back to Brownstown, Indiana, to be near the larger Stilwell family scattered through Jackson County. Disappointed, Stilwell returned to the army only to meet what was perhaps his most dangerous assignment.

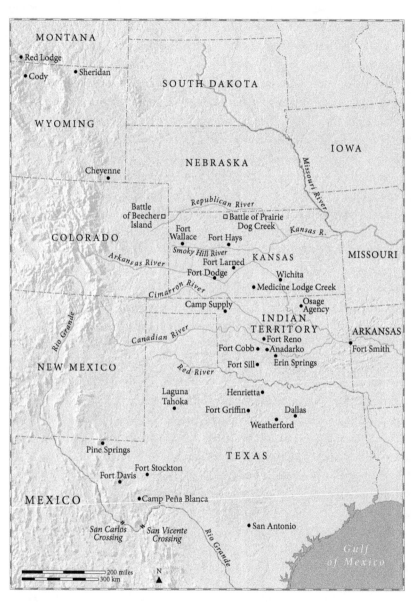

Forts and places at which Jack Stilwell worked and lived. *Map by Carol Zuber-Mallison.*

CHAPTER 4

THE BATTLE OF
BEECHER ISLAND

Among the most memorable military engagements between U.S. soldiers and Plains Indian warriors, the Battle of Beecher Island was the signal event in the frontier career of Jack Stilwell. It occurred in September 1868 on the Arickaree (Arickara) Fork of the Republican River in extreme northeastern Colorado. For nine days Cheyenne, Arapahoe, and Lakota warriors lay siege to American scouts and frontiersmen under the command of Maj. George A. Forsyth, Ninth Cavalry. Many died on the shallow little island, including Cheyenne war leader Roman Nose and army officer Lt. Frederick Beecher, Third Cavalry. But for young Stilwell the battle brought praise and recognition.[1]

In the aftermath of Hancock's War, Stilwell had taken a brief respite from military activities. That changed in August 1868 when he enrolled in a special company of frontiersmen and scouts headed by Major Forsyth at Fort Harker. The frontiersmen, most of whom were recent recruits from the area, were anxious to join Forsyth's command, which included orders to operate against Cheyenne and Arapahoe warriors in western Kansas. Many recruits had heard of—or experienced firsthand—Indian raids on frontier settlements along the Saline and Soloman Rivers in 1868, and they sought revenge and hoped to clear the region of Indians.[2]

Forsythe's special unit was the brainchild of the Commander of the Department of Missouri, Gen. Philip H. Sheridan. This superb combat officer knew the army needed more mounted troops in Kansas, and he knew that getting the state of Kansas to raise a regiment of cavalry would take time, so he determined to establish a mobile force of scouts for immediate service on the frontier. Accordingly, on August 24, 1868, he directed Major Forsyth to employ fifty "first class hardy frontiersmen" to serve against Indians. Thirty men, including Stilwell, enrolled at Fort Harker.[3]

At the time of his enlistment, according to Adolph Roenigk, Stilwell "was a light haired youth of eighteen . . . with big blue eyes and a smooth face. [He was] well mounted. [He arrived at] Fort Harker just in time to be selected as a member of the troop where he was the youngest man in the company. . . . Most of the men were well mounted and equipped for service."[4] Years later, Fletcher Vilott, one of Forsyth's frontiersmen, gave this description of Stilwell: "He was a boy of not more than eighteen years of age . . . fair complexion, rather tall, slender and straight." Vilott said that he "was young in years but old in experience; a stranger to fear and always acting where duty called him, taking upon his young shoulders responsibilities under which those much older than himself would have shrunk."[5]

Allison J. Pliley, who had served out of Fort Hays with Jack in 1867, also enlisted with Major Forsyth. Stilwell had great respect for Pliley, who had set a good example as a scout in the battle at Prairie Dog Creek the previous year. After they had enlisted, Pliley, Stilwell, and the other new recruits boarded a westbound train at ten o'clock in the evening. They reached Fort Hays the next morning and camped along Big Creek about a mile from the famous post. They waited there for two days for their horses and equipment; meanwhile twenty more scouts signed up.[6]

The enlistment at Fort Hays proved timely for a young New Yorker named Sigmund Schlesinger, who was broke and in need of work. Schlesinger's age and lack of experience left Major Forsyth doubtful of the recruit's usefulness, but after a recommendation by Richard Parr, whom Forsyth respected, he told his second in command, Lieutenant Beecher, to sign him up. That afternoon eighteen-year-old Stilwell introduced himself to Schlesinger. Sigmund asked Jack if he had any experience with Indian campaigns. Jack said he had some experience but indicated that he had been knocking around on the plains in years past, and he had become well accustomed to roughing it. Jack and Sigmund, the two youngest men among the frontiersmen, became friends and stuck together. Later that day Sigmund walked over to Jack's quarters and helped him sew a collar on the buckskin shirt Stilwell wore on the expedition. The visit started a friendship that lasted a lifetime.[7]

At Fort Hays the army outfitted the Forsyth command. Each frontiersman received a seven-shot Spencer repeating carbine and Colt revolver, although some of the better marksmen were issued Springfield rifles. Each scout was given tack and camp equipment including a saddle, bridle, lariat, picket pin, canteen, haversack, knife, tin plate, tin cup, and blanket. The army also offered some of the men ponchos, boots, shirts, trousers, and coats, with such items charged against their pay. According to the quartermaster's records, Stilwell checked out one poncho and one haversack, and Schlesinger received one poncho and one canteen.[8]

In addition to Forsyth and second-in-command Lieutenant Beecher, the force included William McCall as first sergeant. A Civil War veteran, Dr. John H. Mooers, who hailed from the new town of Fort Hays, became the unit's acting assistant surgeon. The officers wore military uniforms, while the scouts wore various homespun apparels. Stilwell wore buckskin clothing, an attire that quickly became his regular dress during his years as a scout and guide.[9]

Each frontiersman received fifty dollars per month and an additional twenty-five dollars a month if he provided his own horse. Seasoned guides included Louis McLaughlin, Allison J. Pliley, and Pierre Trudeau. Stilwell was not yet among the select group. Many of Forsyth's men had served in the Union army and responded to military discipline. Two men had seen service in the Confederate army. Others were bullwhackers, teamsters, laborers, and farmers. A number of farmers from the valleys of the Saline and Solomon Rivers were Union veterans who called themselves the "Solomon Avengers."[10]

On the afternoon of August 29, 1868, the frontiersmen broke camp on Big Creek, mounted up, and headed to Fort Hays, a mile distant. Led by Lieutenant Beecher, they sprinted full speed past the headquarters building, breaking into loud cheers when they caught sight of General Sheridan standing on the portico with Major Forsyth at his side. A few minutes later Forsyth and Sheridan shook hands, then Forsyth mounted his horse and signaled to his men. They rode north.[11] Soon rain began to fall, and it continued overnight. About ten o'clock the next morning the wet frontiersmen went into camp. The following day, August 31, they rode into a large herd of bison; from morning until night the command rode past thousands of the beasts. In addition to bison, the men saw herds of pronghorn and elk at a distance. A special detail of hunters provided meat for the command.

With Lieutenant Beecher acting as chief guide, they rode northwest toward Beaver Creek. On September 2 they camped along its banks. They had not encountered any Indians, and the abundance of game in the area indicated that there had not been any in some time, but as they continued up Beaver Creek signs of Indians became apparent. Major Forsyth encouraged greater caution. The outfit followed the creek southwestward, and on September 5, Fort Wallace, located on the upper Smoky Hill River in far western Kansas, came into view.[12]

The frontiersmen now saw a line of objects on the bluffs to the southeast. Beecher believed it was Indians, and Forsyth decided to charge them. The frontier command galloped across a level area of prairie before realizing the supposed enemy was nothing more than a hay train on its way to Fort Wallace. The men followed the train into the post, where one of the ablest plainsmen of his day, scout and guide Abner T. "Sharp" Grover, joined the command as chief scout. Fletcher Vilott soon noticed Grover's unusual ability to follow a trail that no one else but Beecher could see and follow.[13]

As the company was about to depart Fort Wallace, news arrived of an attack on a wagon train some seventeen miles to the northeast at Sheridan, Kansas, the latest end-of-track of the Kansas Pacific Railroad (formerly called the Union Pacific, Eastern Division). Two teamsters died in the raid, which included the theft of thirty head of cattle that had been grazing to the north. Forsythe's command pursued the raiders, although eventually the trail disappeared and neither Beecher nor Grover could pick it up again. Forsyth then decided to move northwest toward the Republican River in hope of finding the Indians who had struck the wagon train. Occasionally the men saw movement in the distance, activity that led them to believe that warriors were watching every step they took.[14] With this in mind, Forsyth consulted with Lieutenant Beecher, Sargent McCall, and Chief of Scouts Grover as to whether the command should proceed or turn back. Grover and McCall believed that if pursued, the Indians would return to their villages, gather reinforcements, and overwhelm the command. Despite such counsel, Forsyth determined to press forward.[15]

On September 14 the scouts found a small, fresh trail that led them up the Arickaree Fork of the Republican River. As they progressed, the trail became a wide track leading toward an Indian encampment. According to John Hurst, some of the frontiersmen questioned the wisdom of proceeding farther, but Forsyth asked: "Did they not enlist with him to fight Indians?" The question ended the discussion, but the scouts and frontiersmen doubted the wisdom of their course.[16] Sharp Grover warned Forsyth that if they found the enemy, they would encounter a large force of Indian warriors who would offer strong resistance. The warning did not change the commander's mind; he wanted to attack at the first opportunity. Forsyth, one of Sheridan's staff officers, hoped to prove to Sheridan that he, as a line officer, could command troops in the field. But Forsyth had no experience fighting Indians.[17]

On September 16 the frontiersmen went into camp on the north bank of the Arickaree Fork, in a spot ill-advised for setting up a defense. Although it offered water and wood in abundance, to the north spread a level plain that terminated at a sharp ridge arising about two hundred feet above them, offering the Indians a vantage point for observing the command's strength and movements. Behind the ridge, canyons served as hiding places. On the river's south bank, a plain about two miles wide covered the empty valley. In the middle of the stream, a narrow, shallow island about three hundred yards long and fifty to one hundred feet wide contained a few willows, tall grass, and small cottonwood trees. On either side of the sandy island, the clear water ran only a few inches deep.

At the camp on the riverbank, the frontiersmen spent a long, restless night. During the evening, in fact, Sharp Grover and Stilwell scouted the sandy island to see if it could be a place of safe retreat in case of a large strike. Fearful of an attack, the men remained close to their picketed horses. After midnight the company heard "coyote" howls and correctly interpreted them as Indians signaling one another. Just before daylight the howls multiplied and moved nearer the camp. Finally, at daybreak, eight Indians on horseback appeared at the east end of the encampment and stampeded one horse and six mules. Camp sentinels fired and signaled the alarm.[18]

The Battle of Beecher Island had begun. Indian warriors—an alliance of Cheyennes, Arapahos, and Brule Lakotas—quickly surrounded Forsyth's company. Forsyth, either at the suggestion of Grover or Stilwell (John Hurst, who was there, said it was Stilwell) ordered his men to the island. Hurst later reported that he heard no command to retreat to the island; instead he claimed that when Stilwell suggested he was going to the island, the men around him followed. They led their mounts over and tied them to the small trees. The movement confused the Indians, who briefly stopped their attack. Stilwell and the group that had followed him dug depressions in the wet sand on the east end of the island. Others had followed Jack Donovan to the west end, where they, too, dug shallow trenches to fortify their position and prepare for defense.[19]

Schlesinger remembered the evacuation differently, recalling that "Forsyth and his advisors, Lieutenant Beecher, 'Sharpe' Grover, [Sargent] McCall, Jack Stilwell, and others, chose the island to be our best position to give battle. It was situated," he said, "that we were far enough removed from the zone of gun fire directed from the surrounding hills. To reach us the Indians had to come down nearer to our level, and here the sandy bottom proved our protection."[20]

Another eyewitness, George Oaks, stated that early in the battle Major Forsyth sent Stilwell and five other scouts to the east end of the island. Because the upper west end of the island was well defended, apparently, the Indians tried to take the lower end. Oaks also claimed that Stilwell and his companions found little cover on the east end, so they splashed across the narrow channel to hide in the tall grass on the riverbank. Indian sharpshooters, he said, prevented the men hidden on the riverbank from returning to the main body of soldiers.[21]

Whatever the case, the frontiersmen soon faced a large force of mounted warriors surrounding and bearing down on them. A desperate battle began. Indeed, early in the fight Forsyth was shot in the left thigh and thereafter took a bullet to his lower left leg. Lieutenant Beecher was shot in the back, and Dr. Mooers was shot in the head. Men who rose to shoot at the charging Indians risked being hit. In such a way Indian warriors killed a frontiersman named Culver and wounded Sargent McCall. Indian warriors also shot the horses, but Forsyth's men soon learned to use the dead mounts for protection while digging deep into the island's sand.[22]

Some years later Stilwell described the fight. In an interview with Fred L. Wenner, he recalled that on the night of September 16, the expedition had "camped on a flat and narrow sandbar near the stream. Early the next morning we were attacked by a few Indians who attempted to run off our stock. While we were saddling our horses, a larger party began a more vigorous fight upon us. The sun was just rising [on the 17th] when it was decided that we should move upon the sandbar which was an island in wet weather and when the river was high."[23]

Stilwell noted that the men "quickly took possession to the upper end of the island, while Indians swooped down upon the lower end." He reported that "Forsyth detailed me and five other men to go bushwhacking and capture, if possible, the position held by the Indians." The men succeeded, "but the Indians," noted Stilwell, "had by this time stationed their sharpshooters in the hollows nearby" and "prevented us from returning to the main force."[24]

After about ninety minutes, Stilwell, Forsyth, and the entire command got some relief. As Stilwell noted, "At this time we discovered that the Indians were wrangling as who should command them. . . . At ten o'clock old Roman Nose, [leader] of the [Cheyenne Elk Scraper Society], and the most celebrated Indian fighter of that day, assumed command. He wore the same headdress which I had seen on his head in previous fights—a contrivance with a buffalo horn standing on its end just above the forehead and flanked on either side by stuffed birds."[25]

Roman Nose carried a feathered lance that he used to direct his troops. Then, according to Stilwell, sitting "squarely on his horse with his . . . lance up lifted," he led a charge through the island. His warriors bore down the center and "dashed almost half way to the main party" of frontiersmen before a bullet from behind him struck Roman Nose and pierced his stomach. A "young warrior," Stilwell reported, "whom I believe was a relative of Dull Knife, now assumed command. He . . . succeeded in rallying his horsemen, nearly all of whom were dismayed at the fate of Roman Nose," who died "from a [second] bullet in his head." The Indians, recounted Stilwell, "didn't seem to recognize any commander, but kept up the fight in a haphazard way until after three o'clock when they received reinforcements and a new man in command." Despite the new leader, the fight continued in Stilwell's "haphazard way" as each of the frontiersmen was "so busy with his own affairs that he paid no attention to the movement of his neighbor."[26]

All day and into the late evening the fight continued. About midnight Major Forsyth requested that Pierre Trudeau and Stilwell make a fast run to Fort Wallace, some eighty-five or more miles away, and get help. Indeed, Stilwell volunteered for the assignment. Trudeau, an old trapper, former "mountain man," and an excellent marksman, accepted reluctantly. To look like Indians and help conceal their tracks, the two men wrapped themselves in stinking saddle blankets and put on moccasins made from the tops of their boots. They "crept out among the Indians, whose camp . . . extended in a direct line" south toward the post.

With "a chunk of raw horse meat for food," the men "succeeded in making three miles the first night," during which they walked backward to obscure or confuse any Indians who might try and follow them. At daybreak they "hid in a washout in a ravine where the grass had grown so tall that it hung over the ledges." Here, in an old buffalo wallow, with Indians not far away and an excited rattlesnake in their faces, one of the men, Stilwell probably, drove the snake away with a huge spit of well-aimed tobacco juice. They stayed there all day, "listening to the fighting on the island" and "powerless" to go for help or return to the command.[27] When Major Forsyth had asked for volunteers to run through Indian lines, Sigmund Schlesinger, Stilwell's young friend, remembered that "Jack was the first to announce himself."[28] Schlesinger was worried that he would never see his friend alive again. In the hours following the scouts' departure, Schlesinger and the other men under siege listened for a war hoop announcing the Indian discovery of Stillwell and Trudeau. They heard no such celebration.[29]

Years later Stilwell wrote in a letter to Schlesinger that he thought "the sun would never go down on that 18th of September 29 years ago when I was [lying] in a washout listening to you fellows fight only 3 miles away." With each volley, he wrote, he and Trudeau "thought it would be the last," but Pierre, "hard headed old man that he was, would swear a while in French and English and then throw in a word or two in Spanish just for good measure." We "took heart," he said, "when we still heard firing from the island."[30]

At nightfall they again "made tracks toward Fort Wallace." Now, however, according to historian Ralph Andrist, "their feet were in such bad condition from cactus spines . . . they wound strips of blanket around their feet" to keep going.[31] A few hours later Trudeau and Stilwell found themselves "within half a mile of the main village of the Indians on the south fork of the Republican River." They slipped into a marshy swampland near the river and hid until morning, when they saw that they had arrived "at the head of Goose Creek on a high rolling prairie."[32]

Here "Indians were so thick all around us," according to Stilwell, "that we had to hide in the carcasses of two buffaloes. The beasts had been killed the winter before so that it was an easy matter to crawl into the shells formed by the bleaching ribs. . . . There was just enough hide on the bones to conceal us, and so we lay there and waited for the night to come." Although those tight quarters smelled unpleasant, their hiding places served the men well.[33]

The third night, September 20, Stilwell and Trudeau once more set off for Fort Wallace. According to Franz Huning, a Santa Fe trader from Albuquerque, on the 21st the men reached a stagecoach and mail station known as Kiowa (perhaps Cheyenne Wells) between Fort Lyon on the Arkansas River and Fort Wallace on the Smoky Hill and waited there for the eastbound stage. Huning, a passenger on the stage, remembered that the two soldiers "had their guns but were without shoes." He wrote, "They told us they were messengers from Forsyth's command that was surrounded by Indians on the Republican. . . . The name of one of them was [Stilwell]."[34]

As the Stilwell and Trudeau trudged toward Fort Wallace, Forsyth, although badly wounded, remained in charge on the island. His men deepened their defenses, cut meat from the dead horses, and dug a well to get fresh water without exposing themselves along the shallow stream. They put up a heavy barrage of gunfire each time Indian warriors made their charges, but their position remained vulnerable. They could not flee without horses; moreover, on foot the wounded men would slow their retreat. Thus they waited. Beecher and a few others, including Dr. Mooers, died. Wounded men called out in pain. The dead horses began to stink. Forsythe sent out two more couriers, Donovan and Pliley, for he did not know if Trudeau and Stilwell had made it through the Indian lines.

Food began to run short. Fortunately for the frontiersmen, many of the Indians began to leave after the fourth day of the siege. Others remained, dug their own rifle pits, and kept their eyes on the soldiers.[35]

On September 22 Trudeau and Stilwell reached Fort Wallace. Upon hearing their story, post commander Col. Henry Bankhead immediately sent two couriers to find Capt. Lewis H. Carpenter, Company H, Tenth Cavalry (Buffalo Soldiers), who was encamped about sixty miles west of Fort Wallace near the Cheyenne Wells stage station on the Smoky Hill Road. When the messengers arrived, the dispatch they carried directed Carpenter to proceed at once with his troops to the Arickaree Fork. In response Carpenter and his command left the stage road and traveled north at about six miles per hour. He had been under orders to return a Dr. Fitzgerald to Fort Wallace, but he kept the surgeon with his troopers in case he was needed at Beecher Island.[36]

Colonel Bankhead and his command left Fort Wallace on September 23, the morning after Trudeau and Stilwell's arrival. The two scouts rode with his column back to the island. Scouts Donovan and Pliley arrived at Fort Wallace shortly after Bankhead left with Stilwell and Trudeau. Thereupon Donovan left to seek out either the Carpenter or Bankhead columns, and Pliley rode north, seeking help in a different direction.[37]

Donovan soon found Captain Carpenter and told the commander that to reach Forsyth he needed to move his troops farther north, which Carpenter did. On September 25 the arrival of the Tenth Cavalry lifted the siege. Carpenter's men found Forsyth in his island trench with a copy of *Oliver Twist* in his hand. They fed the survivors, rendered medical treatment, and sheltered them in tents away from the battleground. Meanwhile Pliley hurried north and found Lt. Col. Luther P. Bradley and Maj. James S. Brisbin with two cavalry troops, who also rode to Forsyth's rescue. Pliley, however, severely exhausted by his ordeal, returned to the Fort Wallace hospital.[38]

Soon after Carpenter's arrival at Beecher Island, Bradley and Brisbin appeared with their troops. Bankhead's command came a day later. Schlesinger, whose story Cyrus Townsend Brady included in his *Indian Fights and Fighters*, said, "After [Captain] Carpenter came to our relief Jack was not with him and this made me and others feel very uneasy." The next day a mounted sentinel signaled from a hill about three miles away that a body of men rode nearby. Schlesinger said, "As the horsemen approached one of them was Jack Stilwell. Nearly all of us ran to meet the party. Soon Jack jumped from his horse and in his joy to see so many of us alive again, he permitted his tears free flow down his good honest cheeks."[39] Men of the three rescue detachments spent two days nursing wounded frontiersmen before evacuating them to Fort Wallace, where everyone arrived on September 29.

The fight at Beecher Island was over. Forsyth's command suffered six men killed and fifteen wounded. Fifty horses died. All of the surviving frontiersmen suffered extreme exhaustion. Although Forsyth reported Indian casualties numbering thirty-five killed and one hundred wounded, Indians reported six dead. About the battle, Stilwell years later concluded simply: "That fight was fought on the Arickaree fork of the Republican. I don't know how to spell that word and I never saw a man who did but that don't make any difference about the fight."[40]

The battle apparently ended Sheridan's plan to use fifty-man volunteer units in the field. Otherwise, according to historian Robert M. Utley, except for those involved, it had been "an action of little consequence, but one that would be long remembered and glorified in the annals of the Indian-fighting army."[41] Accounts of the battle filled newspapers of the day, giving the impression that most fighting in the West followed a similar pattern. It did not, but young soldiers entering the army often saw reflected in the battle their own self-image as Indian fighters: outnumbered and surrounded but steadfast and heroic under heavy siege as Indian warriors thundered down around them through several days of furious combat.[42]

As is frequently the case, those engaged in battle have different recollections as to exactly what happened. Stilwell, for example, recounted that Roman Nose appeared in the morning, but according to George Bent (the son of William Bent of Bent's Fort and Owl Woman, a Cheyenne) the famous war leader fought later in the day. Bent remembered that Roman Nose advanced with fewer warriors than he had in the morning battles and that he rode near frontiersmen lying in a hole on the riverbank and was shot in the small of the back as he passed.[43]

However he remembered it, the praise and recognition Stilwell earned from the Beecher Island fight marked an important point in his life. In his memoir Major Forsyth recalled that in selecting men for the rescue mission, he chose Trudeau "and a young fellow named Jack Stillwell, a handsome boy of about nineteen with all the pluck and enthusiasm of an American frontier lad. Two better men for the purpose it would have been difficult to find. I gave Stillwell, as he was by far the more intelligent and better educated man of the two, my only map."[44]

For Stilwell the Battle of Beecher Island determined his destiny. His action in leading the scouts to defend the east end of the island during the first day of the battle got high praise from military leaders. Alongside Trudeau, he readily volunteered to risk his life to rescue his fellow scouts. Such valor did not go unnoticed. The latter action came to the attention of General Sheridan. According to Michael V. Sheridan, Philip Sheridan's brother, who endorsed Stilwell's pension petition, "Your service as a scout . . . was highly appreciated by my brother . . . [who] on more than one occasion commented on the bravery and skill by which you got through the Indian lines . . . to carry the news of Forsyth's predicament to Fort Wallace."[45]

Meanwhile, on October 8, 1868, General Sheridan directed his quartermaster at Fort Hays to pay scouts Stilwell, Donavan, and Trudeau $150 each. A. J. Pliley received $100. The extra pay, Orvel Criqui indicated, "represented services in stealing through the Indian lines surrounding Forsyth and his men on the Arickaree Fork and conveying information to Fort Wallace in a perilous situation." On October 31 Sheridan directed that Stilwell be paid $100 per month as a military scout.[46]

Sheridan, it turns out, had additional plans for Stilwell. Having gained the confidence of the commander of the Department of Missouri, Stilwell soon became one of the first scouts hired for service in the field and one of the last to be discharged. He served with honor and distinction for the next twelve years. His first new assignment placed him in Sheridan's winter campaign on the southern Great Plains.

CHAPTER 5

SCOUTING WITH CUSTER

S hortly after the Indian triumph at Beecher Island, Jack Stilwell found himself in the middle of a cold winter operation on the southern Great Plains. Following the treaty signed at Medicine Lodge in the fall of 1867, most fights between Indians and soldiers, including at Beecher Island, occurred because Indians of the southern and central plains continued to live as they had for several generations: hunting, raiding, and refusing to limit those pursuits to the reservation lands designated by the government. General Sheridan had learned to his chagrin that his roving bands of "fifty hardy frontiersmen" were not an effective deterrent; he and his superiors, including General Sherman—the often-unmanageable commander of the Division of Missouri—determined to strike with force during the winter of 1868–69. When Plains Indians "resort to acts of war," as they had at Beecher Island, Sherman argued, one has "no alternative but to punish them as a whole tribe."[1]

Army policy at that time insisted that southern Plains Indians who were deemed hostile (those off reservations) return to their Indian Territory reservations. To force them to do so, Sherman and Sheridan planned a winter campaign using three converging columns of U.S. troops to sweep through Cheyenne, Arapaho, Comanche, and Kiowa camps located in the upper Canadian and Washita River valleys and around the Antelope Hills in western Indian Territory—even though Comanches and Kiowas and several bands of Cheyennes and Arapahos had not taken part in the Kansas raids of the previous summer. The plan relied on finding the Indians "hunkered down," as was their practice in winter, when they often reduced or ceased altogether their raiding activities and seldom expected attacks on their own villages. The army's plan involved encircling Indians' winter camps from different directions during the months when weather conditions meant Indians did not venture far from their villages and there was less forage for livestock. Of course, the difficulty of cold-weather travel and shortage of feed for horses hindered the army as well, limitations that meant it had seldom initiated winter operations against the Plains tribes.[2]

Sheridan's winter campaign on the plains became a punishing endeavor—for both Indians and soldiers. Stilwell remembered that during the winter of 1868–69, "I suffered great hardships while carrying dispatches from Camp Supply [in western Indian Territory, on the North Canadian River near the junction of Beaver River and Wolf Creek] to what is now Fort Sill" on the Comanche-Kiowa Reservation, as well as to other points.[3] Besides the privation, suffering, and death one expects in warfare, the snow-filled campaign produced lasting controversy and precipitated the military and political demise of former Kansas governor Samuel J. Crawford, an Indian-bashing politician who early in the effort became head of a Kansas cavalry regiment.

The many-sided and sometimes disturbing campaign began in the fall of 1868. On October 9 Sheridan asked Governor Crawford to raise a volunteer Kansas regiment of twelve companies to participate in winter maneuvers. The next day Crawford sent out a call for volunteers, and he quickly filled his cavalry. Indeed, by November 4 officials had organized, armed, and mustered his entire troop, the Nineteenth Kansas Volunteer Cavalry, into federal service. Crawford, "a fire-snorting believer in the benefits to be gained by killing Indians," resigned as governor to serve as colonel of the organization. Horace J. Moore, who in 1867 had successfully commanded the Eighteenth Kansas Volunteer Cavalry during Hancock's War, became lieutenant colonel of the twelve-hundred-man volunteer regiment.[4]

While Crawford filled out his cavalry, Stilwell received orders from Sheridan to join a command led by the controversial, flamboyant Lt. Col. George Armstrong Custer, Seventh Cavalry, who had just returned to the plains from his parents' home in Michigan. Custer's troops rode south from Fort Hays to Camp Supply, the stockade under construction in northwest Indian Territory (in what is now Woodward County, Oklahoma). From that stronghold Sheridan and Custer planned to move against Cheyenne, Arapaho, Kiowa, and Comanche villages along the Canadian and Washita River valleys in the eastern Texas Panhandle and western Indian Territory. Stilwell transferred temporarily to Lt. Silas Pepoon's scouts in the Tenth Cavalry, now part of the Custer command. After Beecher

Island, Sheridan did not allow volunteer detachments to operate without federal troops, and Pepoon assumed command of the reorganized frontier scouts.[5]

Two other men joined Pepoon's Tenth Cavalry scouts: George W. Brown and William "Apache Bill" Semans. Because Brown was out of work, Stilwell, who had met him in Hays City, Kansas, encouraged him to ride to nearby Fort Hays to see about work with the scouts, and Pepoon signed him up. Semans, chief of scouts at Fort Dodge in the summer of 1867, had been one of Stilwell's mentors during that summer. Stilwell's friend Allison J. Pliley, a former scout, became captain of Company A in Crawford's Nineteenth Kansas.[6]

Stilwell and Semans received orders from Sheridan to proceed by train to Topeka, Kansas, and guide Crawford's Nineteenth Kansas to Camp Supply, which would serve as base of operations for Sheridan's southern plains campaign and the Sheridan-Custer winter offensive.[7] In Topeka, Colonel Crawford ordered Capt. Richard Lander's Company G and Capt. John Q. A. Norton's Company D to take a train west to Fort Hays. They were assigned to escort overland supply trains between Fort Hays and Camp Supply.[8] The ten remaining companies of the Nineteenth left Topeka on horseback heading south. They rode to Burlingame and from there pushed southwestward past Emporia and El Dorado before reaching Camp Beecher, a small post near the mouth of the Little Arkansas River at present-day Wichita.[9]

Here trouble started. Infantry troops already at Camp Beecher had consumed part of the rations meant for the Nineteenth Kansas Cavalry, and a wagon train with feed for their horses and mules had not arrived from Fort Riley. Although short of both rations and forage, Colonel Crawford continued southwestward with his regiment. The move turned out to be a mistake, and shortly afterward Crawford lost confidence in his young guides, Stilwell and Semans.[10]

Indian trader James R. Mead was responsible for the loss of confidence. He called the command "a splendid body of men [with] an able and honored commander." Upon making inquiries, however, he discovered Crawford's destination and told the colonel, "You cannot get through that country at this season of the year unless you know just where to go. It is exceedingly broken and difficult." Mead then talked to Stilwell and Semans and determined—incorrectly—that neither had scouted or served south of the Arkansas River. He believed they "were absolutely ignorant of the country where . . . they were attempting to guide a regiment through."[11]

Mead was partly wrong. In traveling the Santa Fe Trail 1863–67, Stilwell had been south of the Arkansas. On two occasions he had followed the Crooked

Creek Route in southwestern Kansas, which started south of the spot where Fort Dodge was later constructed. The trail followed Crooked Creek south, crossed the Cimarron River, and continued south across the Beaver River and over to the head of Wolf Creek in the Texas Panhandle. From there it headed south to Adobe Walls, just north of the Canadian River. Stilwell also had wintered in New Mexico. He often took part in bison hunts near the head of Wolf Creek and close to Beaver River, which joined to form the North Canadian River not far from the location of Camp Supply. Stilwell understood much of the country below the Arkansas River, and his friend Allison Pliley, captain of the Nineteenth's Company A, likewise knew it.[12]

Mead, hoping for a chance to make money from the expedition, offered to supply his own guides to Crawford. The colonel refused. Crawford held no authorization to hire additional scouts, nor did he have money with which to pay them. He had to rely on the men Sheridan provided—Stilwell and Semans. Mead, however, had planted significant doubt in Crawford's mind as to their competency. Such doubt later came into play when the Nineteenth Kansas got bogged down and delayed in the canyons, bluffs, and washes along the Cimarron River.[13]

Although still without adequate food for the troops and forage for their animals, Crawford pushed ahead. He led the Nineteenth Kansas out of Camp Beecher on November 14, and two days later the command camped on the Chikaskia River southwest of present-day Wichita. Riding southwest, the men pitched their tents on Medicine Lodge Creek on the night of the eighteenth, near the site of the major peace talks in 1867. That night the horses stampeded, and some of the animals were not recovered. The regiment, now short of mounts and still without extra food and forage, left the next day. Complicating the shortage of provisions, as the force moved into the uncharted bluffs and draws of the Cimarron River valley—a maze of steep gorges and abrupt ridges that were already covered with snow—it encountered a severe early-winter blizzard.[14]

The command now struggled southwestward, its men subsisting on buffalo meat provided by their hunters, including Stilwell. On November 20 they camped at a place called Hackberry Point on the Cimarron River, where another storm struck. The bad weather continued all day, forcing Crawford and his Nineteenth Kansas Cavalry to wait out the snow and cold. By this time many of the horses and mules had become too weak and exhausted to be ridden. The men were cold, wet, and hungry. In desperation they ate hackberries and as a result suffered severe constipation.[15]

With exhausted stock, sick men, and the train stuck in the snow at Hackberry Point, Crawford needed his guides to get help from Camp Supply. Because he thought the regiment had become lost in the eroded river valley, Crawford conferred with his scouts about a route to follow. Apache Bill Semans, according to Pvt. Henry Pearson of Company I, believed "Camp Supply lay due south of where we were camped," and on November 20 he "took twenty-five men and started south." Unable to find the stockade post, Semans and the men returned the next day less two horses.[16]

Stilwell believed the elusive post lay to the southwest. When Semans started south on the twentieth, "Johnny Stilwell," as Pearson called him, took "two hundred cartridges, two carbines and two revolvers, an extra horse and started southwest alone." The men of the Nineteenth put a lot of trust in "Johnny Stilwell[,] even though he was but a boy of twenty years. For days and nights we wondered if Johnny Stillwell had succeeded in finding Camp Supply." Stilwell reached the new post on November 27.[17]

After Apache Bill Semans and his men had returned to Hackberry Point, Colonel Crawford, unsure if he should wait for Stilwell, decided on another course. On November 22 he ordered Captain Pliley of Troop A to take fifty of the best-mounted men to seek out Camp Supply and send relief to the stranded troopers at Hackberry Point—or as some men called it, "Camp Starvation"—on the Cimarron River.[18] Two days later, still worried, Crawford and 450 men with healthier horses pulled out of the dismal camp, leaving behind some 500 men. Crawford and his group crossed the Cimarron River and headed southwest, the same direction Stilwell had taken, hoping to strike the North Canadian River and follow it upstream to Camp Supply. On November 28 they reached the post, one day after Stilwell. While Crawford had not lost a man, he had lost many horses, and the regiment was too late to participate in Custer's operation.[19]

General Sheridan oversaw the winter campaign from Camp Supply. He had become concerned when the ten companies of the Nineteenth Kansas failed appear on time. Accordingly, on November 24, the same day Crawford and his 450 men left Hackberry Point, Sheridan sent scouts out fourteen miles to try to locate the Kansas volunteers, but they failed to find a trace of the missing regiment. Late in the afternoon of the next day, however, a second scouting party from the post returned with Captain Pliley's detachment. Pliley reported that his regiment had been snowed in and stranded on the Cimarron. The following day, November 26, Pliley's volunteers, Lieutenant Pepoon's scouts, and a wagon train with supplies left the camp to rescue the troops on the Cimarron and return them to Camp Supply.[20]

On November 28, the day that Crawford and his 450 men arrived at Camp
Supply, Pliley, Pepoon, and three wagons carrying provisions arrived at Hackberry Point.[21] Men of the Nineteenth Kansas still at the desolate camp gorged
themselves on the food and after a brief rest packed up their tents, blankets, and
other equipment before heading to the elusive post. The men walked and led
their horses, which were too exhausted to be ridden. On the twenty-ninth, as
they moved toward Camp Supply, Quartermaster Luther A. Thrasher obtained
forage for their mounts at Lieutenant Pepoon's camp, and two days later the last
company of the stranded regiment arrived at Sheridan's camp. Like others of
the Nineteenth Kansas, they were too late to take part in the Custer's infamous
fight on the Washita River.[22]

The Custer expedition, as noted above, formed the main column of Sheridan's
three-column plan.[23] Another of the columns, led by Maj. Eugene A. Carr and
guided by "a daredevil young plainsman" named William "Buffalo Bill" Cody,
rode southeast out of Fort Lyon, Colorado. Carr's column aimed to operate in
the area of the Antelope Hills, near the Canadian River along the border between
the Texas Panhandle and Indian Territory. Carr led his troops north and west
of the Washita River valley hoping to drive Indians back to their reservations.
For several weeks, he and his men kept Comanches and Kiowas on the move
in the Texas Panhandle. No major engagements occurred, and Carr's troops on
February 19, 1869, returned to Fort Lyon.[24]

Stilwell made only indirect contact with Major Carr's command. Its troopers
rode into the Texas Panhandle, camped at Palo Duro Creek in "severe weather
with snow and blizzards," and then continued south to the Canadian River. From
there Carr sent Edmund Guerrier, a French-Cheyenne trader, with dispatches
to Sheridan at Camp Supply. Because Sheridan had gone south, Guerrier fell in
with some of Custer's scouts, including Stilwell, and returned with them to Fort
Sill with the dispatches to Sheridan.[25]

The remaining column involved in Sheridan's campaign was led by Maj.
Andrew W. "Beans" Evans; it left from Fort Bascom, New Mexico, and pushed
east along the South Canadian River. Major Evans established a base camp on
the Canadian River, left about 260 soldiers of his command there, and headed
southeast with 300 men of the Third Cavalry and two mountain howitzers. On
Christmas Day he found a Comanche camp at Soldier Springs on the North Fork
of the Red River west of the Wichita Mountains. Using the howitzers, his troopers
cleared the village of Indians and moved into it. As his men destroyed tipis,
food stores, weapons, and other supplies, the Comanches, supported by Kiowa

reinforcements, struck back. A fight raged most of the day before the Indians withdrew. Evans and his Third Cavalry continued to search out Indian camps, but they became lost and ended up bivouacking only twenty miles from Fort Cobb, established in 1859 and located along the Washita River at the northern edge of the Comanche-Kiowa reservation in what is now Caddo County, Oklahoma.[26]

On December 30 Stilwell and three other scouts from Fort Cobb reached the temporary camp with a message for Major Evans. In "very cold and tempestuous" weather, wrote Evans, "we were about going into camp, when four men came up in rear on our trail." Stilwell remembered that Sheridan had sent him to ride west from Fort Cobb "to ascertain what expedition there was between the Washita River and the Wichita Mountains." He found Evans with his Third Cavalry.[27] Evans's location only twenty miles from Fort Cobb surprised Stilwell. He thought that after the fight at Soldier Springs, Evans's guides had "mistaken the Washita for the Canadian" and got "completely lost." He figured that they must have left the Canadian and passed around the head of the Washita without knowing it. "It is the only way we could account for their being in there and not knowing the Washita River."[28]

Whatever the reason for Evans's location, the message Stilwell carried ordered him and his troops back toward New Mexico. In response, early the next morning Evans and the Third Cavalry headed west and spent much of January seeking additional Indian villages before returning to their base camp. From there they headed back to Fort Bascom and reached the post about February 7. As Evans started west, Stilwell and other scouts guided a small detachment of the Third Cavalry led by Lt. Edward Hunter, in charge of the howitzer unit, to Fort Cobb. Evans wanted General Sheridan to know the condition of the Third Cavalry, which badly need food and forage. Because of cold temperatures and a rainy night, Stilwell, the scouts, and the detachment made only slow progress toward the post, which by this time had become the center of the Sheridan-Custer campaign.[29]

Custer's column (Sheridan's main column) left Camp Supply on November 23 without the Nineteenth Kansas Volunteers. It included eight hundred men and a long string of supply wagons. A foot of wet snow covered the ground that morning, and more fell throughout the day, slowing the march but not stopping Custer's command as it pushed south toward the Antelope Hills and across the Canadian River. Through several wet, miserable days the men continued south, reaching the upper Washita on November 27—the same day Jack Stilwell had belatedly reached Camp Supply. While it was still dark very early the next morning, and without making a reconnaissance, they struck the first Indian camp they reached.

What followed proved controversial. Custer's men had attacked the Cheyenne camp of Black Kettle, a peace advocate—although some of his young men had participated in the previous summer's raids in Kansas—and routed them. Cheyenne warriors fought back as they tried to get their families to safety, but within ten minutes Custer's men had control of the village. During the day they fought off Indian sorties as they gathered captives, burned tipis, and destroyed whatever food and other possessions, such as robes, weapons, and utensils, the dwellings contained. They also slaughtered 875 Cheyenne horses and mules.[30]

Toward evening Custer turned back to Camp Supply, unaccountably leaving behind a small detachment led by Maj. Joel Elliott, whose fate remained unknown. Slowed by his captives and his wounded, Custer reached the post on December 2. He reported 103 Indians killed—an exaggeration—plus tipis, supplies, and horses destroyed. He had captured 53 women and children. He had lost an officer and four men; Major Elliott and his fifteen men were missing; and three officers and eleven men were wounded. Later Sheridan discovered that Indians had killed Elliott and his entire detachment, increasing the number of men Custer lost to twenty-one.[31]

After the Seventh's return Sheridan decided to leave Camp Supply and move his headquarters south to Fort Cobb, located on the Washita River well below the battle site, taking with him Custer's cavalry and five hundred troops of the Nineteenth Kansas. Stilwell, who had joined Custer's guides and scouts (including Moses "California Joe" Milner, Jack Corbin, Raphael Romero, Ben Clark, James Morrison, and Henry Bradley) would ride with them. Some 250 other men of the Nineteenth, short of horses, stayed behind. They spent the rest of the winter garrisoning the post and escorting supply trains to Fort Dodge and back.[32]

On December 7, with some 1,500 men, the Sheridan-Custer command pulled out of Camp Supply. The temperature fell below zero, and the storm that blew in soon turned to a blizzard. The men rode south, crossed the South Canadian River, and approached within eight miles of the Washita battle site, where they camped. Sheridan, Custer, and a small escort rode over to the scene of the battle, found the mutilated remains of Major Elliott's detachment, and buried them, as well as the bodies of a white woman and child.[33]

The large force continued toward Fort Cobb, scouting for Comanches and Kiowas as they moved down the Washita. Hearing about the approaching force, Gen. William B. Hazen, commanding Fort Cobb, sent a courier and several Kiowa chiefs with their families to Sheridan; they carried a dispatch that suggested Sheridan and Custer should not attack Indians south of their present position, for such Indians lived at peace.[34] Unhappy with the message, Sheridan compromised. He did not harm the Indians with the courier, but he "arrested" two Kiowa chiefs, Satanta and Lone Wolf. Sheridan, Custer, and their captives reached Fort Cobb on December 18, ten days after leaving Camp Supply. Later Sheridan announced that he would hang the two captives unless all Kiowas scattered across the region went back to the reservation and Fort Cobb. Runners went out with the information, and the Kiowas quickly returned to the fort.[35]

As Indians arrived at the post, camping and grazing land around Fort Cobb became crowded. Such was always an issue in winter. Thousands of Indians and soldiers were camped in an area of sparse grass that soon gave way to barren ground, and, after snow or rain, to muck and mud. Such conditions led Sheridan in early January 1869 to order his soldiers, the Indians, and Indian agency personnel to relocate some thirty miles south to a new post, Fort Sill, under construction east of the Wichita Mountains in the heart of the Comanche-Kiowa reservation. Here spread a clean, wide plain with plenty of grass to support both Indians' and soldiers' horses.[36]

Through much of January and early February, Custer, sometimes with Stilwell as a guide, led small units of cavalrymen in search of additional Cheyenne, Arapaho, Comanche, and Kiowa bands. In one instance, with Stilwell as the chief scout, his men moved west of the Wichita Mountains, located some bands, convinced a few to ride to Fort Sill, and learned that others, especially Cheyennes, had moved farther west toward canyons on the eastern edge of the Llano Estacado, a huge tableland about three hundred feet above the land surrounding it.[37] Sheridan determined to go after the Cheyenne "fugitives." He left Fort Sill for Camp Supply, where he arranged logistical support for a large Custer expedition west toward the Canadian River and the North Fork of the Red River. On March 2, 1869, the same day that Custer and the Seventh Cavalry (reinforced by the Nineteenth Kansas Volunteers) left Fort Sill, Sheridan received orders to proceed to Washington, D.C.[38]

Thus Custer was left to finish the winter campaign. After leaving Fort Sill, he and his command scoured the eastern edge of the Llano Estacado looking for Cheyennes but found only a few. Consequently, he sent part of his force back to the Washita River and with eight hundred men continued his search toward Indian Territory. On March 15, along Sweetwater Creek near the Texas Panhandle border with Indian Territory, he found a large Cheyenne village. He did not attack, for the Indians, led by Little Robe and Medicine Arrow, held two white women as captives. After three days of negotiations and promises on both sides, Custer turned his men north to Camp Supply and on March 28 reached the post.[39]

Sheridan's winter campaign was over. The winter had taxed Stilwell's strength as he rode through blizzards and freezing temperatures to guide troops and deliver messages. On January 2, 1869, Sheridan had placed him on Lt. Col. A. J. McGonnigle's quartermaster roll as a scout and guide in the field. His pay remained $100 per month.[40] The next day, Sheridan sent Stilwell, Ben Clark, Jimmie Morrison, and Jack Corbin from Fort Cobb to Camp Supply. At the supply post Stilwell, Morrison, and Corbin received the mail and with fresh horses delivered it back to Sheridan's headquarters at Fort Cobb. Ben Clark guided a wagon train back to the post.[41]

The three mail carriers experienced a difficult and hazardous return trip. In a letter to his wife, Libby, dated January 14, Custer wrote, "I want to tell you about the courage of one of the guides." He was referring to Jack Stilwell. "Nearly naked," Stilwell "was mounted on a mule and riding through camp. . . . He had just returned" through frigid weather and snow with the mail, and he was close to unconsciousness. "I began calling to him in [delicate] tones," Custer wrote, "and we soon had him in my tent. After pouring a gill of whiskey down him . . . he was able to speak."[42]

According to Custer, "Heavy rains for several days had filled the streams to overflowing. . . . Stillwell with his party and their pack mules reached the opposite bank about a mile above camp, [and] found the stream impassable for loaded pack mules bearing the mail." Thereupon, Custer continued, Jack with his horse plunged in the river, and "swam the stream" that was "nearly frozen with ice water." Then he rode into the camp along Medicine Bluff Creek and told Custer that "owing to the rapid current, it was impossible to bring the mail over till morning, when it was hoped that the water would fall and render swimming unnecessary."[43]

Custer had great respect for his couriers. A month after his return, Stilwell, Corbin, and Morrison made another cold, winter ride to Camp Supply and back, and in another of his many letters to Libby, this one written on February 20, Custer wrote that as he sat alone in his Sibley tent, he heard riders approaching. "Three muffed figures," he explained, "human in shape, mounted on mules and leading two pack mules, rode up to my tent and dismounted." They carried mail that Custer anxiously sought. "Shaking hands all around and asking them to set down by my sheet-iron stove and warm, I called the adjutant to distribute the mail that they brought." The three mail carriers were "daring men," he said. "I could have hugged them when I thought that they braved the perils of two hundred miles through Indian country, in order to bring us . . . news from our loved ones."[44]

Clearly, Stilwell had served the army well. His one big disappointment during the winter campaign was the failure of the Nineteenth Kansas to reach Camp Supply in time to march with Custer's November expedition. No records survive in which he mentions his responsibility in guiding the Nineteenth Kansas from Topeka to Camp Supply. He remained too embarrassed about the regiment becoming lost in the breaks and washes of the Cimarron River to talk about it, and at least one observer, the trader J. R. Mead, blamed the debacle on him. In a 1908 letter to a colleague at the headquarters of the Kansas Historical Society, Mead wrote, "Stillwell [sic] was the most overrated man there was on the plains. He is the man probably responsible for the disaster" that befell the Nineteenth Kansas Cavalry in 1868.[45]

Mead was wrong. Eight officers and nine enlisted men wrote about the march from Topeka to Camp Supply. Their opinions, of course, differ, but most officers, including Colonel Crawford and Lt. Col. Horace Moore, blamed scout and guide Apache Bill Semans for the problems. Stilwell bore little fault for the disaster of the Nineteenth Kansas Cavalry's troubles along in the Cimarron River valley.[46] Most enlisted men, like their officers, also blamed Semans for becoming lost, but several of them believed that Colonel Crawford was responsible for the calamity. The sergeant of Company M, Major A. Victor, writing to the editor of the *Emporia News*, attributed the regiment's problems to Crawford. He wrote that if the regiment had a voice in choosing a commander, S. J. Crawford would not get any votes. If Crawford again ran for civilian office, he would get few votes from the regiment's troopers.[47]

George W. Brown, who with Stilwell's help had joined Pepoon's scouts at Fort Hays, likewise believed Colonel Crawford and the other officers were liable. They had no experience in frontier life, he argued. The "green" officers distrusted Semans and "from time to time would call him in and show him their maps and compass and declare that he was off course."[48] Sgt. James A. Hadley of Company A (wrongly) stated that "not an officer or a man in Crawford's command had ever been south of the Arkansas River." He also blamed the unusually harsh winter weather, acknowledging that the command met "conditions unforeseen" with inadequate supplies. Such conditions "would confuse anybody. The very maps were wrong, and this added to the confusion." He believed that "the cold weather and the lack of stores were the causes of the catastrophe. . . . The universal ignorance of that country was at the bottom of it all."[49]

In his 1888 memoirs Philip Sheridan criticized Crawford for becoming lost because he did not rely on the advice of his guides.[50] Conversely, Pvt. Joseph Phelps Rogers of Company F held Sheridan responsible. "If General Sheridan had known anything about the country and what we were to encounter that time of the year," Rogers noted, "he would never have given the order to make that march. He had been misinformed by his scouts."[51]

Responsibility for the Cimarron River question aside, by riding southwest from the snow-filled valley, Stilwell had made it to Camp Supply alone with his weapons intact and his horses fit. Then, on December 7, he had ridden south with Sheridan and Custer to Fort Cobb and for the next three cold months he had served as guide and courier with both commanders. The winter campaign of 1868–69 had secured Stilwell's future as an army scout and guide on the Great Plains of the American West.

CHAPTER 6

WITH BUFFALO SOLDIERS
ON THE SOUTHERN PLAINS

Following Sheridan's winter campaign of 1869, Jack Stilwell worked intermittently for the next two years. When he worked for the army, he served as a scout, hunter, and guide, shifting between the commands of Lt. Col. Anderson D. Nelson, Fifth Infantry, at Camp Supply and Custer's Seventh Cavalry at Fort Hays. When he was off duty he went home to Baldwin City, relaxed with friends at Hays City, or went east to Lawrence. A transfer to Fort Sill in the summer of 1871 led to active duty with the Tenth U.S. Cavalry, a Buffalo Soldiers regiment.

Stilwell's contemporaries left vivid word portraits of his appearance and bearing during these years. John Hurst described him as "a beardless youth . . . but a veteran in frontiersmanship and plains craft and one of the bravest, nerviest, and coolest men in the command." Lt. Robert G. Carter said he "was a very boyish, modest, quiet-appearing and soft voiced man." Describing his appearance, Carter wrote that he "was of medium height, slim, rather sallow complexion, light chestnut-brown hair . . . very deep-set, penetrating grey blue or steel blue eyes, a firm jaw and sharp nose."[1]

April 1869 had seen the Nineteenth Kansas Volunteer Cavalry released from federal service, putting Stilwell out of work—although not for long. The young scout's knowledge of the southern plains and the terrain surrounding the northwestern portions of Indian Territory convinced Colonel Nelson to hire him to serve as guide at Camp Supply, which had become the interim agency for the Cheyenne and Arapaho tribes. Nelson served as temporary Indian agent at the post, and Troops F, H, I, and K of the Tenth Cavalry provided military support.[2]

As both military commander of Camp Supply and Indian agent, Nelson faced myriad difficulties. The most pressing related to feeding Cheyenne and Arapaho people as they arrived at the post (or, because they wanted to live away from the soldiers, at camps nearby). It fell to the army and the Department of War to feed and support people of both tribes until the government established a permanent reservation and the new civilian agent, a Quaker named Brinton Darlington, arrived. Through the summer of 1869 more Arapahos and Cheyennes camped near the post, compounding the problems. Capt. Seth Bonney, in charge of issuing rations, reported early in the summer that his men had distributed food, particularly beef, to 1,335 Arapahos and 165 Cheyennes. As time passed and more Cheyennes arrived, every fifth day or so he delivered supplies to an additional 1,200 people, for a total of about 2,500 people.[3]

Nelson also faced an Indian attack. On June 11 a large party of Kiowa and Comanche warriors struck the post, and soldiers responded. The short fight that followed turned deadly; six of the attackers died, and ten received wounds before the Indians retreated. No Cheyennes or Arapahos participated in the quick but lethal battle.[4] The new Quaker agent brought further headaches. Nelson and Darlington did not get along. They disagreed over a good location for the reservation's permanent agency: Nelson wanted it to remain at Camp Supply, and Darlington proposed moving it to Pond Creek, east of the temporary agency. The Indians would not agree to that site. Darlington, who had the support of the Interior Department's Indian service (which by September 1869 controlled government-Indian relations), countered by selecting a spot on the North Canadian River about 125 miles southeast of Camp Supply. Called the Darlington agency, the place became the administrative center for the Cheyenne-Arapaho reservation.[5]

Stilwell was only cursorily involved with such decisions. For the most part he hunted wild game, especially bison and deer, to help feed reservation people; served as a guide for troopers and others seeking a permanent location for the reservation agency; and acted as courier for Colonel Nelson by carrying messages from Camp Supply to Fort Hays in Kansas and to Fort Sill, near the Comanche-Kiowa reservation agency. Not long after the government moved the Cheyenne-Arapaho reservation to the North Canadian River, Stilwell's responsibilities diminished, and in January 1870 he left Camp Supply and rode north to Fort Hays.

In the spring of 1870 Jack visited his family. From Fort Hays he made his way east by rail to Lawrence, Kansas, and from there he traveled to Baldwin City. He found his aunt and uncle, Rhoda and Jacob Stilwell, still farming the northern half of the original Stilwell homestead about a quarter mile west of Baldwin City. All of Jack's cousins—William, age twenty-two; Phoebe, age twenty; Olive, age fifteen; and Clara, age seven—were still living at the farm with their parents. Jack's brothers Howard and Millard lived in Palmyra Township near their Uncle Jacob; brother Frank resided in eastern Kansas.[6]

From Baldwin City Jack traveled east to visit his mother, Charlotte, and two younger sisters, Clara May, now eleven, and Elizabeth Ann, nine. By 1870 Charlotte Stilwell had sold her half of the Palmyra Township claim, and with her daughters moved to Mooney in western Jackson County, Indiana, where she could draw financial and familial support from the very large Stilwell family in the Brownstown area and from her own Winfrey family in nearby Lawrence County. Charlotte was thirty-six years old and a divorced single mother.[7]

Stilwell probably had no interest in visiting his father, a man whose name he rarely mentioned. Nor did he wish to see his stepmother, Jennie Pike, who had mistreated his younger brothers Howard and Millard. William Henry Stilwell and his second wife lived in Buchanan County, Missouri, where in 1870 the forty-five-year-old had resumed his work as a carpenter. Jennie, who as Sarah Jane Brenner had "married" William in 1865 for the second time (their 1863 marriage was invalid because William Henry and Charlotte were not legally divorced), turned thirty-two in 1870. The couple supported her daughter from her first marriage (Mary, sixteen) and seven-year-old Ella, their shared daughter.[8]

When he returned to Kansas in the spring of 1870, Stilwell headed for Fort Hays, where Custer was eager to employ him. "Stilwell I knew well," wrote Custer, "having employed him as a scout for many years." According to Custer, the young scout possessed "a trim figure which was set off to great advantage by a jaunty suit of buckskin which he wore, cut and fringed." In his belt he carried "a large sized revolver and hunting knife. These with his rifle constitute his equipment." Stilwell was "a capital shot whether afoot or on horseback, and a perfect horseman."[9]

Stilwell reported to Custer at a large camp on Big Creek, two miles east of Fort Hays. Lack of space at the post and Custer's independent spirit accounted for the Seventh Cavalry's encampment away from the post. Custer and his wife Libby had spent the summer of 1869 at the camp and returned there in late spring of 1870. They had wintered at Fort Leavenworth, away from the cold and windy plains.[10] Stilwell enrolled for work on June 4. Custer required of him two separate duties: to serve as a scout for Seventh Cavalry detachments sent into the field from Fort Hays and Big Creek; and to guide—as well as entertain—Custer's guests and visitors who poured in from the East on the Kansas Pacific Railroad.[11]

On June 7, only three days after he arrived at Big Creek, Stilwell rode off on assignment. Custer sent him and two other scouts to find missing Seventh Cavalry detachments reconnoitering the plains in western Kansas. Cheyenne warriors, twenty in number, spied the three men on the North Fork of the Solomon River in what is now Sheridan County and attacked, pinning them down. Stilwell and his companions kept them at bay for about two hours, until some of the Indians left to find reinforcements. The scouts made their escape and headed south for Grinnell Station, near the upper Saline River. From there they returned to the Big Creek camp, reaching it two days later. The reconnaissance units they had been sent to find reached camp, unaided, on July 15.[12]

Custer's guests at Big Creek included British aristocracy, army generals and their wives, political leaders, wealthy businessmen, and newspaper reporters, among others. That summer about two hundred guests appeared—so many, in fact, that Libby became bored with them. Bison hunting was the most popular pastime for the visitors, and Stilwell, when not out with troopers, served as their guide, finding herds, locating campsites, and protecting them from possible Indian attacks. He enjoyed hunting and shot many bison during the summer's expeditions.[13]

Stilwell's bison-hunting duties also included relaxation, storytelling, and other amusements. On occasion Libby Custer provided a romantic environment for regimental officers, inviting single women to join their entourage. The summer of 1870 Annie Roberts was among them. Roberts was the niece of Col. George Gibson, who was commander at Fort Hays in 1870. Her father, W. Milnor Roberts, was an engineer who had built a railway in Brazil from Rio de Janeiro into the interior jungle. While with him in Brazil, Annie became fluent in several languages; she also developed into a master equestrienne and a superior markswoman. In Kansas she participated in several Custer-arranged bison hunts, and because she was skillful in bringing down the big animals she acquired the nickname "Buffalo Annie."[14] In her diary Roberts described Stilwell as a "celebrated character." She noted that he "wore a beautifully embroidered buckskin suit and had several pistols at his belt."[15] It is likely that Stilwell's western-style garb, or "jaunty suit," as Custer called it, factored into what became his growing popularity among the eastern visitors.[16]

In any case, Roberts wrote about a hunt in which she and at least two other single women participated. On July 4, she noted, Custer sent Stilwell and Companies D and F of the Seventh to Selma Creek, thirteen miles from Fort Hays, to establish a hunting camp. The next evening the hunting party departed the Big

Creek camp in four ambulances but they were waylaid by a heavy rain. Soaked, the party took unsatisfactory shelter beneath some trees. The next morning Stilwell found the wet, cold hunters and led them to the Selma Creek camp. In her diary Roberts described the large camp as beautiful: tents stood in the shade of elms along the bank of the creek, and soldiers had already dug several fire pits.[17]

Custer, Roberts, Lt. W. M. Yates, and Stilwell joined other greenhorns and soldiers in the sport, charging after a herd of a hundred bison and killing many before the rest escaped. The men butchered the dead animals in the field, including delicacies such as tongues, hind quarters, back strap, and other special cuts, before heading back to camp where soldiers prepared several wonderful meals of bison meat. In another hunt Roberts was galloping alone after a bison when she saw a dismounted man, who—to her surprise—turned out to be Custer. His horse had stepped into a prairie dog hole and tripped, throwing him. He was not hurt, but he was on foot. Custer's quandary lay in the fact that many people in the 1870s, especially enlisted men, viewed an officer on foot as something of a humiliation. Stilwell, apparently trying to divert Roberts's attention away from Custer's predicament, rode up and advised her to go back; the rough country contained all sorts of hazards for a horse and rider going at great speed. She would have none of it. Greatly embarrassed, Custer tried to get Roberts to maintain a discreet silence regarding his fall. She did not, and back in camp Custer had to admit the accident, which required him to buy champagne for the entire party.[18]

During the hunts along Selma Creek, Lieutenant Yates, who later married Roberts, paid her close attention. After one hunt, in an effort to spend more time with her, he led her back to Big Creek by a route different from that of the main party. Stilwell accompanied them, but other than an unsuccessful attempt by the two men to scare Roberts about Indians in the vicinity, nothing of consequence occurred.[19]

Throughout the summer and fall of 1870 Stilwell continued to enjoy his time on bison hunts and assisted additional hunting parties. He also guided detachments of Seventh Cavalry troopers in western Kansas, although he did not get involved in major engagements with Indians. By early winter, however, he was again jobless, if only briefly: many years later he wrote, "In the spring of 1871 I was employed as a post guide at Fort Sill."[20]

Being an army scout or guide was at best a part-time job, work that was usually offered in the summer and fall. The pay ranged from fifty to seventy-five dollars per month. When cavalry regiments moved in the field, Stilwell or other scouts served under the direction of the unit's field commander. Stilwell wrote that in "the summer months of 1871, 1872, and 1873, I was in the field with different scouting parties almost constantly, taking part in nearly all if not every fight between United States troops from Fort Sill and hostile Indians along the border of Texas."[21] In 1871 he was the only guide hired by the Fort Sill quartermaster, Capt. Almon Rockwell. Stilwell got the position because he knew the country well, for, as John McBee of the Nineteenth Kansas Volunteers had suggested three years earlier, "Jack Stillwell [had been] with Custer all the way around."[22]

Events in Texas in the spring of 1871 led to the army's need of Stilwell's services. As early as March, Fort Sill's Indian agent, Lawrie Tatum, requested that the southern boundary (i.e., the Red River) of the Comanche-Kiowa reservation be patrolled to prevent, as far as possible, Indians from crossing into Texas to find horses, cattle, or other "treasures" they might covet. Tatum wanted the army to arrest any Indians found attempting to cross into Texas, and troopers from Companies L and M of the Tenth Cavalry, commanded by Maj. David Bell McKibbin, received orders to proceed south, camp at the mouth of Cache Creek on the Red River, and from there patrol the border.[23]

The patrols did not always work. On May 18 about one hundred Kiowas led by Satanta, Satank, Big Tree, and Maman-ti attacked a train of several wagons owned by freighting contractor Henry Warren, in what became a significant turning point in Indian-soldier relationships. Bound west on the old Butterfield Overland Mail route from Fort Richardson, the wagons carried corn and other supplies to Fort Griffin. At Salt Creek Prairie in present-day Young County, Texas, the Indians descended on the teamsters, killing the wagon master and six of the twelve teamsters. One Kiowa warrior died and six suffered wounds. A wounded teamster, Thomas Brazeal, escaped and made his way twenty miles to Fort Richardson, where he reported the attack.[24]

Often called the Warren Wagon Train massacre, the incident quickly got the attention of General of the Army William T. Sherman, who had on the previous day followed the Overland trail east from Fort Griffin and had just arrived at Fort Richardson. Sherman had received numerous reports of Indian depredations in Texas, and he wanted to check the region for himself. When Kiowas hit the wagon train, he had just completed the long inspection tour and recognized that only by chance had he and his small military escort not been targeted.[25]

Sherman was not happy. On hearing Brazeal's account, he determined to shift U.S. Indian policy and abandon the "defensive stance" the army had been using in favor of more aggressive action. He planned to act deliberately until he could convince President Grant to end the so-called "Peace Policy" in U.S. relations with American Indians in the West.[26] The shift in policy began immediately—if gradually. Sherman ordered Col. Ranald S. Mackenzie, post commander at Fort Richardson, to take his Fourth Cavalry troops to the site of the attack and pursue the Kiowa raiders—even up into the reservation. Mackenzie met with little success and lost the trail of the raiders near the Red River. Thereupon he headed for Fort Sill.[27]

As Mackenzie continued to search the Red River border country, Sherman and his inspection party (including Maj. Randolph B. Marcy, inspector-general of the army, two aides, and a detachment of seventeen Tenth Cavalry soldiers) left Fort Richardson for Fort Sill. When he arrived at the post, Sherman reported the raid to Indian Agent Lawrie Tatum and requested his aid in finding the Indians who led the attack. Tatum thought that he could help when the Indians came in for rations. Four days later, in fact, many Kiowas, including some who had been in the wagon train raid, appeared at the agency. Tatum asked them about the tragedy in Texas, and the great orator Satanta spoke up to claim credit for leading the attack. Kiowa chiefs Satank, Eagle Heart, and Big Tree confirmed Satanta's story.[28]

Tatum informed Sherman and Col. Benjamin H. Grierson, post commander at Fort Sill, of Satanta's speech and requested that Satanta and some others be arrested and sent to Texas to stand trial for murder. Accordingly, on May 27, 1871, Kiowa leaders met with Sherman on the front porch of Grierson's quarters. After heated discussion, Sherman, as expected, indicated that Satanta, Satank, and Big Tree would be sent to Texas. When several angry Kiowas appeared, Tenth Cavalry soldiers unhooked their carbines and raised the weapons. In response most Indians backed down and left for their camps elsewhere on the reservation. Troopers placed the three leaders in irons and led them to cells at barracks near the southwest corner of the post's parade ground.[29]

Not long afterward, Sherman left Indian Territory for Washington, D.C. His plan, as indicated, was to convince Grant to abandon the Peace Policy, also known as Grant's Peace Policy or the Quaker Peace Policy. He was successful and shortly afterward he turned loose the troops, instructing military officers to begin offensive operations against all Indians off their reservations.[30] As part of the new plan, Sherman determined to increase the presence of soldiers along the Red River, which formed the southern border of the Comanche-Kiowa reservation. In addition to the established base at the mouth of Cache Creek, the Tenth Cavalry would set up a military camp on Otter Creek southwest of Fort Sill. Soldiers, according to the plan, were to use the camps to patrol the river.

The quartermaster at Fort Sill hired Stilwell as scout and guide to help with these maneuvers, and on June 1 Stilwell went to work.[31]

This assignment meant Stilwell was often in the saddle. On August 1 he rode from Fort Sill with Troop B, Tenth Cavalry, led by Capt. John B. Vande Wiele, to escort a wagon train loaded with supplies to establish the camp on Otter Creek. Two days later he joined Troop G, commanded by Capt. Phillip L. Lee; Troop H, led by Capt. Lewis H. Carpenter; and Troop I, led by Capt. Theodore A. Baldwin, after they had departed Fort Sill to search the Red River borderlands. Within the week he was back at the Otter Creek camp when Colonel Grierson; his quartermaster, 1st Lt. William H. Beck; Troop D, led by Capt. James W. Walsh; and Troop K, under 1st Lt. Robert G. Smithers, arrived at the recently founded camp.[32]

In the meantime, five days after General Sherman had left Fort Sill, Mackenzie returned to the post and reported that he had lost the Indian raiders' trail. To his surprise the three Kiowa chiefs he had been pursuing sat in irons in the post guardhouse. Mackenzie was ordered to escort the prisoners to Fort Richardson and Jacksboro, Texas, to stand trial. He and the Fourth Cavalry were also directed to participate in Sherman's new offensive against Indians who left their reservations.[33]

Mackenzie met with Colonel Grierson at the Otter Creek camp to discuss plans for the new action. The two campaigners were both successful military men, but their philosophies for dealing with the Indians were fundamentally opposed: Mackenzie subscribed to Sherman's new aggressive strategy; Grierson preferred the now-abandoned Peace Policy. Nonetheless, Grierson and Mackenzie agreed on a plan of action. First, they would find Kicking Bird's Kiowa band, which hunted off the reservation. Then, with approval and confirmation of their superior officers in the Military Division of the Missouri, headed by General Sheridan, they would pursue other absent Indian bands. To find Kicking Bird, Tenth and Fourth Cavalry troopers crossed the North Fork of the Red River with pack trains before splitting into two columns. Mackenzie and his regiment followed the Salt Fork of the North Fork, while Grierson's detachments of Tenth Cavalry rode up the main branch of the North Fork.[34]

Both cavalry regiments patrolled from August to November, but not all went according to plan.[35] Stilwell rode with Colonel Grierson's command; they followed the North Fork, roughly paralleling Custer's post-Washita battle route of March 1869. Along the trail Stilwell showed Grierson part of an old wagon bed abandoned by Custer and, for whatever reason, pointed out that it had been at one time repaired by Maj. Henry Inman of Fort Harker.[36] Stilwell and Grierson became friends, and Grierson often asked his guide to join his mess.[37]

Grierson did not find Kicking Bird. On September 6 he returned to Fort Sill, leaving the bulk of his command at Otter Creek to continue scouting the along the Red River and toward Fort Griffin in Texas. At Fort Sill he learned that Kiowas had returned all mules stolen in the Warren Wagon Train raid to Indian Agent Tatum. With that knowledge Grierson, who as indicated above favored the now-abandoned Peace Policy, sent the post's interpreter, Horace P. Jones, to find Kicking Bird's Kiowa band and warn them to move back into the Wichita Mountains on the reservation. Jones found the band, and the Kiowas returned. Mackenzie, when he learned that Jones had been successful, turned his attention to Kwahada Comanches on the Llano Estacado.[38]

Stillwell then returned to the Otter Creek camp, where he joined Captain Vande Wiele and Troop B of the Tenth Cavalry on patrol along the Red River. On September 19 at Foster Spring in Indian Territory, Indians attacked the Buffalo Soldiers, killing Foster Larkin, a wagoner, before fleeing the soldiers' counterattack. After the skirmish Vande Wiele returned to Otter Creek and sent Stilwell to Fort Sill with a report of the clash.[39]

Stilwell remained at the reservation post for the remainder of the month. He dined with Colonel Grierson, exchanged war stories with Tenth Cavalry Buffalo Soldiers, tended to his mounts, and visited with Horace Jones, the post interpreter. On September 30 he left Fort Sill, having once again been discharged for want of assignments.[40] Three and a half months later, on January 15, 1872, Stilwell settled at Fort Larned, Kansas, where the post quartermaster hired him as a guide for the Third Infantry regiment. His first assignment with the Third involved guiding a detachment to Medicine Lodge Creek to locate and recover the body of Pvt. Franklin Winston, who recently had been killed by Osage warriors while Winston and Pvt. Isaac K. Larkin searched for three lost army mules.[41]

Stilwell and the infantry detachment arrived at Medicine Lodge Creek on January 18. They took affidavits from Larkin, who had escaped the attack, two bison hunters in the area, a wolf hunter named Henry Floyd, and a rancher named G. Watson Griffin, to whose home they had all fled when the Osage warriors appeared. On being shown the burial place of Private Winston, members of the Third Infantry exhumed the man's body and returned it to Fort Larned for reburial in the post cemetery.[42]

With the task completed Stilwell's employment at the post ended. Such was the life of a civilian guide and scout. Briefly Stilwell found work leading cattle drovers and their herds north from Texas to railheads in Kansas. In testimony given in 1897 at Anadarko, Oklahoma Territory, he said that he "took a couple herds up the trail along in 1872, from Texas to Kansas."[43] That spring many drovers followed the Chisholm Trail north to a railroad shipping point at Wichita. Stilwell was familiar with the main trail as well knowing as its various alternate routes, he spoke Spanish, and he knew Kiowas, Cheyennes, and Comanches who might be encountered as the herds passed through Indian Territory, so he proved to be an excellent guide.[44]

On July 8 he returned to military service at Fort Sill. For the next two months he again rode with detachments of Buffalo Soldiers who scouted from the temporary camps along the Red River. Their responsibilities included keeping Texans out of Indian Territory and Indians, especially Kiowas and Comanches, on the reservation.[45] In September Stilwell got a different assignment. It arose from government plans to send a delegation of Kiowa chiefs to Washington, D.C. Special commissioners to Fort Sill Indians Henry E. Alvord (formerly a captain in the Tenth Cavalry) and Edward Parrish of Philadelphia visited the reservation to set up the tour. Because the chiefs had agreed to travel to the capital only if Satanta and Big Tree were brought to Fort Sill so that the tribe could see them, Alvord and Parrish lobbied successfully to have the Indian prisoners returned to the reservation agency. Accordingly, Lt. Robert G. Carter and Troop E, Fourth Cavalry, picked up the prisoners in Dallas and began transporting them to Fort Sill.[46]

Anticipation of the return of Satanta and Big Tree roused the Kiowas. Maj. George W. Schofield, temporarily in command at Fort Sill, interpreted the excitement negatively as "bad attitude" and believed such conditions made the post unsafe unless officials released Satanta and Big Tree. With most of the Tenth Cavalry on patrol along the Red River, Kiowas outnumbered and surrounded the post's small military garrison.[47]

To ensure the safety of Indians and soldiers at Fort Sill, Major Schofield sent Stilwell to find Lieutenant Carter and deliver a message that included a plea that Carter, despite his orders, should not bring the prisoners to Fort Sill but instead deliver them to Commissioners Alford and Parrish at Atoka, a depot along the Missouri, Kansas, and Texas Railroad (known as the Katy) in southeastern Indian Territory. From Schofield's point of view, the post situation seemed highly volatile, and the appearance of the Kiowa leaders would add fuel to the supposed fire.[48]

Stilwell rode south into Clay County, Texas, and then took a trail southeast toward Denton County. Instructed to hurry, he galloped fast and hard enough that before reaching Carter his first horse died from exhaustion, forcing Stilwell to borrow a second horse from a rancher along his route. On September 10 Stilwell found Carter, his troops, and the prisoners camped at Denton Creek on the Fort Sill trail and delivered Schofield's message. Although Carter described his meeting with Stilwell as "a midnight council of the Fort Still Trail," he was reluctant to change course. His orders instructed him to deliver the prisoners to Fort Sill. According to Carter, Stilwell convinced him otherwise. The scout "spoke slowly and deliberately with a slight soft drawl, saying 'I an't no soldier, but have been in some pretty tight spots in my life. As sure as you take these Chiefs into the Fort Sill Reservation you will be taking very big chances of getting them out. . . . My best judgement and advice would be . . . not to take them there. . . . I know the mood of all those Indians pretty well and I believe Major Schofield's fears are correct.'"[49]

Stilwell's argument convinced Carter to alter his course, and he, Stilwell, the troops, and the prisoners left the Fort Sill trail and turned northeast toward the Red River. They passed through Gainesville, Texas, and crossed the river near Preston on September 14. From there they rode north to Atoka and the railroad depot. Here Carter sent Stilwell to find the Indian commissioners, who had recently arrived from Fort Sill. Jack located them and interpreter Horace Jones on a Katy train in a "Pullman Special"; Kiowa spokesman Lone Wolf and many of the Kiowa chiefs and their families were with them.

Soldiers removed the shackles that had secured Satanta and Big Tree and brought the men to the train. The Kiowas enjoyed a brief but happy reunion with fellow tribe members before the train continued northeast to Saint Louis, and from there, minus Satanta and Big Tree, to Washington. Stilwell left for Fort Sill. Carter later wrote that he missed "the good common sense, wisdom and modesty of Stilwell."[50]

After returning to the reservation post, Stilwell had little to do. He escorted a few Buffalo Soldier detachments to and from their temporary scouting camps along the Red River, but he spent a lot of time in idleness. He hunted some, especially at the edges of the Kiowa-Comanche reservation, and consumed too much alcohol. Not surprisingly, on December 31 the army discharged him.

Three months later, on April 1, 1873, the army again employed Stilwell, placing him under the "direction of the commanding officer" at Fort Sill.[51] The new commander was Lt. Col. John W. "Black Jack" Davidson, a West Point–trained and very demanding "spit-and-polish" officer. Davidson did not always get along with the Tenth's staff officers, who preferred the less ridged style of former commander Benjamin Grierson. Stilwell's relationship with Davison remains unknown, but as the commanding officer hired no additional scouts, Davidson must have at least trusted him. Indeed, on May 25 Davidson and an escort of twenty men under Capt. Phillip Lee left Fort Sill for a five-day reconnaissance in the direction of the North Fork of the Red River, and Stilwell was their guide.[52] They found no Indian warriors. On August 19, again with Stilwell as scout and guide, Davidson led a six-troop expedition to scour some of the same country west of Fort Sill, following the Red River and its North Fork. The men traveled up the North Fork as far as the Elm Fork before turning back. The expedition returned to post on September 14. They rode four hundred miles and saw no Indians.[53]

Later in the fall Stilwell served as guide on a bison hunt out of Fort Sill. Two businessmen, Wall Street broker A. W. Dimock and his friend J. Q. A. Ward, arrived at the post carrying letters of introduction from Division of the Missouri commander Philip Sheridan and other military officers. Post soldiers and civilian employees entertained the easterners for two days with a formal party, a wolf hunt, a ride to beautiful Medicine Bluff near the post, and a visit to some Kiowa camps.

While Dimock left on business for a few days, several Tenth Cavalry officers applied for leave to escort Ward on a bison hunt with Comanche chief Quirtz-quip. Upon his return to the post, Dimock insisted on joining his friend Ward in the field. Davidson advised him not to go alone, but Dimock was insistent. Thereupon Davidson offered him the best horse on the post, and, according to Dimock, Stilwell jumped at the opportunity to join the hunting party, telling the easterner that he "could find the hunting party if anyone living could." The two of them started after dusk.[54]

After they had ridden many miles, Stilwell suggested that they halt until morning. When ask why, the young guide said he did not want to ride up to an Indian camp—even though it was Quirtzquit's village—at night for fear of being shot. Stilwell believed the busy little camp spread across a nearby creek. He slid from his saddle, placed it on the ground as a pillow, and tied one end of his rope around his pony's neck and the other end around his wrist. Dimock did the same, and Jack told him get some sleep, for Jack's pony would warn them of trouble. For safety Dimock and Stilwell did not build a fire.

As they stretched out on the ground, the men exchanged stories. Stilwell related his experiences in the Beecher Island fight and reported on Lt. Frederick Beecher's last camp. In turn Dimock reported on Beecher's "first camp," as he called it. In a surprising coincidence, many years previously Dimock and Beecher had camped in deep snow during a February storm in some New England mountains. The men, it turns out, had been schoolmates in Andover, Massachusetts. The next morning Dimock woke up bruised and sore, courtesy of the long ride, the hard saddle, the Spencer rifle, and the large army revolver secured to his waist. After mounting his horse, he and Stilwell rode into the Quirtzquip's camp ready for the bison hunt. Stilwell returned to Fort Sill with several officers.[55]

On October 8 Stilwell appeared at a government conference with Indian leaders. The meeting took place at the Comanche agency about a mile and a half from Fort Sill. Commissioner of Indian Affairs E. P. Smith chaired the meeting, which was attended by Indian Agent James Haworth, post interpreter Phillip McCusker, a number of clerks and recorders, and about sixty Indians—Kiowas and Comanches—among them Quirtzquip, Black Horse, and Cheevers. Stilwell and A. W. Dimock, the latter having returned from the bison hunt, came to testify as witnesses.[56]

At the meeting, which occurred in the agency commissary building, Commissioner Smith demanded that Comanches turn over to the government five young men who had been raiding in Texas—although Smith could not name the alleged raiders. Several Comanches, led by Black Horse, refused, citing the fact that just three days earlier the government had released from prison Kiowa leaders Satanta and Big Tree, both of whom had led deadly raids in Texas. Smith, who had encouraged release of the Kiowa leaders, nonetheless foolishly pressed his demands for the Comanche arrests. The meeting grew contentious and then turned worse. Outside the small commissary building, Indians loaded their rifles or tested their bowstrings.

Dimock was worried. Years later he remembered Jack Stilwell sitting on a bench by a window, and he asked him, "How does it look, Jack?"

"Bad," was the reply.

"What are you going to do about it?" Dimock asked.

"This is my pony by the window," Stilwell answered. "If I am alive after the first shot, I'll be through the window and on his back."

"Is it that bad?"

"Look for yourself," Stilwell said. "See how they are all armed. . . . Who is likely to start trouble? The Commissioner. If he does not change his tune he'll never see Washington again."[57]

As Stilwell leaned toward his escape window, Iron Mountain, Quirtzquip, and their followers massed around Dimock for his protection and pushed him into a corner of the room. At that point a wise Comanche leader (the Penateka headman Tosaway) spoke up, cooled tempers, quieted passions, and prevented a massacre. Agreements were reached, and attendees at the meeting dispersed.[58]

As in previous winters, after that October meeting Stilwell's duties slowed, and accordingly at the end of February 1874 the government again discharged the twenty-three-year-old. Capt. Theodore Baldwin of the Tenth Cavalry stated years later that Stilwell had performed his duty faithfully and that every officer with whom he served on the Great Plains recommended him.[59] Those recommendations were confirmed during his next service—in the Texas Panhandle's Red River War.

CHAPTER 7

THE RED RIVER WAR

The last major engagement between Indians and soldiers on the southern plains occurred in the Texas Panhandle in 1874 and 1875. The Red River War brought to the Panhandle some three thousand federal troops in five converging columns. Those columns operated more or less independently, attacking and burning Comanche, Kiowa, and Cheyenne camps amid the deep canyons and steep breaks on the eastern edge of the Llano Estacado.[1] Throughout the conflict Jack Stilwell served as a scout with the Tenth Cavalry Buffalo Soldiers. "I was in the field with . . . [Lt. Col. John W.] Davidson's command," Stilwell later recalled, "and accompanied nearly all of his detachments" during the campaign.[2]

Multiple and tangled problems related to corruption and incompetence in the Bureau of Indian Affairs and to indifference on the part of congress after 1867 led to shortages on reservations in Indian Territory: food, supplies, equipment, and material goods promised Native Americans were often late (if they arrived at all) and of poor quality. Indians grew hungry, resentful, and restless. Younger warriors—eager to gain honor, respect, and rank—sought success by fighting, raiding, and hunting. They left reservations to strike ranches and isolated settlements, seeking trophies and the accolades that came with them. These problems were compounded by white outlaws and horse thieves from Kansas and Texas who stole ponies from reservation herds. Other unscrupulous whites ran guns and trafficked liquor, increasing Indian unrest. By the early 1870s the southwestern plains had become a tinderbox.

In addition, bison hunters intruded onto Texas Panhandle land reserved for southern Plains tribes by the Treaty of Medicine Lodge, signed in 1867. Having destroyed most of the herds in the upper Arkansas River country of western Kansas and eastern Colorado, the hide-seekers in 1872 moved south into Texas. Two years later, led by J. Wright and John W. Mooar, hunters and businessmen established a village on the Canadian River at the old Adobe Walls trading post and planned to use the place as a base from which to strip hides. Southern Plains Indians, especially Comanches and Cheyennes, resented the illegal intrusion into their favorite hunting grounds, and on June 27, 1874, a group of warriors attacked the village. The ensuing fight is often referred to as the Second Battle of Adobe Walls. (The first battle at the site involved the Kit Carson–led expedition of 1864 described in chapter 2.) Twenty-eight men at Adobe Walls held off the assault, but over the following weeks angry and frustrated Indian warriors struck smaller bison-hunter camps and targeted isolated settlers over a wide area of the southwestern plains.[3] The army, led by Gen. William T. Sherman and Military Division of the Missouri commander Gen. Philip H. Sheridan, struck back in force. The subsequent Red River War—a series of some twenty-four engagements (fourteen of which were pitched battles) between the army and warriors from Comanche, Kiowa, Cheyenne, and Arapaho tribes—lasted nearly a year.

Even before the fight at Adobe Walls, Stilwell's services were needed on the frontier. On February 26, 1874, he guided Capt. Caleb H. Carlton and Troop K, Tenth Cavalry, out of Fort Sill. The detachment, including a wagon, an ambulance, and twenty loaded pack mules, left the post bound for Camp Augur. Located southwest of Fort Sill, east of another temporary encampment at Otter Creek, and near a military road on the north side of the Red River, Camp Augur was one of the border posts used to guard the southern edge of the Comanche-Kiowa reservation. The soldiers held orders to block Comanches and Kiowas from raiding in Texas. The men of Troop K pushed to Camp Augur as hard as the loaded pack mules could withstand and reached the post without incident. The next day Stilwell and a lone packer, William Welsh, returned to Fort Sill with the unloaded mules, leaving the wagon, the ambulance, and the men at the camp. Upon the scout's return to Fort Sill, the post quartermaster discharged him, and Stilwell was once again unemployed.[4]

About two weeks before Stilwell's trip to Camp Augur, his mother had remarried in Jackson County, Indiana, where she had moved after her divorce from William Stilwell. On February 14 in a small, private ceremony conducted by Justice of the

Peace Anthony J. Drewell, Charlotte married Isaac Wiseman, a local farmer. In the nineteenth century such marriages provided some financial security to women like Charlotte, who had been raising Stilwell's sisters Clara and Elizabeth Ann alone, as well as benefitting widowers like Isaac by furnishing comfort and support.[5]

Stilwell's whereabouts remain unknown between the time of his discharge in February and his rehire in July. Apparently he stayed close to his old base at Fort Hays, Kansas, but he very likely traveled to the Kansas City region to visit family members, including his uncle Jacob Stilwell and his three brothers. Perhaps he learned of his mother's marriage. The record is mute, unfortunately, but the "Indian troubles" that began in earnest in June at Adobe Walls again brought Stilwell into military service as a civilian guide.

As noted above those "troubles" endured a long gestation. Trespassing bison hunters, food shortages, undelivered supplies and equipment, and Texan horse thieves plagued the Indians. For their part, Indian leaders could not prevent their younger warriors from crossing the Red River into Texas to steal horses or collect other treasure.[6] Sometimes the warriors struck close to home. On July 3, 1874, for example, Indian raiders attacked a supply train on its way from Wichita, Kansas, to the Cheyenne-Arapaho agency at Darlington, located on the north side of the North Canadian River near modern-day El Reno, Oklahoma. About sixty miles north of the agency, they hit a train of twenty wagons belonging to Patrick Hennessy. The raiders, probably Cheyennes, killed and mutilated Hennessy and his teamsters and after taking what goods they could haul on horseback, they burned the wagons.[7]

An increasing number of similar Indian attacks and Anglo counterattacks kept Stilwell busy. He guided Charles E. Campbell, an employee of the Indian service, from Kansas to the Cheyenne-Arapaho agency at Darlington. Campbell had been sent to investigate the difficulties and the mounting unrest on reservations. Upon reaching the agency about July 5, Stilwell and Campbell found Agent John D. Miles and his employees agitated and fearful of a larger Indian attack. They apparently had heard about the recent Adobe Walls fight and had just learned from cattlemen about the killing of Hennessey and his teamsters. To get military protection for his agency, Miles asked Stilwell to ride at once to Fort Sill, about seventy miles distant, report the death of Hennessey, and ask that troops be sent to Darlington.[8]

Stilwell accepted—although it was a dangerous mission. The tired scout left the agency near sundown on July 5 and rode hard southwestward, crossing in turn the North Canadian River, the wide main stream of the Canadian River with its beds of quicksand, and the Washita River. He changed horses at the Wichita agency at Anadarko and just after reveille on the morning of the sixth he reached Fort Sill. Years later, in 1896, Capt. Owen Jay Sweet, Twenty-Fifth Infantry, commented on the assignment. In a sworn statement Sweet said that a large number of war parties "infested" the country through which Stilwell had passed. To him, Stilwell's ride was an incredible feat.[9]

At Fort Sill, Stilwell reported to Colonel Davidson, the post commander. He described the cattlemen's tale of the attack on Pat Hennessy's wagon train and conveyed Miles's request for military protection.[10] Davidson had also recently obtained from Horace Jones, the post interpreter, some details of the battle of Adobe Walls. In an official report dated July 7, he relayed to his superiors the information he had received from Stilwell and Jones.[11] The accounts confirmed that southern Plains Indians were leaving their reservations, and Davidson worried that worse trouble might follow. In response, he instructed the quartermaster to hire Stilwell, back-dating the enrollment to July 1.[12] The post commander, in response to the Miles request, wanted his new scout to accompany 2nd Lt. Mason Marion Maxon and Troop M of the Tenth Cavalry back to Darlington and the Cheyenne-Arapaho agency.[13]

The simple plan and its subsequent action did not work. Although both agencies were within the army's Division of the Missouri, the Darlington agency was in the Department of Missouri and the Wichita agency at Anadarko was in the Department of Texas. Army regulations did not allow Lieutenant Maxon's squad to cross the South Canadian River, which formed the border between the two southern plains military departments. He and Troop M stayed south of the river at the Wichita agency. Such bureaucratic inefficiency often frustrated commanders in the field, and Charles Campbell, the Indian service employee, called it a beautiful example of "military red tape."[14] Agent Miles, however, did not need be concerned. Members of the Cheyenne and Arapaho tribes liked their agent and his employees, and they assured Miles that they would not attack Darlington as long as the employees remained close to the agency. The Cheyennes kept their word.[15]

Stilwell, as a civilian employee, could and did return to the agency at Darlington. Once back, he left again—immediately—with inspector Campbell, bound for Fort Sill. Accompanying them was a young man (possibly a Quaker, as he carried no weapons) on his way to the Wichita agency. To Campbell any man in their situation without a weapon was a burden rather than a help. As Captain Sweet later explained, the country they needed to cross from the North Canadian River to the Canadian River was hostile territory.[16]

As they rode into a ravine on their way south, they saw a cloud of dust coming toward them. Fearing an attack, Stilwell and Campbell dismounted their horses, threw the bridle reins over their left arm, drew Winchesters from their scabbards, and stood behind their horses. But the dust rose from a heard of loosely grouped horses being driven by two peaceable Arapahos on their way to their agency. The Arapahos reported that two war parties of Cheyennes were headed northeast. Stilwell and his companions then remounted and continued their journey without incident, happy to reach the south bank of the Canadian River and escape the roaming bands of raiders and avoid the quicksand of the river.[17]

While Stilwell guided Indian service personnel and troops in Indian Territory, Generals Sherman and Sheridan determined to end the "Indian troubles" once and for all. Some years earlier they had decided to define "peaceful" (noncombatant) Indians as those who remained on reservations; "hostile" (combatant) Indians were those who left the reserves. Now they ordered military officers in the field, with help from agents, to enroll noncombatant Indians and thus divide them from the hostiles. Accordingly, at Fort Sill on July 17 Davidson issued an order that his troops must be able to tell friendly from hostile Indians and resolved that noncombatants should camp on the reservation east of Cache Creek.[18]

At the end of July, Davidson left Fort Sill with Troops B, H, and E, Tenth Calvary, and rode ten miles north to enroll friendly Indians. He and his men encountered no difficulties in registering the bands of Comanche chiefs Horseback, Cheevers, and Quirtzquip. At the Kiowa camp a few miles away, however, Davidson's subalterns found a more difficult situation. Some Kiowas who were known to have left the reservation wanted to sign up as friendly Indians, and Kiowa leader Kicking Bird could get only a few men to cooperate in the enrollment. Davidson's men, led by Capt. George Sanderson, asked the Kiowas to come to Fort Sill to complete the enrollment.[19] Simultaneous with the enrollment activities, Davidson sent additional Tenth Cavalry troops to patrol between temporary camps along the Red River. He also moved Company C, Twenty-Fifth Infantry, northeast to guard the Wichita agency. Stilwell served as a guide in many of the maneuvers.

In early August problems arose at the Wichita agency. Combatant Comanches and Kiowas demanded rations and exhibited threating behavior. When notified, Colonel Davidson left Fort Sill for the agency on the twenty-first with four troops of the Tenth Cavalry and one company of the Twenty-Fifth Infantry. Stilwell served as scout. Davidson's command arrived the following morning and immediately engaged the warriors in a struggle that lasted well into the next day. It became known as the Battle of Anadarko.[20] Stilwell was part of the heavy action; he helped drive Comanche and Kiowa hostiles from the sutler's store and then settled in to protect the building and its contents. He fired through a window at some Kiowas—at least one of whom he recognized—but missed. When it was over the combatant Comanches and Kiowas left Anadarko, presumably to join others off the reservation. Four of Davidson's men and six of his horses suffered wounds. Fourteen Indians, Davidson reported, had been "shot from their horses" and four of their ponies killed.[21]

A few days after the battle, James W. Grahame, a teamster with the Tenth Cavalry, saw Stilwell at the sutler's store and described the scout's reaction to seeing one of the Kiowa warriors who had participated in the battle on the post grounds. According to Grahame, Stilwell pointed out the man as the "very stinker, I shot at twice last Thursday here at the Wichita Agency out of the Sutler's house."[22]

Stilwell, said Grahame, hardly slept a wink, wondering how he missed the Kiowa warrior. The guide confronted the warrior and asked for an interpreter to translate their exchange. Later the "stinker" laughed in Stilwell's face. Stilwell replied that he was tired of hearing Texans complain about Kiowas, and if he had another opportunity, he would make his shots count. Grahame described Stilwell as tall, well built, with a light complexion, and under thirty years of age. He noted that Jack was a "good natured, rollicking, dare devil sort of a fellow who while following his dangerous calling had lived constantly in the saddle." Stilwell, he added, had a reputation as someone who could go farther and get more out of a horse than any man on the border.[23]

As such events unfolded, Generals Sherman and Sheridan finished plans to gain control of the southern plains once and for all. As in the winter campaign of 1868–69, they wanted to strike at Indians in the Texas Panhandle from several directions. This time troops under the command of Col. Nelson A. Miles rode south from Fort Dodge; Maj. William R. Price led soldiers riding east from New Mexico; Lt. Col. George P. Buell and his troops rode west from Fort Griffin, Texas; Col. Randal S. Mackenzie and the Fourth Cavalry moved north from Fort Concho; and Col. John W. Davidson rode with his men, the "Fort Sill column of Buffalo Soldiers," from Fort Sill.[24]

By late August 1874 the converging columns had commenced engaging the Indians. Davidson's column, however, owing to the fight at Anadarko and the need to provide troops at the agency, did not leave Fort Sill until September 10. His column consisted of Troops B, C, H, K, L, and M, Tenth Cavalry; three companies of the Eleventh Infantry; a company of mountain howitzers; and forty-four scouts, including Jack Stilwell and his friend John Kilmartin, under the supervision of Lt. Richard H. Pratt, who later established the Carlisle Indian School in Pennsylvania. Forty-six wagons carrying supplies and rations for the men and forage for the animals accompanied the troopers.[25]

When Davidson and his command left Fort Sill, they moved northwest toward old Fort Cobb on the Washita River. The troopers then followed the divide between the Washita River and the North Fork of the Red River. Stilwell, Kilmartin, three other white men, and thirty-nine friendly Indians served as scouts and guides. Their duties included becoming the eyes and ears of the command, scouting ahead, watching each flank and the rear of the column, and reporting immediately any Indian trails they found or evidence of the location of combatants.[26]

Nothing was easy for Davidson's column—or for any of the participants in the Red River War. The summer of 1874 was hot: August temperatures often exceeded 100 degrees. Water holes, playa lakes, and shallow streams upon which soldiers depended for water were dry. Much of the water that they did find contained high levels of alkali. Drought also raised havoc with grass, stifling its growth, turning it dry and brown, and cutting its use as forage for animals. The flammable forage proved to be advantageous to Indians, who often set fire to the prairie to slow the soldiers' advance. Poor and untimely delivery of supplies limited the army's mobility, and columns ran short of rations. As summer turned to fall and winter, cold temperatures, rain, ice, and snow also limited mobility. Such conditions were likewise hard on Comanche, Cheyenne, and Kiowa families trying to flee their canyon homes and avoid soldiers in the field.[27]

Stilwell was not without his own problems. Just as Davidson's command was about to march from Fort Sill, for example, James Henry, a local thug, stole his horse.[28] Because of the expedition's demands and the scarcity of serviceable mounts, the theft left the scout on foot just as the Fort Sill column was leaving post. Fortunately, Capt. A. S. B. Keyes, Troop D, found a good, sound animal and provided the horse for Stilwell's use.[29]

Because of supply problems, Davidson's command made two expeditions to the Panhandle country. As described above, they first rode along the Washita River divide. On September 22 Davidson sent scouts to inform Colonel Miles of his whereabouts, and the two officers met that evening. After a day's rest Davidson crossed south of the North Fork of the Red River and from there scouted along the eastern edge of the Llano Estacado.[30]

With his stock short of forage and his men on half rations, on October 2 Davidson detached guides Stilwell and Kilmartin and ten Indian scouts to find Mackenzie's supply camp on Wanderer's Creek to get provisions. Three days later the guides returned without finding the campsite, but they had found a camp under Colonel Buell's command. Unfortunately, it could not spare extra stores for the Fort Sill column. After hearing the news, Davidson turned east toward Fort Sill to refit and recuperate the stock on Herd Creek nearby.[31]

On October 21, with his command resupplied and rested, Davidson left the Fort Sill area on his second expedition. He headed west again, riding to the North Fork of the Red River in the eastern Texas Panhandle, where he established a base camp on the north side of the stream. From his headquarters there he sent troops to seek out Indian parties and either attack them or prevent them from escaping. Perhaps the major activity occurred in early November. On the eighth Lt. Frank D. Baldwin of Miles's command discovered the camp of Grey Beard. Baldwin and his troops attacked, forcing Grey Beard and his one hundred Cheyenne followers to move. On the same day Major Price encountered the Indians crossing his front as they fled from Baldwin. Price and his troops, for "some reason not yet satisfactorily explained," reported Miles, failed to attack.[32]

Davidson took up the chase. Grey Beard moved northwest, apparently hoping to hide in the breaks and side canyons of the Canadian River. At the edge of the Llano Estacado, Davidson halted his column and instructed Capt. Charles D. Viele to pick 120 troopers of the Tenth and with Lieutenant Pratt's scouts, including Stilwell, to continue the pursuit. Robert M. Utley noted that in "two days of hard riding they wore out their horses without overtaking the Cheyennes. Veile called off the pursuit and turned back."[33]

Miles kept after Grey Beard and his Cheyenne families, but cold temperatures and wet weather changed the complexion of the Red River campaign. Through the rest of November and December harsh weather battered the region. For both Indians and soldiers there seemed, as Utley wrote, "no relief from the torture of rain, sleet, snow, and freezing cold." Horses died and men suffered debilitating frostbite. Columns moved slowly in the snow and ice and mud—when they moved at all.[34] From his base camp in the eastern Panhandle, Davidson reported that "on the morning of the 15th began a violent rain storm that changed to sleet and snow which lasted until the morning of the 19th freezing to death nearly one hundred animals and freezing the feet of twenty-six men."[35]

Stilwell, Davidson's guide, was among those who endured pain from the cold and ice. The rain and melted sleet and snow had filled many of the Panhandle streams, and a thin layer of ice had formed on them. When word of the location of a Comanche camp arrived at the Tenth's temporary headquarters on the north bank of the North Fork, Davidson on November 20 put Stilwell into action. He ordered the scout to take a message south to Lt. William Davis Jr., Troop F, notifying him of the Indians in his area. Stilwell mounted his horse and rode out of camp in the cold and sleet. At the river he dismounted and began leading his horse over the ice-bound stream. He and the horse broke through the thin ice and fell into the raging, freezing water. He returned to camp cold and wet and altogether miserable, but he changed clothes and headed out again to deliver the message.[36]

On November 29 Davidson and his command returned to Fort Sill. His second expedition into the Texas Panhandle was over. Lieutenant Pratt's scouts had stayed busy. They saw duty with different officers of the Tenth and their troops, and scouts acting as couriers maintained daily communications with troops in the field. On October 29, for example, four scouts rode to the camp of Colonel Miles to deliver messages. Two of them, Stillwell and Kilmartin, engaged two Indians for several hours in the valley of Sweetwater Creek. They performed well. Pratt wrote that "in performance of their duties he would mention by name as especially meritorious [scouts] Kilmartin, Stilwell, [Michael] Gordon, and [Phillip] McCusker."[37] Pratt was a bit mistaken, however, for Gordon's name was not on the quartermaster's roll at Fort Sill, although he had been hired on August 22 to carry a dispatch from troops at the Wichita agency at Anadarko to Fort Sill.[38]

After the rough time "in the field service" with the Fort Sill column, scouts Stilwell, Kilmartin, and James N. Jones went to Henrietta in Clay County, Texas, for Christmas. They must have been having a very good time, for they were arrested on December 26 and charged with disturbing the peace by firing their pistols on the streets of Henrietta. The case was presented to the Texas grand jury, and a trial was recommended before the Clay County District Court. A trial date was set for the first Monday of December 1875.[39]

Their cases, numbers 44, 45, and 46, were tried in the Clay County Courthouse at Henrietta on December 7, 1875, nearly a year after their arrests. Each of the defendants, out on bail and working as scouts for the U.S. Army, pleaded guilty. Kilmartin and Stilwell each received a fine of one dollar and court cost. Jones received a fine of five dollars. Because Stilwell was serving as a guide for the Fourth Cavalry in Indian Territory during the hearing for case no. 45, *The State of Texas vs. Jack Stilwell*, he did not appear in Henrietta. A local attorney represented him.[40]

The Red River War grew cooler as 1874 came to a close. Some of the Indians had returned to Indian Territory as early as October, surrendering at Fort Sill. Others, suffering from cold and lack of food and material goods, held out until December. Of those remaining, many returned to the reservation in January and February 1875. Yet those who had never agreed to live on a reservation still lingered in Texas.[41]

As early as December 3, 1874, however, Gen. C. C. Augur, commander of the Department of Texas and part of Indian Territory, wrote to General Sheridan from Fort Sill, saying that two days previous two young sons of Mowway, a Comanche headman, came in and stated that their father was on the plains. He added, "Last night three [Kwahadas] went into the Wichita Agency and surrendered their arms. When they were brought to Fort Sill they claimed that [Mowway] and his people were anxious to return to the Reservation."[42]

As Indians were returning to reservation lands in early 1875, Comanche noncombatant leaders Tabenanica, Red Food, and Cheevers approached Colonel Davidson. They indicated that if a few of their men were permitted to go out to the hostile Kwahadas and tell them that they may come in without fear of soldiers attacking, the combatants would return. The Comanche leaders believed that the hostiles would gladly come in to escape the cold weather and hunger they were experiencing on the Llano Estacado. Davidson concurred, telling his superiors, "I believe they will give up without the use of force."[43]

But events moved slowly. To confirm his opinion that Kwahada Comanches were ready to return to Fort Sill, Davidson, probably sometime in early March, sent Stilwell and Kilmartin with two Comanche guides, Esa-Rosa (White Wolf) and Habbewithcut (Habby wake), to Mowway's camp on the Llano Estacado. In his 1896 pension petition to Congress, Stilwell wrote, "In March 1875, I made a trip with one white man . . . into the Staked Plains and induced the [Kwahada] Band of Comanche under the leadership of [Mowway] and Quanah to come in and make peace, they being the last of the Comanches to surrender."[44]

Officers agreed it was best to wait until March or early April for them to come. Indian ponies needed to feed on spring grass to give them enough strength and stamina to reach Fort Sill. Moreover, Scout John Kilmartin and Lena Baker had been married before Clay County, Texas, Justice of the Peace J. M. Stratton on February 13, 1875, so an earlier trip would have been unreasonable. The couple needed a brief honeymoon, and a long separation so soon after their marriage might have caused some unnecessary personal conflict.[45]

On their trip to the plains, Stilwell, Kilmartin, Esa-Rosa, and Habbewithcut followed what became a familiar route. They traveled west from Fort Sill below the Signal Station and the Wichita Mountains, and then crossed Otter Creek, the North Fork of the Red River, and the Prairie Dog Town Fork of the Red. In Texas they crossed the Pease River and its branches, always moving southwest and trending toward the edge of the Llano Estacado. They might have camped at Roaring Springs south of present Matador. Their southwest course took them into Blanco Canyon, and they probably crossed the White River at Silver Falls near present-day Crosbyton. From here, they likely moved onto the Llano Estacado and then down into Canyon de Rescate (also known as Ransom Canyon or Traders Canyon) to cross the North Fork of the Double Mountain Fork of the Brazos River (or Traders Creek as it was called). From that prominent stream they again climbed onto the Llano and moved south to Mowway's camp at Laguna Tahoka, a large lake near the modern-day town of Tahoka in what is now Lynn County.[46]

On their trip to the plains, the emissaries encountered no trouble. Upon reaching the Comanche's camp, they conferred with Mowway and his warriors, presented surrender terms, and promised that food and warm clothing were available at the reservation. Mowway agreed to return to the reservation, and shortly afterward the move back to Fort Sill was underway. The women pulled down tipis and packed up camp gear and supplies while the men rounded up the huge horse herd. As they began their return, the band of Wild Horse joined them but remained a day behind Mowway's people. The move was slow, and the two Comanche bands did not reach Fort Sill until April 18, 1875, meaning that Stilwell, Kilmartin and the two Indian guides were out at least a month and a half on the important mission. For their service Stilwell and Kilmartin each received twenty Indian ponies. Esa-Rosa and Habbewithcut got four mounts each. Agent James Haworth reported to the commissioner of Indian Affairs that their "mission was partially successful," meaning presumably that not all the Kwahadas had agreed to return.[47]

While the scouts were gone, Col. Ranald S. Mackenzie, who had participated in the Red River War, assumed leadership at Fort Sill and brought to the post his Fourth Cavalry. Mackenzie was a Civil War veteran and one of the most successful military officers in the West. He welcomed Mowway and his band to Fort Sill on the eighteenth and three days later reported that 36 men and 147 women and children from Mowway's band also arrived with the chieftan. The number of ponies, mules, and colts totaled 699.[48]

Because of Stilwell and Kilmartin's success in bringing in Mowway's band, Mackenzie decided to send a second group of messengers with peace overtures to the plains. The second group included Dr. Jacob J. Strum, the Fort Sill field interpreter, and three Comanches: Wild Horse, Habbewithcut (who had just returned from the plains), and Toviah.[49] The messengers departed Fort Sill on April 23 and followed a route similar but not identical to that taken by Stilwell,

Kilmartin, and their guides in March.[50] When they reached the camp of Quanah and Isahatai, located below the High Plains near Muchaque Peak in modern-day Borden County, the Indians received them well. After some preliminary speeches and discussions, Quanah's group agreed to return to the reservation, and, upon leaving a note for some of their band members absent hunting bison, they left for Fort Sill.[51]

There is more to Strum's famous story. In correspondence with Robert G. Carter, a Fourth Cavalry aide who wrote about military activities in Texas, John B. Charlton, Troop F, stated that in April 1875 he was asked by Colonel Mackenzie to bear a message to Mowway, the Kwahada chief, asking him to surrender and bring his band into Fort Sill. Mackenzie, according to the note, told Charlton that such a trip could be dangerous. Charlton went ahead anyway, taking with him a person he called his "half breed interpreter" and a man named "Storms or Sturm, who lived somewhere on the Washita [River]. Storms and I with two Comanches left Fort Sill on April 24." They reached Mowway's camp, the note indicated, and "there they were confined for three days [before] Mackenzie's terms were accepted." The return trip to Fort Sill was made in four days. In his note to Carter, Charlton stated that "the few times I told the story (upon request) I have been accused of telling 'a romance.'"[52]

Perhaps Charlton's story is fiction. If not, is "Storms or Sturm" actually Dr. Strum? However, consider that Stilwell, Kilmartin, and their two Comanche guides needed some forty-five days to reach Mowway's band and bring them back to Fort Sill. They returned even before Strum had left the post on his mission to the Llano Estacado. Dr. Strum, led by three Comanches, took thirty days to complete his round trip to Quanah's camp and back. Charlton claimed that he, "Storms or Strum," and their guides made the round trip in about sixteen days.

During the Red River War, Jack Stilwell had performed capably with Colonel Davidson and his Tenth Cavalry Buffalo Soldiers. He endured relentless heat and fierce winter cold while handling many of the most dangerous reconnoitering assignments, and he had completed them with the skill and ability expected of a seasoned frontier scout. Perhaps his principal contribution to the war's outcome had been his service as a messenger to the Kwahada Comanches on the Llano Estacado, an effort that provided for their peaceful return to Fort Sill, thus signaling the end of the last major confrontation between soldiers and Indians on the southern plains. The army, however, was not finished with one of its favorite scouts.

Simpson Everett "Jack" Stilwell at Fort Sill, ca. 1869–71. Only nineteen or twenty years old when this photo was taken, Stilwell was already an experienced plainsman and frontier scout. *Photograph by Will Soule. Fort Sill Museum, Fort Sill, Oklahoma, P1879.*

Opposite, top: "Old Castle" School House, Baker University, Baldwin City, Kansas, where Jack Stilwell attended school in 1863. *Kansas East Commission on Archives and History, Baker University, Baldwin City, Kansas.*

Left: George Armstrong Custer in winter uniform during the Washita campaign, ca. 1868. Custer often called upon Stilwell's skills as a civilian scout and buffalo hunter. *Photographer unknown. National Park Service, Little Bighorn Battlefield National Monument.*

Right: Col. Benjamin Grierson, commander of the Tenth Cavalry at Fort Sill, 1871. He is shown wearing his Civil War general's uniform. *Fort Davis National Historic Site, Fort Davis, Texas.*

John "Jack" Kilmartin served with Stilwell as a civilian scout at Fort Sill, 1872–76. Stilwell witnessed his murder when Kilmartin's wife shot him in Clay County, Texas, in 1876. *Photograph by W. P. Bliss. Fort Sill Museum, Fort Sill, Oklahoma, P1881.*

Scouts Jack Stilwell (*right*) and James N. Jones at Fort Sill, 1876. Photograph by
W. P. Bliss. *Courtesy R. G. McCubbin Collection, Santa Fe, New Mexico.*

Top, left: Fr. Isidore Robot, founder of Sacred Heart Mission in Indian Territory. He and Stilwell enjoyed a lucky encounter when Father Robot was lost on his first trek into Indian Territory. *Oklahoma Historical Society Photograph Archives, 6174.*

Top, right: Esa-Rosa (White Wolf), 1875. This Comanche chief accompanied Stilwell and Jack Kilmartin in their search for Mowway's Comanche band on the Llano Estacado in 1875. *Fort Sill Museum, Fort Sill, Oklahoma, P4113.*

Left: Mowway, Comanche chief. After the Red River War, Mowway brought his band to Fort Sill in April 1875. *Fort Sill Museum, Fort Sill, Oklahoma, P1785.*

Opposite, top: Lt. William Henry Beck, commander of Company B, Tenth Cavalry, at Camp Peña Blanca, Texas, 1878. Stilwell was a witness for both the prosecution and the defense at Beck's court-martial in January 1879. *Fort Davis National Historic Site, Fort Davis, Texas.*

Jack Stilwell, 1885. Photograph by Marable and Caldwell, Henrietta, Texas. *Oklahoma Historical Society Photograph Archives, 19654.*

Top: El Reno Police Judge Stilwell, October 1893. Stilwell is wearing an overcoat given to him by William F. "Buffalo Bill" Cody. *Courtesy Tenal Stilwell Cooley III.*

Right: Sigmund Schlesinger, ca. 1872, one of the survivors of Beecher Island and a friend of Stilwell's. He is show here at age twenty-one, approximately four years after the battle. *American Jewish Archives, Hebrew Union College, Cincinnati.*

Top, left: Dan W. Peery, editor of the *El Reno Democrat,* often reported on Stilwell's exploits in his newspaper. Peery went on to found the town of Carnegie, Oklahoma. *Oklahoma Historical Society Photograph Archives, 1994.*

Top, right: Lewis N. Hornbeck, editor of Indian Territory's *Minco Minstrel.* Hornbeck acted as something of an unofficial press agent for Stilwell and was the author of many stories promoting "Comanche Jack." *Oklahoma Historical Society Photograph Archives, 20196.0M.11.5–6.11.1.*

Left: Capt. Jesse M. Lee, temporary Indian agent on the Cheyenne-Arapaho reservation 1885–86. *National Archives, Washington, D.C., 90511.*

Left: Quanah Parker standing on the front porch of his home west of Craterville, Indian Territory. *University of Oklahoma Libraries, Western History Collections, Irwin Brothers Studio Collection, 48.*

Opposite, top left: Buffalo Bill (Hon. William F. Cody), Denver, Colorado, ca. 1895. Stilwell and Cody were both scouts at Fort Hays during the 1868 Indian campaigns. *Photograph by C. H. Wells. Buffalo Bill Historical Center, Cody, Wyoming, P.69.915.*

Opposite, top right: Maj. Frank D. Baldwin served as a temporary Indian agent on the Kiowa-Comanche reservation at Anadarko, Oklahoma Territory, from 1894–98. *University of Oklahoma Libraries, Western History Collections, Martin Luther Turner Collection, 2.*

Deputy U.S. Marshal Frank Farwell and three Indian policemen: (*right to left*) Charlie Ohettaint, Kiowa; Police Captain Bert Arko, Comanche; and Jack Watsemomsoakawat, Comanche. *Courtesy Kit C. Farwell III, Burke, Virginia.*

Waiting for the beef issue on the Cheyenne-Arapaho reservation at Cantonment, ca. 1890. During the years when the beef allotment came on the hoof, the day of issue was one of celebration for the Indians. *University of Oklahoma Libraries, Western History Collections, Division of Manuscripts, 456.*

Right: Esther Stilwell Hammitt, whom Stilwell married in 1895. After Jack's death, Esther married Carl Hammitt of Cody, Wyoming. *Park County Archives, Cody.*

Bottom, left: Fred L. Wenner, ca. 1900. Wenner, a Guthrie newspaperman, interviewed Stilwell at Anadarko, Oklahoma Territory, ca. 1896, to get his story of the 1868 Battle of Beecher Island. *University of Oklahoma Libraries, Western History Collections, Wenner Collection, 190.*

Bottom, right: John H. Burford, the federal judge under whom Jack Stilwell served as U.S. commissioner at Anadarko, 1895–98. Oklahoma Historical Society *Photograph Archives, 4395.*

Top: Group picture with Buffalo Bill in front of Irma Hotel in Cody, Wyoming, ca. 1902. (*Standing, left*) Jack Stilwell and (*standing, right*) Buffalo Bill in front of the white horse. At the far left is Jack's two-pony buggy, described by Frederic Remington in his article in *Collier's Weekly*. In the background is the Medicine Lodge stagecoach. *Park County Archives, Cody.*

Bottom: In 1984 the town of Cody honored Stilwell's memory with a reburial at Old Trail Town, alongside other noted western icons. His grave is to the left. *Photograph by Clint Chambers.*

CHAPTER 8

WITH RANALD MACKENZIE
AT FORT SILL

For nearly two years following the Red River War, Jack Stilwell served as an army scout in and around Fort Sill, Indian Territory. He guided detachments of Fourth Cavalry troops on military maneuvers, carried messages to soldiers in the field, and performed significant other duties for post commander Col. Randal S. Mackenzie, a West Point graduate. In addition, Stilwell aided several Comanche friends, found himself accused of stealing mules, and acted as an emissary for cattlemen driving herds to market through the territory.

The southern plains saw historic changes in the years following the Red River War. Comanches and Kiowas settled into a new way of life on their reservations. Bison numbers declined sharply; the once-massive herds on which the Plains tribes had depended for food were depleted by hide hunters who loaded tons of hides on eastbound railroad cars. Indians went on few, if any, raids, and their hunters' and warriors' societies transformed in meaning and purpose. Some Indian families tried farming, but as time passed more and more came to rely on the food, clothing, equipment, and supplies promised them by the Treaty of Medicine Lodge in 1867. Many Indians successfully raised cattle and horses, and some herds grew large.

Because Comanches and Kiowas commonly loose-herded horses, their stock attracted thieves and rustlers. Horse stealing and related crimes were not uncommon on the reservations, and non-Indians engaged in most of the nefarious activities, especially horse stealing. To get close to the herds, some thieves near Fort Sill posed as employees of hay, wood, and beef contractors. Military authorities had no jurisdiction over civilian crimes in Indian Territory, so any felony suspects they arrested had to be transported to the nearest federal court in Fort Smith, Arkansas, a journey that required more than a week's hard travel.[1]

At first Stilwell had little to do with stopping horse rustlers. Soon after his return to Fort Sill from the Llano Estacado with Mowway's band (April 1875), his scouting work for Colonel Mackenzie commenced. On April 27 Mackenzie ordered Capt. Wirt Davis and Companies A and F of the Fourth Cavalry to move to the Cheyenne agency at Darlington.[2] Ten days later, on May 7, Mackenzie sent Stilwell to Davis with a message telling him that Indians had been seen north of the agency on the Caldwell, Kansas, road and ordering him to return them to the reservation. In that message Mackenzie also authorized the captain to retain "Mr. Stilwell as long as you deemed it essential." With eighty men and Stilwell serving as guide, Captain Davis rode in pursuit, but he and his troopers found no Indians. After a week in the field they returned to the agency.[3]

Stilwell stayed near Fort Sill until August 27, when Thomas A. Campbell, an employee of a Fort Sill hay contractor and a former teamster with the Tenth Cavalry, died in a gunfight at a hay camp.[4] The incident related to horse theft. Four people, names unknown, identified Stilwell and his friend John Kilmartin as the shooters, and on September 8 the U.S. commissioner at Fort Smith issued warrants for their arrest.[5] Fortunately for Stilwell, who had not been at the hay camp during the shooting, authorities dropped his name from the indictment but added the name of James N. Jones, another Stilwell associate. Jones and Kilmartin did not appear at Fort Smith for their first court date of November 8, 1875, whereupon officials changed the date to November 13, 1876.[6] By the time the government's case finally proceeded on December 9, 1876, Kilmartin was dead. Jones appeared for trial, and the court found him innocent of murder.[7]

Shortly after the hay camp murder, Stilwell became involved in the army's attempt to settle a difficult situation on the Osage reservation, which extended north and west of present-day Tulsa, Oklahoma. Problems among the Osages began in the summer of 1874 with the start of the Red River War. To keep Osage people away from the fighting, Agent Isaac T. Gibson sent couriers to warn all bands of Osages absent on their annual summer bison hunts to return to the reservation. Because of the hostilities, unfortunately, word did not reach a party of twenty-nine men, women, and children who had roamed into south-central Kansas. About forty white men from settlements near Medicine Lodge attacked the peaceful hunting party. Four Indians died. The others lost their personal belongings, and the white attackers captured several Indian ponies. After the assault the governor of Kansas, rather than bringing the assailants to justice, mustered them into the Kansas Militia and back-dated their papers, thus making the incident appear legal.[8]

Understandably, even the Osages who had not been attacked were unhappy about having to return from their hunt. They needed whatever meat they could procure from remaining bison herds to get through the winter. When they heard the fate of their tribesmen in Kansas, some Osages became angry and over time their resentment grew. In 1875, after the Red River War, they learned of a new regulation requiring them to work in order to receive rations, and they rebelled. Some warriors showed up at the agency in war paint. Other leaders took their families and left the reservation without authorization. In response, in mid-September and again in early October, troops of the Fourth Cavalry were sent to locate the absent Osages, but the detachments of searchers could not find them.[9]

On the reservation resentment continued to mount, and Gibson, fearing an outbreak of trouble, sent couriers to Fort Sill asking for additional troops. On October 28, with "the well-known scout, Jack Stilwell," as his guide, 2nd Lt. John W. Martin departed with Troop B from the Cheyenne agency at Darlington and moved northeast to the Osage reservation. The troops arrived on November 1, but by that time the Osages had restored peace among themselves, making outside force unnecessary.[10] Thereupon Martin sent Stilwell back to Fort Sill to inform Mackenzie of the Osage situation and request further orders. By November 8 Stilwell was at the post. It was an eight- to ten-day horseback ride between the Osage agency and the fort. To reach Fort Sill so quickly Stilwell must have ridden his horse hard to the east to the Gibson Station on the Katy Railroad. From there he could have taken the train to Caddo, Oklahoma. From Caddo, a two-day stage ride would have delivered him to Fort Sill.[11]

According to Stilwell, Agent Gibson was unable to decide whether he wanted to arrest the Osage troublemakers. Mackenzie advised that unless Gibson accepted his responsibility in such an action, no arrests should be made. He further suggested that a sergeant and six enlisted men from nearby Fort Gibson should be able to maintain order at the agency, but officials in the Department of Missouri wanted a company of Fourth Cavalry troops posted there.[12]

Upon his return to Fort Sill, Stilwell did not have much time to relax. Having problems feeding reservation Indians, Mackenzie on November 26 took unusual action. He assigned 2nd Lt. Joseph H. Dorst and Troop H with a few men from Troop K to escort Mowway's Comanches toward the Texas Panhandle on a buffalo hunt. Stilwell served as guide.[13] Over the next few months Mowway's long hunt met with enough success that Mackenzie sent an additional wagon pulled by a team of horses to Dorst and Mowway. They used the wagon to haul extra bison robes and meat back to the agency. The colonel warned Dorst to take special care of the horses, as they were needed at Fort Sill. He also told the lieutenant to be on the lookout for Indians who might slip off to go raiding, but no such problems developed.[14]

Stilwell was on the hunt with Mowway's band of Comanches until early March 1876. During the extended hunt he improved his knowledge of both the Comanche language and Indian sign language, and he deepened his understanding of Comanche society and culture. He pursued bison with the hunters, perhaps using a lance as he had as a young man in New Mexico, and the Comanches came to view the twenty-five-year-old Stilwell as a friend and comrade.[15]

Back at Fort Sill, Mackenzie faced some serious problems. First, he needed to keep Indians on the reservation, a difficult assignment as the agency was often short of rations and other Kiowas and Comanches wanted to hunt as Mow-way's band had done. Too often Agent James Haworth, who was responsible for supplying his reservation inhabitants, needed to borrow rations from the army and turned to the commander at Fort Sill. Mackenzie wrote to his superiors: "In order to give these people an opportunity to work they must be fed. . . . It is all very well to say you ought not to run away or behave badly to people who are driven to do so by the pangs of hunger."[16]

White rustlers also infested Indian Territory and committed repeated raids. In fact, on February 18, 1876, Mackenzie wrote the U.S. marshal for the Western District of Arkansas at Fort Smith, informing him that two prisoners, cattle thieves, were expected from Cantonment on the Sweetwater (Fort Elliott) and that he would hold them until he received orders.[17] On March 6, having just returned with Mowway to Fort Sill, Stilwell received new orders. He was to proceed on detached service to accompany a Mr. Russell from Cantonment on the Sweetwater in pursuit of some stolen mules and the men who took them. He was to give Russell, an agent for the powerful trading firm of Lee and Reynolds, all possible assistance. Cpl. William Wilson and two privates of Troop J, Fourth Cavalry, with five days' rations and one pack mule, were sent with Stilwell to help find the thieves. The pursuers soon captured Hank Jones, one of the rustlers, and brought him in to Fort Griffin, Texas. From Fort Griffin, Russell conveyed Jones to Fort Sill, where officials transferred him to U.S. Marshal James F. Fagan of Fort Smith, Arkansas.[18]

During this time Stilwell also helped to lay out two roads from Fort Sill to Fort Elliott in the Texas Panhandle (on Sweetwater Creek in what is now Wheeler

County). Workers made them as straight as practicable. Where necessary they cut away brush, moved large rocks, removed dead tree branches from riverbeds, graded stream crossings by cutting banks down to allow wagons easier access, and otherwise improved the trails. The roads took similar tracks from Fort Sill to the North Fork of the Red River. From there the wider road, the northern route, followed the North Fork upstream where there were more camping sites and water. It then turned west and crossed some sand hills to Sweetwater Creek. The southern route followed Elk Creek and crossed the North Fork at Comanche Springs; it then followed the North Fork to the mouth of Sweetwater Creek. Here the two roads met again before continuing to Fort Elliott.[19]

At Fort Elliott, William "Billy" Dixon, a bison hunter who had gained fame during the fight at Adobe Walls in 1874, served as a scout and guide. One of Dixon's recollections was that "all old timers in the southwest remember Jack Stilwell, scout, guide and good fellow." Once when Dixon and Stilwell were out on the Llano Estacado with nothing to eat, Stilwell persuaded Dixon to kill a wild horse for food, and they built a fire and cooked some of the meat. Dixon, however, was not able to swallow a single bite, for it stuck in his throat. He preferred to go hungry rather than eat horseflesh. While the meat looked good, the name was too much for him.[20] Stilwell had spent a lot of time with Comanches and therefore had no problem eating horse meat, a regular menu item among the tribe.

Once the Fort Elliott roads were improved, Stilwell headed to Fort Sill. During the trip he experienced a memorable encounter with two Catholic missionaries. In March and April of 1876, Lazarus Alexia Robot, known in religious circles as Fr. Isidore Robot, journeyed through the Chickasaw Nation to Fort Sill. Born in Burgundy, France, on July 7, 1836, Robot took his vows in a Benedictine Monastery and was ordained a priest in 1862. He determined to enter the missionary field in America, and he became the first permanent Catholic proselytizer among native people of Indian Territory. He also established the first Catholic schools for Indians in the region. The schools, both located in Pottawatomie County, included St. Mary's Academy for girls and the Sacred Heart Boys School.[21]

Father Robot and his companion, Brother Dominic Lambert, started their expedition through Indian Territory from Caddo, on the Katy Railroad in modern-day Bryan County, Oklahoma. On foot, they traveled first to Tishomingo, capital of the Chickasaw Nation. They then moved to Cherokee Town (present-day Pauls Valley, Oklahoma) and followed the Washita River up to Erin Springs across from present-day Lindsay. From Erin Springs they walked to Rush Springs (present Grady County, Oklahoma) and then hiked west toward Fort Sill.[22]

In 1885, years after the Benedictines' long walk, Stilwell recalled meeting Father Robot. He said that one evening in 1876 on the road to Fort Sill, he heard two men singing. The song was not familiar, and neither was the language; he knew it was not Spanish, German, or French. He thought it might be an Indian funeral chant. As he rode into their camp, Stilwell saw two men lying on their backs, either sick or asleep. He asked if they were lost or ill. One of the men, Father Robot, replied that no, they were not sick, but they were hungry. They had lost their way and for two days had eaten nothing. Stilwell asked them about the song they were singing: What kind of song was it, and in what language? Father Robot told him that it was the "Salve Regina"—prayer to the blessed virgin—in Latin.

In turn, Stilwell gave them cheese and crackers from his saddlebag. Then he went into the timber and shot a rabbit. After skinning it, he built a fire and roasted the meat, and they all enjoyed the meal. Father Robot and Brother Dominic thanked Jack and stated that he had saved their lives. They vowed to never forget his kindness. Stilwell always believed that his hearing them sing in Latin may have saved them. As they were bound for Fort Sill, Jack put them on the right road and he on horseback rode ahead toward the fort.[23]

Sometime after June 25, 1876, news of Custer's defeat on the Little Bighorn River in Montana reached Fort Sill. In fact, Stilwell heard it first and broke news of the disaster to John R. Hughes, a reservation trader, at the sutler's store. About the same time, an Indian stole a mule from the post, and Mackenzie sent the scout to retrieve the animal. Several days later Stilwell returned empty-handed and reported the mule must have died and the Indian would steal no more. Later Hughes and Dan McCarty, another trader, ran across the trail of the mule and thief while returning from an Indian camp where they had business. They followed the trail and came upon an Indian camp. A fire-fight followed, and they got the mule and returned it to Fort Sill.[24] After the traders arrived at the post leading the stolen mule, Stilwell became the butt of many jokes. Apparently he took the jokes in good humor. Mackenzie's reaction can only be surmised, but Stilwell may have been protecting a Comanche friend.[25]

Stilwell was not above taking advantage of opportunities that presented themselves. On one occasion Mackenzie sent him to notify some cattlemen that they would not be allowed to take a herd through Indian Territory on their way to market in Kansas. What he discussed with the cattlemen is unknown, but Stilwell backed the cattlemen. He returned to Fort Sill and, remembering Mackenzie's conflicts with Indian agent Haworth, he used that to needle the colonel. When Mackenzie repeated that the herd could not pass through, Stilwell replied, "Of course not, Agent Haworth won't allow it." With much spirit, the post commander answered, "The Agent won't allow it, we will see." He immediately sent Stilwell to pilot the cattlemen and their herd through the territory.[26]

Not all of Stilwell's interactions that year would be so lighthearted. In early July 1876 John B. Charlton, sergeant of Troop F, Fourth Cavalry, rode out on a scout with Stilwell and John Kilmartin. Comanches had reported that some horses were stolen from their camp on Cache Creek. Officials sent Charlton, Stilwell, and Kilmartin with two Comanche trackers to follow the horse thieves' trail, which did not prove difficult, at first. They moved south to the Red River, about thirty miles above the spot where the Jacksboro Road crossed it. Because the Comanche trackers would not cross the Red River into Texas, Charlton, Stilwell, and Kilmartin continued without them to the Big Wichita River, where they discovered that the trail had been obliterated by a herd of buffalo. After camping overnight, they were still unable to find the thieves' route the next morning, so the men determined to ride forty miles to Henry Whaley's Clay County ranch and stay overnight. The idea of a home-cooked meal sounded good.[27]

Kilmartin and Whaley were partners in the ranch, and Kilmartin's wife, Lena Baker Kilmartin, served as housekeeper there. The record indicates that Mrs. Kilmartin was much more than a domestic employee. In August 1874 Lena Baker and Henry Whaley had been charged with adultery. In April the following year, a Clay County court found them guilty of the charge. At the time—March and April 1875—John Kilmartin was searching for Mowway and his band on the Llano Estacado, and he and Lena had been married only a few weeks.[28]

When they arrived at the Clay County ranch on July 15, 1876, the men found Lena Kilmartin alone. She prepared an excellent meal, but it was apparently spoiled by her bad temper: she raged at Kilmartin throughout the evening. Charlton and Stilwell did not know the exact reason for the quarrel. It may have been because Kilmartin wanted his wife to return north with him to live at Fort Sill, and Lena did not want to go and said so. After the meal Charlton and Stilwell retired to the barn for the night. Shortly thereafter Kilmartin left the house and made his bed near the back door. The men then spent a quiet and restful night.[29]

According to Clay County court records, shortly after dawn on July 16, Lena Kilmartin shot and killed her estranged husband. Stilwell and Carlton heard the shot and ran toward the house. They saw Lena, pistol in hand, turn away from her husband, who still lay in his bedroll. Both rushed to Kilmartin's side only to discover that he was dead. She had shot him in the head. Sargent Charlton screamed at Lena, "You she-devil, you have killed him while he was asleep!"

Stilwell asked: "What made you do that?" Mrs. Kilmartin backed into the house and locked the door. Stilwell and Charlton wrapped Kilmartin's body in a blanket and buried him beside a mesquite tree.[30]

The men returned to Fort Sill and reported the murder to Colonel Mackenzie, who stated that Clay County, Texas, was not within his jurisdiction. Civil officials later confined Lena Kilmartin to jail, and the Clay County grand jury interviewed seven people. Kilmartin's partner Henry Whaley and three members of his family testified, but they were not eyewitnesses like Charlton and Stilwell. Lena claimed at her trial that her husband had made her marry him, had threatened to kill her on numerous occasions, and had made her fear for her life. She pleaded self-defense, and the jury found her not guilty. John Kilmartin had no will. His estate, valued at $1,300, was awarded to Lena.[31]

During this period Sergeant Charlton also assisted Stilwell in the capture of Joseph "Red" McLaughlin, a former teamster turned outlaw. McLaughlin had been a wagon master in October 1874 for troops out of Fort Sill during the later stages of the Red River War.[32] Stilwell knew him in that capacity. After the Texas Panhandle fighting ended, McLaughlin turned to crime and was considered to be one of the worst outlaws in Indian Territory. He was a horse thief and made his headquarters at "Widow Mcgee's" ranch, a hideout for outlaws along the western border of the Chickasaw Nation.[33]

While looking for McLaughlin, Stilwell and Charlton rode together to Ten Mile Creek, east of Fort Sill. There they separated; Stilwell went northeast toward the Washita River, and Charlton headed directly east on the road to the Rush Springs stage station. About eight miles from the stage stop, McLaughlin surprised the sergeant at the top of a hill, pointed a gun at him, and said, "Keep riding Yankee." Charlton responded, "Yes Sir if you will kindly let me by." As Charlton passed and rode on toward Rush Springs, McLaughlin kept him covered until Charlton vanished from sight. But Charlton wasn't finished. He followed the outlaw, keeping out of sight, and determined that McLaughlin was riding to Widow McGee's ranch. Charlton then returned to the main road. A bit later he met Deputy U.S. Marshal J. J. McAllister, who was also after McLaughlin. They rode to Rush Springs together, where they met Stilwell. After talking things over, they decided to send one of McAlister's men to ask Mackenzie at Fort Sill for a detail of enough men to surround the McGee ranch house.[34]

In response to the request Mackenzie sent a detachment from Troop E, Fourth Cavalry, who arrived at Rush Springs about eleven o'clock that night. Before daylight the next morning Stilwell, McAllister, Charlton, and the cavalry troopers rode to the ranch and surrounded the house. One of the McGee boys, Charles, came out of the little log building. He could see that they were hemmed in. Stilwell and Charlton laid down their guns and approached the young McGee for a discussion. It ended when McGee said, "If you want us, come and get us." With that, he reentered the house and closed the door.[35]

The posse of lawmen and troopers began firing on the house. When plaster began to fall off the walls inside, McLaughlin and the two McGee brothers, Charles and David, surrendered. Like McLaughlin, the Widow McGee's sons had taken horses belonging to someone else. Most recently, on February 2, 1876, they had stolen two horses from a man named T. F. Drake. McAlister arrested the three thieves and transported them to Fort Smith, Arkansas, for trial.[36]

After Custer and the Seventh Cavalry's destruction in southeastern Montana Territory, change came to Fort Sill. On July 25 General Sheridan ordered Mackenzie and six companies of the Fourth Cavalry to move north to the Red Cloud Agency, then located in northwestern Nebraska.[37] Lt. Col. John Porter Hatch became the new Fort Sill commander. He held orders, dated August 5, 1876, from the Department of Missouri that directed him to reduce salaries and discharge employees if practical—especially guides, interpreters, and scouts. Hatch wanted to keep Stilwell and another scout, James N. Jones, but he informed them that their salaries were to be cut. Jack elected to leave.[38]

Stilwell headed east into the Chickasaw Nation. At Erin Springs, located across the Washita River from modern-day Lindsay in Garvin County, he became a member of the Elm Springs Masonic Lodge No. 7.[39] The lodge, organized by John Coyle, was chartered on September 6, 1876, and the first meeting was held on September 30. Coyle helped build a two-story building, the upper story of which served as the lodge hall while the bottom floor served local residents as a school and church. The Elm Springs Lodge served most of the western part of the Chickasaw Nation for a radius of fifty miles. They met on the last Saturday of the month. After initiation, Jack became a master mason.[40]

Troubled followed Stilwell to Erin Springs. J. L. Jelem, a freighter from Caddo, Indian Territory, accused him of stealing a mule on or about September 15, 1874; on February 2, 1875, Stilwell got word of the charges. About the time of his supposed crime the previous fall, Stilwell had been serving with Colonel Davidson in the Texas Panhandle during the Red River War, so those charges were dismissed.[41] Yet Jelem again charged Stilwell with having stolen two mules on December 1, 1875. On that day Stilwell had just arrived at the Osage Agency with Lieutenant Martin and Troop B of the Fourth Cavalry. Nonetheless, on September 19, 1876, a month after the second charge had been filed, Stilwell received a summons by writ of subpoena to appear before U.S. Commissioner Stephen Wheeler in the district court for the Western District of Arkansas.[42]

On October 5 Special Deputy Marshal J. W. Mullen of the Chickasaw Nation and another legal official, Wallace Bennett, arrested Stilwell. They locked him in a local jail, but not long afterward Stilwell's friends Asberry S. Fowler and William H. Buckley bonded him out for $500. Four days later Mullen delivered at Fort Sill a writ of subpoena to Jelem, Harry Heck, and William Gordon.[43] Stilwell's court "examination" began on November 9 before Commissioner Wheeler. Jelem, Gordon, and a man named Fowler gave testimony. Their information did not prove or substantiate Stilwell's guilt. In fact, Gordon and Fowler stated that as far as they knew Stilwell had a good reputation at Fort Sill. But after their testimony Commissioner Wheeler postponed the testimony for four days. The trial ended on November 13 with Wheeler stating, "The defendant is discharged, no further evidence having been produced against him."[44]

Thus ended Stilwell's two active years of service at Fort Sill. During his tenure he had become a friend of the Comanches, supported civilian cattlemen, helped catch Anglo horse thieves, weathered some serious charges—and he had become one of the better-known and most successful military scouts on the southern Great Plains. By early 1877 Jack Stilwell was ready to seek new adventures; he headed for Arizona Territory.

CHAPTER 9

IN ARIZONA AND WEST TEXAS

After leaving Fort Sill and the scouting service in late 1876, Jack Stilwell rode east into the Chickasaw Nation. Twenty-six years old and widely known on the southern plains, the scout and guide settled temporarily at Erin Springs, a settlement on the Washita River about fifty-five miles south of present-day Oklahoma City. Here he made important economic and political connections and turned skills he had gained as a scout and guide into new job opportunities. In one instance his knowledge of Comanche customs and language led to work with the U.S. Marshals Service. Because few people who knew the Indian language were available as translators, he was hired to be a court interpreter during a trial in the district court of the Western District of Arkansas at Fort Smith.

In January 1877 he earned $2.50 per day (and received $17.75 for mileage between Erin Springs and Fort Smith) to interpret the testimony of Indian witnesses in the case of one William Alden, who was charged with larceny for stealing two saddle horses in Indian Territory.[1] The Indian witnesses in the case included both Kiowas and Comanches. Stilwell, as indicated above, could handle the Comanche language without difficulty, but he found the Kiowa tongue impossible to understand. Thus when the Kiowas testified, a Comanche witness translated the Kiowa into Comanche, which Stilwell then translated into English. At the end of the trial, the court found William Alden guilty. He was sentenced to serve one year in the Arkansas State Prison at Little Rock.[2]

The trial over, Stilwell, accompanied by several Comanche friends, headed home. He rode through Caddo, in modern-day Bryan County, before reaching his destination. The local paper in Caddo on January 13 reported: "Mr. S. E. Stilwell, U.S. Interpreter, an affable gentleman and fine looking man passed through town last Thursday with a party of Comanches, who had been to Fort Smith attending court. These people will have traveled a distance, when they get back home, of six hundred seventy miles."[3]

A more settled life allowed Stilwell better contact with his family, particularly his brother Frank.[4] In early 1877 he learned that his mother Charlotte and her second husband still lived in Indiana and that his sister Clara May had married William Alexander in Jackson County, Indiana, in October 1876.[5] Frank was living in Kansas near his Uncle Jacob and his large family. Jacob still owned and farmed the north half of William Henry Stilwell's original 1854 quarter section. Frank was a farmhand, according to the 1875 Kansas State Census, living with William Heffner in Irving Township in Brown County.[6]

Not all was well for Frank Stilwell. By early 1876 he had left the farm in eastern Kansas and moved near Wichita. That September a Wichita policeman named C. B. Jones arrested Frank for drunkenness. Frank was enjoying the company of several cowboys who had driven a herd of Texas cattle to market at the Wichita railhead. The group was celebrating the end of the long drive, and they had obviously consumed too much alcohol. Shortly after his arrest Frank appeared before Judge J. M. Atwood, who pronounced him guilty and fined him three dollars. The judge collected only two dollars, all that Frank had in his possession.[7]

Hoping to keep his brother out of further trouble, Stilwell arranged for Frank to receive a pass, dated March 4, 1877, to visit the Kiowa reservation. Frank arrived on March 31. Shortly afterward the brothers left the Anadarko agency and started for Arizona, where they hoped to make their fortunes in the Arizona goldfields.[8] They traveled southwest on what Stilwell called the Whipple Route (or as the army called it, the Whipple Road), named for Maj. Gen. Amiel Weeks Whipple. The road followed the Washita River from Indian Territory into the Texas Panhandle, where it crossed over to the Canadian River, which led travelers to Fort Bascom in eastern New Mexico Territory. From there the road struck west to Albuquerque and continued into Arizona Territory and Fort Whipple, north of Prescott.[9]

Jack and Frank Stilwell arrived in Prescott in late spring 1877. The town was a fascinating community, in part because of its history. After the discovery of precious metals in the nearby San Francisco Mountains, officials in 1864 had made Prescott the territorial capital.[10] Political maneuvers relocated the office to Tucson a few years later, but by 1877, after a ten-year absence, it was once again the political center of the territory and a very busy place.[11]

Ellen McGowan Biddle, who arrived there about the same time as the Stilwells, called it a pretty little frontier outpost. Ellen was the wife of Maj. James Biddle, Sixth Cavalry, who was stationed at Fort Whipple. At first she was sad to be far from the East Coast, where her sons were in boarding school. Upon nearing Prescott, though, she began to change her mind, likening the entrance to the town to a beautiful garden. She observed it was a small but well-built town with a plaza in the center surrounded by stores on each side: "One side of the plaza was given up to saloons but it was fairly orderly considering it was a mining town."[12]

Jack went to work in July as a teamster at Fort Whipple.[13] His work paid sixty dollars per month and centered around the quartermaster's corral, stables, and shops adjacent to Whipple Barracks, which served as headquarters of the Military Department of Arizona.[14] His major responsibility as a teamster was driving private (as opposed to military) teams at Whipple Depot and delivering military supplies under the direction of Assistant Quartermaster John Simpson. As a boy Stilwell had walked beside oxen pulling wagons on the Santa Fe Trail. At Whipple Depot, he drove an army wagon pulled by mules.

Although not yet thirty years old, Jack's health had deteriorated. Rheumatism, which he had first suffered in the cold winter months of the Red River War, surfaced again. It is possible that the long, hard ride to Arizona caused it to flare up. According to Major Biddle, Jack was hurting. In his endorsement of Stilwell's pension petition, he wrote, "I have known Mr. S. E. Stilwell for over a year. . . . He is a good and able man when physically fit for duty but was completely broken down with rheumatism. . . . [He is] a man who has seen much hard service. . . . [I have] heard of him as a competent man."[15]

While Jack's rheumatism sidelined him, Frank's quick temper got him in trouble with the law. In October he was employed as a teamster on a wagon train belonging to George Young. While in camp on the eighteenth, Frank confronted the newly hired cook, Jesus Bega, because he served tea rather than coffee with the meal. Frank asked why he had not made coffee. When Bega replied that he was not aware that coffee was preferred over tea, Frank insulted Bega's nationality, his ability to cook, and his mother. Outraged, Bega hit Frank over the head with a shovel. In response Frank shot the cook through the lungs. That afternoon Frank turned himself over to law-enforcement officials in Prescott, where the justice of the peace questioned and promptly acquitted him.[16]

Afterward Frank found work in a variety of occupations, including as a teamster and cowboy. Four years later, while living at Charleston Village near

Tombstone, he became associated with the "Clanton Cowboy Faction," a group of Arizona ranchers and cowhands who operated on the edge of the law. For reasons no longer extant, but probably to enhance his cowboy reputation, he claimed in the 1880 U.S. census that he had been born in Texas.[17]

Jack Stilwell remained in Arizona for a year. In March or April 1878 he gave up on trying to make his fortune as a teamster at Whipple Depot. Unable to control Frank's temper and keep him out of trouble, he left his younger brother behind and headed for Texas. With his rheumatism in remission, he probably made his way via the discontinued Butterfield Overland Mail road that led from Tucson to El Paso and from there to Fort Davis, in the upper Big Bend region of Texas. From Fort Davis he rode east and north to the old Comanche War Trail at Fort Stockton, located at Comanche Springs in present-day Pecos County.[18]

In late April, Stilwell hired on as chief packer for Buffalo Soldiers of the Tenth Cavalry, stationed at Fort Stockton. The army depended heavily on the services of good packers, because expeditions and patrols failed without a steady supply line; the position showed their confidence in Stilwell's abilities. Happy once again to work with the black troopers, he functioned more as a guide for troops in the field than as a packer.[19]

He did not wait long for new field service. On April 18, a few days before his hire, news had arrived at Fort Stockton that Indians, probably Mescalero or Lipan Apaches, had attacked a rider carrying mail from Fort Concho to Fort Davis. The assault occurred about three miles east of Escondido Station. The rider got away, but the eleven Indians involved captured his horse and the mail. A man accompanying the mail carrier died, and Indians also took his horse. Stilwell's old Fort Sill commander, Gen. Benjamin Grierson, was now commander of the District of the Pecos, and he ordered the commanding officer at Fort Stockton, Capt. David Dougall Van Valzah of the Tenth Cavalry, to send out a detachment of the Tenth Cavalry to locate and pursue the raiders, and if possible destroy them.[20]

On April 25, two days after Stilwell's hire, Captain Van Valzah got a report that twelve Indians were camped near lower Escondido (or hidden) Springs. Stilwell suggested to the post commander that a scout not be sent until evening. He reasoned that by waiting until nightfall, troopers might find the Indians camped at one of three Escondido Springs.[21] Agreeing, the commander assigned Jack to join recently commissioned 2nd Lt. John Bigelow Jr., an 1877 graduate of West Point, and a detachment of thirty enlisted men from Troop B. They rode out of Fort Stockton in the evening, scouted the road for twenty miles to the vicinity of Escondido Springs, and then ranged farther east to the Pecos River. They encountered no Indians. On May 3, after having been gone eight days, they returned to Fort Stockton.[22]

On May 12 Lieutenant Bigelow, with twelve enlisted men, two noncommissioned officers, and Stilwell as a guide, rode west from Fort Stockton to Fort Davis. Upon reaching the well-established post in the beautiful Davis Mountains, Stilwell found his former boss, Colonel Grierson, in charge. Grierson remembered Stilwell from their experiences together when he had scouted for an expedition up the North Fork of the Red River in 1871. The colonel recalled Stilwell as an able and intelligent man who spoke Spanish and Indian languages. He was also, Grierson suggested, an excellent trailer and scout.[23]

Grierson determined to put Stilwell's skills to use in a new operation. The colonel planned to keep multiple detachments of Tenth Cavalry troopers continuously in the field during the summer. He wanted them to explore the District of the Pecos in West Texas and while doing so locate water sources and campsites, including places where Indians stopped overnight. In addition he instructed his troopers to strike any bands of Indians they found off the Fort Stanton Apache reservation in New Mexico.[24] Accordingly, Grierson sent Stilwell northeast through Wild Rose Pass in the Davis Mountains to Barilla Springs. There he was to join Capt. Stevens T. Norvell and Troop M of the Tenth Cavalry. Stilwell held orders to serve as a guide for Norvell during the captain's operation along the upper Butterfield Overland Mail road.[25]

Captain Norvell's command, with Stilwell as a guide, moved north via Point of the Rocks, Toyah Creek, and Apache Springs to Independence Spring near the head of Delaware Creek.[26] From there the men rode west past Delaware Springs to Pine Springs (now part of the Guadalupe Mountains National Park), where they camped. They found each of the important water sources located just off the upper road of the old Butterfield Overland Mail route, which traced the Texas–New Mexico border east to west through the Guadalupe Mountains in far West Texas.[27] Pine Springs bubbled up near the summit of Guadalupe Pass on the north side of the road. Independence Spring was six miles east of Pine Springs, and the men found Delaware Springs about twenty miles farther east.[28]

From the main camp at Pine Springs, Captain Norvell stood in a good position to watch for Indian movements either north toward the reservation in New Mexico Territory or south into West Texas. On June 17 Norvell, 2nd Lt. Millard F. Eggleston, and thirty men from Troop M, with Stilwell as their guide, left the camp at Pine Springs and marched west. The next evening they camped in the Cornudas Mountains at a place that had been occupied by Apaches on the seventeenth.[29]

At four o'clock in the morning on the nineteenth, Norvell's command rode north, following an Indian trail that led in from the south. They tracked it for fifty-two miles into the Sacramento Mountains of New Mexico, but lost the trail after a rainstorm obliterated the tracks. The soldiers scattered to search for fresh signs, and at the summit of a mountain, they found multiple hoofmarks going in different directions but no fresh trail. With his animals short of water, Norvell gave up the chase and returned to Pine Springs on June 23. On the twenty-fourth, to improve grazing conditions for the expedition's horses, he moved the camp three miles north to a place called Bull Springs. His command had marched 150 miles in four days in very hot weather.[30]

During the remainder of June and the first half of July 1878, Novell kept small scouting detachments constantly in the field looking for active Indian trails. Along a 170-mile line from the Pecos River in the east to Hueco Tanks in the west, they found few signs of Indians. Those they did find were Apaches migrating north to south.[31] It is clear that the Indians the soldiers were seeking were keeping watch on Norvell's troops; they knew their locations and avoided areas where they might encounter Tenth Cavalry soldiers.[32]

While Norvell and his men patrolled far West Texas, Capt. Henry Carroll rode south from Fort Stanton in New Mexico with fifty troopers of the Ninth Cavalry and thirty Navajo Scouts. The expedition scouted several southeastern New Mexico mountain ranges without finding Indians. Carroll's troops then moved into camp at Pine Springs, only three miles south of Novell's little command. Carroll, discouraged at not finding Indians and a long way from his post, soon determined it was time to return to Fort Stanton.

On July 20 Lieutenant Bigelow and Troop B, Tenth Cavalry, arrived at the Bull Spring camp. They had completed a scout along the Pecos River from Horsehead Crossing to the southern boundary of New Mexico. After resting and refreshing his mounts for a day, Bigelow returned to Fort Stockton. Stilwell, who was out hunting for fresh Indian trails, missed Bigelow, his former colleague—but not for long.[33]

The two men soon became reunited in ways neither expected. After a hot summer searching for Apaches across much of southern New Mexico and West Texas, Stilwell received orders to proceed "to Fort Stockton before September 1 . . . for duty with Company B, Tenth Cavalry, in the field." He was probably pleased to get the new assignment.[34] One of the new officers of Troop B was 1st Lt. William

Henry Beck, who had served as the regimental quartermaster at Fort Sill. Beck had received a field command that put him in charge of Camp Peña Blanca (White Cliff Springs), located many miles due south of Fort Stockton and about ten miles southeast of present-day Marathon. His junior officers at the little camp included West Point graduates Lieutenant Bigelow and 2nd Lt. John McMartin of the Twenty-Fifth Infantry.[35]

Maj. Napoleon B. McLaughlen, the Fort Stockton commanding officer, was displeased with the choice of Lieutenant McMartin. He did not think that infantry officers should be stationed with cavalry at Camp Peña Blanca, and he wanted McMartin to serve as his post quartermaster. "I have ordered Lieutenant McMartin as directed," he wrote, "but believe it is all wrong."[36]

In addition, the army assigned Marshall F. Price, a civilian physician, as the medical officer to Troop B. It was Price's first field assignment, much to the regret of Lieutenant Beck, whose son, Willie, was to accompany him. At the little scouting camp, Price, Stilwell and Bigelow would share meals in one mess. Lieutenants Beck and McMartin and Willie Beck would eat together in the second.[37]

The expedition left Fort Stockton on September 4, 1878, and arrived at Camp Peña Blanca two days later. On arrival the detachment found the camp filthy and in disarray. Troop L of the Tenth Cavalry, under the command of 1st Lt. Mason Maxon, and had spent the summer of 1878 scouting the lower Big Bend from the camp, and after officials called Maxon away, the remaining troops left the camp a mess when they rode out a month later. It took two days for Bigelow and his Buffalo Soldier detail to clean the campsite of empty cans, bottles, heaps of manure, and rubbish.[38]

During a break in cleanup duty, Stilwell and McMartin "went out riding," according to Bigelow, "and came to a water hole which Mac's horse walked into and sunk. Mac was pulled out by Stilwell who threw him a lariat. The water was so deep that Mac could not touch the bottom. McMartin did not know how to swim, and lost his carbine." Afterward, Stilwell reported the incident and apparently embellished its details. In any case, Bigelow commented, "Stilwell like most guides can spin yarns and is afraid of nothing."[39]

Soon afterward there occurred more serious trouble. Troop B was tasked with checking for Indians deep in the Big Bend region near the San Carlos Crossing of the Rio Grande River. Army officials believed Apaches were camped in the area, and they wanted Troop B to find them. Accordingly, on September 18, 1878, Troop B left Camp Peña Blanca for the Rio Grande. The party included

Lieutenants Beck, Bigelow, and McMartin, assistant surgeon Price, and Stilwell as their guide, as well as several troops. The command rode south but stopped at the water hole where McMartin had lost his carbine. There a trooper who could swim dove into the water and recovered the rifle.[40]

That chore accomplished, the column continued south to the base of Mount Santiago, where the terrain turned rugged. A pack mule carrying supplies for Bigelow, Price, and Stilwell fell from a steep slope and rolled down a forty-five-degree incline. The mess kit broke and scattered over the slope, but the mule survived uninjured.[41] The accident was a minor difficulty compared to the problems caused by the absence of a map of area they were scouting. Not only was there no map, but Beck, the column's leader, had failed to consult former camp commander Lieutenant Maxon for directions to the San Carlos Crossing. Maxon, as noted above, had spent all summer scouting in the Big Bend from the base at Camp Peña Blanca. Moreover, Stilwell, the guide, had never been in the lower Big Bend country.[42] Beck chose to march away from San Carlos Crossing. He turned his column west, planning to strike the Fort Davis–Presidio del Norte road and then ride south to Presidio del Norte, where he hoped to get directions on how to reach the crossing.[43]

According to Bigelow, on September 21 the Troop B command met a Mexican who accompanied the men part of the way to Presidio del Norte. During the ride Bigelow tried to ask him questions about landmarks in the distance. Although both Bigelow and Stilwell spoke Spanish, neither man could get helpful answers from him. Perhaps he feared Apache reprisals if they saw him helping American troops.[44] After reaching the post, Beck's command camped at Fort Leaton, a trading post along the Rio Grande. From there they commenced southeast along the north bank of the river. With no discernable road, travel here became very difficult, but with help from a second Mexican guide, Beck's soldiers made their way downstream, moving past "mountains and canyons" before reaching the San Carlos Crossing on the twenty-fourth.[45]

The trek was hard on the horses, and one became so weak that the men abandoned it. Several of the mounts showed signs of serious fatigue. Accordingly, Beck ordered a three-day rest. Afterward, Beck's scouting column broke camp and headed north. It reached Mount Santiago on September 28 and its home station at Camp Peña Blanca two days later. On October 1 the surgeon Price wrote to Major McLaughlen requesting that he be relieved from duty with Lieutenant Beck.[46] The request had resulted from a thorny clash between the doctor and Beck. It began when Price accused Beck of marching his men to the point of exhaustion. It increased when the surgeon questioned Beck's ability as a troop commander. Beck lost his temper. The two men exchanged bitter words, and Price threatened to make a report of Beck's behavior to the medical department. Price's request to be relieved of duty was denied.[47]

Back at Camp Peña Blanca, Stilwell had a tent but no chairs. Thus he and Beck spent a lot of time with Bigelow in his tent, where there were chairs. They often talked until midnight. Stilwell may have been trying to teach Bigelow Spanish. "By study and talking with Stilwell," the lieutenant wrote, "I may make considerable progress."[48] On at least one occasion, Beck, Stilwell, McMartin, and Bigelow spent a good deal of time drinking whiskey, not studying Spanish. In the midst of this party, Bigelow undressed and went to bed, telling the others that he wanted to get some sleep. They left, but it was after midnight. Price overheard the late-night carousing. On another night Price found Bigelow, McMartin, and Stilwell discussing the prospect of war with Mexico, particularly dwelling on the issue of clashes in northern Mexico between Mexicans and American troops who had been crossing the Rio Grande. All were opposed to war out of sympathy for the Mexican people.[49]

Amid such talk, on October 7 Lieutenant Beck started a second scout into the lower Big Bend country. His son Willie, Stilwell, Lieutenant McMartin, and twenty-five enlisted men accompanied him. The purpose of the foray was to search for a route across the Rio Grande to the abandoned Presidio de San Vicente. Beck headed southeast along San Francisco Creek and reached the river on October 9. During the march over this difficult and broken landscape, the men endured the extreme heat of southwest Texas. Beck tried to ride upriver, but harsh terrain blocked his movements. He sent Stilwell to scout a route, but the craggy country proved impossible to navigate. Afterward the lieutenant sent Stilwell to locate San Vicente, but he was unable to find the old Spanish colonial fort. Separated from Beck's men, Stilwell rode to the San Carlos Crossing and from there continued to Mount Santiago before returning to Camp Peña Blanca, where he arrived on October 21.[50]

Meanwhile Beck struggled as his men, horses, and mules became worn and haggard. His supply of rations dwindled and became dangerously short. Worried about Stilwell but no longer able to wait for the scout's return, Beck turned back. He retraced his old trail to Camp Peña Blanca and arrived on October 18, three days before Stilwell. Upon learning that his wife, Rachel, was dreadfully ill, Beck left Camp Peña Blanca for Fort Stockton on October 23, accompanied by his son and McMartin. They made a rapid trip in an army ambulance drawn by four mules. Unfortunately, one mule died during the exhaustive ride and another was injured. The animals' death and injury angered Major McLaughlen, the Fort Stockton commander, who was responsible for the well-being of the mules, and he would not forget Beck's sorry treatment of them.[51]

At Fort Stockton Beck discovered that Rachel was too ill to care for herself or their young children, Mamie and Paul. Mrs. Fanny McLaughlen was caring for the family. Beck, affected by the stress of the circumstances, began to drink. While drunk, he rode his horse into the trader's store. On the twenty-sixth, he applied for a leave of absence, but soon withdrew it.[52] On October 28, finding his wife's health improving, Beck, his son, and McMartin returned to Camp Peña Blanca, just ahead of August Hannahan, a contract hauler and sutler, and his supply train. Hannahan's camp stood near to the officer's tents, and that evening Beck and Stilwell visited Hannahan, who carried among his stores a liberal supply of whiskey. The men consumed plenty of alcohol, reportedly drinking and singing late into the night. Dr. Price again reported the late-night activity to Major McLaughlen, who later wrote: "Lieutenant Beck's conduct has not been commendable and his example to the young men at the post is very bad."[53]

By this time the scouting season was getting late, even for southwest Texas. Even so, on November 8 Colonel Grierson arrived at Camp Peña Blanca from Fort Davis with plans to search for Apaches who were supposed to be near the San Carlos Crossing of the Rio Grande. Accordingly, along with Lieutenants Beck and Bigelow, Stilwell, and fifteen enlisted men, he pushed south to Maravillas Creek in present-day Brewster County. After establishing a temporary camp there, Grierson, Beck, Bigelow, Stilwell, and seven enlisted men rode south and struck the Rio Grande between the San Carlos Crossing and San Vicente.[54]

Lieutenant Beck's problems, whatever they were, must have continued during the trek. Bigelow indicated that he watched and heard Grierson give Beck "a cussing." He also indicated that he "saw several hot and cold water springs, swam in the river, and saw San Vicente," which Stilwell believed "was an old Aztec ruin of adobe."[55] The men eventually found the long-sought ford that crossed the Rio Grande. It was shallow enough that wagons could cross, and Bigelow confirmed its use by swimming across the river. The findings supported Grierson's plan to build a wagon road from Fort Davis and Fort Stockton into the Big Bend. Thus, they returned to the temporary camp on Maravillas Creek, picked up the men left there, and returned to Camp Peña Blanca.[56]

Shortly afterward, on November 20, Colonel Grierson sent Beck, Stilwell, and several men of Troop B south once again. This time they were to locate a tract for the wagon road Grierson wanted. Little was accomplished, and on November 25 a heavy snow interrupted the men's work. Beck returned to Camp Peña Blanca and ordered the camp dismantled. Troop B returned to Fort Stockton for the winter.

Now came more trouble for Lieutenant Beck, much of it stemming from his quarrel with Dr. Price. Price had charged Beck with causing the exhaustion of his men and animals during one of the return rides from the San Carlos Crossing. When Brig. Gen. Edward O. C. Ord and his staff read Price's report of the charges, they fussed, because the incident recalled Capt. Nicholas H. Nolan's questionable judgement in leading men of Troop A, Tenth Cavalry, across the desert-dry and largely uncharted Llano Estacado a year earlier. The Nolan incident had led to the death of four men and most of the horses. It also had received national attention from America's newspapers, and Ord did not want another disaster during his command of the Department of Texas.[57] Ord called William Henry Beck to San Antonio for a general court-martial. Beck arrived in December. But the troubled lieutenant continued to swim in turmoil, and he did not help his military cause when he got drunk shortly after arriving in the city. General Ord placed him in close arrest and restricted him to the Menger Hotel, located near the Alamo.[58]

Beck's court-martial convened on January 29, 1879. The charges and specifications seemed damaging, indicating that Beck engaged in "conduct unbecoming an officer and gentleman," drunkenness on duty, marching his men to the point of exhaustion near the San Carlos Crossing, and ignoring the medical officer's pleas to rest the troops. While intoxicated he had ridden his horse into the trader's store at Fort Stockton. Back at Camp Peña Blanca, Beck had visited the teamsters' camp, where there was singing, shouting, and whiskey drinking. He appeared drunk at evening stable duty and drove the ambulance mules to Fort Stockton so fast that one mule died and another mule was injured. Beck pleaded not guilty to the charges.[59]

Prosecution officers presented sixty-one pages of testimony and called several witnesses, including Stilwell, who had been ordered to San Antonio on December 31 to serve as a trial witness.[60] Among other testimony, Stilwell indicated that he had been present when Price and Beck argued over the extent of exhaustion among Buffalo Soldiers of Troop B. In testifying for the prosecution, Stilwell said Beck asked the surgeon "why he had mounted the command." He then indicated that Lt. John Bigelow answered, saying, "Dr. Price said because they were exhausted." Stilwell further testified, "Lieutenant Beck cursed, turned away with the remark that the whole outfit was worthless."[61]

As first witness for the defense, Lt. John McMartin maintained that when Beck and Price had their confrontation near the San Carlos Crossing, Beck was angry but his language was polite. McMartin also stated that the expedition was Dr. Price's first scout, and he was not acquainted with the usual manner that a surgeon performed in the field—meaning, apparently, that Price had no business confronting Beck. Defense counsel also asked McMartin about the loud singing or noises "after the Indian fashion" in Camp Peña Blanca. Who made the noise and where was it? he wanted to know. McMartin admitted it was Jack Stilwell trying to sing and the incident occurred "in my tent."[62] Lieutenant Bigelow testified that Dr. Price was ill disposed and prejudiced toward Beck. When counsel asked him about the singing after the "manner of Indians" at Camp Peña Blanca, Bigelow replied, "Yes, it was my guide Mr. Stilwell. The singing was noisy and discordant."[63]

On March 1 Stilwell testified for the defense. When asked about the second scout with Beck and the trip he took to look for San Vicente, he replied that he rode alone, missed San Vicente, and moved over to San Carlos Crossing. He then returned to Camp Peña Blanca after riding a distance of about 180 miles. When asked about Beck's leadership, Stilwell said, "I think he was able to command and did it." He also said the lieutenant was good at handling stock.[64]

Beck took the stand in his own defense. When asked about the bottles of whiskey in his tent, he replied, "I paid no attention to it myself but told Stilwell the box with the liquor in it was in my front tent if he wanted any, he might go and get it which I presume he did." Beck also alluded to his friendship with Stilwell. When asked about the subject of a conversation around a campfire, he said, "A good deal of it was on the subject of Indians, Indian country and the Pecos. . . . I was alluding to Mr. Stilwell's personal experience, I was always interested, he and I having been together in Indian Country [near Fort Sill]."

Much more testimony and many additional arguments followed, of course, but final statements came on March 20. Afterward, officials closed deliberations and cleared the court. The verdict came down six days later. The court found Lt. William Henry Beck guilty of most charges and specifications. It recommended he be dismissed from the service of the U.S. Army.[65]

As with nearly all such courts-martial, Beck's case underwent a review. General Ord and his staff looked at the trial records and accepted the court's findings, but they recommended leniency, as did his superiors, including General Sherman. After a final review, President Hays commuted the sentence to "suspension of rank on half-pay for one year."[66] Following the court-martial, Lieutenant Beck served in the field as aide-de-camp and acting assistant adjutant to Colonel Grierson. The assignment allowed the effective and obliging officer to monitor Beck's behavior.[67]

In March 1879, the court-martial over, Jack Stilwell left San Antonio for Indian Territory. During the two years he had lived in Arizona and West Texas, he had engaged in a number of activities, none of which had added greatly to his stature as a scout and guide—or as a teamster, for that matter. Admittedly, his work in the Big Bend proved largely unsuccessful, but the experience he gained in traversing a hard and difficult country added to his and the military's knowledge of the area.

After being caught in the middle of the unpleasant Beck court-martial, he must have been relieved when he boarded a train in San Antonio and turned north toward "home." Once back in familiar surroundings near Fort Sill in Indian Territory, he found work as a cowboy on the Chandler-Conover Ranch along the Little Washita River east of the military post.[68] Here "Comanche Jack," as he was now often called, remained free to sing Comanche songs where they were appreciated.

CHAPTER 10

CHASING CATTLE, TROUBLE, AND WYATT EARP

After the court-martial of Lt. William Henry Beck in March 1879, twenty-eight-year-old Jack Stilwell left Texas and headed north for Indian Territory and the Comanche-Kiowa reservation at Fort Sill. By the end of the 1870s, conflicts between soldiers and Indians in the Southwest had largely concluded, so the army no longer needed civilian scouts and guides. Accordingly, Stilwell shifted easily into life as a cowhand on an Anglo-owned ranch in the territory.[1]

Stilwell's work as a cowboy was not easy, of course, but it kept him in the saddle, kept him in a region that had become his home, and kept him close to both his Comanche contacts on the reservation and his Anglo friends at Erin Springs in the Chickasaw Nation. His life during the next four years proved busy as he juggled time spent on family issues with watching over herds of cattle, branding them, and moving them to better pastures and to market.

When Stilwell left San Antonio in early 1879, he had boarded a Katy Railroad train and traveled north to Caddo, Indian Territory. From Caddo he took a stagecoach west toward Fort Sill and bounced along a military supply road for several days on the 135-mile journey. He may have stopped briefly at Erin Springs to attend a monthly meeting of the Elm Springs Masonic Lodge, where he had become a member in 1876 (following the tradition of his grandfather Joseph Everett Stilwell, who had joined a Masonic lodge in Brownstown, Indiana, many years earlier). While working as a cowboy in 1879 and 1880, Stilwell remained active as a Mason, and near the end of his first year back in Indian Territory, he won election to the office of senior warden in the Masonic order.[2]

Complicated family issues intruded on his cowboy life. When his father, William Henry, married Jennie Pike for the second time in 1865, she had used her maiden name, Sarah Jane Brenner. The name change apparently stemmed from a scheme in which she and William hoped to receive an inheritance from her family. Results of the maneuver are unknown.

During the 1870s, while Jack was scouting for the army, William Henry had remained in and around Saint Joseph. According to census records, he continued to work as a carpenter to support the family he had created with Jennie Pike. It included a teenage step-daughter, Mary (Jennie's daughter from a previous partner), and Ella, the couple's own child. How much Jack kept in touch with his father's second family is unknown; the records are not available.[3]

Stilwell's sister Clara May—who as a teenager in October 1876 had married William Alexander—died young, possibly in childbirth or of an infectious disease. There is an unmarked burial of a teenage girl named Sarah [Clara?] and an Alexander in the Wayman–Pleasant Grove Cemetery, Brownstown Township, in Jackson County, Indiana. An obituary in the local newspaper, the *Brownstown Banner*, indicated Clara died around November 10, 1878. In the same cemetery Stilwell's uncle Gustavous B. and aunt Catherine Stilwell are buried along with his cousins Annie Stilwell Wallingford and David E. Stilwell.[4]

Stilwell's youngest sister, Elizabeth Ann, on November 23, 1879, married Joseph Cooley.[5] William Henry might have been present for the wedding, as he was in Jackson County about that time. On October 1, 1879, he filed a court action, "Notice to Non-Residents," in a case titled *William Henry Stilwell vs. Simpson E. Stilwell, Frank C. Stilwell, Howard C. Stilwell, and William O. Stilwell*. He wanted "to ascertain the residence of said defendants"—his sons and a nephew.[6] After all the years of being absent, William Henry's purpose in contacting members of his first family remains a mystery.

William very likely discovered the family was scattered. According to the 1880 U.S. census, Jack's mother, Charlotte Stilwell Wiseman, was a widow living in Hamilton Township, Jackson County, with her youngest daughter, Elizabeth Ann, and her son-in-law, Joseph Cooley. He may have discovered that his son Frank was keeping a livery stable in Charleston Village, Pima County, Arizona. He may have learned also that his son Howard was working as a laborer in Baldwin City, Kansas, and that his nephew William O. Stilwell (the son of William Henry's brother Jacob) lived with his parents in Kansas on the half quarter section near Palmyra Township that Jacob Stilwell had bought from William Henry in 1861. He may have given up on the lawsuit: in the fall of 1880 William Henry, Sarah Jane (Jennie Pike), and their daughter Ella moved to Joseph, in Union

County, Oregon.[7] Over the next two years conflicts consumed their marriage. Court documents filed by Sarah Jane paint William as jealous, insulting, and threatening to her; in September 1882 he deserted her. Their daughter Ella had in the meantime married a man named Roberts.

In Indian Territory, Stilwell had hired on as a cowboy on the Conover Ranch, named for George W. Conover. Located below Rock Crossing of the Little Washita River along the 98th meridian, the ranch spread across many acres in the eastern part of the Comanche-Kiowa reservation—in an area that is now western Grady County.[8] The Conover Ranch had its start as the 320-acre Chandler Ranch, created during the winter of 1871–72. It was the first land allotment on the Comanche-Kiowa reservation authorized by the Treaty of Medicine Lodge in 1867. Encouraged by the Quaker Indian agent Lawrie Tatum, Joseph Chandler and his wife Tomasa applied for and were awarded an allotment thirty miles northeast of Fort Sill, just west the 98th meridian. Chandler was part Cherokee, and Tomasa, originally a member of the Carissa tribe of Mexico, had been captured by Comanches and carried north.[9]

Tomasa's story is a bit unusual. When she was a small child, Comanche warriors raided her home in Mexico and carried her away into captivity. A Comanche family adopted her and treated her kindly. After a few years with the family, American officials ransomed her and sent her back to Mexico, where she became something of a slave. She ran away and after much difficulty returned by chance to the same Comanche band with which she had grown up. She was happy to return to the lodge of her Comanche foster mother. But as she grew into womanhood, she refused to marry an older Comanche man, Blue Leggings, and instead chose trader and ranchman Joseph Chandler.[10]

Because of their long association with Comanches, Tomasa and Joseph Chandler were of great service to Fort Sill's Indian agency. Agent Tatum and Josiah Butler, the first teacher at the Fort Sill agency school, put them to work. In 1870 Tomasa became an interpreter at the school as well as one of its first students. Besides Tomasa, other early students included two small boys, one small girl, and three young women. Since it was a boarding school, Mrs. Butler and Tomasa oversaw the girls while Mr. Butler watched over the boys. Tomasa's help in the establishment of the agency school was greatly appreciated by the Butlers.[11] Lawrie Tatum also had great respect for Tomasa and Joseph and for their children Lotsee, Solomon (Bud), Joseph (Boone), and George.[12]

The elder Joseph had lived near the Comanches for many years. He served as a trusted interpreter and became one of the ranchers/contractors who supplied beef to the government. But his tenure at the ranch was short-lived; Chandler died in January 1873. He was only fifty years old. Former Fort Sill commissary sergeant and Indian agency employee George W. Conover was then working on the ranch. Shortly before Chandler died, Conover took over operations. He eventually became its official manager, and in 1875 he and Tomasa married.[13]

Conover and Tomasa owned the ranch by the time Stilwell went to work there as a cowboy. They knew or learned that Stilwell had previous experience with cattle: he had accompanied two herds up the trail from Texas to Kansas in the early seventies.[14] To Conover, Stilwell was a man of "rather formidable personal appearance." Stilwell worked about two years on the Conover Ranch.[15] According to William F. Dietrich, who had married Lotsee Chandler, Stilwell "rode lines" on the ranch for only one year.[16] Stilwell, on the other hand, maintained that he worked on the Conover Ranch for nearly four years and held responsibility of the management of the cattle.[17]

Although he kept busy as a cowboy on the ranch, Stilwell had time for extra-curricular activities—such as horse racing. One year during the large spring round-up, a Northern Cheyenne named Chief Buffalo challenged the cowboys to a matched horse race in which his rangy, mouse-colored animal with numerous burrs in his main and tail would run. The cowboys saw it as the "hardest looking horse" they had seen. Chief Buffalo's horse was matched with Old Tim, the best three-hundred-yard horse that the cowboys owned, but for whatever reason the participants selected a distance of four hundred yards for the race instead of three hundred. Many Indians arrived ready to bet all their goods. The cowboys had great confidence in Old Tim and so put up their last dollars, all the property in camp, and even their private horses on his winning.[18]

Charles F. Colcord rode Old Tim, and a seventeen-year-old Indian boy rode Chief Buffalo's horse. The race track was a two-rut wagon road. Colcord got a good start and during the race he made several efforts to block the Indian boy by pulling Old Tim over into the Indian's lane. Finally, the boy guided his horse out of the road and went around Colcord like "the wind" and beat Old Tim by ten feet. After the race the Indians went wild. The cowboys went broke, as some of them had bet part of their blanket rolls. According to Colcord, the judges of the race were Jack Stilwell and Amos Chapman, a former scout like Jack.[19]

The Conover Ranch gained acreage while Stilwell worked there. Kiowas, Comanches, and Kiowa-Apaches saw their agency at Fort Sill eliminated in 1879. Afterward, government officials consolidated it with the Wichita agency at Anadarko, hoping a merger would reduce expenses. The fact that all three Indian groups who lived there could speak Comanche, the "court language," also played a role in the decision.[20] In response to the consolidation, George Conover, hoping to return to agency work, left the ranch on the Little Washita and in 1880 moved to Anadarko about two miles south of the agency.[21] William Dietrich, the husband of Lotsee Chandler, and their sons Tom and Burke continued to manage the Conover Ranch on the Little Washita Ranch until 1884, when they too moved to the Anadarko area.[22] Stilwell continued to work with the Dietrich family on the ranch.

Even as he worked as a cowboy, Stilwell found additional employment. He secured temporary work in September 1880 at the Cheyenne and Arapaho agency, an act noted in the local newspaper: "Mr. Stillwell is at present butchering for the Agency."[23] Jack also worked again briefly for the U.S. Army. He served as a guide at Fort Reno in Indian Territory for just over a month, December 9, 1880—January 22, 1881. Carried on the quartermaster rolls as Jack Stilwell (rather than S. E. or Simpson E., as he had been in the past), he found the work easy. In early December he guided Company I of the Sixteenth Infantry, under the command of Capt. William H. Clapp and bound for the Department of Texas, to the nearest station of the Katy Railroad in eastern Indian Territory. On Christmas Day he guided Company B, commanded by Capt. Evart Stinson Ewing, to the same station, where they too headed south to Texas. These two short trips represent Stilwell's last assignments as a guide with army troops in the field.[24]

Toward the end of his service as a guide, Stilwell found himself in a bit of a pickle. He and J. R. Cook, a teamster at Fort Reno, got drunk one evening on the Cheyenne reservation, barged into a tipi (tent home), and demanded lodging. Normally, the incident would have gone unnoticed, but Mollie Hauser, the Cheyenne daughter of the tipi owner, was there. Educated in the East, Mollie had once lived at Fort Sill, where she agreed to marry Herman Hauser, an old soldier who had financed her education. However, after the marriage she refused to live with him and returned to the reservation to be with her mother. Mollie filed a complaint against Stilwell and Cook. On January 20, 1881, in a letter to the Cheyenne and Arapaho agent John D. Miles, Mollie stated that two men came in on Monday evening to her mother's tipi and demanded lodging for the night. Jack, according to the complaint, became abusive and drew his pistol, scaring everyone enough that, despite cold weather, they left the place. Mollie closed her letter: "Please let these men know that we are under your protection which knowledge will probably prevent similar outrages in the future."[25]

Indian police arrested the men and took them to the agency headquarters. Jack protested and he and Cook showed a letter they claimed was from the commanding officer at Fort Reno to Capt. Hanson H. Crews of the Fourth Cavalry, the commander at Fort Sill. Stilwell claimed that it was important to deliver the letter as soon as possible. Fortunately for Stilwell and Cook, the Indian policemen released them to continue their journey.[26] Agent Miles wrote to the commander at Fort Reno, Capt. George M. Randall of the Twenty-Third Infantry, about the incident. He stated that Stilwell and Cook were not employed at the Indian agency. Ms. Hauser's complaint was then referred to Captain Crews at Fort Sill. He in turn wrote to Miles for information and an explanation. Indeed, Captain Crews wanted some clarification. He asked Stilwell to explain the situation. Stilwell, however, would not explain, and as Crews pressed him for information, the former scout became evasive, obfuscated, and then became silent on the matter. Crews then ordered legal affidavits taken.[27]

The matter of affidavits and Mollie's complaint went to her estranged husband, Herman Hauser, at Fort Reno. Hauser was the quartermaster clerk as well as U.S. commissioner, and he administered all affidavits.[28] In one of them Crews said that he was in the dark about Stilwell's alleged troubles. Fortunately for Jack, Captain Crews, at the time of the affidavits, had not yet received a letter, a telegram, or other information he had sought from Miles concerning Stilwell's misbehavior as reported by Mollie.[29] Except for the affidavits, no other action was taken.

Not long after the Hauser problem was behind him, Stilwell and Thomas Donnell, the Fort Reno scout, stopped for dinner at a wayside station operated by Caddo George Washington. Caddo George, a leader of the White Bead band of Caddos, served meals to travelers at his little stop located on the Canadian River along the trail between the Darlington agency and the Anadarko agency. After Stilwell and his traveling companion finished eating and were about to leave, the owner charged Donnell one dollar for his meal but asked nothing from Stilwell. Donnell, a bit indignant, asked how it was that he was charged a dollar and Stilwell was charged nothing. With all the frankness and truthfulness he could muster, Caddo George stated, "Jack he is my friend, I no charge him but I charge you one dollar, so you pay for both."[30] The incident once again illustrates that Stilwell maintained friendships among the Indians.

These episodes aside, Stilwell also traveled on business for his employer, George Conover. In the summer of 1881 he rode north to Caldwell, Kansas. The *Caldwell Post* noted his presence in town. The paper's editor wrote, "Mr. Stilwell, who was in the employ of 'Uncle Sam' as a scout is here having some fun mit de b'boys. Mr. Stilwell is in the employ of Mr. George Conover of the Washita agency."[31] Obviously, Jack had gained some fame (or at least notoriety) while living in Indian Territory.

In the spring of 1882 Stilwell left the Conover Ranch, moved to action by the death of his brother Frank at the hands of Wyatt Earp's band of law enforcement agents in Tucson, Arizona Territory. The shooting occurred at the Tucson railroad depot shortly after seven o'clock on the evening of March 20.[32] Just when Jack, at work on the Conover Ranch, was informed of Frank's death is not known, but the shooting was reported on the Cheyenne reservation in the *Cheyenne Transporter*, published at the Darlington agency, on the twenty-fifth.[33]

The newspaper article indicated that Frank Stilwell's body was found riddled with bullets beside the railroad tracks near the depot. Frank had been seen earlier at the railroad station with Ike Clanton, a leader of the "Cowboy Faction," some of whose members had engaged in the bloody street battle at the O.K. Corral in Tombstone the previous fall with the Earp brothers' faction. The Darlington paper further indicated that a westbound train had arrived in Tucson with an armed party of Earp's friends and the body of Morgan Earp, who had been ambushed and killed on March 18. Four members of the Earp bloc followed Stilwell down the track and shots were heard. The *Cheyenne Transporter* article concluded, "Frank was the brother of Jack Stilwell so well known in these parts."[34]

Frank's murder stunned the Stilwell family. It may have contributed to William Henry's further mental deterioration. Living far from his Stilwell kin in northeast Oregon, he was already a bit unhinged and paranoid. His second wife, Sarah Jane, would claim in her divorce filing in 1884 that he did not work to support the family, gambled often, drank to excess in local bars, and was always in conflict at home.[35] William Henry wrote to Jack in 1882, but the contents of the letter are unknown; by September of that year he had deserted Sarah Jane. Jack briefly saw his father again in Arkansas, but they did not discuss what became of Sarah Jane Stilwell. William never returned to Oregon.[36]

In any case, Jack Stilwell headed to Arizona Territory to investigate his brother's death.[37] He traveled first to Baldwin City, Kansas, to outline his plans for his time in Arizona for his Uncle Jacob. Years earlier Jacob had looked after Frank, as well as Charlotte and the boys' two sisters before Charlotte and the girls had moved back to Indiana.[38] After explaining his plans, Stilwell took the Atchison, Topeka & Santa Fe Railroad from Kansas southwest through Albuquerque to Deming, New Mexico. At Deming he transfered to a westbound Southern Pacific train to Benson, Arizona Territory.[39] There he boarded a stagecoach to Tombstone; from that legendary boomtown he rode southwest to Charleston Village, where Frank had lived. He expected trouble, for he remembered Frank's temper and habit of settling arguments with a gun, as he had in 1877 when he shot Jesus Bega.[40]

Stilwell soon learned his brother Frank's Arizona history. After working as a teamster at Signal, Mohave County, in 1878, Frank had gone to work as a teamster for Charles Hamilton "Ham" Light. Light's company held a contract for hauling ore from surrounding mines to the mills at Millville-Charleston. His wagons were pulled by sixteen-mule teams and loaded with twelve and a half tons of ore at three dollars per ton.[41] Frank, Jack discovered, had been implicated with others in the killing of one J. Van Houton at the Brunckow Mine near Charleston Village in November 1879, but had been acquitted for lack of evidence. Later Frank rotated through several businesses in Charleston and Bisbee, owning at different times a saloon, wholesale liquor business, livery stable, and a stage line, among others. He had been a partner with Pete Spence in a saloon at Bisbee, and there Frank in September 1881 had been implicated in the hold-up of the Bisbee stage. Frank was in jail at the time of the Earp-Clanton showdown at the O.K. Corral in Tombstone on October 26, but he was alleged to have been involved in the ambush of Virgil Earp on December 28. In addition, Jack learned that plenty of citizens in Arizona believed that Frank had taken part in the ambush-murder in Tombstone of Morgan Earp.[42] Clearly, the Earp family and their friends did not like Frank Stilwell. Josephine Sarah Marcus Earp later described Frank as in a "class by himself." She remembered that he "acted like a daring boy playing cops and robbers."[43] (As it turns out, Josephine and her editor, Glenn G. Boyer, fabricated much of her story.) Wyatt Earp call Frank a coward. He told a Denver newspaper reporter in 1893 that Frank "could not shoot," and that when Earp and the others chased him down in the Tucson railyard, "Frank stood helpless as he begged for his life and clutched at Wyatt's shot gun as he was being shot with both barrels."[44]

In Charleston Village and in Tombstone, Jack Stilwell heard both sides of the Earp-Clanton conflict as told by supporters of each faction. He also learned that Frank's murder was noted in California by the *Los Angeles Times* and the *San Diego Union*. The *Los Angeles Times* was outraged by Frank's assassination and demanded that the guilty parties be apprehended and brought to trial. The *San Diego Union* also pointed out Frank's possible involvement in the Bisbee stage robbery and the murder of Morgan Earp.[45]

Even before the March 1882 murder of Morgan and the assassination of Frank Stilwell, lawlessness in parts of Arizona Territory, especially Cochise County, came to the attention of President Chester A. Arthur. On February 2, 1882, Arthur sent a message to Congress noting problems in the territory. Moreover, he pointed out suggestions that had been made—by Secretary of the Interior S. J. Kirkwood and the acting governor of Arizona Territory John Gosper—about enacting legislation to allow the federal government to assist territorial and local authorities in restoring and maintaining order in the territory.[46]

As Stilwell ascertained the details of his brother's involvement in the Earp-Clanton feud, he also closed out his brother's livery stable business and other interests, including the bar in Bisbee. These errands took him from Charleston Village to Bisbee to Tombstone, where he made the Grand Hotel his base for further investigations related to Frank's death. He was there often in April 1882.[47]

John B. Charlton, who had served with Jack Stilwell at Fort Sill, also knew Frank. Charlton was among many people in the area who believed that Wyatt Earp killed Frank at the Tucson railway depot. He noted that after Frank's murder, he saw Jack Stilwell in Benson, Arizona, as Jack sought information about his brother. Perhaps Stilwell was seeking Wyatt Earp as well.[48] In the end Stilwell determined that Frank's association with outlaws had made him an outlaw himself, and the realization disappointed him. Within a month he had closed out Frank's livery business, but he lingered in the territory for a time, perhaps hoping Wyatt Earp might appear. Stilwell considered riding with Sheriff John Behan's posse in pursuit of Earp and his associates, but he checked into the Grand Hotel instead. The posse left Tombstone on March 27 and returned on April 2: "It was a fruitless search of the absconding Earps," a local newspaper reported. On the day of his return, Behan filed his expense voucher naming the entire posse. Stilwell was not listed on the roll.[49]

In the meantime, the brothers' Uncle Jacob in Kansas worried about the fate of his nephews. As early as April 9 Tucson's *Arizona Daily Star* printed a letter from Jacob indicating that he was the uncle of Frank and "Texas Jack" Stilwell. The letter noted that he was "anxious to get information about the latter and deplores the fate of the former."[50]

The eldest Stilwell brother, it turns out, became popular in Arizona Territory. Tombstone's *Arizona Weekly Star* on May 4, 1882, published a long article about Stilwell and his life in the Tombstone area. It said, among other things, that Jack was still in town and "a general favorite." It noted that he was the brother of Frank, who had been "murdered in Tucson a few weeks ago." The paper indicated that "Jack is a genuine" frontiersman, "every inch . . . a gentleman." It reviewed Jack's background as an eighteen-year military scout and stated that he was presently a cattleman who preferred to be seen as a cowboy. It described him as an "amiable and good-natured man, tall and robust with . . . small hands and feet." The author wrote that Stilwell held letters of introduction that stated he "comes recommended by army officers and other prominent citizens of his section," and added that he "is master of the Elm Springs Lodge No. 7, F. & A. M. of Indian Territory." By "all appearances" he "is a man moving in good society."[51]

The newspaper article also suggested that "of course the Earp Party put him down as a desperado at once, but then according to their code anyone who will cheer for outlaws cannot be a good citizen." The article summed up Stilwell's peaceful purpose in the territory: he had come "to look after his brother's effects and to enquire into the cause of his murder and if possible bring his murderers to justice." Although, the writer concluded, while Stilwell "is a downright law and order man, I would hate to be in Wyatt Earp's place if they met face to face on the open prairie."[52]

Unable to find Wyatt Earp (who had left Tombstone for Colorado ahead of an arrest warrant) or others responsible for Frank's death, Stilwell took leave of Arizona. He could do no more. Thus, in the early summer of 1882 he returned to Indian Territory and resumed cowboy work on the Conover Ranch.[53] Stilwell appreciated his work on the ranch along the Little Washita, far removed from his family's problems. Now operated by Lotsee Chandler's husband, William Dietrich, the range was still "open" and unfenced. Stilwell worked cattle, of course, but in winter he also had to "ride line." Line riders on the ranch usually stayed south of the Little Washita River to keep the cattle from drifting south. It was not hard work, but it was monotonous, particularly when riders were alone all day. On many days a rider might not see another human, but it was a great day when he met another rider, probably coming from the opposite direction, and upon meeting have someone with whom he could talk and smoke.[54]

A good line rider could identify where wayward cattle left the range. If cattle strayed off the Conover Ranch, the rider must be able to pick up the tracks. At that point he would turn them back and herd them across the river back onto the ranchland. Certainly identifying new trails from old ones was a problem. Such problems were exacerbated by drought, when the cattle would be more inclined to look for water. In a winter storm cattle drifted south, and on the Conover Ranch they often crossed the Little Washita. The ranch kept its southern line on the south bank of the river, where it maintained "line shacks," or houses for the riders. Stilwell, as all cowhands, worked spring and fall round-ups when the men separated and counted cattle, branded calves, and castrated the new-born bulls.[55]

Stilwell enjoyed his ranching life, and he was happy on the Comanche-Kiowa reservation. Over the years it had become his home, a little corner of the world where his singing in the Comanche language might be appreciated rather than land him in jail, as had happen some years previous. Yet not all was well for the thirty-two-year-old. His hip bothered him during the winter of 1882–83, and he wanted to seek treatment. He worried about his father's sorry emotional condition and wondered about the fate of his father's second wife in Oregon. He wondered about the status of his half-sister, Ella, who had married but remained in Oregon near her mother.[56]

Moreover, Frank's death and what Stilwell considered his own unsettled situation continued to bother him. He realized that Frank, with his livery stable and his bar in Charlestown Village, had made a terrible mistake in connecting and siding with Ike Clanton and his cowboy cronies, an association that led to his death. Jack believed that Frank was little more than a Kansas farm boy who got in way over his head with the grizzled Wyatt Earp and his family. Unlike Jack, his brother had no experience dealing with such killers.

With such problems on his mind and troubled by physical pain, Jack Stilwell remained a troubled and unhappy man for the next several months. Nonetheless, he stayed with his duties as a cowhand at the Conover Ranch on the Comanche-Kiowa reservation, making the best of his life as a cowboy.

Chapter 11

A COWBOY IN INDIAN TERRITORY

W hen he returned to Indian Territory from Arizona in 1882, Jack Stilwell was not in good health. Only thirty-two years old, he suffered from rheumatism in his right hip and shoulder. He appeared worn out and aged beyond his years. Still strong of mind, determined, and unafraid of responsibility, he settled restlessly and painfully back into cow work at the Conover Ranch on the Comanche-Kiowa reservation. Besides his physical afflictions, Stilwell found that family issues intruded on his well-being. According to Sarah Jane Stilwell's petition for divorce, Jack's father William Henry exhibited many symptoms of paranoia. Moreover, he did not work or otherwise support his family; she also claimed he abused her.[1] Late in the year, William wrote to Jack, asking to see him, among other things. They arranged to meet sometime in the spring.[2]

Meanwhile, for twelve dollars per month Stilwell continued his line-riding duties on the southern edge of the Conover Ranch, despite his aching body. Each day he rode out along the river for half a day before circling back, heading downstream for one circuit and upstream the next. He stayed in a line shack at night.[3] Unwell and often unable to work, Stilwell found the fall and winter of 1882–83 a difficult time. His recurrent rheumatism frequently kept him out of the saddle. He spent time in Anadarko with such Comanche friends as Red Tail and Hickory. An account in his name at the A. J. Reynolds store at the Anadarko agency showed that on November 30, 1882, he purchased merchandise for twelve dollars, and on February 28, 1883, he made a fifty-cent purchase, spending some of the money on his friends. He gained weight, as well, from inactivity and too much alcohol, among other things.[4]

Spring's warmer temperatures brought no relief from his hip and shoulder pain. At that point Stilwell and his local physician determined he should seek alternate treatment for his maladies. Thus, in April 1883 he resigned his position with the Conover Ranch, climbed into a stagecoach, and rode north to Caldwell, Kansas, where he boarded a train to Hot Springs, Arkansas. Once there he began a therapy regimen that included soaking in the hot baths of the popular and already-famous spa.[5]

While he sought relief from his rheumatism at Hot Springs, Stilwell's father joined him. Jack had not seen William Henry since the latter had been drafted for service in 1864, some nineteen years previous. Many details of the meeting are unspecified, but during their talks, which must have spread over several days, William Henry did not discuss his second wife, his child with her, or their relationship. Jack did not wish to talk about such matters with his father.[6] How long Jack remained at Hot Springs is unknown, but the therapeutic baths must have helped. By January 1884 friends reported him in Darlington, the town that hosted the agency for the Cheyenne-Arapaho reservation.[7]

By the time Stilwell had returned to Indian Territory—and likely before he had left—he became assistant foreman of the Kansas City–based Word-Bugbee Cattle Company. This large ranch stretched through the Washita River valley in the heart of the Cheyenne-Arapahoe reservation. Rather than riding line, his main duties were concentrated on keeping peace among various Indian factions connected with the ranch through leases and on securing ranch rights vis-à-vis other lease holders. Such leasing of grazing land on the reservation had begun in late 1882 and early 1883, part of an effort to stabilize and perhaps improve economic conditions and living standards for Cheyenne and Arapaho people whose troubles were significant and complicated.[8]

As early as March 1882, before Stilwell had left the Conover Ranch to head to Arizona and settle Frank Stilwell's estate, John D. Miles, the tall, thin, and heavily bearded agent at Darlington, had been facing a crisis. Congress had failed to appropriate enough funds to purchase beef and other rations to feed Indian families properly, and Miles was at a loss as to how he should reply to an aged Cheyenne's plea: "It is meat and bread we need."[9]

In response to the Cheyenne's plea, Miles wired Commissioner of Indian Affairs Hiram Price. He suggested that after setting aside funds for schooling,

Congress should take other monies and apply them to the purchase of additional beef. Miles suggested as well that as agent he be authorized to locate rancher-owned livestock—"drift cattle," he called them—at remote points on the reservation and collect a reasonable tax on the animals. He also wanted to establish a leasing program whereby cattlemen for an annual fee might lease grazing rights to Cheyenne and Arapaho pastureland. Price immediately refused the request.[10]

Maj. George M. Randall, commander of Fort Reno near the Darlington agency, stepped in. Randall wrote in July 1882 to Brig. Gen. John Pope at Fort Leavenworth, who directed army affairs on the plains (especially the southwestern plains). The Fort Reno commander recommended that Agent Miles's proposed lease plan be implemented. Pope forwarded Randall's recommendation to Secretary of War Robert T. Lincoln, who in turn recommended to Secretary of Interior H. M. Teller that the leasing of reservation grazing lands to cattlemen was a good idea and should move forward. Such correspondence between the War Department and the Interior Department eventually brought political pressure on Commissioner Price, and he resented it; he did not think the military should dictate Indian policy.[11] Price may have been embarrassed by "outside interference," but he did not capitulate.

As the summer and fall months of 1882 passed, Agent Miles in Darlington fumed about bureaucratic delay. Then he acted. In early December he called together a council of Cheyenne and Arapaho chiefs and the representatives of several interested cattlemen. He wanted them, especially the Indian leaders, to decide if 2.4 million acres of the reservation pastureland should be leased to Anglo ranchers for grazing. George Bent, Robert Bent, and Ben Clark encouraged the Cheyennes to agree to lease, while John Poisal, Jack Fitzpatrick, and Mary Keith sought Arapaho approval. The Indians agreed. On December 12, 1882, seventeen Cheyenne and nine Arapaho leaders signed the accord, which called on cattlemen to pay two cents per acre per year for grazing rights. Also, according to the agreement, each member of the Cheyenne and Arapaho tribes was to receive ten dollars twice a year.[12]

At the Darlington agency six days later, former army scout and Indian interpreter James "Jesse" Stewart Morrison applied for a lease. Morrison had been married to a daughter of Arapaho chief Big Mouth. After fifteen years of marriage, his wife died, and Morrison was left with two children whom he placed in school at Lawrence, Kansas. On January 15, 1883, he obtained a lease that included 138,240 acres in the southeast corner of the reservation located on the west border of the Wichita and Caddo reservation and the north border of the Comanche-Kiowa reservation.[13] Within six months Morrison had sublet his entire lease to the Word-Bugbee Cattle Company.[14]

Charles W. "Charlie" Word was a Texan who had previously established a ranch in Colorado. Yet not long after starting this venture in 1872, he returned to Texas and began trailing livestock on the Great Western Trail to Dodge City, Kansas. In 1881 he purchased a Texas Panhandle ranch with a partner, but less than two years later Word sold out and moved his family to Kansas City.[15] Thomas S. Bugbee and his wife Molly moved into the Texas Panhandle from Kansas in late 1877 and established the Quarter Circle T Ranch along the Canadian River in what is now Hutchinson County. In 1882, when their herd numbered around 12,500 head, they sold the ranch and cattle for some $350,000 and moved to Kansas City.[16]

Word and Bugbee soon met in Kansas City, and with banker John S. Chick they established the Word-Bugbee Cattle Company. The owners quickly secured grazing rights to Jesse Morrison's lease and made plans to operate a steer ranch on their "Cheyenne and Arapaho lease," as they called it. In addition they obtained entitlement to an adjacent grazing lease of 121,660 acres that Lewis M. Briggs of Muscotuh, Kansas, had acquired. Thus, by the close of 1883 they controlled leasing rights to nearly 260,000 acres of good pasture—at least in years with adequate rainfall. According Bugbee's daughter Helen, they placed 26,000 steers on this land with plans to fatten them out for market.

As the ranch developed, Word and Bugbee split their responsibilities. Charlie Word brought steers from South Texas and placed them on ranges near Wichita Falls, Texas.[17] Here cowboys branded the animals with the UU brand, and then Word and his ranch hands moved them across the Comanche-Kiowa reservation and onto the Word-Bugbee lease on the Cheyenne-Arapaho reservation. Once steers were ready for market, Word oversaw trailing operations to Caldwell, Kansas, where he sold the animals and readied them for shipment east by rail.[18] To give an example of the scale of operations, in 1883 Word-Bugbee cowboys at Wichita Falls received and took charge of twelve thousand head of one- and two-year-old steers. They burned the UU brand on the bullocks and then in separate groups of three thousand animals drove them across the Comanche-Kiowa reservation before turning them out to graze on the big pastures of the Word-Bugbee lease.[19] Thomas Bugbee handled responsibilities associated with lease payment. For instance, he carried two suitcases of silver dimes to the Darlington agency from Kansas City two times a year to pay the Indians their lease money. Bugbee's twice-yearly trip by train and stagecoach worried his wife, Molly, for she was fearful of robbers. Bugbee always returned unharmed.[20]

The Word-Bugbee ranch headquarters stood 35 miles up the Washita River from the Wichita agency at Anadarko.[21] To keep its cattle on leased land, the company installed 65 miles of barbed-wire fence at a cost of two hundred dollars a mile.[22] Most likely John H. Seger and several Indian coworkers built the fence. Over the next two years they constructed as much as 240 miles of additional fence. The fenced acreage included a strip on the south side of the leased lands between the Washita River and the North Fork of the Red River.[23]

Some grazing land in the Briggs lease went to the Washita Cattle Company, which also owned the Seven K Ranch in the Texas Panhandle.[24] Frank Biggers was the company's foreman. Oliver Nelson, a contemporary, described Biggers as six feet, six inches tall and weighing nearly two hundred pounds. As a foreman, he was tough, capable, and fearless but not mean-spirited.[25] West of the Word-Bugbee lease, the Austin Cattle Company, managed by T. J. Webb, leased grass for cattle. All three ranch operations suffered from cattle rustling, and Kiowas from the Comanche-Kiowa reservation proved the most troublesome, at least as reported to Cheyenne-Arapaho agent John D. Miles.[26]

F. M. "Mose" Tate was the Word-Bugbee foreman. Before his position with Word-Bugbee, he had worked in the Texas Panhandle, where some observers indicated that he managed more men with fewer words than any other man in the Panhandle. Tate was indeed a quiet leader. One story highlighting his taciturn nature told of a time when he was ill but still went to work. Another cowboy, who barely knew Tate, asked him one morning "How do you feel?" No answer came. They worked all day without a word. As they rode up to the bunkhouse that evening, Tate said, "I feel much better today."[27]

Stilwell, as indicated, was the assistant foreman for the Word-Bugbee opera-tion. He was very familiar with the Washita River valley. He had been there as early as 1868 with General Sheridan, and four years later he had taken a "couple of herds" up the Chisholm Trail to Kansas. In 1879 and afterward he had worked at least part-time as a cowboy on the Conover Ranch along the Little Washita River. In fact William Dietrich, who had managed the Conover operation while Jack was there, thought that "Jack was hired by Word-Bugbee as a kind of peace maker between the cattlemen and the Kiowa."[28]

Hiring Stilwell to act as a mediator signaled an important moment in the land-lease program, for trouble had erupted between the ranchers and Kiowas. As a result Stilwell worked closely with Frank Biggers, foreman of the Washita Cattle Company, and T. J. Webb, of the Austin Cattle Company, as well as with his own foreman, Mose Tate. Everyone had their own interests to protect: cowboys, cattle, horses, and mules. In addition, Stilwell and Tate also needed to protect John Seger and the Word-Bugbee fence-builders. Stilwell and Biggers became friends, and Stilwell also cooperated diligently with Webb and Tate.

Ranching on the Word-Bugbee lease was neither routine nor safe. In addition to the dangerous work associated with rounding up and branding livestock, riders could fall from their horses while they rode their circuits alone, or they could run into trouble when they came across men—Indian and Anglo—butchering a stray cow. Sometimes line riders were killed. Such was the fate of William Munn, a rider for the George and Robert Bent Ranch, located sixty-five miles northwest of the Darlington agency. Munn was twenty-six years old and married. He and his wife had two young children. Before going to work on the Bent Ranch, he had been a soldier at Fort Sill, a member of the Fourth Cavalry.[29]

Evidence suggests that Munn rode out on a cold, windy afternoon in early January 1884 to inspect his line and check on cattle. At sundown his horse returned to the ranch without him. Other cowboys immediately searched for Munn but did not find him. It was noon the next day before they found his frozen body. He lay facedown in tall grass, and a partially butchered calf lay nearby. Munn's Winchester carbine, leggings, and hat were missing. They brought Munn's body to the ranch, where it was received by his terror-stricken wife and children.[30]

Friends carried Munn's remains to the agency's doctor's office in Darlington, and local authorities convened a six-man coroner's jury, which included Jack Stilwell. Examination of the body revealed a bullet hole in his back that exited near the right nipple. A gunshot wound to the forehead, fired at close range (shown by powder burns), was evidently a finishing touch. Authorities surmised that Munn came upon some men (whether they were Indian or Anglo is unknown) butchering the calf and got in a serious quarrel with them. As he turned his horse to leave, evidence suggested, the cattle butchers shot Munn in the back. He fell from his horse and then was shot in the forehead. How he came to be facedown was not explained. The coroner's jury discovered that Munn, unfortunately, was unpopular with Indians and previously had several disagreements with them. The jury went through the evidence as presented by reservation authorities and the coroner, but they could reach no consensus about parties responsible for Munn's death.[31]

One wonders how the tough and combative Stilwell would have reacted if he had come across men butchering cattle for which he was responsible. If the culprits were Indians, he most likely would have spoken Comanche to them or used the universal sign language of the plains. He would likely have inquired whether their families were hungry. It is also likely that if they had been Indians, he might then have ridden by and paid no attention. Stilwell understood the reservation belonged to these people, many of whom were his friends.

Most of the cattlemen with leases in Indian Territory had more trouble with Anglo cattle thieves than Indian rustlers, but this was not always the case. On March 26, 1884, a couple of months after the Munn killing, a party of Kiowa riders drifted north onto the Word-Bugbee and Austin Cattle Company leases on the Cheyenne-Arapaho reservation and began moving some two hundred head of cattle back south. Trying to stop them, cowboys fired at the cattle thieves. A brief melee followed in which one Kiowa raider was wounded and seven steers were shot. No cowboys suffered injuries. If Stilwell was present during the shooting, he failed on this occasion to keep the peace, one of the reasons the Word-Bugbee company had hired him.

Foremen Mose Tate and T. J. Webb sent a report of the trouble to Cheyenne-Arapaho agent John Miles. In turn Miles wrote to the Fort Reno commanding officer, Maj. Thomas B. Dewees. He told Dewees that Kiowas camped inside the southern boundary line of the Cheyenne-Arapaho reservation were making frequent depredations. Miles also asked that a troop of cavalry be sent to the area to keep the peace. Major Dewees sent the report and request up the military chain of command. Eventually it reached Secretary of War Henry M. Teller, who at least in this instance did not think the difficulty Miles described was an "occasion for military interference."[32] As a result, Stilwell and cowboys of the Word-Bugbee had no help as they watched for thieves and sought to protect ranch steers from poachers. In addition, of course, they handled the customary duties associated with a large ranch.

One of Stilwell's responsibilities involved hauling ranch supplies. More than once he made the thirty-five-mile trip by wagon from the Word-Bugbee head-quarters down the Washita River to buy food staples and other goods from the traders at Anadarko. He bought provisions at different stores, but he often used Dudley P. Brown's busy establishment. There he secured the required merchandise, transacted company business, and exchanged gossip.[33] Such supply runs offered Stilwell opportunities for socializing. On May 10, 1884, the *Cheyenne Transporter* in Darlington noted that "Jack Stilwell, one of the old-timers, was hand shaking about the Agency on Wednesday. He has been among the western Indians since before war times and is ever where known among them."[34] When off duty in Darlington, Stilwell had money to spend. As the principal peacekeeper between Indian leaders and ranch employees, Jack was well compensated by the Word-Bugbee outfit. From May 31 to July 31, for example, Jack spent $104.50 in Anadarko—$49.50 of it on assorted merchandise, including clothing. On September 30, again in Anadarko, he spent $5.75 for various items, and in the months of October and November he spent a total of $135.65. At the end of December, he held a balance of $225 in his account at the Reynolds store in town.[35]

Financial compensation aside, sometimes Stilwell endured physical injuries. He suffered from rheumatism, of course, but as with most cowboys, other maladies intruded. He had broken his right leg in the summer of 1883, for example, and in early August 1884, during a Word-Bugbee cattle drive to Caldwell, Kansas, he again injured the leg, caused, apparently, by a "fractious" horse. The *Cheyenne Transporter* indicated: "S. E. Stilwell, more familiarly known as 'Jack,' had been laid up at the Agency . . . with a badly wrenched limb." The paper further noted that his "right leg had not healed completely from the break received over a year ago. He was not in shape to stand the hard knocks connected with range work. . . . After a long painful ride he came to the Agency at Darlington for medical treatment." Although crippled, Jack "still possessed that happy spirit and fun-loving disposition which attracts so many friends to him."[36]

The injury kept Stilwell in Darlington for some time. The *Cheyenne Transporter* described him as "popular and distinguished for his courage and love of adventure." During his rehabilitation he spent plenty of money in August and September with his agency friends, particularly the Cheyennes, but his glad-handing, his friendly manner, and his general cheerfulness won for him great respect and caused residents in the town to seek him out.[37] While Stilwell recovered in Darlington, Charlie Word delivered the cattle herd to Caldwell. The *Caldwell Journal* on August 21, 1884, reported: "C. W. Word, the irrepressible little cowman of the Word-Bugbee Company, was in the city several days supervising the shipment of 14,000 head of UU beef."[38]

When his injury had healed, Stilwell returned to work. Plenty of the old troubles remained. Kiowas still crossed into the southern portions of the Cheyenne-Arapaho reservation, they still refused to recognize the border between their reservation and that of their neighbors to the north, and, as they had for some time, they still opposed the use of fences to distinguish boundaries. Cattle rustling continued.

In addition to the boundary dispute, other issues intruded on the companies raising cattle on reservation land. Cheyennes, who had not signed the lease agreement back in 1882, had become disgruntled and unhappy. They opposed the leasing system. Cattlemen, likewise irritated, presented the local agent with multiple requests—demands, even—and often complained to Congress about the rustling, the boundary issue, and the fight over fencing.[39] In December 1884 Jesse Morrison, through whom Word-Bugbee held its lease, addressed the problems before a congressional committee. Kiowas and Comanches left their reservation, he indicated, to disturb occupants of some leases on the Cheyenne-Arapaho reservation. He suggested that Kiowas in particular did not acknowledge the south boundary line of the Word-Bugbee lease, claiming the line was too far south. Nor would the Kiowas allow fencing.[40]

Efforts to resolve the impasse reached back at least a year. In 1883 agents from the boarding reservations and leaders of the Kiowas, Comanches, and Cheyennes met. Their discussions prompted the agents to recommend a government survey to establish reservation lines, but Hiram Price, the parsimonious Indian commissioner, saw no reason for a survey and claimed no funds were available for it. The Cheyenne-Arapaho agent at Darlington, John Miles, replied on December 13 that his Indians at Darlington would pay for the survey.[41]

Thereupon officials asked army representatives to provide military surveyors, as Indians would have strong confidence in them. On February 8, 1884, the army agreed but requested that $1,168.75 for expenses be provided by the Bureau of Indian affairs. On February 21 Price blocked the request for the survey when he stated that no funds were available. On April 17 John Miles stated that he had access to the funds needed for the survey. His action forced the Department of the Interior and the Bureau of Indian Affairs to agree to the survey, but the two agencies wanted it done with government, not private, funds.[42]

The army completed the survey during April 1885. As reported by the *Cheyenne Transporter*, "Jack Stilwell, the interpreter, guide and scout who came in yesterday from the southwest, [reported] that everything was quiet out there. The surveying corps that has been running the line between this reservation and the Kiowa had completed their work and had gone to the Creek country to do some more surveying."[43]

Stilwell was over-optimistic. The survey did not solve troubles on the reservation borders. About May 5 he was in camp with some surveyors on the north side of the Washita River in the southeast corner of the Cheyenne-Arapaho reservation. At this location five Kiowa leaders and sixty or seventy followers met Stilwell. The leaders asked him for a beef, and he said that he would not give them any as last fall he had given them a beef. The Kiowas laughed in Stilwell's face and said they would take the beef by force if necessary. He could not stop them. When Stilwell threatened to have them arrested, the Kiowas called him a fool and stated that their arrest was impossible. They told Stilwell to leave the surveying party and go home or they would kill him. Jack left.[44]

The next morning, Kiowa rustlers slaughtered more steers, this time near the camp of Kiowa leaders Co-mate (Komate), Po-lante, Tope-deer, and others. Their camp and the killing field were within the Cheyenne-Arapaho reservation on the Word-Bugbee lease. A cowboy line rider, Curley Smith, discovered where Kiowas had killed the cattle and immediately reported it to Stilwell, who quickly mounted his horse and visited the butchering site. Tracks led directly to the Indians' campsite of the previous night, and near there Stilwell found portions of hides that had been cut to pieces and thrown into a shallow creek. By piecing them together Jack discovered the UU brand of the Word-Bugbee Cattle Company. He then trailed the Indians and soon overtook them. There he found Co-mate and Tape-deer bands with freshly slaughtered beef in their possession. After a tense parlay, the Kiowa leaders promised they would not allow their young men to steal additional Word-Bugbee cattle. Outnumbered, Stilwell then backed off and returned to his camp. Kiowas continued to harvest Word-Bugbee beeves without permission.[45]

On June 13, while riding a southern boundary fence line, two Word-Bugbee cowboys, J. S. Jack and Tol Bohannon, discovered three more head of cattle had been killed. They followed tracks to a point where barbed wire stretching across a small ravine had been raised to allow exit from the pasture. They continued to follow the trail and shortly arrived at Tape-deer's camp, where freshly slaughtered beef hung. Nothing was done, but the next day Tape-deer met Bohannon on the fence line and asked the line rider if he had or intended to inform Stilwell. Bohannon replied that Stilwell had already been informed.[46]

Despite the large number of thefts, Charlie Word continued to find steers for his lease property. On July 4 he had written on Henrietta [Texas] National Bank stationary to Agent P. B. Hunt at the Comanche, Kiowa, and Wichita agency and requested permission to drive a herd of one thousand cattle across and through the Comanche-Kiowa reservation. The cattle would have the UU brand. He requested a permit be sent to Ben Cobb at the Henrietta Nation Bank.[47]

Government changes followed. In July 1885 the government replaced agent Miles with D. B. Dyer, a brusque bureaucrat who had been an agent with the Modocs. Dyer proved unable to check the increasing tension between Cheyennes and cattlemen, and he came quickly into conflict with Indians, who soon did not trust him.[48] The disorder and confusion that had characterized the reservation leasing system for years continued. This eventually brought Indian Inspector

Frank C. Armstrong to Darlington. Shortly after his arrival in July, he found that Cheyenne leaders were demanding the removal of the cattlemen from the reservation and asserting that there were too many unauthorized Anglos on Cheyenne and Arapaho land. He believed that Agent Dyer could not carry out his duties without military support, and Dyer would be helpless to manage the reservation if troubles arose. He recommended Dyer be replaced.[49]

Quickly thereafter Gen. Phillip H. Sheridan and Col. Nelson A. Miles intervened. In mid-July, Sheridan interviewed leaders of the dissident Cheyenne faction. Their inspections and Sheridan's interviews led to a twenty-four-page report to President Grover Cleveland. In it Sheridan seemed to confirm the findings of Inspector Armstrong that Agent Dyer had to be relieved and that the cattlemen, because they had no legal claim to their leases, should leave the reservation as soon as possible.[50] Before the month was over, Dyer resigned. The government quickly replaced him with Capt. Jesse M. Lee, Ninth Infantry, as acting Indian agent. General Sheridan was pleased. He believed an army officer would have the force necessary to keep the Indians under control and remove the cattlemen off their leased pastures.[51]

President Cleveland also took drastic action. Hearing in July that cattlemen were responsible for the reservation trouble and that a permanent farm settlement was not possible until the Anglo ranchers were gone, he issued on July 23 a proclamation that directed the removal of all Anglo-held cattle from the reservation within forty days. The proclamation proved a problem. Many cattlemen could not find a market for their livestock or move thousands of cattle within the required time. When the deadline was not met by early September 1885, officials sent military personnel to each ranch to investigate and report the progress in cattle removal to Agent Lee at Darlington. 1st Lt. Edwin Proctor Andrus, Fifth Cavalry, rode from Fort Supply to the Word-Bugbee Cattle Company. He learned from foreman Mose Tate that 3,900 cattle had been removed from the lease. There were twenty men and forty horses rounding up the 8,000 head remaining.[52]

On September 7 Tate reported to Agent Lee that a conflict had erupted between ranch hands and Kiowas on the Word-Bugbee range and at the Washita Cattle Company. Both cowboys and Indians had fired shots. Stilwell was probably involved in the confrontation and, if so, failed again as a peacemaker with the Kiowas. Fortunately, no one was killed or wounded, but the fight delayed cattle removal. The skirmish also led to visits to the ranches by an agent from the Comanche, Kiowa, and Wichita agency and by 1st Lt. George Allen Dodd, Third Cavalry, who had ridden in from Fort Sill with a troop of solders. In Dodd's report on the confrontation, he stated that a deputy U.S. marshal from Texas, Word and Bugbee, and the Comanche-Kiowa agent were expected to make appropriate arrests the next day.[53]

Such difficulties further delayed the removal of Anglo livestock and resulted in additional rustling. On October 2 Comanche-Kiowa agent Captain Hall, a generous and hospitable agent who drank to excess, stated the Word-Bugbee Cattle Company had suffered the loss of a total of fifteen hundred beeves taken from their pastures recently. Not coincidentally, Kiowas held a large number of hides bearing the UU brand, which they later sold to traders in Anadarko.[54]

Nonetheless, in August and September 1885, the huge Word-Bugbee Cattle Company, one of the largest cattle operations in the country at the time, began leaving its grazing leases on the Cheyenne-Arapaho reservation. After the removal of Word-Bugbee steers from the reservation, Jack Stilwell was out of work. He climbed into the saddle and once again followed the Washita River downstream to Anadarko, one of his favorite places on the southern Great Plains. In Anadarko he found a room in a small hotel, a two-story, wood-frame house kept by a Mrs. Tieman, a Catholic lady. He planned to stay for several days before heading to Wichita, Kansas, to visit members of his family. Quanah Parker, recognized in 1885 has one of the principal Comanche leaders, was also staying at the little hotel for a couple of days.[55]

While Stilwell visited friends in Anadarko in October, Fr. Hilary Cassal, a determined Catholic missionary, traveled through western Indian Territory. His purpose was to visit a few military posts, such as Fort Sill and Fort Reno. After stopping at Fort Reno, he traveled to Anadarko, reached the town well after dark, and found a room at Mrs. Tieman's hotel. The next morning Father Cassal said mass and then sat down to breakfast. On his right sat Quanah Parker. On his left sat a large, soldierly-looking white man with a moustache. Mrs. Tieman introduced him as "Captain Stilwell the chief of the Scouts." Father Cassal expressed surprise to hear Quanah Parker speak English. The men exchanged a few pleasantries before Stilwell asked Father Cassal to consider building a school on the reservation for Indian children. Quanah Parker said he would do all he could to help establish such a school in Anadarko.[56]

Before the end of breakfast, Stilwell asked the priest if Fr. Isadore Robot was still at the Sacred Heart Mission. Thereupon he launched into his story of finding Father Robot and Brother Dominic singing a prayer in Latin, a prayer he thought was an Indian funeral chant. He was happy once again to recall the time that he played the Good Samaritan while serving as a scout at Fort Sill.[57]

After several days in Anadarko, Stilwell headed for Wichita. As he rode away from the agency town and his Comanche friends on the reservation, perhaps he looked back on the two years he had spent with the Word-Bugbee Cattle Company. The outfit had hired Stilwell, a powerful, strong-willed, and self-confident leader, to serve as a peacemaker with the Kiowas, their cattle-rustling neighbors to the south. He had failed his mission. He had been severely injured at least twice, spent plenty of time rehabilitating his injuries in Darlington, performed all manner of ranching duties, took part in driving cattle to market, and fought with Kiowas on the Cheyenne-Arapaho reservation. He had made good wages as a cowboy for the large ranch, but while in town he had spent freely in friendly amusement. Through most of 1885, his account at Reynold's store in Darlington remained active, but near the end of the year, when the money in his tally sheet decreased, his spending dropped off.[58]

Perhaps as he rode away from Anadarko, Stilwell also wondered about his family. The year 1885 had proved significant for his siblings. Their mother Charlotte had died in Brownstown, Indiana. His brother Howard remained single and lived in Topeka with the A. G. Potter Family.[59] Millard had recently married Emma A. Lathaw at Jefferson, Illinois.[60] Their youngest sister, Elizabeth Ann Stilwell Cooley, moved to Caldwell, Kansas, with her growing family, and there her husband Joseph made a living as a stonemason. Their father, William Henry, now sixty-three, lived with Joseph and Elizabeth Ann and their children and worked as a carpenter.[61] On his way to Wichita, Jack planned to stop in Caldwell to visit his younger sister. He would be happy to see her. He may not have been as happy to see his father.

Stilwell must have contemplated other matters as he left his Comanche friends behind. The livestock and grazing changes on the reservation, for which he was at least partially at fault, put him out of work as a cowhand, but that loss now freed him to find work as a deputy U.S. marshal.

Chapter 12

DEPUTY U.S. MARSHAL

For seven years, from 1885 to 1892, Jack Stilwell served as a deputy U.S. marshal in the Northern District of Texas. His responsibilities included arresting thieves (both Anglo and Indian), testifying at trials, investigating shootings and murders, and trying to prevent so-called "boomers" and "sooners"—mostly unlawful home-seekers—from claiming land in Indian Territory before it was made available for settlement. During these years Stilwell also spent time in Wichita, Kansas, and served as a hangman in the execution of two Native Americans. He got involved in politics and became something of a legend during his own lifetime. Yet his health continued to fail him: by mid-1892, at the age of forty-one, osteoarthritis, severe rheumatism, and debilitating injuries from his past had begun to take a serious toll on his body.

Before he joined the Marshals Service in 1885, Stilwell tied up his responsibilities with the Word-Bugbee Cattle Company. In one bit of last-minute work as assistant foreman, in May he filed affidavits against two Kiowa headmen, Po-lante and Comate, accusing them of killing cattle on the Word-Bugbee range in Indian Territory. The accusations were only one part of a whole series of difficulties in Indian Territory's western regions, although many of the problems related to trouble between Indians and the ranchers who ran cattle on leased reservation lands. In July the Bureau of Indian Affairs fired Cheyenne-Arapaho agent D. B. Dyer, a stubborn, impatient employee who could not get along with the Cheyennes. He was replaced by Capt. Jesse M. Lee of the Ninth Infantry, who would serve as the acting agent.[1]

Captain Lee realized early in his tenure that Cheyenne and Arapaho problems were significant, complicated, and often not of their own doing. He sympathized with them and took up their cause with the Bureau of Indian Affairs and the army, but to little avail. As described in chapter 11, Lee was ordered to end the grass and grazing leases on the Cheyenne-Arapaho reservation and remove all Anglo-owned cattle from Indian land, and army officials sent military detachments from Forts Reno, Supply, Elliott, and Sill to oversee a smooth removal, to report on progress, and to prevent conflicts between cowboys and Indians.[2]

Soon after he took charge of the Cheyenne-Arapaho agency, the acting agent met Stilwell, and they got along well and respected one another. They became friends during the difficult removal period, and Stilwell's past service as a government scout stood him in good stead with the captain. Stilwell worked for Lee throughout the latter's tour of duty at the agency—until September 1886. According to Captain Lee, Stilwell did "his full duty and more with intelligence, zeal and fearlessness."[3]

A new Comanche-Kiowa agent also was appointed during the removal period. Former Texas Ranger Jesse L. Hall was described as "generous, hospitable, and a heavy drinker"; based on the evidence presented in Stilwell's affidavits, he arrested Po-lante and Comate. Hall held them only briefly before releasing them. From the agent's point of view, the arrest and release of the headmen was insignificant. To the Kiowas, however, it meant a great deal, and the event appeared on George Poolaw's Kiowa Calendar for 1884–85.[4]

During the cattle-killing spree in May that led to Stilwell's accusations against Po-lante and Comate, Agent Hall, like his counterpart Captain Lee, also came to respect the former scout. Indeed, on November 21, 1885, Hall requested from Gen. W. L. Cabell, U.S. Marshal for the Northern District of Texas, a deputy marshal commission for the former Word-Bugbee foreman.[5] After receiving the appointment, one of Stilwell's first official acts was the arrest of Joseph Leonard, an Anglo, about thirty-five miles from Anadarko. Leonard, at least according to Stilwell and Agent Hall, had proved for some years to be a reservation troublemaker. He had married a Caddo woman and subsequently prompted a Wichita-Caddo boundary dispute with the Cheyennes and Arapahos. Leonard hired Luther H. Pike to act as legal counsel for the Wichitas and Caddos. The two men promoted dissatisfaction among the Indians, and in 1883 Caddo agent P. B. Hunt ordered them off the reservation. However, two years later Leonard continued to promote discord. It was then that Stilwell arrested him, took him to Dallas, and stood him before judicial authorities, who charged him with living in Indian Territory without a passport.[6]

A trial followed, and it was not without controversy. On December 8, 1885, a *Dallas Morning News* article sided with Leonard and maintained that as a U.S. citizen without a passport he should be allowed to return to his Caddo village where he is a "power among the Caddo." During the proceedings the courtroom was crowded with witnesses from Indian Territory, and, the paper noted, those in the crowd included "Deputy United States Marshal Jack Stilwell who could talk Indian . . . and sound the war-whoop like a Comanche."[7]

Stilwell did not stay long in Dallas. On December 9 he passed through Weatherford, Texas, on his way to Graham, where he served as a witness in a federal court case.[8] Back on the Cheyenne-Arapaho reservation, he discovered that cattle stealing and grazing issues continued, as well as horse thieving. In his 1886 annual report, acting Cheyenne-Arapaho agent Captain Lee complained that during the previous fall, winter, and spring, Indians had no fewer than 150 head of ponies stolen. Lee wrote, "Government cattle were considered common property. White men in this country had no regret to burn a brand or steal a calf. The cattle losses last winter were fully twenty-five percent." In response, on June 1, 1886, Lee hired Stilwell to hunt stray cattle on the reservation.[9]

Straying cattle caused plenty of problems. Evan G. Barnard, a cowboy in Oklahoma's Cherokee Strip, which ran along the northwest border with Kansas, remembered some of them. Back in June 1886, he recalled, when the contract to supply beef to the Cheyenne-Arapaho agency expired, T. Cornell and J. W. Butler decided to move their cattle to Kiowa, Kansas. They started their herd of 1,600 head up the Chisholm Trail before stopping for the evening just north of present-day Kingfisher. A hard rainstorm that night caused the cattle to scatter, and the Cornell-Butler cowboys spent the next morning rounding up livestock before putting the animals on the road again. They drove them to the Red Fork Road Ranch, located just north of the Cimarron River. There they held the cattle for Jim Decker, a government employee who would check the herd for stray Bar CA cattle, which belonged to Cheyennes and Arapahos. After the storm, some of the Bar CA livestock had strayed and got mixed up with the Cornell and Butler's herd.[10]

At this point Deputy Marshal Stilwell got involved. He arrested the Cornell-Butler foreman, Samuel Matthews, for stealing Cheyenne and Arapaho cattle. As Stilwell and Matthews headed for Fort Reno, Butler and his cowboys drove the cattle onto the Kiowa Trail west of the Bull Foot Road Ranch. Here the men learned that Butler was needed at the fort to serve as a witness in Matthews's hearing. Butler left promptly, going by buckboard to Bull Foot Ranch and then, as

instructed, to Fort Reno. At the fort he was arrested and placed in the guardhouse
with Matthews. The government planned to try the men in a U.S. federal court
in Wichita.[11]

Meanwhile, after hearing news of the Matthews and Butler arrests, the
cowboys back on the Kiowa Trail grew angry and decided to blame Stilwell.
They planned to waylay the deputy marshal at Buffalo Springs, just north of the
Bull Foot Road Ranch, as he took the two men to Wichita. When the cowboys
approached Stilwell, Butler told his men that he had done nothing wrong and
convinced them not to make further trouble. Indeed, he told them to return to
their camp and take the cattle herd to market at Kiowa.

With that incident averted, Butler, Matthews, and Stilwell continued toward
Wichita in a spring wagon and reached the city without further incident. Stilwell
delivered the cattlemen to jail, but they soon made bail and were released from
custody. In early September 1886 the accused drovers returned to Wichita for
the trial. Wichita lawyer Dennis Flynn was engaged to prepare the defense.
At the last minute, however, because Butler could not pay his legal fees, Flynn
refused. The next day a lawyer named Bentley, who was willing to accept Butler's
promissory note, took on their case.[12]

At ten o'clock on the morning of September 6, the trial began. Samuel Matthews stood accused of stealing thirteen head of cattle from the Cheyenne
and Arapaho tribes in Indian Territory, and J. W. Butler was named a willing
accomplice to the theft. Deputy Marshal Stilwell, Agent Lee, George Johnson,
Burt Griffin, and J. G. Chapin appeared as witnesses for the United States. Several
of Butler's cowboys appeared for the defense.[13] The trial only lasted an hour, after
which the jury acquitted both suspects. But the defense had been expensive.
After paying the lawyer, Butler and Cornell were unable to pay their cowboys
back in Kiowa, Kansas, for all their work.[14]

As for Stilwell, after the trial he returned to the Cheyenne-Arapaho agency.
Employed by the federal government as a deputy marshal, he represented "the
law"; that is, he was the single law enforcement officer in the agency. Stilwell
was forced to go to Wichita when necessary to get a U.S. commissioner to issue
arrest warrants. To avoid the long delay and hard travel, Agent Lee requested the
appointment of a U.S. commissioner at Darlington, but the decision was delayed.[15]

Meanwhile, on July 16, 1886, a local officer at Fort Reno accused Barney Cooper,
a soldier, of murdering a Cheyenne woman, Metowi, near the Indian Agency.
Captain Lee placed Cooper under arrest, and Stilwell transported the suspect to
Wichita. On August 4 officials locked Cooper in the Sedgwick County jail on a

charge of murder and held him over for trial, which, because of delays in August and September, did not take place in the U.S. federal court until September 1887, the next court session.[16]

From September 17 to the end of the month, Stilwell also served as a "cattle hunter" on the Cheyenne-Arapaho reservation.[17] The new Indian agent, Gilbert D. Williams (who had replaced acting agent Captain Lee), was a "man with little imagination or energy." He authorized Stilwell "to recover possession of any agency cattle in the hands of unauthorized persons within the borders of this territory." Williams feared that too many ranchers, as they moved their cattle off the reservation, might appropriate stray cattle, as had Sam Matthews and J. W. Butler.[18]

The record of Stilwell's movements over the next several weeks is largely mute. Yet a cryptic and unexplained article about him appeared on November 9 edition of the *Wichita Daily Eagle*: "S. E. Stilwell, Deputy U.S. Marshal in Indian Territory made a call yesterday." Rather mysteriously, the article noted Stilwell was "touching the gold and silver discoveries down there [in the Wichita Mountains of Indian Territory], that they are so big he couldn't afford to stop to pick up a twenty-dollar gold piece." Obviously, Stilwell was pulling the reporter's leg. By 1886 Stilwell's wit and sense of humor were famous and attracted a lot of people to him. He knew that others had tried to find mineral wealth in the Wichita Mountains, and the newspaper editor, red-headed Marshal M. Murdock, recognized Stilwell's lighthearted spoof when he featured the comment in his reporting.[19]

On December 6, 1886, in an unusual duty for a deputy U.S. marshal, Stilwell served as Issue Clerk at Cantonment, a former military post on the North Canadian River that had lately become a beef distribution center for Cheyennes. Since the treaties of 1867 and 1868—and even perhaps before then—the government had delivered live cattle when it supplied the so-called "beef ration" to Indians. At Cantonment, officials, including Stilwell, released the animals from a pen. Cheyennes on horseback chased after the cattle for perhaps a half-mile and shot them. Women followed. They butchered the animals, divided the meat, and saved the hides to sell to the agency traders. This celebratory and, from the Cheyenne point of view, happy event recalled bison hunting days, but it ended in the early 1890s when the government no longer issued its beef ration as live animals.[20]

After distributing beef at Cantonment, Stilwell may have spent Christmas at the home of his younger sister, Lizzy Cooley. In 1886 the family had moved from Caldwell, Kansas, to the Chickasaw Nation, west of Purcell, Indian Territory, where they operated a farm on Dibble Creek. This was not far from Jack's Darlington and Anadarko territory.[21]

In any case, back at work after a brief winter break, Stilwell stayed busy during the first half of 1887. His major new responsibility was to detect and prevent liquor from being sold to Indians.[22] His duties also included transporting those persons charged with crimes from Indian Territory to Wichita, where they were committed to the county jail until they could be tried. He also delivered subpoenas to the witnesses so that they would know when to appear before the U.S. federal court at Wichita. After a federal commissioner was established at the Cheyenne-Arapaho agency, Stilwell saw that all cases went to the commissioner first to determine if arrest warrants should be issued; if charges were necessary, the case went to the Wichita federal court.[23]

Accordingly, on May 31, 1887, Stilwell committed "Mexican Joe" (a local Hispanic employee whose full name is unknown) to jail. Joe had been accused of stealing a wagon, a horse, and a mule from George Bent, the mixed-race son of William Bent and Owl Woman of the Cheyennes, who after 1863 lived most of his life with his mother's people. After being arrested, Joe appeared before the U.S. Commissioner James F. Samson at Fort Reno; Samson referred his case to the District of Kansas federal court in Wichita for trial.[24]

About the same time that he had arrested Mexican Joe, Stilwell committed Riley Garrison to the Sedgwick County Jail. Officials had accused Garrison of attempted rape. On July 16 he committed Morris Wilson, charged with being a horse thief, to the county jail. Four days later he brought in W. B. Smith and Abe Linscott, charged with stealing horses. On September 8, in a more serious case, Stilwell jailed Wesley Warren, from Cantonment in Indian Territory. Warren had been charged with murder. Clearly, the deputy marshal was busy and spent a lot of time in the saddle. The distance from Anadarko, Indian Territory, to Wichita, Kansas, for example, was over 150 miles.[25]

The District of Kansas federal court began hearing cases in early September 1887. Shortly afterward, it disposed of several of them. With George Bent and Jack Stilwell serving as prosecuting witnesses, the jury found Mexican Joe guilty of theft. Joe thereupon put up a five-hundred-dollar bond, which entitled him to be released temporarily. Because of separate legal issues, however, he would need to appear at the next regular term of the U.S. federal court of the Northern District of Texas at Graham.[26]

Barney Cooper's long-awaited trial for the murder of Metowi occurred on September 7, 1887. When the court in Wichita opened for its fall session, an article appeared in the *Wichita Eagle*: "A band of Indians, twenty in number and comprising members of the Cheyenne and Osage tribe, are camped in the rear of the Richey house under the charge of Jack Stilwell, deputy U.S. marshal from Fort Reno, and Ben Clark, the Cheyenne Interpreter." There was no mention of why Cheyenne and Osage people were under Stilwell's "charge," but presumably they were in the area to support Metowi's family, and they felt safe with Jack.[27]

A number of Indians spoke for the prosecution, including Cheyenne chief Whirlwind and his wife, who were Metowi's in-laws. Other Cheyenne women testified against Cooper, as did a Mr. O'Bar and a Mr. Cummings, engineers at the Fort Reno pump station near the site of the murder. Ben Clark and Capt. Jesse Lee also testified for the prosecution. Two soldiers testified in Barney's defense. After final arguments, Judge C. G. Foster instructed the jury and sent it out to deliberate. Because the jury was unable to agree on a verdict, however, Judge Foster declared a mistrial. A second trial, in September 1888, convicted Copper of manslaughter and sentenced him to five years in a Kansas prison.[28]

Riley Garrison and Wesley Warren, whom Stilwell had arrested in July, got lucky. During the September 1887 federal court session, officials dropped charges of attempted rape against Garrison and on the thirteenth released him from jail. Likewise, the court dropped murder charges against Warren and a day after Garrison's release, Warren walked out of the jail a free man.[29]

Even as the trials moved forward, problems with white men using reservation lands to graze livestock continued. On December 8, 1887, government authorities asked Stilwell to round up and count cattle not owned by Indians on the Cheyenne-Arapaho reservation. In conjunction with Stilwell's survey, they asked for the army's help in removing from the reservation unauthorized cattle and horses found grazing in the area. The new assignment proved dangerous for the deputy marshal. Indian Territory was a refuge for outlaws, cattle thieves, and fugitives wanted for murder, bank robbery, and other crimes, and some of the cattle he found "belonged" to them. He held warrants to arrest criminals, but he was not always successful, and sometimes, especially when he was out-numbered and out-gunned, he did not try.

One day a couple of thieves heard that Stilwell was on his way to a cow camp to arrest the "Sleeper Kid" for stealing horses. In response, two men named Bryant and Hunt sat on a bench by a table near the Kid's tent. They assumed that should Stilwell show up, he would enter the tent to get the Kid. That afternoon Stilwell approached the camp riding a big gray horse. When Stilwell rode in, Bryant asked him to sit down. Stilwell dismounted and sat across the table from Bryant and Hunt, who had placed their six-shooters on the table and Winchesters by their sides. They talked to Stilwell about the weather, stock, and other mundane topics. After a bit, the Kid left the tent and walked to his horse. Stilwell saw him but did not move; he knew he was outnumbered. Even though he had warrants to arrest all three men, he understood he would not succeed this time. He soon got up and left the camp.[30]

On February 8, 1888, Stilwell went on vacation to Canadian, Texas. He called on Frank Biggers, whom he had met while working as a cowboy on the Word-Bugbee lease. He met other old friends and acquaintances, got plenty of rest, and visited scenes of his exploits near Wolf Creek in the Texas Panhandle in the winter 1868–69, when he carried dispatches from Camp Supply to General Custer.[31]

Worked awaited, however, and when Stilwell resumed his duties he found himself a busy man. On March 27 he arrested Kias Williams, a liquor smuggler he had first arrested in August 1887. Both arrests arose from Williams bringing liquor into Indian Territory. Williams, however, found plenty of folks to bond him out of jail. Among them were George Bent and W. B. Barker, a friend of Bent's who helped distribute Williams's whiskey. In March 1888, after the second arrest, George E. Reynolds and Barker once again put up a five-hundred-dollar bond for the alcohol smuggler's release. Reynolds and Barker were making plenty of money from the illegal liquor dealer and wanted him out of jail.[32]

The Williams trial occurred in September. Stilwell had made the arrest and had served subpoenas to witnesses, including two Indian women and Cheyenne-Arapaho agent Gilbert Williams, and he sat through the court proceedings. In the end the jury found Kias Williams not guilty and he was released. Clearly, a demand existed for Williams's product and services.[33] In fact, in February 1888 Agent Williams reported to the Commissioner of Indian Affairs on a noted character named James Jones, alias Whiskey Jim, who peddled whiskey on the outskirts of the Cheyenne agency and to soldiers at Fort Reno. Jones had eluded both Indian police and the army for a long time. But after a desperate struggle, two Indian policemen, Lieutenants Coyote and Sleeping Wolf, captured him. Authorities took him to Wichita for trial, and there Stilwell served as a witness for the prosecution. In September the jury convicted Jones for selling liquor to Indians and stealing George Bent's gold watch. He received a sentence of one year in the penitentiary.[34] Morris Wilson, W. B. Smith, and Abe Linscott, whom Stilwell had apprehended the previous summer, were tried in September for horse stealing. The court found Wilson guilty and sent him to prison for one year. It found Smith guilty and sentenced him to two years of hard labor in the penitentiary. Linscott was acquitted and released.[35]

On November 21 Stilwell was handed perhaps his most dreadful and difficult assignment. Three years earlier, brothers Joseph and Jacob Tobler, who were Creek Indians, had killed two well-known Indian Territory cattlemen, A. P. Goodykountz and Frank Cass. A federal court had tried and convicted the brothers for the murders and sentenced them to be hanged. Stilwell, as deputy marshal, was charged with hanging the Toblers. The regrettable but well-attended event would occur outside the Sedgwick County jail in Wichita.

A *Wichita Eagle* reporter observed the hangings and wrote:

Old Jack Stillwell got a little bit excited at one time and made a lapus lingua that meant well enough but was not exactly well put. Just while the cap was being adjusted and old Jack was fussin around over the platform the prisoners wanted to say good-bye to the officers. Their hands were tied behind them but they managed to raise their hands. Old Jack grabbed hold of a finger of each and shaking it said, "Good-bye, good-bye, be good boys, be good boys" and hurried over and in a second he pulled the lever. The remark was noticed by several, but the surrounds were too ghastly to even create a smile at the time.[36]

The hangings were the last such legal executions in Wichita.[37] A few years later, Stilwell complained of the incident to a newspaperman associated with New Mexico's *Eddy Argus*. The reporter wrote that Stilwell told him "the hangings were the worst job that he ever had and that he would rather take a three-month cut in pay."[38]

In the more immediate aftermath of the hangings, Stilwell got a lot of attention in the press. In December the *St. Louis Post-Dispatch* reprinted an article about the executions from its Wichita correspondent. The newspaper piece, entitled "Comanche Jack's Record," stated that Stilwell had shot thirty-one men and helped hang seventeen others—a reporter's exaggerations to make a more sensational story. On the other hand, the writer indicated that Stilwell was not a desperado but was "retiring in his disposition. . . . Only when drinking did he boast of his deeds."[39]

Over the next few months, several newspapers from across the country picked up "Comanche Jack's Record." On February 24, 1889, for example, the *Chicago Daily Tribune* ran it. Others followed: the *Atchison* (Kansas) *Daily Champion* on

March 6; the *Wichita Daily Eagle* a day later; the Fort Worth *Gazette* on March 9; and in Hagerstown, Maryland, the *Herald and Torch* ran the story on March 28. There were others.[40] These stories about Stilwell's exploits, embellished by a newspaper reporter's over-enthusiasm, led to the "Jack Stilwell myth." Like the hanging articles, the "myth," which also appeared in national newspapers, promoted Stilwell as a trigger-happy shootist, a willing hangman, a heavy drinker, a grand storyteller, and a tough, no-nonsense lawman who got results.[41]

Not long after the "Comanche Jack's Record" articles appeared, Stilwell's work took on new complications. On April 22, 1889, former Indian Territory lands were opened to Anglos for settlement. The "land rush" in weeks and months that followed led to many conflicts. Stilwell soon learned that it was easier to deal with Indians in Indian Territory than with the so-called boomers and sooners and their disputed land claims in what was soon to become Oklahoma Territory. Sooners were those new settlers who slipped in and claimed land before the April 22 official opening. In towns they included lot jumpers, who seized city lots ahead of the rush, and in rural areas they included people who claimed and fought over the same homestead. Dealing with such characters and issues added to Stilwell's workload, for he still had to contend with outlaws in the new towns of Reno City, Guthrie, and Oklahoma City. As no provision had been made for territorial government prior to the 1889 run, Oklahoma was without civilian lawmen—except for the deputy U.S. marshals.[42]

Before the land run Stilwell had served for three years as a deputy U.S. marshal at the Darlington–Fort Reno entry point into Oklahoma Territory. He now began a short stint as a special detective.[43] His job was to look out for "moonlighters," another name for sooners. He also took note of people from the agency or from Fort Reno who went into Oklahoma Territory before the twenty-second to spy out claims for themselves and their friends.[44] Moreover, he continued to search out bootleggers and promptly arrested anyone attempting to haul alcohol into the territory.[45]

In addition to his duties as a deputy marshal, Stilwell later was appointed city marshal of Reno City. Founded in 1889 on the north bank of the North Canadian River and east of the Darlington agency, Reno City represented boundless hope for urban development and success, especially because the Rock Island Railroad survey ran through town.[46] Reno City's first citizens held a great Fourth of July celebration in 1889, just months after they had established the town. Activities included a reading of the Declaration of Independence, an oration, music furnished by Darlington schools, an ox roast, a forty-one-gun salute, and a nighttime fireworks display. The *Wichita Eagle* on July 12 noted that Stilwell and E. E. Mitchell made very efficient and ubiquitous marshals during the celebration.[47]

The high expectations for Reno City were short-lived. The riverbank location suffered heavy spring rains that made the town a sea of mud. When the city founders refused to donate money requested by the Rock Island Railroad for extending tracks through the town, the company relocated the tracks away from the river bottom. The Rock Island thus by-passed Reno City, and people soon abandoned the place. Its residents moved south across the North Canadian to establish what would become El Reno.[48]

In addition to his duties as deputy U.S. marshal, Stilwell spent the next year serving as city marshal in Reno City and El Reno (and, for fifty-three days, in Oklahoma City). Among his duties, he investigated two lot jumpers in El Reno. The first was George A. "Bunky" Lambe, born in Tyrone County, Ulster, Ireland, in 1854. He came to Fort Reno by covered wagon and made the 1889 Oklahoma run. Lambe owned a team and a plow and went to work tilling ground on a lot that would later become Grand Avenue in El Reno. John A. Foreman, a soldier, claimed the lot and had hired Lambe to work the land in exchange for two lots of land as payment.[49]

Payment for Lambe's work did not arrive as he anticipated. Eventually, Lambe concluded that Foreman did not intend to pay him. He contacted E. E. Brown, another land seeker, who stated that Foreman's lack of action represented a fraud, as Foreman did not yet own his own claim. Brown thought the government could handle the problem later. Lambe, Brown, and others placed stakes on unoccupied lots, including two lots staked out by Lambe on what would become El Reno's Bickford Street.[50] Word now spread that Bunky Lambe had organized a group of lot jumpers. Town site officials asked Lambe about his stakes, and he responded that the lots he had staked out were in lieu of the promised payment for work he performed for the El Reno Town Site Company. The company did not own the land, as John Foreman had not proved up on his homestead claim. The town site company men were angry and carried six-guns.

In his capacity as deputy U.S. marshal, Stilwell got involved in the confrontation. El Reno Town Site Company members, including officers and gamblers, asked him to remove Lambe from the lots, but Lambe told Stilwell that the company men were wrong and their activities, such as threatening him, were illegal. He also told Stilwell that he did not want anything that was not his, but he insisted he had as much right to ask for protection as they had the right to evict him from his lots. Lambe noted that he had occupied the lots first and suggested that later, if the court decided in the company men's favor, he would leave. Stilwell then told what had become an angry crowd of company people that Lambe's position was reasonable and the only thing that he (Stilwell) could do was to protect Bunky Lambe.[51]

The second lot jumper, E. E. Brown, had staked out a corner lot on the El Reno town site. Brown, perhaps because he was from Beaver City in what was then called "No Man's Land" (the present-day Oklahoma Panhandle) possessed a reputation of being a "tough" character. Accordingly, the company town site people were less confrontational with him than they had been with George Lambe. They offered to sell him the lot he had staked out, but he did not want to buy. They then asked him to vacate the site, but he refused. The next day, they sent Stilwell to tell him he would have to leave. According to Brown's version of events, he asked Stilwell if he had papers to serve, and Jack replied, "No, I told these folks I would tell you to leave and I have. Good bye." Brown left for Oklahoma City, but not before he received four lots in El Reno in exchange for the corner property.[52]

While Stilwell dealt with lot jumpers in El Reno, his family lived up to its restless reputation. Jack's father, William Henry, returned to St Joseph, Missouri, for example, where he lived in the Great Western Hotel and worked as a laborer. Elizabeth Ann Cooley, her husband Joseph Cooley, and their sons Daniel Clinton and William Clifford, as noted, had moved to Indian Territory and in 1880 settled on Dibble Creek in the Chickasaw Nation. They were living there while Jack served as a deputy marshal, and in September 1889, amid the famous Oklahoma land run, their third son, Walla Owen Cooley, was born.[53]

By this time Stilwell had entered politics. On May 31, 1890, he attended a Democratic Party convention at Frisco, located fifteen miles east of Reno City. There, delegates elected J. M. Sharp chairman. They also selected Stilwell, Frank Farwell, and five others to serve on the committee on resolutions. In addition Stilwell and another man from his township—assigned the number fourteen—became members of the Canadian County Central Committee. As such they also became members of the region's Democratic Central Committee. Among other issues the committee considered, its members resolved that mortgaging of homesteads was undemocratic and contrary to the best interest of the country. The Frisco convention adjourned, and the Democratic Central Committee organized with Stilwell as its chairman. On June 4 the first Oklahoma Territorial Census listed Stilwell as a white male, age forty, living in Reno City, the Fourth District of Oklahoma. On June 5 the *Frisco Herald* noted that "Jack Stilwell, the rustling democrat from Reno City, had been in town on Saturday." Stilwell, of course, had been at the Democratic Party convention.[54]

To protest developments related to what they saw as an undemocratic provisional territorial government at Guthrie, citizens and newspapers in Kingfisher, Oklahoma City, and Norman called for a large gathering—an "Advisory Convention"—to meet on July 15 in Frisco. People in Reno City chose Jack as one of their sixteen delegates.[55] Preparatory to the Advisory Convention, Stilwell, as chairman of the Democratic Central Committee, called a delegate convention on July 14 for county number four (Canadian County) at Bakers Hall in Frisco. Stilwell and others hoped the meeting would promote harmony among its fuming factions. The meeting went well, apparently, and later some party leaders appointed Stilwell to the Committee on Credentials.[56]

Although busy with political issues and party politics throughout most of the summer, Stilwell continued his work as a deputy marshal. He arrested outlaws, sought signed affidavits from witnesses, escorted prisoners to jail, and testified at trials. In October he escorted a man named Bill Bowes and an unnamed woman to jail in Guthrie. He had captured them between Minco and Fort Sill after a short search. Both prisoners, bootleggers, later appeared before U.S. Commissioner J. W. Haddon at Anadarko to plead their case.[57] They were released.

At the end of January 1891, he took another law-breaker, J. H. Curran, to jail, this time escorting him to Wichita. Curran, a picture dealer and sometime dairyman at Fort Sill, had boarded the mail stage at the fort. Some sort of trouble arose between the driver (a young man named Prince) and Curran. During the fight Prince jumped from the stage into the brush, leaving Curran to drive the stagecoach to Anadarko, where he put up the team and went to bed in the local hotel as if nothing had happened. When news of the fight reached them, stagecoach company officials brought charges of assault against Curran. Stilwell found the man, arrested him, and placed him in the local jail. When Curran could not make the five-hundred-dollar bond, Stilwell took him to Wichita. Curran remained in the Sedgwick County jail until April 24, 1892, when Judge Abraham J. Seay of Kingfisher released him.[58]

Stilwell's service as a deputy U.S. marshal shifted over the years. From 1885 to 1889 he served under U.S. Marshal William C. Jones, based in Kansas, who held jurisdiction in Indian Territory. From 1889 to 1890 he answered to Marshal Richard L. Walker, who was stationed in Oklahoma Territory. Once the Oklahoma Territorial government was establishment—in May 1890—William C. Grimes became the U.S. marshal. Stilwell, who had been transporting prisoners to Wichita, now began transporting them to the jail in Guthrie.[59] The most recent changes shifted Stilwell's home base to Minco. Here, after 1891, he became great friends with Lewis N. Hornbeck and his wife Letitia. Hornbeck, well-educated and a superb writer, was editor of the *Minco Minstrel*. Letitia was a schoolteacher. Stilwell and Hornbeck had met in Anadarko, and once both moved to Minco, the editor often wrote about his friend. After news of Stilwell's transfer, Hornbeck wrote, "We hear that Jack Stilwell is to be appointed to Minco as a local deputy marshal. No better selection could be made."[60]

In January 1892, around the time he moved to Minco, Stilwell became involved in a case he could not solve. It involved W. P. Wyatt, who was married to a Kiowa lady. The couple and their young child lived in a small house one mile east of Anadarko. Wyatt was a quiet, inoffensive, and peaceable man with no known enemies. His one-room house was tiny, and he was too poor to tempt a robber. One unseasonably warm night in January, Wyatt was sleeping on the floor while his wife and child occupied the bed. About midnight his wife saw the shadowy shape of a man going out the door and found her husband half-conscious on the floor. He had sustained a broken jaw from a blow with a heavy stick. Mrs. Wyatt ran to a house nearby to seek help. Soon runners went to the agency to fetch a physician and to find police officers, including Stilwell and others, for help in apprehending the offender. The doctor set the broken jaw, and Stilwell found tracks to and from the house, but he found no additional clues. What puzzled everybody was a motive for the assault. There was no robbery, no attack on the wife, and only a failed attempted murder. While Jack successfully cleared many cases as a deputy marshal, the assault on Wyatt remained unsolved.[61]

In the last half of 1892, as his health rapidly deteriorated, Stilwell served as a witness in three long-standing court cases involving land titles for lots in El Reno. In the first case, *William Redder and Jorgen Paterson vs. Isaac Jalonick, Jr.*, Stilwell testified that he saw Jalonick living illegally in Oklahoma Territory before the land rush occurred on April 22, 1889. The testimony made little difference. The court awarded the two lots to Isaac Jalonick, who was clearly in Stilwell's view a lot jumper.[62]

The second case, *D. D. Davisson vs. Henry P. Shimer*, involved title to four lots in El Reno. Davisson was something of a land speculator and town promoter. During his testimony Stilwell reviewed the experiences he had with lot jumpers in the North Canadian River town and noted that he could not arrest them without a warrant. Because there had been no arrest, Davisson got all four lots.[63] The third case again involved Davisson. This case, *David D. Davisson vs. A. C.*

McComb, involved a single lot in El Reno. During his testimony Stilwell stated that he saw McComb in Oklahoma Territory before April 22, 1889, but as an army lieutenant, McComb was there legally, on duty under the jurisdiction of the commander at Fort Reno. At first the court awarded McComb the lot, but a higher court in Washington, D.C., reversed the ruling upon review, and the lot went to Davisson, as he had occupied it first and made improvements.[64]

Stilwell, though only forty-three, was worn down by his job. It required a lot of traveling, mostly on horseback, which wracked his arthritic body. His old injuries also made time spent in the saddle grueling. He walked with a cane and could no longer perform physical labor. Escorting prisoners between Indian Territory and Wichita, trailing after bootleggers, chasing down suspects and witness affidavits were activities he found too painful and hectic. He was physically unable to continue in the Marshals Service. To support himself, he needed to find a new way to make a living.

CHAPTER 13

EL RENO POLICE JUDGE AND FRIEND OF BUFFALO BILL

In 1892 El Reno, Oklahoma Territory, was a wide-open frontier town. Twenty saloons and dance halls on the north end of town employed women (many of them prostitutes) who paid the city an "occupation tax" of five dollars per month. Soldiers from nearby Fort Reno came to town on paydays, and the saloons, gamblers, and girls on the north end quickly separated them from their wages. Indians from the reservation, which bordered on El Reno, also lost plenty of money, especially at the saloons. At night the dance halls did a big business, and "shooting up the town" was a popular pastime. Killings were frequent.[1]

El Reno's "genteel element"—which included its mayor C. H. Hobart, city clerk William McHugh, the saloon owners (always prominent citizens in raw frontier towns), and gamblers—wanted the shootings to stop. They also wanted a police judge who could bring some order, peace, and stability to the town. Jack Stilwell was made for the job. Debilitated by old work injuries and deepening arthritis, he left the risky and dangerous life of a deputy U.S. marshal in 1892 and determined to run for the position of police judge. Known by the political nickname "the rustling democrat," he received a total of 179 votes to win the election and embark on still another chapter in his life.[2] Undoubtedly his success as a deputy marshal enhanced his reputation, which had been boosted even more by newspapermen and their stories of the exploits of "Comanche Jack." Stilwell's new responsibilities as police judge took him out of the saddle and put in him in a courtroom where he dealt with both criminal and civil cases.

Lewis N. Hornbeck, Stilwell's friend since the 1880s when Hornbeck and his wife Letitia taught at the Kiowa school in Anadarko, was editor of the *Minco Minstrel*. During the campaign he became Stilwell's unofficial local press agent. Later he celebrated the new judge's win with pretentious prose:

Jack Stilwell has been elected, as Police Judge in El Reno. There now see with what certainly of precision fate works her mysterious way with poetry of motion to the music of circumstantial harmony. A Judge? And not? Does not that splendid corpulence of this modern Jack Falstaff comport serenely with attending dignity and widespread chair of a noble and just judge? Is he not of that fair minded and expansive capacity . . . and has he served in various capacities, the great U.S. from a stripling with Custer to a Falstaff with Grimes, not to learn at a glance whether a supplicant victim before his throne is rendered palsied with repentance . . . or by an ordinary and premeditated jag? . . . Jovial Jack is a man of many parts and plays them all well. Not a horse back in this entire kingdom was long enough to take a saddle made for the comfort of this very Jack; and once at Anadarko when death had followed him on a long last ride and stood looking in the door. These men did pray only that he might be given a wagon box for a burial casket and allow room for once. Thus did he make merry at the grim spectra which in turn did generously grant him a pleasant reprieve. . . . Now this same merry fellow, this honest Jack is made judge of the police court in the wicked and bibulous El Reno Town. Here's health to thee Jack and may thy shaking sides and broad bosom never grow smaller or perish for lack of humor in the court.[3]

In 1893, the year officials chartered El Reno as a city, the ninety-eighth meridian marked its western edge—which also happened to be the eastern boundary of the Cheyenne-Arapaho reservation. Fort Reno stood nearby, and soldiers of the Third Cavalry and Fourteenth Infantry garrisoned it. The young troopers were a raucous bunch, especially once a month on payday, when the town offered one continual source of pleasure. Charlie Bickford sold whiskey at his place on Bickford Avenue, and Jack Schweltzer had a saloon just down the street, where he served plenty of soldiers and Indians and entertained them with gambling of various kinds, including Mexican Monte. Poker and roulette tables also attracted men from the local military post.

Judge Stilwell, known as "Comanche Jack" Stilwell to town folk, maintained an office with the city clerk above the El Reno fire station. His courtroom was there as well. His responsibilities in that courtroom kept him busy. During his first few months in office, he judged a total of fifty-seven criminal actions: seven in December 1892; forty in January 1893; and ten in early February. The term "criminal actions" covered a variety of misdeeds, including assault, provoking to commit assault, fighting, drunkenness, drunk and indecent exposure, drunk and disorderly, drunk and fighting, carrying a pistol, gambling, vagrancy, and prostitution. In addition to recording the criminal actions for each case in the docket book, Stilwell submitted a monthly written report to the El Reno City Council. It named each defendant, his or her offense, any fines assessed, police judge costs, city marshal costs, city attorney costs, fees paid, and additional expenses paid. Any remaining money was returned to the El Reno city treasurer.[4]

Although kept busy by the town's rowdy elements, Stilwell was not adverse to relaxation. On January 6, the local paper noted, "S. E. Stilwell is taking a day off at present."[5] Later that month Lewis Hornbeck stopped in El Reno to visit Stilwell on his return from Guthrie to Minco. He stated that the judge was at "elegant leisure that day and was telling stories to beat creation." Hornbeck noted, "Jack is a great Stilwell any way you take him."[6]

Hornbeck further noted that by opening the Cheyenne-Arapaho reservation for non-Indian settlement in 1892, Oklahoma Territory had increased in size. New counties had been created from the former reservation lands, and those counties had been given letter designations. He wrote: "Some talk is going on to make the name of 'G' county in honor of Jesse S. 'Jimmy' Morrison. We all know Jimmy is not his name but no one knows what his name really is. Same as with Jack Stilwell whose name is not Jack at all but S. E. Stilwell. All right let 'G' County be known here after as Jimmy Morrison County, O.T." About a week later, Stilwell took the Rock Island train south from El Reno to Minco, where he visited with Hornbeck. Afterward, Hornbeck wrote:

Jack Stilwell, Police Judge at El Reno, was down to see us last Sunday. He is looking better than we ever saw before and carries an evident increase in dignity since his election as Police Judge. He was relating antidotes, as usual and among them was a vivid description of a marriage ceremony he recently performed in his official capacity. His story of the occasion was pretty rich and wound up with the pointed moral that it was a strange thing to him that an ugly, measly scrub of a galoot like that fellow could marry the handsomest girl in all the country after a few weeks acquaintance, when a fine portly gentleman like himself had to remain a bachelor for lack of appreciation by the fair ones.[7]

The elections of November 1892 that had placed Stilwell in office resulted in only temporary positions. Thus in spring 1893 the judge and several other El Reno officials faced reelection. To choose their candidates for the coming elections, a citizens' meeting took place in March in the district courtroom. The El Reno *Oklahoma Herald* noted, "Many of the very best people of El Reno were present." Those citizens nominated Stilwell as candidate for police judge. Of Stilwell, the editor wrote, "Police Judge Stilwell has shown himself to be a man among men and a faithful public servant and just Judge." El Reno's "genteel element," still controlled nominations for City of El Reno offices.[8]

Stilwell continued working even as he sought reelection. On March 23, 1893, he received several visitors from Anadarko in the El Reno court. T. H. Woodard, official agency interpreter, brought in several chiefs from the Kiowa tribe, and they visited Stilwell's court in the morning. Among them was the Kiowa chief justice, Chaddle Kaung-ky. He had replaced Lone Wolf, who had resigned the position. One of three chief judges on the Comanche, Kiowa, and Wichita reservation, Chaddle Kaung-ky was Lone Wolf's brother and a former Indian policeman. Chaddle Kaung-ky stated that he was pleased with Stilwell's method of punishment by locking up anyone who would not work.[9] On April 4 the city elected C. F. McElrath mayor, William J. McHugh city clerk (by a majority of one vote), and Stilwell, who retained his position as police judge.[10] Perhaps support from some of the Indian leaders, who probably did not have a vote, helped secure Stilwell's reelection.

In May, Stilwell traveled north to attend the Columbian Exposition—the Chicago World's Fair. An article about his attendance at the grand event appeared in the May 25, 1893, edition of the *Chicago Tribune:*

Jack Stilwell, official hangman for the Indian Territory, is here to see the world fair. He has his rifle with him, although he has no idea that he will be compelled to use it while in Chicago. The gun which is in his room at the Palmer [House] Hotel is a curiosity. . . . Stilwell's only regret is that his late partner, also a deputy United States Marshal, is not here to see the fair with him. Carr was this man's name and he was called one of the bravest men . . . in Indian Territory. A year ago he went into the country from Caldwell, Kansas, to arrest a Mexican horse thief. Three days after both men were found dead in a field, each with his gun in his hand. They had fired together.

Stilwell had great admiration for the beauties of Chicago's Jackson Park but he had contempt for the Columbian guards and thinks that all but one of them should be set at menial work.[11]

No mention is made of William F. Cody in the *Tribune* article, and Stilwell may not have contacted Buffalo Bill while in Chicago, where Cody's Congress of Rough Riders of the World exhibition had opened on April 3. Because the Columbian Exposition's management would not allow a Wild West display on the fairgrounds, Cody and Nate Salsbury, one of his managers, picked a fourteen-acre site opposite the main entrance of the fair and laid out their camp, which included an arena and a forest. Many people thought that Cody's show was part of the World's Fair. As noted in a previous chapter, Stilwell had served with Cody following the Battle of Beecher Island, and they worked together at Fort Hays, Kansas, in October and November 1868.[12] But Stilwell's judicial duties meant he could not stay long in Chicago, so he may not have visited his longtime friend.

Back in El Reno, Judge Stilwell remained very busy. Travis F. Hensley, editor of the *El Reno Democrat*, and members of the Jennings family became bitter over the election results. Alphonso J. "Al" Jennings, who would later earn notoriety by robbing trains, had defeated Hensley in the race for county attorney. (Jennings would later write a book about his experiences with Texas author William Sydney Porter [O. Henry].[13]) Hensley used the pages of his paper to write bitter screeds about the election and about Jennings in particular. The conflict steadily grew worse. The editor lost friends by his persistent attacks. Finally, in late June an intense fight between the men started at the post office; pistols were freely drawn and exhibited, but no shots were fired. When two of Jennings's brothers jumped into the fray, the three of them overpowered the editor. Hensley fought hard but was terribly beaten. His face was battered and cut. A large plate-glass window in the post office was broken in the fight.[14]

The three Jennings boys and the editor were arrested. They later appeared in Judge Stilwell's court, where all were placed under bond to appear the next day. Although badly beaten, the stubborn editor gained no sympathy from the public, and Hensley continued his aggressiveness. After the pistol-whipping, he swore out warrants for the arrest of city police chief U. S. Waltermire, policeman E. J. Waltermire (the chief's brother), and Deputy U.S. Marshal William McCall, arguing that they assisted the Jennings boys in the beating he received.[15]

The Jennings-Hensley case, as it was called, came before Judge Stilwell on June 28, 1893. Frank Danford represented the Jennings brothers, and T. C. James took on Hensley's defense. Hensley pleaded not guilty to charges of carrying a concealed weapon and disturbing the peace. The court dismissed the case for disturbing the peace, but it postponed the concealed weapon charge until July 7. On the appointed day, seven witnesses testified as to what had occurred, and each gave a different version of events. In the end Stilwell fined Hensley twenty-five dollars for carrying a concealed weapon. Hensley appealed, but the outcome is no longer extant. Al Jennings pleaded guilty to disturbing the peace, and Stilwell fined him ten dollars. He fined John and Ed Jennings one dollar each for disturbing the peace.[16]

Stilwell also faced plenty of problems generated by El Reno police officer E. J. Waltermire. The policeman was coarse and rough, and some folks wanted him removed from office. After a series of run-ins, Waltermire came before Stilwell's court, where he was fined for language tending to provoke an assault. When the next city council met, the mayor ordered Waltermire's fine remitted. A couple of months later, however, Stilwell found some relief when both E. J. Waltermire and U. S. Waltermire resigned their law enforcement positions with the city of El Reno on September 4.[17]

On September 16, 1893, the government opened the Cherokee Strip for settlement. Stilwell participated in the land run, and a week later an El Reno newspaperman reported: "Judge Stilwell is happy in the belief . . . that he out stripped the strippers by arriving at Enid thirteen minutes after the opening, secured a claim just two miles from town and staked the finest corner lot in the new city before the sooners dared to come out of the bush."[18]

Even as he claimed newly available land, Stilwell made plans to return to the Chicago Exposition—or so it seems. A story from the *Chicago Herald* was reprinted in the *El Reno Eagle* on September 28. The original was probably intended to call additional attention to Cody's Wild West show in Chicago. The story, apparently written at the suggestion of Cody's long-time press agent Maj. John Burke ("Arizona Bill"), carried the title "Recalls an Old Fight." It was an interview with Stilwell that covered his participation in the Battle of Beecher Island, called by Gen. James B. Frye the "Island of Death." The article describes Stilwell's walk to Fort Wallace and the rescue of Forsyth's frontiersmen. It states that although Stilwell "has had a 'checkered career' since then," he had still been "one of the fastest friends of Buffalo Bill. He knew and followed the great scout (Buffalo Bill) in those days and remembers him now." According to the article, Jack on August 29 had written Buffalo Bill the following letter:

It has been so long since you have heard from me that you will be surprised to learn that I am still on earth. News reached this part of the country the other day that you had bought out a town called Chicago, and had some buffaloes grazing on the prairies there. A white man told me the other day

that if I would get on a Railroad train, he would take me to your town. I am
selling off buckskin trying to get enough nickels and dimes . . . to take me
up there. How would I know your camp, or does the Train stop there? Do
you still keep a quarter of buffalo hanging in front of your camp, or I had
better bring dried meat to last me? If the grazing was better between here
and there I would rather steal a horse and come that way.

The Indians don't watch their horses as close as they used to.

I know you have plenty of whisky up there but is it as strong as the kind
we like, or had I better bring up a jug of the real good stuff for morning
drink? I find that by putting poison oak into whiskey we get from the east,
it adds greatly to its strength and flavor. But if you don't doctor it in some
way it will take all night to get drunk. I have two red flannel shirts. Will
that be enough to last me the trip? . . . We are short on clothes. Now Bill
you are posted on matters of civilization by this time. . . . I don't want to
appear green. If you have an extra neck tie up there please save it for me
as I want to put on lots of style. . . . In case I should get broke up there and
you don't know where I can get a job of whacking bulls for a few days,
please have some good horses spotted so I can steal them and get home.
What is the fine in that country for killing a man or two?[19]

Buffalo Bill answered Stilwell on September 1:

Yours to hand. I should have answered sooner but it took me so long to get
over the surprise of "knowing that you are still alive" that I was unable to
get my cinch pulled up. I haven't bought the whole town of Chicago, but
what I have not bought I have an option on. . . . You won't have any trouble
finding my camp. Ask anybody after you pass St. Louis and they will show
you the trail to the mess wagon. Don't bring any "dried meat" with you,
you can get it in any restaurant. . . . If you do "steal a horse" to come on
don't steal one with a brand on and I will find you a market for him.

You will find the whiskey here all right. This is a cow camp and we
keep stuff on hand that would stiffen an Oklahoma Sheriff. . . . You need
not be afraid of appearing "green." This town is full of people who are so
green that the horses bite them as they walk past.

There is positively no time for killing a man here—in fact I think scalps
are at a premium this year. . . . Come up, there is a fine chance for you to
make a record.[20]

The article about Beecher Island and the Stilwell-Cody correspondence were written in preparation for Stilwell's return to the Chicago fair and Buffalo Bill's Wild West extravaganza. The long-running Chicago season for the old scout's Wild West meant that Major Burke's press staff needed to provide reporters with "new news" so they would continue to write about the Wild West and stimulate public interest in attending the exhibition.[21] Perhaps the Stilwell-Cody letters were part of that effort to beef up interest in Cody's show.

In any case, on October 13 Stilwell was back in Chicago, where he was received as a guest of his old friend Buffalo Bill. While in the city Stilwell visited Cody's Wild West and strolled through the campgrounds, ate at the mess tent, and saw the arena show. A reporter from the *Chicago Herald* interviewed him.[22] Cody bought him a fine warm coat to protect him from the cold winds blowing off Lake Michigan. Stilwell also received a first edition of *Seventy Years on the Frontier: Alexander Majors Memoirs*, which Cody paid to publish after Col. Prentiss Ingraham, a writer of dime novels, edited it. Buffalo Bill inscribed the book: "To: Jack Stilwell with compliments of his Old Pard, W. F. Cody, 'Buffalo Bill,' Chicago, Ill., Oct. 14, 1893."[23]

On October 20 the *El Reno Eagle* announced Stilwell's return to Oklahoma. "Judge S. E. Stilwell, Comanche Jack," the article said, "returned Monday from a visit to the World's Fair where he stopped with his friend Wm. Cody known as 'Buffalo Bill.' 'Jack' was delighted with the fair and the treatment that he received at the hands of 'Bill.'"[24]

On November 3 the *Eagle* announced that Gen. Nelson A. Miles, whose headquarters were in Chicago, and William F. Cody would arrive in town within ten days. The newspaper further indicated that Miles and Cody planned a hunting and pleasure trip to the Indian reservation southwest of El Reno. Judge Stilwell, the newspaper article indicated, had received the hunting information from his friend Buffalo Bill, and the paper hoped that the people of El Reno would give "Bill" a warm welcome.[25]

Upon his arrival in El Reno, Cody stayed at the recently opened Kerfoot Hotel, and indeed he received a warm welcome. El Reno general store clerk J. E. Penner remembered one morning in late November when Buffalo Bill and Stilwell routed him out of bed at three A.M. They were pounding on the door, and Penner recognized Stilwell's voice. Stilwell explained that he and Cody were going on a long hunting trip and needed supplies. They ordered blankets, quilts, other bedding, and a good supply of food. It took thirty minutes to fill the order. The bill amounted to about sixty dollars. When they had everything, Buffalo

Bill paid in cash. Penner observed that Cody was a splendid-looking man. He also noticed that Judge Stilwell was about the same size as his famous friend.[26] Cody showed his regard for Stilwell in many ways. In Chicago he had noticed Stilwell's limp and the deformity of his right hip and shoulder. Determined that he needed a walking cane on the hunt, Cody presented Stilwell with an inscribed silver-headed cane: "To Jack Stilwell from Buffalo Bill Cody." It carried the date of November 14, 1893.

On the fifteenth, "Buffalo Bill" and "Comanche Jack" left El Reno with General Miles. To make his appearance an official visit, Miles inspected both Forts Reno and Sill before joining the former scouts on their hunt.[27] First Lt. Hugh L. Scott of Fort Sill and two troops of cavalry rode escort for the general. In fact, Miles had organized the foray. He brought along his wife, Mary, and several other former scouts, including Ben Clark and Horace Jones. Pony Bob was also in the party: years earlier he had carried the news of Abraham Lincoln's election from Saint Joseph, Missouri, to San Francisco in seven days. While on the prairie, Buffalo Bill kept his own tent. He was aided by military orderlies, who were generally available to him at a moment's notice. In addition, Lieutenant Scott called on some Indians of various tribes to help with camp logistics. Thus, adversaries from the not-too-distant past hunted and worked peacefully together on the southern plains.[28]

Members of the large hunting party settled into camp along Cobb Creek west of the Anadarko agency in what is now Caddo County. Scott's Indians took charge of preparing the camp. After dinner on the first evening, Miles, Scott, Stilwell, Clark, and Jones gathered in Scott's spacious tent to hear the Indians reminiscence about the past. The story-telling continued every night for the next three weeks.

Lieutenant Scott prepared each day's hunt. Every evening he assigned guides for each party, arranged porters, and laid out directions the various parties should take. He also assigned horses, dogs, and Indians to each group. General Miles, Cody, Ben Clark, Horace Jones, and others rode out looking for deer, pronghorns (antelopes), and bison. Stilwell, unable to hunt because of his disabilities, stayed at the base camp during the day, but every night at the campfire he listened to stories and told a few of his own.[29]

The hunters were not always successful. Long before 1893 hide hunters had eliminated most of the bison. Other southern plains animals had also been reduced. The pronghorns scattered. Elk had retreated into the mountains. Thus the hunters were reduced to searching for deer, turkeys, ducks, geese, prairie chickens, and grouse. After the group had returned to El Reno, the *El Reno Democrat* reported on the trip. It indicated that "a splendid time was had by all." The hunters, it noted, killed many ducks, geese, and turkeys. "Buffalo Bill killed one deer," the paper concluded, "but General Miles was not successful" in getting such larger game.³⁰ A year later, Cody described the hunt in *The Cosmopolitan* magazine. He gave a brief overview of the venture, noted its successes, and relayed some of its stories. He closed the article by relating the increasingly famous yarn of Jack Stilwell's bravery and achievement in the rescue of Maj. George A. Forsyth's frontiersmen after the Battle of Beecher Island.³¹

Back to work in November, Stilwell held court, heard cases of various kinds, and when necessary made decisions about punishment. Articles in the December 21, 1893, issues of the *Norman Transcript* and the *Blackwell Record* indicated that "'Comanche Jack' Stillwell, the old Indian scout of the sixties, is the city judge of El Reno. He says he accepted the office because he did not know any law and could therefore make an impartial judge."³²

That month Stilwell also got word about his family: William Henry Stilwell had died suddenly of heart disease in Kansas City, Missouri, on December 1. He was seventy years old.³³ Jack's father, who had lived with three or more women over the years, had last visited his oldest son in El Reno in 1892. In 1888 William Henry had met a widow, Mariah Brownell, at Greencastle, Indiana. He asked her to move to Kansas City with the promise of marriage, but the old man refused to marry Mariah after she arrived. Jack's brother Howard had lived with the couple for about three months in Kansas City before relocating to El Reno, where Jack was living.³⁴

In the meantime, other family news came Stilwell's way. Millard, the youngest brother, and his wife Emma lived in Moline and Rock Island where Millard worked as an insurance agent.³⁵ His sister Elizabeth Ann Cooley and her family were well and happily settled near Purcell. Perhaps William Henry's death and a sense of his own mortality—in addition to his occasional opportunities to perform marriages as police judge—got Stilwell thinking about his own chance at marriage. In any case, the *El Reno Democrat* in February 1894 noted that an article in the *Kansas City Star* commented on the judge's bachelorhood. It said of Stilwell: "He is a bachelor, but is willing to be married. Any woman with a taste for heroes can secure a game husband in Mr. Stilwell."³⁶ He may have met a woman in Chicago and fallen in love with her, for in March the *El Reno Democrat* stated: "Jack Stilwell says that a girl not a thousand miles from El Reno would prove a capital speculation for a fortune hunter of the right sort. Her voice is of silver, her hair of gold, her teeth of pearl and her eyes of diamonds. Jack is about the right age to judge these things."[37] About the same time, an article in the *Wichita Daily Eagle* noted:

> Jack took a leave of absence from the trials and tribulations of the supreme bench of the city of El Reno about three months ago and went up to the North Platte to visit Buffalo Bill, who invited him to spend a week or two with him on his ranch. The two old frontiersmen had a great time together going over the old ground and fighting their battles . . . over again. They would wander out among the Buffalos of Bill's Herd and the remembrance of all the fun they had in there [*sic*] time with the now almost extinct bison, almost made them weep. . . . Judge Stilwell returned last night to El Reno where he will resume the active regulation of the morals of that community.[38]

Not long after his return to El Reno, Stilwell got involved in the struggle between Texas and the United States over Greer County. The land in question was bounded on the south by the main fork of the Red River, on the east by the North Fork of the Red River, and on the west by the hundredth meridian. Texans believed it belonged to them. The United States claimed it was part of Oklahoma Territory. A court case, *United States vs. the State of Texas*, eventually settled the issue in favor of the United States and Oklahoma Territory.[39]

During preliminary hearings in April 1894, Stilwell testified for the United States. The attorneys took his deposition at the El Reno Kerfoot Hotel, and it amounted to more than twenty pages of type-written material. According to Dan W. Peery, who wrote an article on the whole business in the *El Reno Democrat*, Stilwell proved a good witness for the federal government's position. Among other issues under consideration was the status of trails and wagon roads; Stilwell stated that there was no old trail running from New Mexico down the North Fork of the Red River into Texas. According to Peery, Stilwell's knowledge, experience, and testimony strengthened every allegation made by the United States in the case.[40]

Even as Stilwell testified in the Greer County case, other developments eventually brought his service as a police judge in El Reno to an end. A grand jury in El Reno in early June returned indictments against several city and county officials, including Stilwell, who had been accused of receiving money from local gambling houses, which was a felony. On the positive side, in May 1894 he received a monthly salary (beginning in June) of $75.[41]

It is possible that the indictments were politically motivated, as the grand jury had targeted only those El Reno city officers who were up for reelection in a few months. When the accused came up for trial, authorities in each case quashed the indictment. Travis Henley, editor of the *El Reno Democrat*, who earlier had attacked the Jennings family, complained about the dismissed indictments: "What else can you expect," he wrote in his paper, "when the courts are in the hands of robbers? Why shouldn't they turn each other loose?"[42]

Despite such legal difficulties, Stilwell once again left town, this time to visit Buffalo Bill in New York, where he had set up his Wild West and Congress of Rough Riders of the World exhibition at Ambrose Park, South Brooklyn. Attendance in New York did not reach the lofty numbers logged the previous summer in Chicago, and expenses for Cody's extravaganza reached about $4,000 a day. With frequent rain cutting attendance, the show suffered financially.[43] Yet these financial problems did not keep Cody from inviting Stilwell to spend two weeks with him in New York. Once there, he accompanied Cody and Major Burke to Thomas Edison's Laboratory in New Jersey. Cody also took an Indian dance troop to the "invention factory" to be filmed by the Edison's kinetoscope camera. The Indians performed an Omaha war dance as the instrument successfully recorded them.[44]

On the trip home Stilwell visited friends in Pittsburg. The lady of golden hair and "eyes of diamonds" he mentioned to editors of the Wichita paper lived nearby. He also stopped in Quincy, Illinois, in October to see Sam Baldwin, an aeronaut whom he had met many years earlier at Fort Davis, Texas. The local paper ran a short article about Stilwell, suggesting that the "scout, laughing, denied that he had come to find a wife . . . though he admits that he is still a bachelor."[45]

Visiting aside, Stilwell lost his bid for reelection as police judge. In fact, he lost his bid for reelection during the nominating convention at El Reno in March 1895, where at least five candidates were seeking his position.[46] In April, W. H. Waring became the new police judge; the people El Reno presented Stilwell with a handsome gold-headed cane for his public service.[47] Stilwell was not without work, however. During the few weeks that Cody had spent in El Reno participating in the big hunt with General Miles in 1893, he had purchased about $3,000 worth of El Reno real estate. Cody, according to Oklahoma Territorial Chief Justice John H. Burford, bought the business property and gave Stilwell living quarters in it and a salary to manage the building.[48]

In fact, Stilwell had lived in the building and perhaps supervised it on a part-time basis while he was police judge. But a national financial panic and depression in the 1890s—perhaps the worst of the nineteenth century—led to economic difficulties in El Reno and for the building. With business falling off and his physical condition worsening, Stilwell grew depressed. Finally, he wrote to Cody asking what should be done. Cody telegraphed Jack, instructing him to sell the property, pay the taxes, and draw on Cody for the balance.[49]

Shortly afterward, Stilwell left El Reno. He had worked hard there, serving the people of his city to the best of his abilities. He made little money during his time as police judge, but his fame as a military scout, as a friend of Buffalo Bill, and as an impartial court official gained him respect and renown not only in the former Indian country but also across the United States. As a judge he proved tough, honest, and fair-minded. After his public service, in the spring of 1895 he had tried managing Cody's real estate full time, but as his health failed and the business collapsed amid a widespread economic depression, he sought new employment opportunities.

Chapter 14

FEDERAL COURT COMMISSIONER
IN ANADARKO

New employment opportunities came easily for Jack Stilwell. From the time he ran away from his Missouri home to join Santa Fe traders when he was thirteen, he was seldom without work: teamster, scout, guide, cowboy, court officer, deputy U.S. marshal, police judge, and real estate manager among his occupations. When he was without work, he was either on leave or, in modern parlance, on "vacation" visiting family, friends, or health spas.

After losing his bid for reelection as El Reno police judge, Stilwell found work as a U.S. commissioner at Anadarko. The position was open because of a dispute that arose in January 1895. Deputy Marshal Sam Bartel had arrested Sheridan Moacbee and Joseph Beggs for hunting on Caddo reservation lands. He took them before the U.S. commissioner at Anadarko, who jailed them. The deputy marshal then brought the men to El Reno for trial. When he heard of the arrest, Judge John H. Burford, of the second judicial district of Oklahoma Territory, ordered Bartel to his office and lectured the marshal about arresting men without the authority of law. He also released Moacbee and Beggs. The judge obviously intended for these irresponsible types of arrests to stop. Accordingly, he requested the resignation of the U.S. commissioner at Anadarko, home of the Comanche, Kiowa, and Apache agency.[1]

Stilwell's good reputation at the agency and among army officers stationed at Anadarko coupled with his experience as a deputy U.S. marshal made him an attractive candidate for the position, which he accepted in spring 1895. He already understood the duties of a U.S. commissioner—and he knew not to exceed their limits. A commissioner was supposed to treat legal cases before him as examinations, not trials. The purpose of the examination was to determine if evidence was strong enough make the case for probable guilt. When a defendant admitted guilt, no further examination was necessary, and the commissioner sent the suspect to El Reno for trial in a U.S. district court. When a defendant did not admit guilt, the commissioner needed to hear from witnesses and examine other evidence. If, after such an assessment, the commissioner found probable cause, the accused was sent to El Reno, where, during the time Stilwell served as commissioner, federal judges Burford and John Taraney presided.[2]

Stilwell was at his new post before the end of April 1895. On his move south from El Reno to Anadarko, he stopped briefly in Minco, where his friend Lewis Hornbeck remained editor of the *Minco Minstrel*. Hornbeck wrote in his paper, "For the benefit of many inquiries I'll state that Jack Stilwell is here, gold headed cane and all." He also noted that Stilwell "is U.S. Commissioner now and I must refer to him with all due and official courtesy lest I might be fined for contempt. These Oklahoma federal officials are always on the watch for cases and contempt."[3]

Stilwell moved into a little cottage at the Anadarko agency, but he was soon gone on something of a vacation. He traveled by stagecoach to Chickasha, about twenty miles east of Anadarko. At Chickasha he boarded the northbound Rock Island train for Chicago. Once in the city, he boarded an eastbound train for Pittsburg, and from there he traveled to the home of William Sherwin in Braddock, Pennsylvania. He had been there before in 1894, when he had stopped by after visiting Cody's Wild West exhibition in New York.[4]

Stilwell's purpose in making the trip was to visit Esther Hannah White. Born in England, White had come to America at age nine after her mother Rebecca died in 1880. In the United States she made her home with her mother's sister Ann, her husband William Sherwin, and their five children. Jack and Esther probably first met at the 1893 Chicago World's Fair or at Buffalo Bill's Wild West exhibit. They evidently corresponded afterward, and they met again in 1894 when Jack stopped in Pittsburg to "visit friends."

Now, on May 6, 1895, Stilwell, age forty-four, was in the Sherwin home again. This time he married twenty-four-year-old Esther.[5] The *Braddock Daily News* reported: "The marriage of Judge S. E. Stilwell of El Reno, Indian Territory, to Miss Esther White was solemnized at 4 o'clock this afternoon at the home of the bride's uncle, ex-burgess William Sherwin." The paper noted, "The wedding was a quiet one, no persons being present but the family." It further indicated that

"Rev. David Speck . . . officiated. The bride was attired in bluelette, trimmed in lace and pearls. . . . She wore a diamond star attached to her necklace, a gift of the groom." The article concluded that after "the wedding dinner, the bride and groom" would go "to their future home on the western frontier."[6]

Stilwell had not shared his wedding plans with his friends in El Reno or Minco. Even Lewis Hornbeck, the editor of the *Minco Minstrel*, was surprised. He wrote: "Jack Stilwell has returned from Pennsylvania, a married man. The happy pair passed down Tuesday on their way to Anadarko." He added, "We presume, of course, this'll add largely to the dignity of Judge Stilwell. It should anyway. The Minstrel wishes Mr. and Mrs. Stilwell a pleasant life and all the good fortune that may attend them."[7] A week later, on May 24, Hornbeck reprinted in the *Minco Minstrel* the wedding announcement first published on May 6 in Esther's hometown paper.[8] After leaving Minco, the couple took the train to Chickasha and from there embarked on a twenty-mile stage journey west to Anadarko. There they settled into Stilwell's small cottage at the agency, where Esther took charge of the home and Stilwell saw to his duties as U.S. commissioner.

Despite their considerable age difference, the marriage worked out well. In July, when Stilwell traveled to Chickasha, the local newspaper reported that "The Hon. Jack Stillwell of Anadarko was doing the town the first of the week."[9] What "doing the town" might mean, one can guess, but he was not unhappy. In November he was interviewed at Anadarko by a Guthrie newspaperman, Ed L. Wenner. Later the reporter noted that "with his charming wife, Jack was living a quite domestic life in a neat cottage at the Indian Agency. Jack was quiet and unassuming with kindly blue eyes and curling hair threaded with silver. There was nothing about him to indicate the warrior." After telling Wenner his version of the Battle of Beecher Island, Jack closed the interview: "That fight was fought on the Arickaree fork of the Republican River. I don't know how to spell that word and I never saw a man who did but that don't make any difference about the fight. Let's go to dinner."[10]

Dinner aside, Stilwell's duties as a federal commissioner kept him busy. He worked alongside the new (but temporary) Indian agent, Capt. Frank D. Baldwin of the U.S. Army. Captain Baldwin had been on detached service at the Comanche, Kiowa, and Apache Indian agency since November 1894, and he was glad to see Stilwell at Anadarko.[11] The two men knew and respected one another, having served in different columns during the Red River War in 1874: Stilwell's column rode out of Fort Sill, while Baldwin rode south from Camp Supply with Gen. Nelson Miles.[12]

As commissioner, Stilwell worked with the deputy U.S. marshals responsible for that district. The two most prominent deputy marshals he worked with at Anadarko were Frank B. Farwell and Dan W. Peery. Farwell had served as a deputy marshal in Oklahoma Territory and was chief of police at the Anadarko agency when Jack became commissioner there.[13] Indian policemen who worked with Farwell included Bert Arko (Comanche), Jack Watsemomsoakawat (Comanche), and Charlie Ohettaint (Kiowa).[14] Peery was well known to Stilwell. In 1894, when he was a reporter for the *El Reno Democrat*, he had given Jack high marks regarding the old scout's testimony in the Supreme Court case *United States vs. the State of Texas*. Peery, after the Comanche-Kiowa reservation was opened to settlement, helped to establish the town of Carnegie.[15]

Unlike previous commissioners, Stilwell was able to establish the Comanche language as the court language at Anadarko, although he struggled with the Kiowa and Apache languages. Comanche speech also contained many Spanish words, and Stilwell's knowledge of Spanish helped him to speak and understand Comanche, something of the lingua franca of southern Plains Indians.[16]

One of the first cases to go before Judge Stilwell at Anadarko was that of Pink Haile, Ike Boston, and Kiowa Johnson. Authorities had recently charged the men with conspiring to prevent the testimony of a witness in a Washita County land contest between Dan Williams and a man named Lemons. The case had been settled in favor of Williams two years earlier, but its troubled aftermath lingered, part of a feud that had developed as early as 1892 with the opening for settlement of the Cheyenne-Arapaho reservation.[17] The rivalry over conflicting land claims in Washita County led to numerous charges and counter-charges of blackmail, intimidation, and corruption. The bad blood led to the death of Bole Moore, one of the feudists. Arrests seemingly without number had been made, and trial after trial had occurred related to the feud. Associated trouble, costs, and danger continued after Moore's murder.

Commissioner Stilwell reviewed the court case against Haile, Boston, and Johnson and then dismissed the men without further action. Afterward he commented on the nature of the whole affair. The courts, he suggested, had helped to worsen the feud instead of stopping it. The rivalry would have died on its own, he reasoned, if continual writs, arrests, or affidavits had not spurred new fits of rage. Apparently, his work got results. Lewis Hornbeck, wrote: "We are glad to know that Stilwell took the course that he did . . . to abolish this feud and restore peace to the land."[18] Stilwell's stature and reputation probably helped to ease tensions: the families listened to and respected him.

In another early case, Stilwell handled a liquor matter. Deputy Marshal J. B. Lilly, assigned to the Comanche-Kiowa reservation, ran across some Comanches who had been drinking. By the time Lilly found them, they had almost emptied a one-and-a-half-gallon jug of whiskey. He placed them under arrest. While escorting them to Anadarko, he came across a party of twenty Indians. The deputy wisely turned his detainees loose, but he took the matter up with the U.S. marshal at Guthrie, E. D. Nix. He also complained to Commissioner Stilwell at Anadarko, who could do little. From Guthrie, Nix wrote to Captain Baldwin, the acting agent, as to what should be done with Indians selling or introducing whiskey on the reservation. He also requested that Stilwell issue warrants only if Baldwin approved.[19]

Meanwhile, Stilwell learned that on August 12, 1895, his Uncle Jacob had died at his home near Baldwin City, Kansas. The judge probably had more in common with his uncle than he had shared with his father. Jacob Stilwell had looked after and cared for Jack's mother Charlotte, his brother Frank, and his two sisters until Charlotte and the girls moved to Indiana. Jacob showed concern for both Frank and Jack when he wrote to an Arizona newspaper in 1882 and asked for information about Frank's assassination and Jack's location.[20]

About the same time, Stilwell became reacquainted with an old friend. An article entitled "A Frontier Fight" appeared in the June 1895 edition of the *Harper's New Monthly Magazine*. It was written by George A. Forsyth, commander of the fifty civilian frontiersmen involved in the 1868 Beecher Island fight. Forsyth, who had been severely wounded in the affair, gave his view of the fight in the piece. Stilwell read it, as did Sigmund Schlesinger, who had served with Jack as a teenage scout under Forsyth. Schlesinger, now living in Cleveland, Ohio, obtained Stilwell's address from Forsyth and immediately wrote to him and recalled the battle they fought as boys some twenty-seven years ago.

On August 7 Stilwell answered Schlesinger. "Your esteemed favor of the 3rd, inst. to hand," he wrote, "and to say it was a surprise to me would be to draw it entirely too mild, for I have often wondered what had become of you and what you are doing. I am so glad to know that you are doing well." Stilwell's letter continued:

As for myself, I am as you see here in Comanche Country. First making a living that's all. Am all botched up with rheumatism. Can't ride on horseback anymore to do any good as I now weigh 262 lbs. so you see I have grown since you saw me last.

No Sam, I wore myself out scouting and am a back number laid on a shelf as it were, no more such work to do and I couldn't do it if there was. I have almost lost sight of all the boys who were with us at the time. Now and then I hear from some of them.

Yes Sam please write me all about yourself. I would like so much to see you once more and talk about old times.

P.S. Don't you think Forsyth used the pronoun I, myself, rather freely in that account of the fight.[21]

About the same time (perhaps a couple of days previous), Stilwell had received a letter from Franklin G. Adams of the Kansas Historical Society in Topeka. Adams had also read the Forsyth article, and he wanted Stilwell's opinion of it. On August 20 Stilwell answered Adams: "I have read the account of the fight you mention. To criticize it, even comment on it would be to rewrite the whole thing . . . and I would leave out four or five hundred pronouns 'I.' I don't feel at this time equal to the occasion. . . . If you see fit to write me again, please tell me the object you have in view in asking for this information; as I am not in the habit of writing for publication."[22]

A short time later Schlesinger wrote again, and on September 5 Jack replied. He indicated that he was busy and apologized that his response took so long. He wrote that he could not travel this fall, for he had to hustle to make a living. Jack explained that he had gone "broke this fall" and then had gotten married. He admitted that he did not have much money to lose but blamed his loss on "Eastern dudes, who were too sharp for us fellows out here." Apparently while visiting Cody in New York in the fall of 1894, he had invested with "Eastern dudes" and lost his money.

In the letter Stilwell indicated that he was thinking about applying to Congress for a pension the next year. He wondered if Sigmund would "handle an Ohio Congressman" for him. Jack also stated that he was "living fat," as for the past two or three weeks he had young prairie chickens or plovers on his table. He did not have much of a house, he noted, "not like the ones back east," but Sigmund "would be as welcome as any man to share what I have got."[23]

Stilwell heard no more from Schlesinger that year, and he returned to his duties as commissioner. He also settled into married life and became, apparently, an attentive husband. Lewis Hornbeck visited Anadarko in January 1896, and afterward wrote: "But say to see Jack Stilwell tamed down to domestic life by a soft spoken demure little woman, is a sight. He takes it in good part, though just as if he had been a married man all of his life."[24]

On March 16, 1896, Stilwell submitted a pension petition to Congress. As a civilian scout he was not eligible for a military pension, but he nevertheless forged ahead. In the petition he outlined his long service record as a scout and suggested that a pension was due because his rheumatism and the resulting deformity of his right knee, hip, and shoulder made it impossible for him to perform physical work and make a living. Fourteen officers endorsed the petition. They included Brev. Brig. Gen. George A. Forsyth, Lt. Col. Lewis H. Carpenter, Lt. Col. Michael V. Sheridan, Maj. Stevens T. Norvell, Maj. William B. Kennedy, Maj. Theodore A. Baldwin, Maj. Joseph M. Kelley, Capt. Marion P. Maus, Capt. Jesse M. Lee, Capt. William Henry Beck, Capt. Owen J. Sweet, Capt. Charles G. Ayres, Capt. Charles E. Nordstrom, and Col. James Biddle. In addition, physicians Allison H. Jackson and C. F. McElrath submitted medical affidavits testifying to Stilwell's health, injuries, and physical condition.[25] In one sense, Stilwell got lucky. The Committee on Pensions approved his petition. Its report recognized his "most remarkable record of scout and guide and although not an enlisted man, he performed services such as to entitle him a pension by a special act of Congress."[26]

Stilwell also did well with his work as a U.S. commissioner, and there were no problems on that front. But there were difficulties at the agency. Jack's friend Captain Baldwin, the agent at Anadarko, came into conflict with reservation traders and "squaw men," as they were unfortunately called—Anglos operating on the reservation and married to Indian women. The issues were complicated. In his efforts to protect Indians on the reservation, Baldwin was honest and not afraid to challenge the special interests of the reservation's traders and the white men who lived there by right of marriage. He stopped allowing Anglos married to Indian women to use free pasture to graze their cattle. He made traders pay Indians more for hides, increasing the cost from one dollar in 1895 to four dollars in 1898. He encouraged Indians to shop in Chickasha where prices were lower. Baldwin also persuaded the Indians to invest fifty thousand dollars of their "grass money"—income from grazing leases—in stock cattle. Reservation whites reacted to the stock cattle purchase as if the agent had taken money from their pockets. It became a major point of contention between the Anglos on the reservation and Baldwin. The efforts of the intermarried whites and traders to get rid of Baldwin continued from 1895 until 1898, when Baldwin was recalled to active duty at the start of the Spanish-American War.[27]

During the long conflict Baldwin had earned the loathing of one of the traders, Dudley P. Brown. Brown started a mudslinging campaign in which he accused Baldwin of excessive drinking. Baldwin retaliated by recommending that Brown's trader's license be canceled. Brown then brought a lawsuit against Baldwin. Additional agency traders joined the conflict.[28] At this point Stilwell became involved. As a cattle inspector appointed by Baldwin, he was responsible for receiving and inspecting livestock. In this instance he was to receive and inspect animals being delivered by John W. Light, part owner of one of the largest cattle-trailing companies of Texas.[29] Accordingly Stilwell received, inspected, and separated Light's cattle pastured at Chickasha. From there cowboys trailed some fourteen hundred year-old heifers and seventy-five bulls selected from Light's herd to Anadarko, where they branded them before Indians at the reservation would accept them for breeding purposes. The action was part of the process to initiate Indian-owned herds. The cattle arrived on May 1, 1896.

Everything went well until May 10, when George W. Conover, who was married to an Indian woman, sent a telegram to his lawyer in Washington, D.C. It stated that the cattle purchased by Captain Baldwin for the Indians were of poor quality and not worth the price of purchase. Authorities sent inspector C. C. Duncan to the agency in June, and a formal investigation was convened. Conover, Baldwin, and Light came with their lawyers.

During his investigation Duncan interviewed seventeen men. Testimony from traders and white men married to Indian women supported Conover's complaint. In the first days of the investigation, Stilwell was not present. He and his wife Esther had gone to Davenport, Iowa, to visit Jack's youngest brother, Millard, who worked as an insurance agent there. From there Esther traveled east to Pennsylvania to visit her family, and Jack returned to Anadarko. Stilwell returned before the investigation was complete, testified, and established that as a cowboy of long standing, he was qualified and able to class cattle. He testified last, but some Conover supporters inferred that he had gone to Davenport to avoid testifying.[30]

Results of the investigation went against Baldwin and Stilwell. Important criticism came in December. That month Indian inspector Province McCormick arrived at the Anadarko agency to make a general inspection and to investigate the Conover charges against Agent Baldwin. Inspector McCormick found many things wrong and excoriated Baldwin as incompetent, a heavy drinker, a poor businessman, and a weak administrator.[31] In addition McCormick criticized Stilwell. He suggested Stilwell was no cattle inspector, even though his appointment had been approved by bureau officials. He also claimed that Stilwell had accepted bribes from his former employer William F. Dietrich and from Louis Bentz for approving cattle for distribution on the reservation. From Stilwell's point of view the charges were groundless. He testified that Louis Bentz came to his house and asked for change for ten dollars. Jack sent him to Dudley Brown's store for change; Bentz had given him no money. Dietrich's five-dollar check, Stilwell testified, was cashed, and some of the money given to Joe Stephenson to build the branding-iron fires. Dietrich testified that this was a bribe, but Stilwell was given the five-dollar check after the Dietrich's cattle had been inspected and accepted. Of significance, perhaps, was that Dietrich, like George W. Conover, was married to an Indian woman and opposed Baldwin.[32]

Stilwell was relieved of his cattle inspection duties, and he was happy to be out of the business. He had other opportunities to pursue. A year earlier, in 1895, Chickasha had become an Indian Territory federal court town for the southern district. The first term was held in Chickasha on the first Monday in September 1895. Judge C. B. Kilgore served the district. With the establishment of the federal court in Chickasha, a total of eleven attorneys practiced law there.[33] As a U.S. commissioner Jack took advantage of an opportunity the large number of Chickasha lawyers presented him. He saw an increasing demand for lawyers in the area, so he studied law for three months and in early 1897 was admitted to the bar at Chickasha.[34]

Stilwell continued to receive attention in area newspapers. Many stories described his life and work as a deputy U.S. marshal. Most exaggerated his activities. Some were more folklore than a representation of authentic events. They told impossible stories of the many men Stilwell had supposedly hanged or killed. The newspapers provided entertaining stories for their readers, and Stilwell made "good copy." A Guthrie newspaper carried this heading: "Daring Jack Stilwell, His Larks were as Audacious as his Exploits were Courageous." The article, as did many about him, started by telling the story of Stilwell's escape from the Beecher Island battle site. It also told of him hiring a hearse to ride around Wichita, Kansas, and his purchase of a barber pole to carry back to Darlington from Wichita.[35]

On September 18, 1897, F. G. Adams, the secretary of the Kansas Historical Society, wrote to Jack about a proposed meeting of the Arickaree survivors to be held at Topeka. Adams's idea was to record an accurate history of the battle. In answer to Adams's inquiry, Stilwell wrote back, stating, "Nothing could please me better, than the meeting suggested especially if the railroads rates were reduced."[36] On the twenty-first, Stilwell, having just received a letter from Sigmund Schlesinger, wrote to his old friend from Beecher Island days. "Dear Sam," he started,

> Yours of the 17th to hand. Yes the 17th, how often when that day comes round do we think of each other and wonder how many are still living and what they are doing. I noted this time that the 18th was not a very long day, yet 29 year ago. I thought that the sun would never go down on that 18th of September when I was lying in a washout listening to you fellows fight only 3 miles away, each volley we thought was your last but old Pete [Trudeau], hard headed old man that he was would swear a while in French and English then throw in a word or two in Spanish just for good measure but at sundown when we still heard firing from the Island, we took heart anew. Yes I am still married and subsisting in the wild and wooly west but my wife don't like the country much if any better than when she first came. . . . Mrs. Stilwell tells of the good time and hearty welcome you gave her [last year in Cleveland]. Give our best wishes to your family and believe me when I say I would like to see you again.[37]

On December 9, 1897, Stilwell made application to open a full-time butcher shop and bakery at Anadarko. Although Stilwell made the application, Agent Baldwin may have endorsed the idea in an effort to block and steal business from the licensed traders with whom he was in constant conflict. On January 3, 1898, Commissioner of Indian Affairs W. A. Jones declined the request.[38]

In May Stilwell received some good news. His application for a pension had passed the Senate and the House of Representatives. The action placed him on the pension roll for distinguished services to the government as a scout in the Indian campaigns.[39] Money associated with the retirement program did not amount to much, but it certainly relieved him from some of his financial difficulties. Unfortunately another problem soon came up. After Captain Baldwin left his position as Indian agent in April 1898 and returned to active duty, Stilwell was left with few allies. By siding with Baldwin he had alienated Anglos with Indian wives and the traders at the agency. The group included James N. Jones, with whom Jack had served as a scout at Fort Sill in 1876; George W. Conover; and W. F. Dietrich, with whom he had worked as a cowboy in the early 1880s.

Not all was bleary. That summer a reunion of military scouts convened at Fort Reno. Stilwell attended and visited many of his former colleagues. Buffalo Bill, Pawnee Bill, Chris Madsen, and others who were prominent characters in their day attended the event. They exchanged stories, caught up one another on their comings and goings, and mourned the loss of several of their buddies.[40] In October, not long after the reunion, Stilwell resigned as U.S. commissioner. Cody, his longtime friend and sometime benefactor, had called him to Wyoming. Financially broke, in poor health, and having no way to make a living, Stilwell accepted the showman's call. He would make his new home in Cody, in the state's far northwest, not far from Yellowstone National Park. Judge Stilwell, the *El Reno Globe* suggested, would no doubt secure a high-paying position but "hundreds of old friends regretted that he had decided to leave the territory."[41]

A review of his record as U.S. commissioner at Anadarko suggests that Stilwell had few problems while serving in the position. A total of eighty-eight cases were brought before him between October 19, 1896, and September 28, 1898. Over half the cases included charges of cutting standing timber on the reservation; of these, eight cases were dismissed for lack of evidence. Of ten individuals charged with introducing whiskey to Indians, six cases were dismissed. Seven cases involved stealing and butchering beef, and three were dismissed. Five people were charged with assault with a deadly weapon. Five were charged with stealing spools of fence wire from the agency. Two were charged for horse theft; two were charged with theft of farm implements from the agency; two were charged with cattle theft. Other cases charged included assault to rob, trade of annuity goods, fugitive from justice, attempt to bribe witness, embezzlement, and purchase of issued cattle from Indians. Of the total cases, about one-third were dismissed for lack of evidence, thus reducing the number of cases sent to the territorial judge at El Reno.[42]

Although he lost the support of some of his old friends by his association with and loyalty to Frank Baldwin, that unfortunate development played out away from his duties as commissioner. Now he no doubt looked forward to moving north with his wife to begin a new chapter in his life in the employ of Buffalo Bill Cody.

CHAPTER 15

IN CODY, WYOMING

Jack Stilwell spent the last five years of his life in northwest Wyoming, where, despite his declining health, he served as the land commissioner for Bighorn County, engaged in real estate ventures, and practiced law. Plans for his and Esther's move to Wyoming developed during the reunion of former army scouts at Fort Reno, Oklahoma Territory, during the summer of 1898. There Stilwell and his old friend William F. Cody found mutual reasons for the move. For his part, Stilwell, needed work. Though he was only forty-eight years old, a life spent in the saddle covering hard miles had aged his body far beyond his years, and his old pursuits were past his physical ability. According to Will Frackelton, a Sheridan dentist who knew Cody, the showman had a "commendable weakness for impoverished Indian fighters, trail blazers, buffalo hunters, and other survivors of the Old West and invented little jobs for them with his Wild West Show or on his ranches." From Frackelton's perspective, "Stilwell was a pensioner on Cody's ranch."[1]

For his part, Cody wanted Stilwell, a lawyer and friend, to fill the position of U.S. commissioner in Bighorn County, a job Stilwell had the experience to back. In such a position he could ensure that people with land-claim fillings in the Bighorn Basin had proper proof and documentation before their applications went to the U.S. Land Office at Lander, Wyoming, for a final decision.[2] Plans in place, after the reunion at Fort Reno, Stilwell returned to Anadarko, where he and Esther packed their trunks. In the fall of 1898 the couple traveled by stagecoach to Chickasha, where they caught Rock Island train. Before joining her husband in Wyoming, Esther journeyed back east to Bradford, Pennsylvania, to visit her family. Jack headed northwest.

Stilwell met up with Cody in October, and the men traveled to Sheridan, Wyoming, where they joined scout J. F. Brown, Gen. Edwin Vose Sumner, and Capt. William Henry Beck in a search for a Sheridan-area winter camp for two companies of soldiers. No doubt during the search Stilwell and Beck exchanged stories about the 1878 scouts they had made from Camp Peña Blanca into the Big Bend of Texas with the Buffalo Soldiers of the Tenth Cavalry. Perhaps they even reviewed the sorry events surrounding Beck's old court-martial.[3]

Upon leaving Sheridan in late October 1898, Cody, Stilwell, and Brown traveled by rail northwest to Billings, Montana. From there they headed southwest for Cody (established in 1895), to look after the entrepreneur's extensive interests in the area.[4] In January 1899 Stilwell appeared before Judge John A. Riner's district court in Cheyenne, where he presented a letter of recommendation to Riner from John H. Burford, chief justice of the supreme court of the Territory of Oklahoma. In his letter Burford stated that Stilwell was a "competent and reliable officer" as well as a "genial and enjoyable companion."[5]

A second recommendation came from Charles F. Manderson, a solicitor for the Burlington & Missouri River Railroad in Omaha, Nebraska. "Judge S. E. Stilwell," Manderson wrote, "who has located in the Big Horn Basin will have charge of the matter of immigration and sale of lands in that section. . . . You will find him in every respect worthy of your confidence and esteem."[6] The U.S. attorney for the District of Wyoming, Timothy F. Burk, was satisfied with Manderson's endorsement of Stilwell as a "competent and suitable person" to receive the commissioner appointment.[7] Judge Riner then ordered that "Simpson E. Stilwell now residing at Cody, Big Horn County, Wyoming, be appointed United States Commissioner for a term of four years after the fourteenth day of January, 1899, unless sooner removed by this court for cause."[8] Stilwell raised his hand, made the appropriated pledge, and then signed the oath of office before Louis Kirk, clerk of the U.S. district court in Cheyenne.[9]

In late January 1899 Esther Stilwell made her way from Pennsylvania to Sheridan, where she met her husband. Together they checked into the Sheridan Inn. Esther remained at the hotel while Jack returned to Cody to attend to business and find a permanent home for them.[10] After spending January and February in and around Cody, Stilwell moved to Buffalo Bill's farm near the village of Marquette, west of town. Marquette had been established prior to Cody's namesake town and stood near the confluence of the North and South Forks of the Shoshone

River, in some of the most beautiful country in the region. (Marquette is now gone, covered by the waters of Buffalo Bill Reservoir.) Although Stilwell rented the farm from Cody, Carl D. Hammett, who would board with Jack and Esther, farmed the land. Farm laborer Robert A. Looney also boarded with them. While such arrangements were being completed, Stilwell made other preparations for Esther's arrival.[11]

In the latter part of March, when the winter weather had moderated, Stilwell left for Sheridan to reunite with Esther and bring her to their new home. On their return, while in Billings, the local paper reported, "S. E. Stilwell who is interested in the Big Horn basin land was here Sunday on his way home to Cody, accompanied by Mrs. Stilwell who has been visiting in Sheridan."[12] After a night spent at Billings's Grand Hotel, the couple boarded the early morning train bound southwest for Red Lodge, Montana. From Red Lodge an arduous trip to Cody faced them: a rough, sixty-five-mile, two-day ride via a stagecoach along the Clarks Fork of the Yellowstone River, including an overnight stop at "Eagle's Nest." Although the route traversed some gorgeous mountain country, the trip proved difficult. At one of the several stream crossings some of the Stilwells' luggage washed away and was lost. They were not injured in the mishap, whatever it was. From Cody they traveled by wagon to the farm at Marquette, which remained their home until 1902.

Among the items lost was an address book. Not an important item, perhaps, but it did have mailing directions to friends and business acquaintances. Accordingly, Stilwell was at a loss to write to many folks until they corresponded with him. Some months passed, for instance, before he could write to his old colleague, Sigmund Schlesinger, from his scouting days. On August 13, 1899, Jack wrote:

You did well to put your address on the wrapper you sent to me for in moving to this country we lost a lot of goods crossing a stream among the rest was your address so you see I could not write to you.

Yes, I live out here but I am not superintendent of any body's 27,000 acres of land and I doubt if there is 50,000 acres under cultivation in the whole country and the country is as big as the state of Rhode Island if not bigger but I am making a living and that is about all, this is the most delightful summer residence in the World, plenty of fish in all the streams, good hunting in the fall, the hottest day we have had this summer was 81 degrees. This is a good stock country and we expect a railroad in the sweet by and by. Cody has some large interest here and is trying to get out a ditch for irrigation purposes.

You see we can't even raise a row in this country without irrigation of some kind.

Just at present Fredrick Remington and wife, Mrs. Cody, two daughters and some friends are camping up here in mountains having a good time.

Sam I would like to hear from you oftener than I do.

With kind regards from Mrs. Stilwell and my best wishes to you and your family.[13]

As Stilwell recounted in the letter, Frederic S. Remington—the famed artist, illustrator, and writer—traveled to Marquette and interviewed him. Remington later authored an article with illustrations that appeared in *Collier's Weekly* that described Stilwell's participation in the Battle of Beecher Island as a teenager and portrayed his and Pierre Trudeau's heroic action in walking to Fort Wallace to bring help to Forsyth's beleaguered frontiersmen.[14]

In the *Collier's* article, "How Stilwell Sold Out," Remington described Stilwell as fat and gray-headed but with a "wonderfully agile mind" and a "beautiful and homely old Missouri humorous talk." He said, "Jack hates many things and loves many people. . . . He will get into his two-pony buggy instantly and pull out if he does not fancy you." He quoted Stilwell as saying at Beecher Island, "When we were bidding the men good-by I (Jack) says, 'Boys, this is a sellout and Jack Stilwell is going to come high. . . . Old man Trudeau he will bring a good price too.'" Remington concluded that after the 110-mile walk to Fort Wallace, "Jack Stilwell never sold out after all."[15]

On February 28, 1900, Stilwell applied for admission to the Wyoming Bar and paid a fee of ten dollars. The subsequent process moved slowly. On May 22 officials referred his application to the bar committee, which referred the application to the larger bar organization, which in turn on September 19 reported favorably for admission. A month later officials sent Stilwell's attorney certificate to him, and on October 14, 1900, Stilwell became a lawyer in Wyoming.[16]

Buffalo Bill needed the old scout's legal expertise. Hudson Darrah, a lumber-hauling contractor, caused multiple problems for Cody and his assistant George T. Beck, who founded the town of Cody. The trouble started at the end of the summer of 1898 when Darrah was not paid for hauling lumber to the site of the Shoshone Irrigation Canal, one of Cody's grand plans for irrigating the Bighorn Basin. In February 1899 Darrah filed a lawsuit against Cody and plowed up the road that he had built to the sawmill. He later lodged a protest with the land office in Lander claiming that the Cody Irrigation Company should not get land patents because they had not irrigated or reclaimed all the land listed on the patents.[17] A hearing on the protest was held on July 21, 1900. Jack Stilwell, the land commissioner and judge, heard the case in Cody. Darrah refused to comply with Stilwell's order for more particulars on the allegations in the affidavit and was unable to produce any confirming witnesses. Stilwell concluded that the case was closed.[18]

The Darrah case aside, Stilwell played a vital role in land settlement in the Bighorn Basin. In November the *Cody Enterprise* reported that "several filings on land were made before Judge Stilwell during the present week."[19] Between November 1900 and December 1901, the U.S. Land Office at Lander submitted several "Notice for Publication" announcements to the Cody newspaper. The notices named the person making the final homestead claim and indicated that proof should be made before "United States Commissioner, S. E. Stilwell." They also stated the place and date to present such proof. The claimant was required to prove continuous residence and cultivation of the homestead land and to provide four witnesses who supported the truth of the claim. Once gathered, all pertinent records would be sent to the federal office at Lander for a final decision.[20]

While Stilwell was busy with such work, on November 23, 1900, Dan Peery, editor of the *El Reno Globe* in Oklahoma Territory, reported this: "A report comes to us via Anadarko that Jack Stilwell . . . had died suddenly at Cody, Wyoming, where he has lived for the past two years. We have no particulars and hope the rumor is not true."[21] Concerned, and not believing the story of Stilwell's sudden death, Peery wrote to the postmaster at Cody, who promptly answered that the judge was in good health and gaining weight. On December 13 a response also came from the *Cody Enterprise*: "The Globe of El Reno, Oklahoma, recently published an elaborate obituary of the sudden death of Judge Stilwell. . . . The judge declares that the statement lacks some elements of truth."[22] Stilwell then wrote to Peery: "I notice among other important locals in your paper that I had died very suddenly." An exchange followed. Peery wrote, "Jack never did anything suddenly and dying was the last thing he wanted to do." Stilwell indicated that he wanted more time in this world and a better send-off than Peery gave him, even if he called on Lewis Hornbeck for help. Peery responded: "We are glad to know for certain that our old friend is not dead; dead men pay no subscriptions. Jack may rest easy, his fame is secure and when he does shuffle off, the Globe will pay a fitting tribute to his memory, . . . and if he should be ready to die the Globe will print an edition befitting the occasion and one the Judge need not be ashamed of."[23]

After the long winter of 1900–1901, in May Stilwell traveled north of Cody to Clark's Fork of the Yellowstone River. There as a U.S. commissioner he reviewed the final proof to support homestead claims and, if he found them satisfactory, sent a report stating so to the federal land office at Lander.[24] While Stilwell attended to his commissioner duties, Carl Hammett and Robert Looney, his farmers, worked hard on raising strawberries. Evidently they raised a substantial crop. "This season Judge Stilwell, the judicial sage and suburban (Marquette) dweller," the *Cody Enterprise* reported in June, "expects the largest kind of a yield from his strawberry farm and is much elated over the prospect."[25]

Stilwell still enjoyed plenty of time away from his farm and legal duties. One of his activities was attending the Cody Club, a sportsmen's club organized by George T. Beck with help from Buffalo Bill. The first meeting, held in Beck's office, was attended by Cody and other notables, including Stilwell. A hunt, in which General Miles participated, followed the meeting.[26] Because they deemed the first meeting a success, participants decided to make the next meeting "Ladies Night." The second meeting of the Cody Club, in September 1901, was also hilarious but without Cody's stories. In his absence, the local paper noted, "Judge Stilwell was called upon and delivered a felicitous speech, congratulating the club upon its success and in his usual humorous manner created much merriment. His remarks were greeted with applause."[27] The recreation notwithstanding, Stilwell dealt with a good bit of land business in Cody. The *Cody Enterprise* announced that because of the local activity, "Judge Stilwell of Marquette, would come to Cody on Tuesday and Saturday to hold court."[28]

Unfortunately, the good times did not last. In December 1901, after an attack of acute gastritis, Stilwell became very ill. In serious condition, he came under the care of Dr. James L. Bradbury of Cody.[29] A few weeks later—in early January 1902—his health status remained about the same: although he rested more easily, there was no improvement in his condition, and he could not work. Worried, he requested hospitalization in Kansas City. Dr. Bradbury and Esther made arrangements that as soon as he gained sufficient strength to travel, he would be moved. During Stilwell's illness Judge C. E. Hayden attended the old scout's legal business.[30]

On January 16 the *Cody Enterprise* reported: "News from the bedside of Judge Stilwell is to the effect that he is slightly better, and will probably be able to undertake the journey to Kansas City in the early future." The paper was correct. In the middle of January, Stilwell left Cody on the newly completed Chicago, Burlington & Quincy Railroad, bound for Kansas City.[31] According to the *Wyoming Dispatch*, Esther was to accompany Jack as far as Toluca, Wyoming, where she would see him safely aboard a Pullman car. She may have, but the *Cody Enterprise* reported that W. O. Snyder, a longtime friend and employee on Buffalo Bill's TE Ranch, traveled with Stilwell. When his train stopped in Lincoln, Nebraska, Jack's cousin Phoebe Stilwell Bare joined him and accompanied him to Kansas City, where he was hospitalized. While he was still in the hospital, Jack's youngest cousin, Clara Stilwell, a Kansas City schoolteacher, looked after him.[32] The *Wyoming Dispatch* in early February reported that Jack showed great improvement following his treatment in Kansas City.[33]

After being released from the hospital, Stilwell traveled to the old family homestead just west of Baldwin City and stayed with his cousin Phoebe. They spent many hours reliving their childhood adventures. They recalled attending the preparatory school at Baker University together in 1863.[34] Jack also recounted the sad time when his mother and father separated, and he was taken to Savanah, Missouri. Then he related his conflicts with his stepmother that led him to join a wagon train bound for Santa Fe. Jack stayed with Phoebe through March.[35]

Stilwell returned to Cody in April. His many friends were glad to learn that he had improved to such an extent that he was able to travel unaided. Cody's *Wyoming Dispatch* on April 18, 1902, reported: "Judge S. E. Stilwell arrived yesterday from his sojourn at Kansas City and Baldwin City, Kansas, much improved in health and will resume the practice of his profession, the law."[36] "Every one of Jack's friends," the *Cody Enterprise* indicated, and all the people in the community around Cody were happy that he had recovered his usual good health and did not cross the "great divide."[37] Yet Stilwell decided to move to Cody, where he would be closer to the care of a physician. He rented a house from local realtor Jake M. Schwoob, and during the last week in May, he and Esther moved into the home. The local paper noted that unfortunately his health was not improving as rapidly as his friends desired.[38]

Even so, Stilwell kept up his correspondence. On July 1 he wrote to Schlesinger:

Your letter to hand today and will answer right away. No the reports are not true that are going around now, but I have been sick now over a year, I have Dropsy but the doctors think they can relieve me, no kidney trouble about it, it is caused by a bad liver.

Yes, there some fellows trying to get up some sort of monument on the old battleground. I hope they will make it, that man Christy who did so much about it is up here now, I don't know much about him.

Yes, Sam I wish I could be at your house for about three weeks then I think I would be well from what my wife tells me but no trip East for me this year.

I tell you that when Wyoming Doctors play with you for a whole year and still have you in the game to say nothing of the trip I made to Kansas City Hospital, it requires but light scales to weigh your money.

The weather is delightful here now. I don't know if they will ever have a reunion of the old Scouts, if they do I shall try my best to attend. I believe I would rather see you than any other one of the old fellows.

P.S. If you have a photo of yourself please send me one.[39]

Stilwell denied that he was near death. He had been ill with dropsy, he said, or generalized edema caused by liver malfunction. He moved to Cody to be near his physician, Dr. Louis Howe. In the letter Jack referred to a monument that would be erected near Beecher Island by the states of Kansas and Colorado in 1905.[40]

By the end of July, Stilwell had recovered enough to get out and attend to his land matters. On August 1 he was in Marquette attending to business. His friends were glad that he had recovered enough to be able to travel and work.[41] On September 5 the *Wyoming Dispatch* indicated that "it was gratifying news that Judge Stilwell was recovering his health. He walked about town and attended police court, heard [a] case, but was not tired. It looked natural to see the jovial Judge back in the court room."[42]

That same month General Miles reported on Stilwell's illness—and on what Miles saw as his impending death. On September 21 he wrote in the *New York Herald-Sun:* "In the shadow of Eagle Mountain, Judge Jack Stilwell the famous Indian scout is dying. He is in the grip of Bright's disease and cannot live many weeks longer. Knowing this he moved from his ranch to be nearer medical treatment, and while the doctors may prolong his life they cannot save it." Miles retold the story of Stilwell's part in the rescue of the Forsyth's Beecher Island frontiersmen in 1868. In addition Miles bragged that Stilwell had studied law and made a brilliant lawyer who would long be remembered for his wit and comprehension of the law.[43] Several major newspapers picked up the article, including the *Denver Republican, Galveston Daily News, Dallas Morning News,* and the *Weekly Times Journal of Oklahoma City.*

General Miles was right about Stilwell's impending death. On February 17, 1903, five months after the *New York Herald-Sun* story appeared, Jack died. The *Cody Enterprise* reported: "Jack Stilwell, age fifty-two, died at his home in Cody on Tuesday morning from pneumonia. He was ill only ten days. He previously had pneumonia on two occasions and in one instance he was nursed back to life by Indians. Jack's physician, Doctor Louis Howe, said that the right lung was very weak owing to his two previous pneumonia attacks." From Dr. Howe's perspective, Stilwell's death was predicated by the onset of his pneumonia.[44]

Esther held the funeral the next day at the new Christ Episcopal Church, which was crowded to the doors with friends and neighbors. Rev. G. W. Van Winkle conducted the service. The church choir led the musical selections: "Asleep in Jesus" and "Nearer My God to Thee." Mrs. Jake Schwoob and Mrs. Walter Schwoob sang a duet: "Jesus Knows our Every Care." After viewing the body, congregation members adjourned to the Riverside Cemetery. As Stilwell was a Mason, local members of the Masonic fraternity had charge of his burial.[45]

Jack's cousin Phoebe Stilwell Bare received word of his death and on February 20 placed a notice in the Baldwin Ledger.[46] In Oklahoma Territory, Stilwell's obituary, as printed in the Cody Enterprise, appeared in El Reno's American News on February 26 and the Guthrie Daily Leader on March 9. The two headings in the Guthrie Daily Leader read: "Old Time Scout Crosses the River" and "Jack Stilwell Succumbs to Death after a Life of Hardship."[47]

Stilwell's story did not end with his burial at the Cody Riverside Cemetery. The pension that he had successfully petitioned for did not extend to Esther, his widow, because of his civilian status. She could not apply for a military headstone for his grave, and therefore she placed a wooden cross as a marker. Stilwell did not leave her completely destitute. Esther, with her husband's help, had filed on an eighty-acre tract near Marquette. But a problem developed after his death—a contest for ownership between Esther and H. D. Barbee. The new U.S. commissioner, J. K. Calkins, took the testimony and sent it to the Lander federal land office, which decided in favor of Mrs. Stilwell.[48] She sold the land and on November 17, 1905, purchased a new residence on Alger Avenue from the Cody Trading Company.[49]

On May 14, 1906, in Omaha, Nebraska, more than three years after Jack's death, Esther Stilwell married Carl D. Hammitt, who had operated Stilwell's strawberry farm in Marquette. Hammitt, who once boarded with the Stilwells, was a deputy sheriff in Park County and a former Cody town marshal. About the Hammitts the Cody Enterprise noted that the "couple will make their home on Alger Avenue in the house previously occupied by Esther Stilwell."[50] While Hammitt continued to serve as a deputy sheriff, Esther remained a highly respected and active member in Cody's Christ Episcopal Church. In June 1906 the ladies of the church formed the Guild of the Episcopal Church. They elected Esther vice president of the organization.[51]

After Stilwell's death, Buffalo Bill Cody did not forget him. He wrote: "Of all the scouts reared in the Far West during the Indian uprisings, Jack Stilwell died with a record of having performed one of the most heroic actions known in the annals of Indian warfare on the American frontier. . . . His wit and philosophical remarks are still a matter of comment out West."[52] Cody also wrote about a so-called debate between Stilwell and another plainsman who had seen a cyclone. The plainsman insisted that he saw a cyclone while riding alone on the plains. Stilwell, Cody noted, insisted that it took two men to see the fast, uncertain movement of a cyclone: one man to say, "Here it comes," and the second man to say, "There she goes." Buffalo Bill then retold the story of teenage Jack Stilwell and his heroism at Beecher Island.[53]

Nor did Esther Stilwell Hammitt forget her former husband. She assisted W. T. Gent in the preparation of a biographical sketch of his life for the *Dictionary of American Biography*.[54] Stilwell was also remembered in Oklahoma. In an article published in the *Daily Oklahoman* on April 16, 1931, Alvin Rucker described Jack as "'The Silk Hatted Marshal of the Prairies' who came in to Darlington from Wichita, Kansas, riding a mule with a jug tied to the saddle horn and being 'lordly drunk.'" Of course, Rucker, like others, told the amazing story of the Battle of Beecher Island and Jack's heroic walk to Fort Wallace to rescue the command.[55]

Stilwell's memory lived on in Cody for decades through efforts to properly mark his gravesite. When he had been a cowboy in the Bighorn Basin, western author John K. Rollinson had known Jack as "Judge Stilwell." He visited Stilwell's grave in Riverside Cemetery in July 1941 and noted that it was marked by a decayed wooden cross. He wrote to the Wyoming History Department of the State Library in Cheyenne and requested that the Wyoming Historical Landmark Committee place a suitable marker at Stilwell's grave. When no such marker appeared, he contacted George T. Beck, William Cody's aide and Stilwell's old friend at Cody, and made a five-dollar donation for a permanent marker for the grave. Although interested in marking Stilwell's grave, Beck died before the feat was accomplished. Rollinson noted that Esther Hammitt, who had died in 1937, was buried beside Jack and had a stone grave marker, but Rollinson failed to get her first husband's grave marked properly before he died in 1948.[56]

In 1984 Cody's Bob Edgar solved the problem of Jack Stilwell resting in an unmarked grave. Edgar appeared before the Board of Trustees of the Riverside Cemetery District on March 12, 1984. He presented Stilwell's background as an army scout and later a judge. Jack was buried in the old section of the cemetery in an unmarked grave, he said. He requested permission to move his remains to "Old Trail Town," a two-acre site west of Cody where other historical frontiersmen are buried. Cemetery trustees approved the move. Preservation of the past was Bob Edgar's goal at Old Trail Town.[57]

To that end, an article by Frank Boyett published in the *Cody Enterprise* on April 21, 1984, stated that "local history buffs Friday unearthed the unmarked grave of Jack Stilwell and plan to rebury the remains at Old Trail Town with appropriate fanfare." The article stated that Stilwell left no descendants, which was true, but it incorrectly suggested that he was an orphan. Nonetheless, Edgar tried to find relatives to ensure that they had no objection to the grave being moved.[58]

Residents of Cody also heard much of Stilwell in May 1984. Many of his exploits were recounted by Linn Lockwood in the *Cody Enterprise* on May 9. A photo essay by Frank Boyett entitled "Burying the Past" appeared five days later. It stated that about 150 people gathered for the reburial and to pay final tributes to Jack. Ed Tarr and Charley Mielke led the funeral possession. Ervin Russell, commander of the Veterans of Foreign Wars Honor Guard, presented a flag that had been draped over the casket by Bob Edgar. Bob Benson conducted the Masonic rites at the burial. A contingent of mountain men then fired a volley over the grave to end the ceremony.[59] Edgar had large native stones placed at the head of the grave, and a flat stone plaque was inscribed with Jack's name, dates of birth and death, and the words "Frontiersman and Scout at Beecher Island, 1868." Finally, after eighty-one years, Jack had an appropriate headstone.

In 2002 descendants of Stilwell's sister Elizabeth Ann "Lizzy" Stilwell Cooley placed a granite marker in Cody's Riverside Cemetery at Stilwell's original resting place next to his wife. The marker reads: "In Memory of 'Jack' S. E. Stilwell, 1850 to 1903." Today, tourists who pass daily through Cody and Old Trail Town can be reminded of Stilwell and the courage that he displayed as a teenager at Beecher Island.

Yet Stilwell's life was more than Beecher Island. His exploits mark the trajectory of the opening of the West to Anglo settlement: on the Santa Fe Trail, with Custer in Kansas and Indian Territory, and opening new roads through the Texas Panhandle. He was an army scout and courier, a hunting guide for eastern thrill-seekers, and a dare-devil who lived constantly in the saddle in the region he understood so well. As railroads crossed the plains and opened the land for development, he rode as a cowboy on ranches spread across Indian reservations. He went "up the trail" on cattle drives to Kansas shipping towns. He inspected cattle and became an aide and interpreter on the Comanche, Kiowa, and Apache reservation at Anadarko. In his later years he became a close friend and associate of Buffalo Bill Cody.

He served as a deputy U.S. marshal and a U.S. commissioner. As such he was a legal courier, a one-time hangman, and a minor federal judge. He studied law, became an attorney, and served as a lawyer in both Indian Territory and Wyoming. After learning that Wyatt Earp had killed his brother Frank, he traveled to Arizona to investigate the shooting and close out his brother's business.

Stilwell was not without faults. He tended to recklessness. He drank too much and too often. He sometimes bullied folks. He was impatient and occasionally overly aggressive. He had little formal education, having quit school and run away from home. He was often broke, and in his late twenties he began having debilitating health issues, particularly rough cases of arthritis, rheumatism, and a pain in his hip that would not go away.

On the other hand, Stilwell was well liked and made friends easily. He looked to the welfare of his brothers and sisters and was always worried about his mother. The same could not be said for his father, whose abandonment of his mother in 1863 initiated the thirteen-year-old's remarkable path on the frontier. Through letters and reunions, he kept in touch with old friends, particularly his former scouting companions. People enjoyed his company. He was a superb storyteller and raconteur in a time when a skillful narrator was highly prized.

Stilwell was intelligent, self-confident, resourceful, and competent. He spoke Spanish and Comanche, and he understood much of the Plains Indians sign language. He knew the land and topography of the southern Great Plains thoroughly, and in that place he became known as "Comanche Jack." Stilwell made Oklahoma—that is to say, Indian Territory—his home for most of his short life. He was neither rich nor powerful, neither a businessman nor an entrepreneur. His fame, such as it was, relates mainly to a few days in September 1868 at Beecher Island in northeastern Colorado when he was still a teenager.

Nonetheless, Jack Stilwell was larger than life. His personal history cannot be contained in the few historical records that track that life. The newspaper accounts and personal letters give us a glimpse of who he was, but only by considering the wide scope and expansive nature of what he did and where he lived can we begin to capture his true essence. He was an acquaintance of, and aide to, such western luminaries as George Armstrong Custer, Buffalo Bill Cody, Nelson Miles, Quanah Parker, and Ranald S. Mackenzie. "Comanche Jack" Stilwell played a meaningful, if often unfamiliar, role on the Great Plains of the American West. His story is a part of the fabric that holds the western frontier together. He should not be forgotten.

NOTES

Chapter 1. Family Background and Youth

1. John E. Stilwell, *The History of Lieutenant Nicholas Stillwell: Progenitor of the Stilwell Family in America* (New York: n.p., 1929–31), 46. Spellings of the family name, Stilwell and Stillwell, have been interchangeable over the years. Nicholas Stillwell, the family's founder in America, used four "ls." Jack's great-grandfather Jeremiah, who settled in Indiana, also used four "ls," but Jack's grandfather Joseph used three "ls," as did Jack's father (William Henry), and Jack's uncle Jacob.

2. Ibid.

3. Teunis G. Bergem, *Register of the Early Settlers of Kings County, Long Island, N.Y.* (Cottonport, N.Y.: Polyanthus, 1973): 277–78.

4. Ibid., 278–79. See also Harry T. Williams, *The History of American Wars: From Colonial Times to World War I* (New York: Alfred A. Knoph, 1981), 13, 14–15.

5. Bergem, *Register of the Early Settlers*, 276.

6. Anson West, *History of Methodism in Alabama* (Spartanburg, S.C.: Reprint Company, 1983), 137.

7. Index to the 1830 Census of Alabama, extracts from Chancery Court Books, Madison County, Ala., 1826–35.

8. Sixth U.S. Census, 1840, Jackson County, Ind., 63.

9. *History of Jackson County, Indiana* (Evansville, Ind.: Unigraphic, 1972), 871, 876.

10. Seventh U.S. Census, 1850, Redding Township, Jackson County, Ind., p. 125; Eighth U.S. Census, 1860, Dallas County, Tex., p. 298, line 24.

11. Marriage Book, Lawrence County, Ind., marriages 1844–51, license no. 907; Seventh U.S. Census, 1850, Pleasant Run Township, Lawrence County, Ind., 433, 444.

12. Seventh U.S. Census, 1850, Johnson County, Iowa, District No. 9, Iowa City, 161; Eighth U.S. Census, 1860, Palmyra Township, Douglas County, Kans., 115.

13. U.S. Department of the Interior, Office of Special Examiner, Bureau of Pensions, Case of Mariah Stilwell, no. 587090, widow of William H. Stilwell, Pvt., Company B, 18th Missouri Infantry, Kansas City, Mo., July 3, 1896, Record Group (RG) 15, National Archives (NA) (hereafter cited as Pension Request of Mariah Stilwell, RG 15, NA).

14. Report of H. M. Burfield, Special Examiner, to Commissioner of Pensions, Guthrie, O.T., August 20, 1897, Pension Request of Maria Stilwell, RG 15, NA.

15. Ibid. The Burfield report included the testimony of Lottie M. Williams, niece of William Henry.

16. William J. Gent, "Simpson Everett Stilwell," in *Dictionary of American Biography*, vol. 9, pt. 2, p. 31.

17. Ibid.

18. "Death of Judge Stilwell," *Cody* (Wyo.) *Enterprise*, February 19, 1902.

19. General Index to Deeds and Register of Deeds, 1854–64, Douglas County, Kans., Land bought and sold by William H. and Charlotte B. Stilwell.

20. Eighth U.S. Census, 1860, Palmyra Township, Douglas County, Kans., Post Office: Prairie City, p. 115, line 6.

21. Kansas Territorial Census, 1857, Calhoun Township (later Palmyra Township), Douglas County; Kansas Territorial Census, 1859, Voter Registration, Palmyra Township, Douglas County; Kansas Territorial Census, 1859, Palmyra Township, Douglas County, p. 15, line 14.

22. Katharine B. Kelly, *Along the Santa Fe Trail in Douglas County, Kansas: A Brief History of the Seven D.A.R. Marker Sites and Town Sites* (Baldwin City, Kans.: n.p., 1987), 12–15.

23. Ibid.

24. John Kingsley Ebright, *The History of Baker University* (Baldwin City, Kans.: Baker University, 1951), 65.

25. Virginia Gatch Markham, *John Baldwin and Son Milton Come to Kansas: An Early History of Baldwin City, Baker University, and Methodism in Kansas* (Baldwin City, Kans.: Baker University, 1982), 325.

26. General Index to Deeds and Register of Deeds, 1854–64, Douglas County, Kans., Book A, July 20, 1858, p. 460.

27. Ibid., Book C, July 13, 1859, p. 64, and July 23, 1859, p. 65.

28. Ibid., Book D, August 30, 1860, p. 336 (Lot 2, Block 67, Palmyra); Book E, October 27, 1860, p. 200 (Lot 2, Block 67, Palmyra); Book E, October 6, 1860, p. 224 (Lot 42, G. Street, Baldwin).

29. Eighth U.S. Census, 1860, Palmyra Township, Douglas County, Kans., p. 115, line 6.

30. General Index to Deeds and Register of Deeds, 1854–64, Douglas County, Kans., Book E, p. 302 (70 acres of NW quarter of Sec. 4, T 15, R 20); ibid., Book E., p. 303 (Lot 42, G Street Baldwin).

31. Ibid., Volume F, p. 15 (80 acres of S. one-half of S. W. quarter of Sec. 33, T 14, R 20).

32. Maxine Kreutzier, Kansas East Commission on Archives and History, Baker University, Baldwin City, Kans., in a letter to Clint E. Chambers, August 12, 1991 (in possession of

authors). Kreutzier wrote, "I have called the public school, our Baldwin Historian and checked the Baker Catalogues and here is what I found . . .: C. A. Stilwell of Baldwin attended Baker University during the school year 1862–63; Phoebe Stilwell of Baldwin attended the school during the years 1862–63, 1863–64, and 1864–65; Anna Stilwell of Baldwin attended Baker during the school year 1881–82; Olive L. Stilwell of Media (western part of Baldwin) was a student in Music; and Clara Stilwell, who started Baker in 1880, was a senior in 1888"; Gent, "Simpson Everett Stilwell," vol. 9, pt. 2, 31.

33. Eighth U.S. Census, 1860, Douglas County, Kans., Palmyra Township, p. 120, line 6.

34. Ibid., line 12; Pension Request of Mariah Stilwell, RG 15, NA; 1900 Oklahoma Census Index, Cleveland County, Lexington, vol. 3, E. D. 28, sheet 9, line 38; *Cody* (Wyo.) *Enterprise*, February 19, 1902. Elizabeth Ann "Lizzy" Stilwell married Joseph E. Cooley on October 21, 1879, in Brownstown, Ind. See Marriage Book, Jackson County, Ind., Book H, 212.

35. See Deposition of S. E. Stilwell, August 19, 1897, Pension Request of Mariah Stilwell, RG 15, NA.

36. Ibid.

37. Ibid.

38. See U.S. Supreme Court, *The United States vs. the State of Texas*, Deposition of S. E. Stilwell, March 31, 1894, O.T., #4, 732, RG 267, NA (hereafter cited as Deposition of S. E. Stilwell, March 31, 1894, *U.S. vs. Texas*). See also Clint E. Chambers, "Using the Deposition of S. E. Stilwell in *The United States vs. the State of Texas* to Scout the Life of 'Jack' Stilwell," *West Texas Historical Association Year Book* 67 (1991): 111.

39. Deposition of S. E. Stilwell, August 19, 1897, Pension Request of Mariah Stilwell, RG 15, NA.

Chapter 2. On the Santa Fe Trail

1. Ray Allen Billington, *The Far Western Frontier, 1830–1860* (New York: Harper & Row, 1956), 28–29.

2. Ibid., 23–40. Marc Simmons, *The Old Trail to Santa Fe: Collected Essays* (Albuquerque: University of New Mexico Press, 1996), 2–21; Marc Simmons, "The Santa Fe Trail as High Adventure," in *Adventure on the Santa Fe Trail*, ed. Leo E. Oliva (Topeka: Kansas State Historical Society, 1988), 1–10.

3. Billington, *Far Western Frontier*, 28–29. By 1833 Franklin had been washed away and Independence was less attractive as the eastern terminus of the trail.

4. Kelly, *Along the Santa Fe Trail*, 12–15; Chambers, "Using the Deposition of S. E. Stilwell," 111–21.

5. Deposition of S. E. Stilwell, March 31, 1894, *U.S. vs. Texas*.

6. Ibid.

7. Ibid.

8. Ibid.

9. Donald R. Hale, "The Old Plainsmen's Association," ed. Mark L. Gardner, *Wagon Tracks* 14, no. 3 (May 2000): 17, 18.

10. Simmons, "Santa Fe Trail as High Adventure," 2–10.

11. Charles R. Strom, *Charles G. Parker: Wagonmaster on the Santa Fe Trail* (White City, Kans.: Village Press, 1999), 42, 43.

12. Mark L. Gardner, "Malcolm Conn: Merchant of the Trail," *Wagon Tracks* 1, no. 2 (February 1987): 7–8.

13. Albert Castel, *Civil War Kansas: Reaping the Whirlwind* (Lawrence: University Press of Kansas, 1997), 124–41.

14. Ibid., 142–53.

15. Lalla Malog Brigham, *The Story of Council Grove on the Santa Fe Trail,* 4th ed. (Council Grove, Kans.: Morris County Historical Society, 1989), 31.

16. David J. Clapsaddle and Leo Oliva, eds., *The Fort Riley–Fort Larned Road: A Phenomenon in the Shift from Trail to Rail* (Woodson, Kans.: Santa Fe Trail Association Publication, 1996), 104.

17. David J. Strate, ed., *West by Southwest: Letters of Joseph Pratt Allyn, a Traveler along the Santa Fe Trail, 1863* (Dodge City: Kansas Heritage Center, 1984; reprint, Dodge City: Village Press, 1999), 37.

18. Chambers, "Using the Deposition of S. E. Stilwell," 111–121; Orval A. Criqui, *Fifty Fearless Men: The Forsyth Scouts and Beecher Island* (Marceline, Mo.: Walsworth Publishing, 1993), 204.

19. Deposition of S. E. Stilwell, March 31, 1894, *U.S. vs. Texas.*

20. Ibid.; Williams, *History of American Wars,* 300–301; Russell F. Weigley, *History of the United States Army* (New York: Macmillan, 1967), 222–23.

21. Deposition of S. E. Stilwell, March 31, 1894, *U.S. vs. Texas.*

22. Deposition of S. E. Stilwell, August 19, 1897, Pension Request of Maria Stilwell, RG 15, NA.

23. Ibid.

24. Deposition of S. E. Stilwell, March 31, 1894, *U.S. vs. Texas.*

25. David Remley, *Kit Carson: The Life of an American Border Man* (Norman: University of Oklahoma Press, 2012), 211–18; Thelma S. Guild and Harvey L. Carter, *Kit Carson: A Pattern for Heroes* (Lincoln: University of Nebraska Press, 1984), 222–24.

26. Leo E. Oliva, *Soldiers on the Santa Fe Trail* (Norman: University of Oklahoma Press, 1967), 145; Gerald Thompson, *The Army and the Navajo: The Bosque Redondo Reservation Experiment, 1863–1868* (Tucson: University of Arizona Press, 1976), 10–17.

27. Charles L. Kenner, *The Comanchero Frontier: A History of New Mexican–Plains Indian Relations* (Norman: University of Oklahoma Press, 1994), 143.

28. Ibid., 98–102. See also Randy Vance, "Comancheros," in *Hidden History of the Llano Estacado,* ed. Paul H. Carlson and David J. Murrah (Charleston, S.C.: History Press, 2017), 33–36.

29. Clifford E. Trafzer, *The Kit Carson Campaign: The Last Great Navajo War* (Norman: University of Oklahoma Press, 1982), 167–69; Remley, *Kit Carson,* 226–31; Guild and Carter, *Kit Carson,* 231–49.

30. Trafzer, *Kit Carson Campaign,* 167–69; Remley, *Kit Carson,* 231.

31. Thompson, *Army and the Navajo,* 10–17; Trafzer, *Kit Carson Campaign,* 167–69.

32. Hale, "Old Plainsmen's Association," 18, 19; Charles Raber, "Personal Recollections of Life on the Plains from 1860 to 1866," *Kansas Historical Collections* 16 (1923–25): 238.

33. Raber, "Personal Recollections," 328.
34. Clint E. Chambers, "Texas Panhandle Branches of the Old Santa Fe Trail in the 1860s," *Wagon Tracks* 28, no. 1 (November 2013): 10–13.
35. Deposition of S. E. Stilwell, March 31, 1894, *U.S. vs. Texas*.
36. George H. Pettis, "Kit Carson's Fight with the Comanche and Kiowa Indians," *Order of the Indian Wars* 1, no. 4 (Summer 1980): 14. See also Remley, *Kit Carson*, 231–36; Guild and Carter, *Kit Carson*, 250–56; Alvin R. Lynn, *Kit Carson and the First Battle of Adobe Walls: A Tale of Two Journeys* (Lubbock: Texas Tech University Press, 2014), 6–20.
37. Gen. James H. Carleton to Maj. Edward H. Bergmann, March 15, 1865, Letters Sent, Department of New Mexico, Arnott Collection, vol. 16, p. 219, Highlands University Library, Las Vegas, New Mexico (hereafter Arnott Collection).
38. Thompson, *Army and the Navajo*, 73.
39. Bergmann to Maj. C. H. DeForrest, May 13, 1866, Letters Sent, Fort Bascom, Arnott Collection, vol. 49, pp. 44–47.
40. Carleton to Bergmann, April 12, 1865, Letters Sent, Department of New Mexico, Arnott Collection, vol. 16, p. 260.
41. In F. Stanley, *Fort Bascom: Comanche-Kiowa Barrier* (Pampa, Tex.: Pampa Print Shop, 1961), 21–24.
42. Ibid.
43. Ibid.
44. Deposition of S. E. Stilwell, March 31, 1894, *U.S. vs. Texas*.
45. Annette Grey, *Journey of the Heart: A True Story of Mamie Aguirre (1844–1907), a Southern Belle in the "Wild West"* (Markerville, Alberta: Greywest Books, 2001), 92; Dorlis A. Miller, "Freighting for Uncle Sam," *Wagon Tracks* 5 (November 1990): 13.
46. Remley, *Kit Carson*, 231.
47. Deposition of S. E. Stilwell, March 31, 1894, *U.S. vs. Texas*. See also Clint E. Chambers, "Jack Stilwell: A Teenager on the Santa Fe Trail, 1863–66," *West Texas Historical Association Year Book* 84 (2008): 20–30.
48. Kenner, *The Comanchero Frontier*, 98–100, 102–5.
49. Marc Simmons, *Coronado's Land: Essays on Daily Life in Colonial New Mexico* (Albuquerque: University of New Mexico Press, 1991), 97–102. See also Fabiola Cabeza de Baca, *We Fed Them Cactus* (Albuquerque: University of New Mexico Press, 1954), 44.
50. Miguel Antonio Otero, *My Life on the Frontier, 1864–1882* (1935; reprint, Albuquerque: University of New Mexico Press, 1987), 35; Simmons, *Old Trail to Santa Fe*, 43–44.
51. C. Robert Haywood, *Trails South: The Wagon Road Economy in the Dodge City–Panhandle Region* (Norman: University of Oklahoma Press, 1986), 6–7; Joseph W. Snell, ed., "Diary of Dodge City Buffalo Hunter, 1872–1873," *Kansas Historical Quarterly* 31 (Winter 1965): 373; George W. Brown, "Recollections," n.p., Manuscript No. 4, Boot Hill Museum, Dodge City, Kans.
52. U.S. Department of War, Quartermaster General Reports, Reports of Persons and Articles Employed and Hired, Fort Dodge, Kans., June 1867, RG 92, NA (hereafter QGR, Reports of Persons Hired).

208   NOTES TO CHAPTER 3

Chapter 3. Scouting for the Army in Kansas

1. George Armstrong Custer, *My Life on the Plains or, Personal Experiences with Indians* (Norman: University of Oklahoma Press, 1962), 191.
2. Ibid.
3. Elizabeth Bacon Custer, *Boots and Saddles or, Life in Dakota with General Custer* (Norman: University of Oklahoma Press, 1961), 120.
4. Leo E. Oliva, *Fort Dodge: Sentry of the Western Plains* (Topeka: Kansas State Historical Society, 1998), 23.
5. QGR, Reports of Persons Hired, Fort Dodge, Kans., March, April, May, and June 1867, #280, Box 345, RG 92, NA.
6. Ibid.; U.S. Department of War, Adjutant General's Office (AGO), Returns of United States Military Posts, 1800–1916, Fort Dodge, Kans., June 1867, RG 94, NA (hereafter Post Returns).
7. QGR, Reports of Persons Hired, Fort Dodge, Kans., May–June 1867, RG 92, NA; Post Returns, Fort Dodge, Kans., June 1867, AGO, RG 94, NA. See also Oliva, *Fort Dodge*, 23–24.
8. U.S. Department of War, Headquarters, Fort Dodge, Kans., July 20, 1867, Special Order No. 85, U.S. Army Continental Commands, RG 393, NA.
9. Quoted in Oliva, *Fort Dodge*, 23–24; Headquarters, Fort Dodge, Kans., Letters Sent, Maj. Henry Douglass to Brev. Brig. Gen. Chauncey McKeever, Assistant Adjutant General (AAG), Department of Missouri, June 18, 1867, AGO, RG 94, NA.
10. Quoted in Oliva, *Fort Dodge*, 23–24; Louise Barry, "The Ranch at Cimarron Crossing," *Kansas Historical Quarterly* 39, no. 3 (Autumn 1973); 353–61; Jack Stilwell, Pension Petition Testimony, "A Bill Granting a Pension to Simpson Everett Stilwell," Senate Bill 2728 and Senate Report 667, 54th Cong., 1st Sess., May 22, 1896 (hereafter Stilwell Pension Testimony, May 22, 1896).
11. Barry, "Ranch at Cimarron Crossing," 353–61; Francis H. Heitman, *Historical Register and Dictionary of the United States Army, 1789–1903* (Washington: Government Printing Office, 1903), 2:428–29; Stilwell Pension Testimony, May 22, 1896.
12. Barry, "Ranch at Cimarron Crossing," 359. See also Sondra Van Meter McCoy, "Central Kansas Trading Ranches on the Santa Fe Trail," in Leo E. Oliva, *Adventures on the Santa Fe Trail* (Topeka: Kansas State Historical Society, 1988), 107–22.
13. QGR, Reports of Persons Hired, Fort Dodge, Kans., July 1867, RG 92, NA; Ramon Powers and Gene Younger, "Cholera on the Plains: The Epidemic of 1867 in Kansas," *Kansas Historical Quarterly* 37, no. 4 (Winter 1971): 379. See also Sarah Keyes, "Western Adventurers and Male Nurses: Indians, Cholera, and Masculinity in Overland Trail Narratives," *Western Historical Quarterly* 43, no. 1 (Spring 2018): 43–64.
14. Samuel J. Crawford, *Kansas in the Sixties* (1911; reprint, Ottawa: Kansas Heritage Press, 1994), 254–60.
15. Ibid.
16. Ibid. See also Elliott West, *The Contested Plains: Indians, Goldseekers, and the Rush to Colorado* (Lawrence: University Press of Kansas, 1998), 309–10; Ralph K. Andrist, *The Long Death: The Last Days of the Plains Indians* (New York: Collier Books, 1964),

135, 143–44; Robert M. Utley, *The Indian Frontier of the American West, 1846–1890* (Albuquerque: University of New Mexico Press, 1984), 107–8, 12–14.

17. Henry M. Stanley, *My Early Travels and Adventures in America* (1895; reprint, Lincoln: University of Nebraska Press, 1982), 138–40.

18. Ibid.; Crawford, *Kansas in the Sixties*, 254–60; Post Returns, Fort Harker, Kans., July 1867, AGO, RG 393, NA.

19. Post Returns, Fort Dodge, Kans., August 31,1867, Record of Events on August 7 and 8, AGO, RG 393, NA; Powers and Younger, "Cholera on the Plains," 379; West, *The Contested Plains*, 310.

20. Henderson Lafayette Burgess, "The Eighteenth Kansas Volunteer Cavalry, and Some Incidents Connected with Its Service on the Plains," *Collections of the Kansas State Historical Society* 13 (1913–14): 536. See also Clint E. Chambers, "Surviving Disease on the Plains," *Wagon Tracks* 20, no. 3 (May 2006): 10–13.

21. Wayne C. Lee and Howard C. Raynesford, *Trails of the Smoky Hill from Coronado to Cow Towns* (Caldwell, Idaho: Caxton Press, 1980), 34–35; "A Hero of America's Gamest Battle Here," *Kansas City Star*, September 5, 1909. The battle referred to in the title of the article was the September 1868 Battle of Beecher Island during Pliley's service as a Forsyth Scout.

22. William Y. Chalfant, *Hancock's War: Conflict on the Southern Plains* (Norman, Okla.: Arthur H. Clark, 2010), 135–45; Robert M. Utley, *Frontier Regulars: The United States Army and the Indian, 1866–1865* (New York: Macmillan, 1973), 114, 115–25.

23. George A. Armes, *Ups and Downs of an Army Officer* (Washington, D.C.: n.p., 1900), 589–93; Stilwell Pension Testimony, May 22, 1896.

24. Utley, *Frontier Regulars*, 119–20; Armes, *Ups and Downs*, 231–56.

25. Col. W. S. Nye, *Plains Indian Raiders: The Final Phases of Warfare from the Arkansas to the Red River, with Original Photographs by William S. Soule* (Norman: University of Oklahoma Press, 1968), 102.

26. Armes, *Ups and Downs*, 231–56.

27. Ibid.; George B. Jenness, "The Battle of Beaver Creek," *Kansas Historical Collections* 9 (1905–6): 443–52; Ron Field, *Buffalo Soldiers, 1866–1891* (Oxford, U.K.: Osprey Publishing, 2004), 13; William H. Leckie and Shirley A. Leckie, *The Buffalo Soldiers: A Narrative of the Black Cavalry in the West*, rev. ed. (Norman: University of Oklahoma Press, 2003), 23–25. Armes and Jenness miscalled Beaver Creek as the site of the battle, which was actually fought on Prairie Dog Creek.

28. Armes, *Ups and Downs*, 231–56; Jenness, "Battle of Beaver Creek," 443–52; Leckie and Leckie, *The Buffalo Soldiers*, 23–25; Organizational Returns, Tenth Cavalry, August 1867, AGO, RG 94, NA.

29. Jenness, "Battle of Beaver Creek," 443–52.

30. Ibid.

31. Ibid., 447–49.

32. Lonnie J. White, *Hostiles and Horse Soldiers: Indian Battles and Campaigns in the West* (Boulder, Colo.: Pruett Publishing, 1972), 49–64.

33. Armes, *Ups and Downs*, 231–56.

34. Maj. Horace L. Moore, Eighteenth Kansas Volunteer Calvary, to Gen. Landon
    D. Easton, Quartermaster, September 23, 1876, Letters Received, Department of
    Missouri, Army Continental Commands, RG 393, NA.

35. Frank N. Schubert, *Voices of the Buffalo Soldiers: Records, Reports and Recollections
    of Military Life and Service in the West* (Albuquerque: University of New Mexico
    Press, 2003), 15–20.

36. See Armes, *Ups and Downs*, 245–48, and Jenness, "Battle of Beaver Creek," 536.

37. Moore, Eighteenth Kansas Volunteer Cavalry, to 1st Lt. J. B. Weir, Seventh Cavalry,
    Letters Received, Department of Missouri, Army Continental Commands, RG 393,
    NA; Stilwell Pension Testimony May 22, 1896.

38. Jenness, "Battle of Beaver Creek," 443–52.

39. Ibid.

40. Utley, *Indian Frontier of the American West*, 114–18; Andrist, *The Long Death*, 145–47.

41. Douglas C. Jones, *The Treaty of Medicine Lodge: The Story of the Great Treaty Council
    as Told by Eyewitnesses* (Norman: University of Oklahoma Press, 1966), 49.

42. Ibid. 38–39; Paul H. Carlson, *The Plains Indians* (College Station: Texas A&M Uni-
    versity Press, 1998), 152–55; Moore to Headquarters, Eighteenth Kansas Volunteer
    Cavalry, September 30, 1867, Letters Received, Department of Missouri, Book 530,
    p. 364, item 996.

43. Jones, *Treaty of Medicine Lodge*, 40–42.

44. Ibid., 45–47. See also Stan Hoig, *White Man's Paper Trail: Grand Councils and Treaty-
    Making on the Central Plains* (Boulder: University Press of Colorado, 2006), 144–49.

45. Burgess, "Eighteenth Kansas and Its Service on the Plains," 537.

46. U.S. Department of War, Department of Missouri, Fort Dodge, Kans., Special Order
    129, October 13, 1867, Army Continental Commands, RG 393, NA.

47. U.S. Department of War, Department of Missouri, Fort Dodge, Kans., Special Order
    141, November 3, 1867, Army Continental Commands, RG 393, NA.

48. Forest B. Blackburn, "The 18th Kansas Cavalry and the Indian War," *The Trail Guide*
    9, no. 1 (March 1964): 12–13; Stilwell Pension Testimony, May 22, 1896; S. E. Stilwell,
    Testimony, March 27, 1879, 408, Court-Martial of William H. Beck, File QQ-1107,
    Judge Advocate Office, Department of War, RG 153, NA.

Chapter 4. The Battle of Beecher Island

1. Utley, *Frontier Regulars*, 147–48; Andrist, *The Long Death*, 148–54. For eyewitness
   accounts, see Peter Cozzens, ed., *Eyewitnesses to the Indian Wars*, vol. 3, *Conquering
   the Southern Plains* (Mechanicsburg, Pa.: Stackpole Books, 2003), 128–237.

2. John H. Monett, *The Battle of Beecher Island and the Indian War of 1867–1869* (Niwot:
   University Press of Colorado, 1992), 58.

3. White, *Hostiles and Horse Soldiers*, 69; see also Utley, *Frontier Regulars*, 147.

4. Adolph Roenigh, *Pioneer History of Kansas* (1933; reprint, Salina, Kans.: Lincoln
   County Historical Society, 1973), 113.

5. Fletcher Vilott, as told to A. Bailey, "Withstood the Siege: The Story of Col. George
   A. Forsythe's Brave Defense at Arickaree Fork," *National Tribune* 26, nos. 4 and 5
   (November 5 and 12, 1896): 1–4, 1–8.

6. QGR, Reports of Persons Hired, Fort Hays, Kans., September 1868, AGO, RG 92, NA.

7. Monett, *Battle of Beecher Island*, 121–22; Sigmund Schlesinger, "Scout Schlesinger's Story," in *The Beecher Island Annual: Sixty-Second Anniversary of the Battle of Beecher Island September 17–18, 1868*, ed. Robert Lynam (Wray, Colo.: Beecher Island Battle Memorial Association, 1930), 75–82.

8. David Dixon and Orvel Criqui, "Forsyth's Scouts: Unit History," *Military Images* 14, no. 6 (May–June 1993): 24.

9. Ibid.; George A. Forsyth, *The Story of the Soldier* (New York: D. Appleton and Co., 1900), 211–12.

10. David Dixon, *Hero of Beecher Island: The Life and Military Career of George A. Forsyth* (Lincoln: University of Nebraska Press, 1994), 70–71.

11. Ibid.

12. Ibid.

13. Ibid.; see also Vilott, "Withstood the Siege."

14. Dixon, *Hero of Beecher Island*, 70–71.

15. Vilott, "Withstood the Siege"; Andrist, *The Long Death*, 149.

16. John Hurst, "Scout John Hurst's Story of the Fight," in *The Beecher Island Annual*, ed. Robert Lynam, 68–73; Lonnie J. White, "The Battle of Beecher Island: The Scouts Hold Fast on the Arickaree, *Journal of the West* 5 (January 1966): 5; Utley, *Frontier Regulars*, 147–48.

17. White, "Battle of Beecher Island," 4–8, Vilott, "Withstood the Siege"; Andrist, *The Long Death*, 149.

18. Vilott, "Withstood the Siege."

19. Hurst, "Scout John Hurst's Story," 68–73; Winfield Freeman, "The Battle of Arickaree," *Collections of the Kansas State Historical Society* 6 (1900), 349.

20. Schlesinger, "Scout Schlesinger's Story," 75–82.

21. George Washington Oaks, *Man of the West: Reminiscences of George Washington Oaks, 1840–1917*, ed. Ben Jaastad and Arthur Woodward (Tucson: Arizona Pioneers Historical Society, 1956), 31.

22. "An Interview with Scout John Hurst," Manuscript 57, Box 4, Walter M. Camp Papers, Interview Notes, September 11, 1916, Special Collections and Manuscripts, Harold B. Lee Library, Brigham Young University, Utah; Andrist, *The Long Death*, 148–54.

23. Jack Stilwell, interview with Fred Wenner, Fred L. Wenner Collection, Western History Collections, University of Oklahoma Library, Norman (hereafter Stilwell interview with Wenner).

24. Ibid.

25. Ibid.

26. Stilwell interview with Wenner.

27. Ibid.

28. Schlesinger, "Scout Schlesinger's Story," 75–82; Cyrus Townsend Brady, *Indian Fights and Fighters* (1904; reprint, Lincoln: University of Nebraska Press, 1971), 121.

29. Monett, *Battle of Beecher Island*, 152.

30. Sigmund Schlesinger Collection (1868–1975), S. E. Stilwell, Anadarko, O.T., to Schlesinger, Cleveland, Ohio, September 21, 1897, MS #130, American Jewish Archives, Hebrew Union College, Cincinnati; U.S. Department of War, Department of Missouri, Report of Col. George A. Forsyth to Bvt. Brig. Gen. Clancy McKeever, Asst. Adj. Gen., Fort Leavenworth, March 31, 1869, U.S. Army Commands, RG 393, NA.

31. Andrist, *The Long Death*, 153; Homer W. Wheeler, *The Frontier Trail, or From Cowboy to Colonel* (Los Angeles: Times Mirror Press, 1933), 36, 37.

32. Stilwell interview with Wenner.

33. Ibid.

34. Franz Huning, *Trader on the Santa Fe Trail: The Memoirs of Franz Huning* (Albuquerque, N.Mex.: Calvin Horn Publisher, 1973), 97; Leckie and Leckie, *The Buffalo Soldiers*, 34–35.

35. Andrist, *The Long Death*, 148–54; Utley, *Frontier Regulars*, 147–48.

36. Monett, *Battle of Beecher Island*, 156–75; Brady, *Indian Fights and Fighters*, 121–22; Returns of Military Posts, Fort Wallace, Kans., September 1868, AGO, RG 94, NA.

37. Returns of Military Posts, Fort Wallace, Kans., September 1868, AGO, RG 94, NA.

38. Department of War, Department of Missouri, Report, Maj. George A. Forsyth to Bvt. Brig. Gen. Chauncey McKeever, March 31, 1869, U.S. Army Continental Commands, AGO, RG 393, NA; Department of War, Organizational Returns, Tenth Cavalry, September 1868; Monett, *Battle of Beecher Island*, 121–22.

39. Schlesinger, "Scout Schlesinger's Story," 75–82; Brady, *Indian Fights and Fighters*, 121–22; Wheeler, *The Frontier Trail*, 36–37.

40. Stilwell interview with Wenner; Utley, *Frontier Regulars*, 148.

41. Utley, *Frontier Regulars*, 148.

42. Ibid. See also Carlson, *The Plains Indians*, 145.

43. George E. Hyde, *Life of George Bent Written from his Letters*, edited by Savoie Lottinville (Norman: University of Oklahoma Press, 1968), 303.

44. George A. Forsyth, *Thrilling Days in Army Life* (Lincoln: University of Nebraska Press, 1994), 60–61; Stilwell Pension Testimony, May 22, 1896.

45. Stilwell Pension Testimony, May 22, 1896.

46. Criqui, *Fifty Fearless Men*, 210.

Chapter 5. Scouting with Custer

1. Jerome A. Greene, *Washita: The U.S. Army and the Southern Cheyenne, 1867–1869* (Norman: University of Oklahoma Press, 2004), 48. See also Philip Weeks, *Farewell, My Nation: The American Indian and the United States, 1820–1890* (Arlington Heights, Ill.: Harlan Davidson, 1990), 143; Carlson, *The Plains Indians*, 156–57; Col. W. S. Nye, *Carbine and Lance: The Story of Old Fort Sill*, rev. ed. (Norman: University of Oklahoma Press, 1974), 60–63. For first-hand accounts, see Cozzens, *Eyewitnesses to the Indian Wars*, 3:256–410.

2. Utley, *Frontier Regulars*, 149–50; Carlson, *The Plains Indians*, 156–57; Andrist, *The Long Death*, 155–57.

3. Stilwell Pension Testimony, May 22, 1896.

4. Horace L. Moore, "The Nineteenth Kansas Cavalry," *Collections of the Kansas State Historical Society* 6 (1897–1900): 38; quote in Andrist, *The Long Death*, 157. See also Stan Hoig, *Tribal Wars of the Southern Plains* (Norman: University of Oklahoma Press, 1993), 253.

5. QGR, Reports of Persons Hired, Fort Hays, Kans., October 1868, RG 92, NA; Paul Andrew Hutton, *Phil Sheridan and His Army* (Lincoln: University of Nebraska Press, 1985), 48.

6. George W. Brown, "The Life and Adventures of George W. Brown: Soldier, Pioneer, Scout, Plainsman, and Buffalo Hunter," ed. William E. Connelley, *Collections of the Kansas State Historical Society* 17 (1926–28): 102; David L. Spotts, *Campaigning with Custer*, ed. E. A. Brininstool (1928; reprint, Lincoln: University of Nebraska Press, 1988), 52; Oaks, *Man of the West*, 33–34.

7. Stilwell Pension Testimony, May 22, 1896; Nye, *Carbine and Lance*, 59.

8. Moore, "Nineteenth Kansas Cavalry," 38.

9. William E. Connelley, ed., "John McBee's Account of the Expedition of the Nineteenth Kansas," *Collections of the Kansas State Historical Society* 17 (1926–28): 361.

10. Ibid.

11. James R. Mead, *Hunting and Trading on the Great Plains, 1859–1875*, ed. Schuyler Jones and Ignace Mead Jones (Norman: University of Oklahoma Press, 1986), 226–27.

12. Deposition of S. E. Stilwell, March 31, 1894, *U.S. vs. Texas*.

13. Mead, *Hunting and Trading on the Great Plains*, 226–27.

14. Henry Pearson, "Campaign against Indians in Oklahoma, Kansas, Colorado, New Mexico, and Indian Territory," *Winners of the West* 7, no. 1 (December 1926): 5.

15. Ibid.; Luther A. Thrasher, "Diary of Luther A. Thrasher, Quartermaster Nineteenth Kansas Cavalry, October 15 to December 31, 1868," *Collections of the Kansas State Historical Society* 10 (1907–8): 660–63.

16. Pearson, "Campaign against Indians," 4–6.

17. Ibid.; Deposition of S. E. Stilwell, March 31, 1894, *U.S. vs. Texas*.

18. Thrasher, "Diary," 660–63.

19. Moore, "Nineteenth Kansas Cavalry," 38–39.

20. De Benneville Randolph Keim, *Sheridan's Troopers on the Borders: A Winter Campaign on the Plains* (1885; reprint, Lincoln: University of Nebraska Press, 1985), 105–7.

21. Spotts, *Campaigning with Custer*, 64.

22. Thrasher, "Diary," 660–63; Utley, *Frontier Regulars*, 149. See also Nye, *Carbine and Lance*, 59–61.

23. Hoig, *Tribal Wars*, 252–59.

24. Quoted in Utley, *Frontier Regulars*, 149; Hoig, *White Man's Paper Trail*, 166–69. See also Don Russell, *The Lives and Legends of Buffalo Bill* (Norman: University of Oklahoma Press, 1960), 110–14.

25. Fred S. Barde, "Edmund Gasseau Choteau Guerrier: French Trader," *Chronicles of Oklahoma* 47, no. 4 (Winter 1969–70): 374; Hoig, *Tribal Wars*, 268.

26. Greene, *Washita*, 176–77; Hoig, *Tribal Wars*, 264–68.

27. Carl Coke Rister, ed., "Colonel A. W. Evans's Christmas Day Indian Fight, 1868," *Chronicles of Oklahoma* 16, no. 3 (September 1938): 286–99; Deposition of S. E. Stilwell, March 31, 1894, *U.S. vs. Texas*.

28. Disposition of S. E. Stilwell, March 31, 1894, *U.S. vs. Texas*; Edward Hunter, "Colonel Evans's Indian Expedition," in Cozzens, *Eyewitnesses to the Indian Wars*, 3:404–6.

29. Rister, "Evans's Christmas Day Indian Fight," 286–99.

30. Hoig, *Tribal Wars*, 252–64; Utley, *Frontier Regulars*, 149–52; Pekka Hämäläinen, *The Comanche Empire* (New Haven, Conn.: Yale University Press, 2008), 325–26.

31. Hoig, *Tribal Wars*, 258; Nye, *Carbine and Lance*, 70.

32. John Ryan and Sandy Barnard, eds., *Ten Years with Custer: A 7th Cavalryman's Memoirs* (Fort Collins, Colo.: Citizen Printing, 2001), 61.

33. Nye, *Carbine and Lance*, 70–71.

34. Ibid.

35. Ibid., 70–74; Moore, "Nineteenth Kansas Cavalry," 40–43; Andrist, *The Long Death*, 162–63.

36. Nye, *Carbine and Lance*, 70–74; Utley, *Frontier Regulars*, 150–51.

37. Andrist, *The Long Death*, 164–66; Nye, *Carbine and Lance*, 88–89.

38. Philip Henry Sheridan, *Personal Memoirs of P. H. Sheridan, General United States Army* (1888; reprint, New York: Da Capo Press, 1992), 2:345–47; Robert Wooster, *The Military and United States Indian Policy, 1865–1903* (New Haven, Conn.: Yale University Press), 134; Utley, *Frontier Regulars*, 155.

39. Nye, *Carbine and Lance*, 94–95.

40. QGR, Record of Persons Hired, Medicine Bluff Creek, Kans., January 2, 1869, RG 92, NA.

41. Headquarters Department of Missouri, Fort Cobb, to Mr. Clark, Morrison, Corbin, and Stillwell, January 3, 1869, box C-46, Folder 4, Fort Reno, I.T., Ben Clark Papers, Western History Collection, University of Oklahoma Library, Norman.

42. Elizabeth Bacon Custer, *Following the Guidon* (1890; reprint, Lincoln: University of Nebraska Press, 1994), 47.

43. Ibid.

44. Ibid., 53.

45. J. R. Mead to George W. Martin, October 10, 1908, Manuscript Division, Kansas Historical Society, Topeka.

46. Criqui, *Fifty Fearless Men*, 211.

47. Lonnie J. White, ed., "The Nineteenth Kansas Cavalry in the Indian Territory, 1868–1869: Eyewitness Accounts of Sheridan's Winter Campaign," *Red River Valley Historical Review* 3 (1978): 170.

48. Brown, "Life and Adventures," 105–6.

49. James Albert Hadley, "The Nineteenth Kansas Cavalry and the Conquest of the Plains Indians," *Collections of the Kansas State Historical Society* 10 (1907–8): 435.

50. Sheridan, *Personal Memoirs*, 2:13, 465–66.

51. Joseph Phelps Rogers, "A few years of experience on the western frontier, 1867–1869,"

7, Collection/Record Group, Manuscripts Collection Miscellaneous, Unit ID-43549, Kansas Historical Society, Topeka.

Chapter 6. With Buffalo Soldiers on the Southern Plains

1. John Hurst, "The Beecher Island Fight: Battle of the Arikaree," *Collections of the Kansas State Historical Society* 15 (1919–22): 532; Robert G. Carter, *On the Border with Mackenzie: Or, Winning West Texas from the Comanches* (1935; reprint, Austin: Texas State Historical Association Press, 2007), 349–72.
2. U.S. Department of War, Organizational Returns, Tenth Cavalry, June 1869, AGO, RG 92, NA.
3. U.S. Department of War, Department of Missouri, Letters Received, 2nd Lt. Silas Pepoon, Tenth Cavalry to 2nd Lt. Louis Henry Coleman, Adj., Camp Supply, I.T., July 22, 1869, Report of Reconnaissance for Post and Cheyenne Agency, Continental Commands, RG 393, NA; Robert C. Carriker, *Fort Supply, Indian Territory: Frontier Outpost on the Plains* (Norman: University of Oklahoma Press, 1970), 31–35.
4. Adjutant General, United States Army, *Chronological List: Actions, &c. with Indians from January 15, 1837 to January 1891* (Fort Collins, Colo.: Old Army Press, 1979), 45.
5. Carriker, *Fort Supply*, 38–39.
6. Ninth U.S. Census, 1870, Palmyra Township, Kans., Roll M593-433, p. 435 (image 418).
7. Ibid., Owen, Jackson County, Ind., Roll M593-326, p. 315 (image 134).
8. Ibid., St. Joseph Ward 1, Buchanan, Mo., Roll 593-762, p. 419 (image 23).
9. Custer, *My Life on the Plains*, 137.
10. Blaine Burley, *Custer, Come at Once! The Fort Hays Years of George and Elizabeth Custer, 1867–1868* (Hays, Kans.: Thomas Moore Prep, 1976), 47–58.
11. U.S. Department of War, QGR, Service Record of Simpson Everett Stilwell, Index to Scouts, 1870, RG 92, NA.
12. Burley, *Custer, Come at Once!*, 94–96; Post Returns, Fort Hays, Kans., June 1871, AGO, RG 393, NA.
13. Burley, *Custer, Come at Once!*, 99–101.
14. Shirley A. Leckie, *Elizabeth Bacon Custer and the Making of a Myth* (Norman: University of Oklahoma Press, 1993), 124.
15. Brian C. Pohanka, ed., *A Summer on the Plains with Custer's 7th Cavalry: The 1870 Diary of Annie Gibson Roberts* (Lynchburg, Va.: Schroeder Publications, 2004), 62–64.
16. Ibid.; Burley, *Custer, Come at Once!*, 99–101.
17. Pohanka, *Summer on the Plains*, 62–65.
18. Ibid.; Leckie, *Elizabeth Custer and the Making of a Myth*, 144–45; Burley, *Custer, Come at Once!*, 99–101.
19. Burley, *Custer, Come At Once!*, 99–101; see also Richard C. Rattenbury, *Hunting the American West: The Pursuit of Big Game for Life, Profit, and Sport, 1800–1900* (Missoula, Mont.: Boone and Crockett Club, 2008), 298–99.

20. Stilwell Pension Testimony, May 22, 1896.

21. Ibid. See also Special Orders No. 97, June 25, 1871, Fort Sill, I.T., 1869–74, vol. 1, U.S. Army Field Artillery and Fort Sill Museum, Fort Sill, Okla. (hereafter Fort Sill Museum).

22. QGR, Service Record of S. E. Stilwell, Index to scouts, 1870, RG 92, NA; QGR, Report of Persons Hired, Fort Sill, I.T., 1871–74, RG 92, NA; William E. Connelly, ed., "John McBee's Account of the Expedition of the Nineteenth Kansas," *Collections of the Kansas State Historical Society* 17 (1926–28): 364.

23. Special Orders No. 54, March 24,1871, Fort Sill, 1869–74, vol. 1, Fort Sill Museum.

24. Nye, *Carbine and Lance*, 123–32; Charles M. Robinson III, *Satanta: Life and Death of a War Chief* (Austin, Tex.: State House Press, 1997), 113–24; Charles M. Robinson III, *Bad Hand: A Biography of General Ranald S. Mackenzie* (Austin, Tex.: State House Press, 1993), 78–86; Benjamin Capps, *The Warren Wagon Train Raid* (New York: Dial, 1974).

25. Utley, *Frontier Regulars*, 209–10; Hoig, *Tribal Wars*, 172–74.

26. Wooster, *Military and United States Indian Policy*, 44–46, 144–46, 151–52.

27. Ibid., 151–53; Utley, *Frontier Regulars*, 210–11.

28. Charles M. Robinson III, *The Indian Trial: The Complete Story of the Warren Wagon Train Massacre and the Fall of the Kiowa Nation* (Spokane, Wash.: Arthur H. Clark, 1997), 77–79.

29. James M. Merrill, "General Sherman's Letter to His Son: A Visit to Fort Sill," *Chronicles of Oklahoma* 47 (Summer 1969): 126–31.

30. Utley, *Frontier Regulars*, 210–11; Ernest Wallace, *Ranald S. Mackenzie on the Texas Frontier* (College Station, Texas A&M University Press, 1993), 30–31.

31. U.S. Department of War, QGR, Record of Persons Hired, Fort Still, I.T., June 1871, RG 92, NA.

32. U.S. Department of War, Post Returns, Fort Sill, I.T., August 1871, Microscopy 617, Roll #1173, NA.

33. Wallace, *Mackenzie on the Texas Frontier*, 33–36.

34. William H. Leckie and Shirley A. Leckie, *Unlikely Warriors: General Benjamin H. Grierson and His Family* (Norman: University of Oklahoma Press, 1984), 192.

35. Gillett Griswold, "Old Fort Sill: The First Seven Years," *Chronicles of Oklahoma* 36 (Spring 1958): 8.

36. Deposition of S. E. Stilwell, March 31, 1894, *U.S. vs. Texas.*

37. U.S. Department of War, Judge Advocate Office, Court-Martial of William H. Beck, File QQ-1107, Testimony of S. E. Stilwell, p. 409, RG 153, NA.

38. Nye, *Carbine and Lance*, 148–50.

39. Ibid., 150; Maj. E. L. N. Glass, *The History of the Tenth Cavalry, 1866–1921* (Fort Collins, Colo.: Old Army Press, 1972), 95.

40. U.S. Department of War, QGR, Reports of Persons Hired, Fort Sill, I.T., September 1871, RG 92, NA.

41. U.S. Department of War, James Ray, Fort Larned Commander, to Asst. Adj. Gen. Fort Leavenworth, January 31, 1872, "Report of Expedition to retrieve Body of Private

Franklin Winston at Medicine Lodge, Kansas," Records of Department of Missouri, Letters Received, Continental Commands, AGO, RG 393, NA.

42. Ibid.

43. Testimony of S. E. Stilwell, December 29, 1896, Anadarko, Okla., Sen. Doc. 34, 55th Cong., 1st Sess., 3559, Investigation of the Affairs at the Kiowa, Comanche and Apache Indian Reservation, 237.

44. Wayne Gard, *The Chisholm Trail* (Norman: University of Oklahoma Press, 1954), 79–81, 182–85.

45. QGR, Report of Persons Hired, Fort Sill, I.T., July 1871, no. 169, RG 92, NA.

46. Nye, *Carbine and Lance*, 158–60; Andrist, *The Long Death*,176–77.

47. Nye, *Carbine and Lance*, 158–60.

48. Ibid.

49. Carter, *On the Border with Mackenzie*, 349–72; quotation on p. 372.

50. Ibid.

51. QGR, Reports of Persons Hired, Fort Sill, I.T., December 1872, April 1873, RG 92, NA.

52. Post Returns, Fort Sill, I.T., May 1873, AGO, RG 94, NA.

53. Homer K. Davidson, *Black Jack Davidson, a Cavalry Commander on the Western Frontier: The Life of General John W. Davidson* (Glendale, Calif.: Arthur H. Clark, 1974), 172, 176; Post Returns, Fort Sill, I.T., August–September 1873, AGO, RG 94, NA.

54. A. W. Dimock, *Wall Street and the Wilds* (New York: Outing Publishing, 1915), 232–64.

55. Ibid.

56. Ibid.

57. Ibid., 279–82.

58. Ibid., 283–84. See also Thomas C. Battery, *The Life and Adventures of a Quaker among the Indians* (1875; reprint, Norman: University of Oklahoma Press, 1968), 195–205; Davidson, *Black Jack Davidson*, 179–83; Nye, *Carbine and Lance*, 168–77; Thomas W. Kavanagh, *Comanche Political History: An Ethnohistorical Perspective, 1706–1875* (Lincoln: University of Nebraska Press, 1996), 5, 437–43.

59. Endorsement of S. E. Stilwell by T. A. Baldwin, March 5, 1896, p. 5, Stilwell Pension Testimony, May 22, 1896.

Chapter 7. The Red River War

1. See James L. Haley, *The Buffalo War: The History of the Red River Indian Uprising of 1874* (Garden City, N.Y.: Doubleday, 1976), 95–168; Leckie and Leckie, *The Buffalo Soldiers*, 113–41; Utley, *Frontier Regulars*, 219–35; Nye, *Carbine and Lance*, 187–242.

2. Stilwell Pension Testimony, May 22, 1896; Post Returns, 1800–1916, Fort Sill, I.T., September 1874, Record of Events, AGO, RG 94, NA.

3. Frederick W. Rathjen, *The Texas Panhandle Frontier*, rev. ed. (Lubbock: Texas Tech University Press, 1998), 122–64; Nye, *Carbine and Lance*, 187–242; T. Lindsay Baker and Billy R. Harrison, *Adobe Walls: The History and Archeology of the 1874 Trading*

Post (College Station: Texas A&M University Press, 1986), 3–74; Hämäläinen, *The Comanche Empire*, 336–40.

4. Special Orders No. 34, February 22, 1874, Fort Sill, I.T., 1869–74, vol. 2, Fort Sill Museum; Post Returns, Fort Sill, I.T., February 28, 1874, Record of Events, AGO, RG 94, NA.

5. Marriage Book, Jackson County, Ind., Marriage License of Charlotte Stilwell to Isaac Wiseman, February 13, 1874, Marriage Book G, p. 123.

6. Leckie and Leckie, *The Buffalo Soldiers*, 113–16; Paul H. Carlson, *The Buffalo Soldier Tragedy of 1877* (College Station: Texas A&M University Press, 2003), 40–46.

7. Nye, *Carbine and Lance*, 191.

8. An endorsement by Owen Jay Sweet, Stilwell Pension Testimony, May 22, 1896.

9. Ibid.

10. Charles E. Campbell, "Down among the Red Men," *Collections of the Kansas State Historical Society* 17 (1926–28): 643–47. There is some confusion in the historical record, for John Murphy, longtime employee at the Cheyenne agency, claimed in his 1918 reminiscences that he rode overnight to carry the dispatch from Miles to Davidson. See John Murphy, "Reminiscence of the Washita Campaign and the Darlington Indian Agency," *Chronicles of Oklahoma* 1 (1921–23): 274.

11. J. W. Davidson to Assistant Adjutant General, Department of Texas, Letters received by office of the Adjutant General (1871–80), filed with 2815 AGO 1874, Microfilm No. 666 (Roll 159), RG 94, NA.

12. QGR, Persons Employed and Hired, Fort Sill, I.T., July 1874, Box 453, No. 55, RG 92, NA; Post Returns, Fort Sill, July 1874, Record of Events, AGO, RG 94, NA.

13. Special Orders No. 102, July 8, 1874, Fort Sill, I.T., 1869–74, vol. 1, Fort Sill Museum.

14. Campbell, "Down among the Red Men," 646.

15. Ibid., Nye, *Carbine and Lance*, 191.

16. Campbell, "Down among the Red Men, 646–47.

17. Ibid.; Post Returns, Fort Sill, I.T., July 1874, Record of Events, AGO, RG 94, NA.

18. Post Returns, Fort Sill, I.T., July 1874, Record of Events, AGO, RG 94, NA; Leckie, *The Buffalo Soldiers*, 118; Utley, *Frontier Regulars*, 213–14, 219–20; Wooster, *Military and United States Indian Policy*, 152–56.

19. Nye, *Carbine and Lance*, 200–205; Post Returns, Fort Sill, I.T., August 1874, Record of Events, AGO, RG 94, NA.

20. John H. Nankivell, *The History of the Twenty-Fifth Regiment United States Infantry, 1869–1926* (Fort Collins, Colo.: Old Army Press, 1927, 1972), 24–26; Leckie, *The Buffalo Soldiers*, 120–25.

21. Nye, *Carbine and Lance*, 206–10; Leckie, *The Buffalo Soldiers*, 120–25; Utley, *Frontier Regulars*, 220–21.

22. James W. Grahame, Tales of the Texas Border manuscript, ch. 19, pp. 463–64, Manuscript Collections, Texas State Library and Archives, Austin.

23. Ibid.; QGR, Persons Employed and Hired, Fort Sill, I.T., October–November 1874, RG 92, NA.

24. Rathjen, *Texas Panhandle Frontier*, 164–66; Andrist, *The Long Death*, 192–93; Wallace, *Ranald Mackenzie on the Texas Frontier*, 124–25.

25. Wallace, *Ranald Mackenzie on the Texas Frontier*, 125–27.

26. Post Returns, Fort Sill, I.T., October 1874, Record of Events, AGO, RG 94, NA; Richard Henry Pratt, *Battlefield and Classroom: Four Decades with the American Indian, 1867–1904*, ed. Robert M. Utley (New Haven, Conn.: Yale University Press, 1964), 68.

27. Utley, *Frontier Regulars*, 219–35.

28. *United States vs. James Henry*, Case No. 88, Western District of Arkansas, Fort Smith, Arkansas.

29. Special Orders 146, Headquarters, Post of Fort Sill, I.T., September 10, 1874, vol. 1, 1874–77, Fort Sill Museum; Post Returns, Fort Sill, I.T., September–October 1874, Record of Events, AGO, RG 94, NA.

30. Joe F. Taylor, ed., "Lieutenant Colonel John W. Davidson, Report of First Fort Sill Expedition to Assistant Adjutant General Department of Texas, October 10, 1874," *Panhandle-Plains Historical Review* 34 (1961): 69–73.

31. Ibid.

32. Miles quoted in Utley, *Frontier Regulars*, 227.

33. Ibid. See also Leckie, *The Buffalo Soldiers*, 133–34.

34. Post Returns, Fort Sill, I.T., November 1874, Record of Events, AGO, RG 94, NA; Utley, *Frontier Regulars*, 227–28.

35. Joe F. Taylor, ed., "Lieutenant Colonel John W. Davidson, Telegram to General C. C. Augur, November 23,1874," *Panhandle-Plains Historical Review* 34 (1961): 109.

36. Stilwell Pension Testimony, May 22, 1896.

37. Joe Taylor, ed., "First Lieutenant Richard Henry Pratt, Report on Scouts in the Second Fort Sill Expedition, November 29,1874," *Panhandle-Plains Historical Review* 34 (1961): 121–26.

38. QGR, Persons Employed and Hired at Fort Sill, I.T., September, October, November 1874, RG 92, NA; Special Order No. 142, Headquarters Fort Sill, I.T., to Post Quartermaster to pay Thirty Dollars to Michael Gordon for services rendered in carrying a dispatch for Wichita Agency to Fort Sill on August 22, 1874, September 4, 1872, vol. 1, 1874–77, Fort Sill Museum.

39. Record of the State of Texas, Clay County District Court, and *State of Texas vs. John Kilmartin, J. Jones, and Jack Stilwell*, charged with disturbing the peace, Grand Jury Indictment, and Trial Record on December 7, 1875, Henrietta, Clay County, Texas.

40. Ibid.

41. Wallace, *Ranald Mackenzie on the Texas Frontier*, 152, 165; Leckie and Leckie, *The Buffalo Soldiers*, 134–35.

42. Carter, *On the Border with Mackenzie*, 520.

43. Joe F. Taylor, ed. "Lieutenant Colonel J. W. Davidson, Fort Sill, I.T. to General C. C. Augur, December 23, 1874," *Panhandle-Plains Historical Review* 34 (1961): 141; and ibid., January 5, 1875, 151.

44. Stilwell Pension Testimony, May 22, 1896.
45. Clay County Register of Marriages, John Kilmartin and Lena Baker, February 13, 1875, Henrietta, Texas.
46. U.S. Department of the Interior, Annual Report of J. W. Haworth, Kiowa and Comanche Agency, I.T., to E. P. Smith, Commissioner of Indian Affairs, September 20, 1875, in Annual Report of the Secretary of the Interior, vol. 1.1 (Washington, D.C.: Government Printing Office, 1875), 774; Post Returns, Fort Sill, I.T., March 1875, Record of Events, AGO, RG 94, NA.
47. Ibid.; Ranald S. Mackenzie to Assistant Adjutant General, Department of Missouri, April 21, 1875, Records of U.S. Army Commands, 1821–1921, RG 393, NA.
48. Mackenzie to AAG, April 21, 1875, RG 392, NA.
49. Ernest Wallace, ed., "The Journal of Ranald S. Mackenzie's Messenger to the Kwahadi Comanches," Red River Valley Historical Review 3, no. 2 (Spring 1978): 229–30.
50. Mackenzie to AAG, April 25, 1875, RG 393, NA; Wallace, "Journal of Mackenzie's Messengers," 227–46; J. J. Strum, "Notes on Travel in Search of the Quah-de-ru band of Comanches," S248/2 DOM 1875 AGO, RG 393, NA.
51. Wallace, "Journal of Mackenzie's Messenger," 230, 238, 241.
52. Carter, On the Border with Mackenzie, 526–29.

Chapter 8. With Ranald Mackenzie at Fort Sill

1. Nye, Carbine and Lance, 243.
2. Special Order 86, Fort Sill, I.T., April 27, 1875, vol. 1, 1874–77, Fort Sill Museum; War Department, Post Returns, Fort Sill, I.T., Record of Events, April 1875, AGO, RG 94, NA; Nye, Carbine and Lance, 231.
3. Mackenzie to Davis, May 7, 1875, Letters Sent, Fort Sill, I.T., Fort Sill Museum; Davis to Mackenzie, May 8, 1875, Letters Received, Fort Sill, I.T., July 11, 1872–June 30, 1875, Fort Sill Museum. See also Wallace, Ranald Mackenzie on the Texas Frontier, 169–71.
4. QGR, Persons Employed or Hired, Fort Sill, I.T., September, October, November 1874, RG 92, NA.
5. Records of District Courts of the United States, Western District of Arkansas, Case File 112, September 8, 1875, RG 21, NA.
6. Ibid., Case File 108, RG 21, NA.
7. Ibid., Case File 408, Common Law Record Book, July 24, 1876–August 1877, RG 21, NA.
8. Post Returns, Fort Sill, I.T., Record of Events, April 1875, AGO, RG 94, NA; Frank F. Finney, "The Osages and Their Agency during the Term of Isaac T. Gibson, Quaker Agent," Chronicles of Oklahoma 36, no. 4 (Winter 1958–59): 426.
9. Finney, "Osages and Their Agency," 245–47.
10. Ibid.; Post Returns, Camp near the Cheyenne Agency, Record of Events, September 1875, AGO, RG 94, NA.
11. V. V. Masterson, The Katy Railroad and the Last Frontier (Columbia: University of Missouri Press, 1988), 132, 143, 172–74; Post Returns, Camp near the Cheyenne Agency, Record of Events, September 1875, AGO, RG 94, NA.

12. Mackenzie to AAG, Department of Missouri, November 8, 1875, Letters Sent, Fort Sill, I.T., Fort Sill Museum; Post Returns, Camp near Cheyenne Agency, Record of Events, October, November, December 1875, AGO, RG 94, NA.

13. Department of War, Fort Sill, I.T., Special Order 270, November 26, 1875, vol. 2, 1874–77, Fort Sill Museum.

14. Mackenzie to Dorst, in the field with Comanche Indians, December 19, 1875, Letters Sent, Fort Sill, I.T., AGO, RG 94, NA.

15. Deposition of S. E. Stilwell, March 30, 1894, *U.S. vs. Texas*.

16. Jean L. Zimmerman, "Colonel Ranald S. Mackenzie at Fort Sill," *Chronicles of Oklahoma* 44 (Spring 1966): 15.

17. Ibid., 13; Mackenzie to U.S. Marshal, Western District of Arkansas, February 18, 1876, Letters Sent, Fort Sill, I.T., AGO, RG 94, NA.

18. Special Order No. 50, March 6, 1876, vol. 2, 1874–77, Fort Sill Museum; Maj. John Kemp Mizner to Capt. Theodore Schwan, Fort Griffin Commander, April 13, 1876, Telegram Sent, Fort Sill, I.T., AGO, RG 94, NA.

19. Deposition of S. E. Stilwell, March 30, 1894, *U.S. vs. Texas*.

20. Olive K. Dixon, *The Life of "Billy" Dixon: Plainsman, Scout, and Pioneer* (Austin, Tex.: State House Press, 1987), 224.

21. Mary Urban Kehoe, "The Educational Activities of Distinguished Catholic Missionaries among the Five Civilized Tribes," *Chronicles of Oklahoma* 24 (Summer 1946): 166, 169, 170.

22. John Michalicka, "First Catholic Church in Indian Territory—1872: St Patrick's Church at Atoka," *Chronicles of Oklahoma* 50 (Winter 1972–73): 482, 483; Joseph F. Murphy, *Tenacious Monks: The Oklahoma Benedictines, 1875–1876, Indian Missionaries, Catholic Founders, Educators, Agriculturists* (Shawnee, Okla.: Benedictine Color Press, St. Gregory Abbey, 1974), 57.

23. Hillary Cassal, "Missionary Tour in the Chickasaw Nation and Western Indian Territory," *Chronicles of Oklahoma* 34, no. 4 (Winter 1956): 408, 409.

24. Chuck Parsons, *Captain John R. Hughes: Lone Star Ranger* (Denton: University of North Texas Press, 2011), 7.

25. Jack Martin, *Border Boss: Captain John R. Hughes—Texas Ranger* (Austin, Tex.: State House Press, 1990), 18.

26. George W. Conover, *Sixty Years in Southwest Oklahoma* (Anadarko, Okla.: N. T. Plummer Book and Job Printer, 1927), 103, 104. Trailing cattle through Indian Territory was not an easy proposition. See Bill Neeley, *The Last Comanche Chief: The Life and Times of Quanah Parker* (New York: John Wiley and Sons, 1995), 187.

27. Robert G. Carter, *The Old Sergeant's Story: Fighting Indians and Bad Men in Texas, 1970–1876* (Bryan, Tex.: J. M. Carroll & Company, 1982), 123.

28. State of Texas, Clay County, A True Bill, No. 37, Foreman of the Grand Jury, Filed August 7, 1874, *The State of Texas vs. Henry H. Whaley and Lena Baker*, charged with adultery, witness for the State, John Whaley, William Whaley, and Lieutenant Cobb.

29. William Charles Taylor, "Henry A. Whaley, First Permanent White Settler of Clay County Texas," *West Texas Historical Association Year Book* 45 (1969):132–35.

30. Ibid.

31. Ibid.

32. Department of War, Records of Person and Articles employed and Hired, Fort Sill, I.T., September, October 1874, Quartermaster General, RG 92, NA.

33. Sharon Standifer Ashton, "Law Enforcement in the Twin Territories: U.S. Marshals, Deputies, and the Indian Police," *Oklahoma Genealogical Society Quarterly* 36, no. 1 (1991): 15.

34. Ibid.

35. Ibid.; Western District of Arkansas, Fort Smith Division, Case File 126, Criminal Defendant Case File for Charles and David McGee, Larceny, 1876, RG 21, National Archives and Records, Southwest Region, Fort Worth.

36. Ashton, "Law Enforcement in the Twin Territories," 15–16; Carter, *Old Sergeant's Story*, 128, 129, 130.

37. General Sheridan, Headquarters, Department of Missouri, to General of the Army William T. Sherman, Washington, D.C., July 25, 1876, Letters Sent, Department of War, AGO, RG 94, NA; Wallace, *Ranald Mackenzie on the Texas Frontier*, 171–72; Zimmerman, "Colonel Mackenzie at Fort Sill," 18.

38. Hatch, Fort Sill Commander, to Assistant Adjutant General, Department of Missouri, Leavenworth, Kansas, August 11, 1876, Letters Sent, Department of War, AGO, RG 94, NA; QGR, Persons Employed and Hired, Fort Sill, August, 1876, RG 92, NA.

39. C. Ross Hume, ed., "Statistical Report of First Ten Years of the Grand Masonic Lodge of Indian Territory, 1874–1884," *Chronicles of Oklahoma* 23 (1945): 171–73.

40. *The Chickasha* (Okla.) *Daily Express*, September 8, 1937; Grand Lodge of Oklahoma Archives, Membership History of S. Stilwell at Elm Springs Lodge No. 7, September 30, 1876, Guthrie.

41. *United States vs. Simpson Everett Stilwell*, Case No. 180, November 11, 1876, U.S. District Court, Western District of Arkansas, Fort Smith.

42. Ibid.

43. Ibid.

44. Quoted in ibid.

Chapter 9. In Arizona and West Texas

1. U.S. Congress, House Executive Document 144, 52nd Cong., 1st Sess., 2955. Claims of Deputy Marshals in Oklahoma, Exhibit L, Claim of S. E. Stilwell, April 22, 1889, to May 2, 1890, p. 13; personal letter from Rodney Krajca, National Archives, Southwest Region, to Clint Chambers, May 31, 2000. The letter stated that there is an incomplete series of oaths sworn by deputy marshals who served in the Western District of Arkansas, and Jack Stilwell's name is not listed there. See also S. W. Harman, *Hell on the Border: He Hanged Eighty-Eight Men* (1898; reprint, Lincoln: University of Nebraska Press, 1992), 46.

2. U.S. District Court, Western District of Arkansas, November Term, 1876, January 4, 1877, Common Law Record Book, July 24, 1876–August 8, 1877, RG 21, NA,

Southwest Region, Fort Worth; U.S. District Court, Western District of Arkansas, U.S. Commissioner Docket 3 W61, 1874–76, Fort Smith, Arkansas, RG 21, NA.

3. *Oklahoma Star* (Caddo), January 13, 1877.

4. Deposition of S. E. Stilwell, March 30, 1894, *U.S. vs. Texas*; Ninth U.S. Census, 1870, Owen Township, Jackson County, Ind., Roll M593, 326, p. 315 (image 134), RG 29, NA.

5. Ninth U.S. Census, 1870, Owen Township, Jackson County, Ind., Roll M593, 326, p. 315 (image 134), RG 29, NA; State of Indiana, Jackson County Clerk, Index to Marriage Records, 1850–1920, Charlotte Stilwell–Isaac Wiseman, February 14, 1874, Book G, p. 123; State of Indiana, Jackson County Clerk, Index to Marriage Records, 1850–1920, Clara Stilwell–William Alexander, October 13, 1876, Book G, p. 415.

6. Kansas Historical Society, Topeka, 1875 Kansas State Census, Microfilm K1-K20.

7. Wichita City Records, 1871–1881, Microfilm #09-1876 XLS, 6096, Kansas Historical Society, Topeka.

8. Kiowa Agency Passes, 1873–74, March 4, 1877, #31, Frank Stillwell, Microfilm KA-K40, Oklahoma Historical Society, Oklahoma City.

9. Constance Wynn Altshuler, *Chains of Command: Arizona and the Army, 1856–1875* (Tucson: Arizona Historical Society, 1981), 126–27; William H. Goetzmann, *Army Exploration in the American West, 1803–1863* (New Haven, Conn.: Yale University Press, 1959, 1965), 287–89.

10. Kitty Jo Parker Nelson, "Prescott: Sketch of a Frontier Capital, 1863–1900," *Arizoniana: Journal of Arizona History* 4, no. 4 (Winter 1963): 22–23.

11. Ibid., 17–19.

12. Ellen McGowan Biddle, *Reminiscences of a Soldier's Wife* (1907; reprint, Mechanicsburg, Penn.: Stackpole Books, 2002), 161–62.

13. QGR, Persons Employed and Hired, Whipple Depot, A.T., July 1877, RG 92, NA.

14. Ray Brandes, "A Guide to the History of the U.S. Army Installations in Arizona, 1849–1886," *Arizona and the West* 1 (1959): 54–55.

15. Stilwell Pension Testimony, May 22, 1896.

16. "Shooting Affray," *Weekly Arizona Miner* (Prescott), October 19, 1877.

17. Tenth U.S. Census, 1880, Charleston Village, Pima, Arizona, Roll 36 (NARA microfilm publication, T9, 1454 rolls), Records of the Bureau of Census, RG 29, NA.

18. See Glen Sample Ely, *The Texas Frontier and the Butterfield Overland Mail, 1858–1861* (Norman: University of Oklahoma Press, 2016), 272.

19. QGR, Persons Employed and Hired, Fort Stockton, Texas, October 1878, RG 92, NA.

20. Col. Benjamin. H. Grierson, Commander District of the Pecos, Fort Concho, Texas, to Assistant Adjutant General, Department of Texas, San Antonio, April 18, 1878, Records of United States Army Continental Commands, 1821–1920, RG 393, NA.

21. Van Valzah, Fort Stockton Commander, to Grierson, Commander District of the Pecos, April 25, 1878, Records of the U.S. Army Continental Commands, 1821–1920, RG 393, NA.

22. Post Returns, Fort Stockton, Tex., April 1878, Returns of United States Military Posts, 1800–1916, Microfilm No. 617, Roll 1230, RG 94, NA (hereafter Post Returns,

Fort Stockton); Gunnar Brune, *Springs of Texas* (Fort Worth, Tex.: Branch-Smith, 1981), 1:362; Marcus Kinevan, *Frontier Cavalryman: Lieutenant John Bigelow with the Buffalo Soldiers in Texas* (El Paso: Texas Western Press, 1998), 124–25.

23. Grierson to Assistant Adjutant General, Department of Texas, September 15, 1878, District of the Pecos, Records of U.S. Army Continental Commands, 1821–1920, RG 393, NA.

24. Ibid.

25. 1st Lt. R. G. Smithers, Assistant Adjutant General, District of the Pecos, to S. E. Stilwell, May 30, 1878, Letters Sent, Records of U.S. Army Continental Commands, 1821–1920, RG 393, NA.

26. Smithers, Assistant Adjutant General, District of the Pecos, to Capt. Norvell, Tenth Cavalry, May 30, 1878, Letters Sent, Records of U.S. Army Continental Commands, 1821–1920, RG 393, NA.

27. See Ely, *Texas Frontier*, 220.

28. Brune, *Springs of Texas*, 1:145–47.

29. Norvell, Camp at Bull Springs, Guadalupe Mountains, Texas, to Acting Assistant Adjutant, District of the Pecos, Fort Concho, June 26, 1878, Letters Received, Records of the U.S. Army Continental Commands, 1821–1920, RG 393, NA.

30. Ibid.

31. Ibid.

32. Ibid.; Norvell to Acting Assistant Adjutant General, District of the Pecos, Fort Concho, July 21, 1878, Letters Received, Records of the U.S Army Continental Commands, 1821–1920, RG 393, NA.

33. Norvell to Acting Assistant Adjutant General, District of the Pecos, Fort Concho, July 21, 1878, Letters Received, Records of the U.S Army Continental Commands, 1821–1920, RG 393, NA.

34. R. G. Smithers, Acting Assistant Adjutant General, Headquarters, District of the Pecos, Fort Concho, to Commanding Officer, Fort Stockton, August 13, 1878, Letters Sent, Records of the U.S. Army Continental Commands, 1821–1920, RG 393, NA.

35. Brune, *Springs of Texas*, 1:90. See also Loyd M. Uglow, *Standing in the Gap: Army Outposts, Picket Stations, and the Pacification of the Texas Frontier, 1866–1886* (Fort Worth: Texas Christian University Press, 2001), 146; Post Returns, Fort Stockton, September–October 1878.

36. McLaughlin, Fort Stockton Commander, to Acting Assistant Adjutant General, District of the Pecos, Fort Concho, Texas, September 4, 1878, Letters Sent, Records of the U.S. Army Continental Commands, 1821–1920, RG 393, NA.

37. Kinevan, *Frontier Cavalryman*, 135.

38. Ibid. 135–36; Uglow, *Standing in the Gap*, 162–164; Post Returns, Fort Stockton, September–October 1878.

39. Kinevan, *Frontier Cavalryman*, 137; Post Returns, Fort Stockton, September–October 1878.

40. Kinevan, *Frontier Cavalryman*, 137–38.

41. Ibid., 138. See also Report of Scouts made by Company B, Tenth Cavalry from September 4, 1878, to November 30, 1878, made by 1st Lt. William Henry Beck to Acting Assistant Adjutant General, District of the Pecos, Fort Concho, Texas, December 21, 1878, U.S. Army Continental Commands, 1821–1920, RG 393, NA (hereafter, Beck, Report of Scouts, December 21, 1878); Post Returns, Fort Stockton, September–October 1878.

42. Kinevan, *Frontier Cavalryman*, 137.

43. Beck, Report of Scouts, December 21, 1878.

44. Kinevan, *Frontier Cavalryman*, 138.

45. Ibid.

46. Beck, Report of Scouts, December 21, 1878.

47. Department of War, the Court-Martial File QQ-1107 of William H. Beck, Judge Advocate Office, RG 153, NA (hereafter, Court-Martial File of William Beck). See also Clint E. Chambers, "S. E. (Jack) Stilwell and the Court-Martial of William H. Beck," *West Texas Historical Association Year Book* 68 (1992): 76–92.

48. Kinevan, *Frontier Cavalryman*, 144.

49. Ibid., 142. For a full discussion of the troubles along the Rio Grande in 1876–78, see Clarence C. Clendenen, *Blood on the Border: The United States Army and the Mexican Irregulars* (New York: Macmillan, 1969), esp. 76–83.

50. Beck, Report of Scouts, December 21, 1878.

51. Ibid.

52. Shirley Ann Leckie, ed., *The Colonel's Lady on the Western Frontier: The Correspondence of Alice Kirk Grierson* (Lincoln: University of Nebraska Press, 1989), 120; Department of War, Endorsements, Maj. N. B. McLaughlin and Col. B. H. Grierson of Lt. William H. Beck's request for a leave of absence, October 26, 1878, District of the Pecos, Record of the U.S. Army Continental Commands, 1821–1920, RG 393, NA.

53. Department of War, Endorsement, Maj. M. B. McLaughlin, of M. F. Price, Assistant Surgeon, request to be relieved from duty under Lt. William H. Beck, Tenth Cavalry, October 1, 1878, District of the Pecos, Records of U.S. Army Continental Commands, 1821–1920, RG 393, NA.

54. Kinevan, *Frontier Cavalryman*, 146–147.

55. Ibid.

56. Ibid.

57. Proceedings of a General Court-Martial, Fort McKavett, Texas, Special Orders No. 169, Headquarters, Department of Texas, San Antonio, September 26, 1877, trial of Sgt. William L. Umbles, convened on October 15,1877; Carlson, *Buffalo Soldier Tragedy*, 131.

58. Alice Grierson to Charles H. Grierson, January 27, 1879, Benjamin H. Grierson Papers, 1927–41 and undated, Southwest Collection/Special Collections Library, Texas Tech University.

59. Court-Martial File of William H. Beck, File QQ-1107, RG 153, NA; Chambers, "Stilwell and the Court-Martial of William H. Beck," 76–92.

60. Post Returns, Orders Received, Fort Stockton, Tex., December 31, 1878, AGO, RG 94, NA.
61. Court-Martial File of William H. Beck, File QQ-1107, RG 153, NA.
62. Ibid.
63. Ibid.; Chambers, "Stilwell and the Court-Martial of William H. Beck," 76–92.
64. Court-Martial File of William H. Beck, File QQ-1107, RG 153, NA.
65. Ibid.
66. Ibid.
67. General Order No. 3, Headquarters, District of the Pecos, July 9, 1880, Records of U.S. Army Continental Commands, 1821–1921, RG 393, NA.
68. George W. Conover, *Sixty Years in Southwest Oklahoma: Autobiography of George W. Conover* (Anadarko, Okla.: N. T. Plummer Book and Job Printer, 1927), 106.

Chapter 10. Chasing Cattle, Trouble, and Wyatt Earp

1. Chambers, "Stilwell and the Court-Martial of William Beck," 90.
2. Archives, M. E. Grand Chapter, Royal Arch Masons of Oklahoma, membership record of S. E. Stilwell, Grand Lodge of Oklahoma, Guthrie.
3. Ninth U.S. Census, 1870, Buchanan County, Mo., Population Schedules, City of St. Joseph, Ward 1, Roll M593–M 762, p. 419, image 23, RG 29, NA.
4. Jackson County Genealogical Society, *Jackson County Indiana, Brownstown Township Cemeteries* (Seymour, Ind.: Rainbow-Miller Printing, 1993), 286.
5. Marriage Book, Jackson County, Ind., Index to Marriages, 1856–1920, Book G, p. 415.
6. State Court Records, State of Indiana, Jackson County Circuit Court, *William Henry Stilwell v. Simpson E. Stilwell et al.*, November Term, 1879.
7. State Court Records, State of Oregon, Union County Circuit Court, *Sarah J. Stilwell vs. William Henry Stilwell*, divorce, May 31, 1884.
8. Conover, *Sixty Years in Southwest Oklahoma*, 104–5; Jim A. Dietrich, *Tomasa: The Tie That Binds: A Story of Three Families* (Owasso, Okla.: private printing, 1993), 14–16. In the authors' personal communication with Jim Dietrich, May 29, 1997, Dietrich described the original Chandler Ranch of 320 acres as east one-half, northeast one-fourth, 33, 5N, 8W (80 acres); northwest one-fourth, 34, 5N, 8W (160 acres); and west one-half, northeast one-fourth, 34, 5N, 8W (80 acres) in Grady County, Oklahoma. See also "The Ranches of Grady County in the last half of the Nineteenth Century as told by George Petty," Anna Lewis Collection, 1803–2005, Series 4, Box 2, Folder 14, Nash Library, University of Science and Arts of Oklahoma, Chickasha.
9. Dietrich, *Tomasa*, 15–16.
10. Hugh D. Corwin, *Comanche and Kiowa Captives in Oklahoma and Texas* (Guthrie, Okla.: Cooperative Publishing, 1959), 105–11.
11. Josiah Butler and J. B. Thoburn, eds., "Pioneer School Teaching at the Comanche-Kiowa Agency, 1870–1873," *Chronicles of Oklahoma* 6, no. 4 (December 1928): 599, 500; William T. Hagen, *United States–Comanche Relations: The Reservation Years* (Norman: University of Oklahoma Press, 1990), 75.

12. Corwin, *Comanche and Kiowa Captives*, 106–7.

13. Dietrich, *Tomasa*, 14–16.

14. Sen. Exec. Doc. 34, 55th Cong., 1st Sess., Investigation of Affairs at the Kiowa, Comanche, and Apache Indian Reservation, Testimony of S. E. Stilwell, December 29, 1896, RG 46, NA.

15. Conover, *Sixty Years in Southwest Oklahoma*, 104–105.

16. Sen. Exec. Doc. 34, 55th Cong., 1st Sess., Investigation of Affairs at the Kiowa, Comanche, and Apache Indian Reservation, Testimony of W. F. Dietrich, December 16, 1896 RG 46, NA.

17. Ibid., Testimony of S. E. Stilwell, December 29, 1896, RG 46, NA. Dietrich had to make Stilwell look bad in order to support George Conover's charges against Baldwin. Stilwell defended Baldwin because of his long association with army officers.

18. Charles F. Colcord, "Reminiscences of Charles F. Colcord, Address at Pioneer Reunion at Medicine Lodge, Kansas, February 9, 1934," *Chronicles of Oklahoma* 12 (1934): 9–10. Stilwell was serving in the Trans-Pecos with the Tenth Cavalry in 1878. In his lecture Colcord told of the Northern Cheyenne band that left the reservation in Indian Territory and moved north through western Kansas in the fall of 1878.

19. Ibid.

20. Grant Forman, "Historical Background of the Kiowa-Comanche Reservation," *Chronicles of Oklahoma* 19, no. 2 (June 1941): 139. See also Robinson, *The Indian Trial*, 182; and Lawrie Tatum, *Our Red Brothers and the Peace Policy of President Ulysses S. Grant* (1899; reprint, Lincoln: University Press, 1970), 202.

21. Conover, *Sixty Years in Southwest Oklahoma*, 121.

22. Dietrich, *Tomasa*, 20–21.

23. *Cheyenne Transporter* (Darlington, I.T.), September 10, 1880.

24. QGR, Persons Hired, Fort Reno, I.T., December 1880–January 1881, Jack Stilwell, guide; and Index to Scouts, Service Record of Jack Stilwell, RG 92, NA.

25. Mollie Hauser to J. D. Miles, January 20,1881, Cheyenne and Arapaho Agents and Agency File, Indian Archives, Oklahoma Historical Society, Oklahoma City. It would be interesting to know if the "J. R. Cook" mentioned in Mollie's letter was John R. Cook, a former bison hunter who years later wrote *The Border and the Buffalo*. Soon after the events described by Mollie, Cook returned to his boyhood home in Kansas and became a temperance advocate. See John R. Cook, *The Border and the Buffalo: An Untold Story of the Southwest Plains* (Austin, Tex.: State House Press, 1989), 2. Mollie Houser was the child of an old army scout, Dick Curtis, who had married a Cheyenne woman. Curtis bet and lost young Mollie in a card game to Herman Hauser at Fort Sill. Houser sent Mollie to a convent in Leavenworth, Kansas, where she was educated and learned to play the piano. At eighteen Mollie and her mother returned to Fort Sill, where she married Hauser, thus keeping an old promise to him. But she refused to live with him as his wife. See Forrestine C. Hooker, *Child of the Fighting Tenth: On the Frontier with the Buffalo Soldiers*, ed. Steve Wilson (New York: Oxford University Press, 2003), 82–86.

26. Hauser to Miles, January 20, 1881.

27. George H. Shrik, "Military Duty on the Western Frontier," *Chronicles of Oklahoma* 47, no. 2 (1969): 124–25; Capt. Hanson H. Crews, Fort Sill Commander, to John D. Miles, Indian Agent, Darlington, I.T., February 21, 1881, Letters Sent, Army Continental Commands, 1820–1920, RG 393, NA.

28. Shrik, "Military Duty on the Western Frontier," 124–25.

29. Crews to Miles, February 21, 1881, Letters Sent, Army Continental Commands, 1820–1920, RG 393, NA; Mollie Hauser to Miles, January 20, 1881, Cheyenne and Arapaho Agents and Agency File, Indian Archives, Oklahoma Historical Society, Oklahoma City.

30. Conover, *Sixty Years in Southwest Oklahoma*, 74–75.

31. *Caldwell* (Kans.) *Post*, July 21, 1881.

32. Roy B. Young, "The Assassination of Frank Stilwell," *Journal, Wild West History Association* 1, no. 4 (August 2008): 16–17.

33. "The body of Frank Stilwell was found riddled with bullets," *Cheyenne Transporter,* March 25, 1882.

34. Ibid.

35. State Court Records, State of Oregon, Union County Circuit Court, *Sarah J. Stilwell vs. William Henry Stilwell,* Divorce, May 31, 1884.

36. Deposition of S. E. Stilwell, August 19, 1897, Pension Request of Mariah Stilwell.

37. Conover, *Sixty Years in Southwest Oklahoma*, 105.

38. Deposition of S. E. Stilwell, August 19, 1897, Pension Request of Mariah Stilwell.

39. Keith L. Bryant Jr., *History of the Atchison, Topeka & Santa Fe Railway* (New York: Macmillan, 1974; reprint, Lincoln: University of Nebraska Press, 1982), 79–81.

40. "Shooting Affray," *Weekly Arizona Miner* (Prescott), October 19, 1877.

41. Richard W. Fulton, "Millville-Charleston, Cochise County, 1878–1889," *Journal of Arizona History* 7 (1966): 17.

42. Roy B. Young, *Cochise County Cowboy War: A Cast of Characters* (Apache, Okla.: Young and Sons Enterprises, 1999), 80, 120; "Frank Stilwell," *San Diego Union*, March 25, 1882; William B. Shillingberg, *Tombstone, A.T.: A History of Early Mining, Milling, and Mayhem* (Spokane, Wash.: Arthur H. Clark, 1999), 320.

43. Josephine Sarah Marcus Earp, *I Married Wyatt Earp: The Recollections of Josephine Sarah Marcus Earp,* ed. Glenn G. Boyer (Tucson: University of Arizona Press, 1976), 68.

44. Casey Tefertiller, *Wyatt Earp: The Life behind the Legend* (New York: John Wiley & Sons, 1997), 227; Paula Mitchell Marks, *And Die in the West: The Story of the O.K. Corral Gunfight* (New York: Morrow, 1989; reprint, Norman: University of Oklahoma Press, 1996), 346–47.

45. "Assassinated," *Los Angeles Times*, March 22, 1882; "Frank Stilwell," *San Diego Union*, March 25, 1882.

46. House Exec. Doc. 58, 47th Cong., 1st Sess., Committee on Territories, Lawlessness in Parts of Arizona, February 2, 1882.

47. "Hotel Arrivals," *Tombstone Daily Nugget*, April 18 and April 23, 1882.

48. "Frank Stilwell," *San Diego Union*, March 25, 1882; "Hotel Arrivals," *Tombstone Daily Nugget*, April 18 and April 23, 1882; Carter, *Old Sergeant's Story*, 116.

49. "The Posse's Pursuit: A Fruitless Search," *Tombstone Daily Nugget*, April 3, 1882; David D. Johnson, *John Ringo, King of Cowboys, His Life and Times from the Hoo Doo War to Tombstone*, 2nd ed. (Denton: University of North Texas Press, 2008), 251.

50. "Letter from Jacob Stilwell," *Arizona Daily Star* (Tucson), April 9, 1882.

51. "Jack Stilwell is here in town," *Arizona Weekly Star* (Tombstone), May 4, 1882.

52. Ibid.

53. Conover, *Sixty Years in Southwest Oklahoma*, 105.

54. David Dary, *Cowboy Culture: A Saga of Five Centuries* (New York: Avon Books, 1981), 311.

55. Ibid.; Philip Ashton Rollins, *The Cowboy: An Unconventional History of Civilization on the Old-Time Cattle Range*, rev. ed. (Norman: University of Oklahoma Press, 1997), 193–95, 206–8; V. H. Whitlock ("Ol' Waddy"), *Cowboy Life on the Llano Estacado* (Norman: University of Oklahoma Press, 1970), 75, 95–98.

56. Court-Martial File of William Beck, File QQ-1107, RG 153, NA; "Account of S. E. (Jack) Stilwell, 1882–1886," in Andrew J. Reynolds Collection, 1880–88, pp. 534, 548, 558, 561, Oklahoma Historical Society Archives, Oklahoma City.

Chapter 11. A Cowboy in Indian Territory

1. State Court Records, State of Oregon, Union County Circuit Court, *Sarah J. Stilwell vs W. H. Stilwell*, Divorce, May 28, 1884.

2. Deposition of S. E. Stilwell, August 19, 1897, Pension Request of Mariah Stilwell, RG 15, NA.

3. Sen. Exec. Doc. 34, 55th Cong., 1st Sess., Investigation of Affairs at the Kiowa, Comanche, and Apache Indian Reservation, Testimony of W. F. Dietrich, December 16, 1896, p. 67, RG 46, NA.

4. "Account of S. E. (Jack) Stilwell, 1882–1886," in Andrew J. Reynolds Collection, 1880–88, pp. 534, 548, 558, 561, Oklahoma Historical Society Archives, Oklahoma City (hereafter "Account of Jack Stilwell," Reynolds Collection, OHSA).

5. Deposition of S. E. Stilwell, August 19, 1897, Pension Request of Mariah Stilwell, RG 15, NA.

6. Ibid.

7. "Shot Dead," *Cheyenne Transporter*, January 28, 1884.

8. See Donald J. Berthrong, *The Cheyenne and Arapaho Ordeal: Reservation and Agency Life in the Indian Territory, 1875–1907* (Norman: University of Oklahoma Press, 1976), 70–71. See also Donald J. Berthrong, "Cattlemen on the Cheyenne-Arapaho Reservation, 1883–1885," *Arizona and the West* 13 (1971): 6–9.

9. Berthrong, "Cattlemen on the Cheyenne-Arapaho Reservation," 8.

10. Edward Everett Dale, "Ranching on the Cheyenne-Arapaho Reservation, 1880–1885," *Chronicles of Oklahoma* 6 (March 1928): 37–40.

11. Sen. Ex. Doc. 54, 48th Cong. 1st sess., Leases of Lands for Cattle Grazing, vol. 4, pp. 72–76.

12. Ibid.; Berthrong, *Cheyenne and Arapaho Ordeal*, 70–71, 75, 77, 92–95.

13. Sen. Ex. Doc. 54, 48th Cong. 1st sess., Leases of Lands for Cattle Grazing, vol. 4, pp. 87–88, 93; Berthrong, *Cheyenne and Arapaho Ordeal*, 94.

14. U.S. Department of the Interior, Records of the Bureau of Indian Affairs, Letters Received, 1881–1907, Special case no. 9, General Philip Sheridan's Report, 1885, and Supporting Documents, RG 75, NA.

15. Dale, "Ranching on the Cheyenne-Arapaho Reservation," 37–40.

16. Helen Bugbee Officer, "A Sketch of the Life of Thomas Sherman Bugbee, 1841–1925," *Panhandle Plains Historical Review* 5 (1932): 18–19.

17. James Cox, *Historical and Biographical Record of the Cattle Industry of Texas and Adjacent Territories* (1895; reprint, New York: Antiquarian Press), 2:534.

18. Lonnie White, ed., "Texas Panhandle News Items, 1877–1885, from the *Dodge City Times*," *Panhandle-Plains Historical Review* 40 (1967): 131.

19. Officer, "Sketch of the Life of Thomas Bugbee," 19.

20. Ibid.

21. Sen. Exec. Doc 34, 55th Cong., 1st sess., Investigation of Affairs at the Kiowa, Comanche, and Apache Indian Reservation, Testimony of S. E. Stilwell, December 29, 1896, p. 237, RG 46, NA.

22. Officer, "Sketch of the Life of Thomas Bugbee," 18.

23. John H. Seger, *Early Days among the Cheyenne and Arapahoe Indians*, ed. Stanley Vestal (Norman: University of Oklahoma Press, 1934, 1979), 89–91.

24. Pauline Durrett Robinson and R. L. Robinson, *Cowman's Country: Fifty Frontier Ranches in the Texas Panhandle, 1876–1887* (Amarillo, Tex.: Paramount Publishing, 1981), 137.

25. Angie Debo, ed., *The Cowman's Southwest: Being the Reminiscences of Oliver Nelson* (Glendale, Calif.: Arthur H. Clark, 1953; reprint, Lincoln: University of Nebraska Press, 1986), 275.

26. John D. Miles, Indian Agent, to Maj. Thomas Bull Dewees, Commanding Fort Reno, I.T., March 30, 1884, Sen. Report 1278, 49th Cong. 1st sess., 1885, Condition of Indians in Indian Territory, vol. 1, p. 632.

27. Laura V. Hamner, *Short Grass and Longhorns* (Norman: University of Oklahoma Press, 1943), 167.

28. Sen. Exec. Doc. 34, 55th Cong., 1st sess., Investigation of Affairs at the Kiowa, Comanche and Apache Reservation, Testimony of W. F. Dietrich, December 16, 1896, p. 60, RG 46, NA.

29. "Shot Dead," *Cheyenne Transporter*, January 28, 1884.

30. Ibid.

31. Ibid. Because Indian women were responsible for the task of butchering and because the carcass was left behind, Stilwell may have argued that Munn was killed by white men.

32. Sen. Report 1278, 49th. Cong., 1st sess., Leases of Land in Indian Territory, Correspondence of John D. Miles, Indian Agent, regarding Kiowa depredations, March 30, 1884, pp. 632, 633.

33. U.S. Department of the Interior, Records of the Bureau of Indian Affairs, Testimony of Dudley P. Brown, Investigation of Purchase of Cattle for Indians by Frank D. Baldwin, Acting Indian Agent for Kiowa and Comanche Reservation, from John W. Light, under Contract, Letters Received, 1881–1907, File no. 26006, 1896, p. 25, RG 75, NA.

34. "Personals Column," *Cheyenne Transporter*, May 10, 1884.

35. "Account of Jack Stilwell," Reynolds Collection, OHSA.

36. "Jack Stillwell," *Cheyenne Transporter*, August 30, 1884.

37. Ibid.; "Account of Jack Stilwell," Reynolds Collection, OHSA, 548, 558, 561.

38. "C. W. Word in the city," and "C. W. Word supervising the shipment of 14,000 head of UU beef," *Caldwell* (Kans.) *Journal*, August 21, 1884.

39. Edward E. Dale, "The Cheyenne-Arapaho Country," *Chronicles of Oklahoma* 20 (December 1942): 365–66.

40. Sen. Exec. Docs. 16 and 17, 48th Cong., 2nd Sess., Leases of Lands in Indian Territory, Testimony of J. S. Morrison, February 1885, p. 162,

41. Sen. Ex. Docs. 16 and 17, 48th Cong., 2nd Sess., Leases of Lands in Indian Territory, Indian Agent John D. Miles to Indian Commissioner Hiram Price, December 13, 1883, p. 110.

42. Ibid., correspondence relating to the military survey of a southern boundary line to settle the dispute between the Kiowa and Cheyenne Indians, pp. 113–18.

43. "Jack Stillwell in from the southwest," *Cheyenne Transporter*, April 30, 1885.

44. Kiowa, Comanche and Wichita Agency, Jesse Lee Hall, Agent, to Charles P. Pearre, Esq., U.S. District Attorney, Waco, Texas, October 2, 1885, Miscellaneous Letters Sent, September 2, 1885–July 15, 1886, Microfilm KA 15, vol. 22, pp. 82–90, Oklahoma Historical Society, Oklahoma City.

45. Ibid.

46. Ibid.

47. Kiowa, Comanche and Wichita Agency, C. W. Word, Word-Bugbee Cattle Company, Henrietta, Texas, to Agent P. B. Hunt, July 4, 1885, Letters Received, Microfilm KA 66, p. 351, Oklahoma Historical Society, Oklahoma City.

48. "Agent Miles' Resignation," *Cheyenne Transporter*, January 28, 1884; Berthrong, *Cheyenne and Arapaho Ordeal*, 98–99.

49. Berthrong, *Cheyenne and Arapaho Ordeal*, 108–13.

50. U.S. Department of the Interior, Records of Bureau of Indian Affairs, Special Case no. 9, Gen. Philip Sheridan's Report, 1885, and Supporting Documents, RG 75, NA; Berthrong, *Cheyenne and Arapaho Ordeal*, 108, 115.

51. "Important Changes, D. B. Dyer resigns, Capt. Jesse M. Lee takes over," *Cheyenne Transporter*, July 30, 1885; Berthrong, *Cheyenne and Arapaho Ordeal*, 115.

52. Berthrong, *Cheyenne and Arapaho Ordeal*, 108–13.

53. Melvin Harrel, "Oklahoma's Million-Acre Ranch," *Chronicles of Oklahoma* 29 (Spring 1951): 74–78.
54. Kiowa, Comanche, and Wichita Agency, Jesse Lee Hall, Agent, to Charles P. Pearre, Esq., U.S. District Attorney, Waco, Texas, October 2, 1885, Miscellaneous Letters Sent, September 2, 1885–July 15, 1886, Microfilm KA 15, vol. 22, pp. 82–90, Oklahoma Historical Society, Oklahoma City.
55. Hillary Cassal, "Missionary Tour in the Chickasaw Nation and Western Indian Territory," *Chronicles of Oklahoma* 34, no. 4 (Winter 1956): 397–409.
56. Ibid. If Quanah Parker spoke English in 1885, it was a largely broken form, for just after the turn of the century he still needed interpreters when he spoke to a group. "Quanah Parker," *The Arrow* (publication of the Carlisle Indian Industrial School, Carlisle, Pa.), March 9, 1905.
57. Cassal, "Missionary Tour in the Chickasaw Nation," 397–409.
58. "Account of the Word-Bugbee Cattle Company, Kansas City, 1884–1885," Andrew J. Reynolds Collection, 1880–88, p. 557, 2006, Oklahoma Historical Society Archives, Oklahoma City.
59. Kansas State Census, Sumner County, Caldwell, 1885, microfilm reels K-1-K-146, Kansas Historical Society, Topeka.
60. *Index to Illinois Marriage Records*, Marriage Index, 1860–1920, Illinois State Public Records, Springfield.
61. Kansas State Census, Sumner County, Caldwell, 1885, microfilm feels K-1-K-146, Kansas Historical Society, Topeka.

Chapter 12. Deputy U.S. Marshal

1. See Berthrong, *Cheyenne and Arapaho Ordeal*, 105–15, 121–23, 127, 130–31.
2. Ibid.
3. Endorsement of Captain J. M. Lee, Stilwell Pension Testimony, May 22, 1896.
4. Alice Marriott, *The Ten Grandmothers* (Norman: University of Oklahoma Press, 1945), 302. The description of Hall is from Wallace and Hoebel, *The Comanches*, 338–39.
5. Kiowa, Comanche and Wichita Agency, Indian Agent Jesse Lee Hall to W. L. Cabell, U.S. Marshal Northern District of Texas, November 21, 1885, Miscellaneous Letters Sent, September 2, 1885–July 15, 1886, Microfilm #KA-15, vol. 22, p. 143, Oklahoma Historical Society, Oklahoma City.
6. "An Interesting Case," *Dallas Morning News*, December 8, 1885; F. Todd Smith, *The Caddos, the Wichitas and the United States, 1846–1901* (College Station: Texas A&M University Press, 1996), 144–46.
7. "An Interesting Case," *Dallas Morning News*, December 8, 1885.
8. "Weatherford," *Dallas Morning News*, December 10, 1885.
9. Capt. Jesse M. Lee, Ninth Infantry, Acting Agent, Cheyenne and Arapaho Agency, Reports of Agents in Indian Territory, August 31, 1886, p. 123, *Annual Report of the Secretary of Interior*, vol. 1, 1886, 332, RG 48, NA. See also Wallace and Hoebel, *The Comanches*, 346–49; Berthrong, *Cheyenne and Arapaho Ordeal*, 113–16.

10. Evan G. Barnard, *A Rider of the Cherokee Strip* (Boston: Houghton Mifflin, 1936), 98–99; "S. E. Stilwell, Hunting Stray Cattle," Records of Employees, Irregular White Labor, Cheyenne Agency, Indian Territory, 1886–89, June 1, 1886, p. 35, Edna May Arnold Archives, Carnegie Library, El Reno, Okla. (hereafter "Stilwell, Hunting Stray Cattle," Arnold Archives, El Reno).

11. Barnard, *Rider of the Cherokee Strip*, 98–103.

12. Ibid.

13. Ibid., 102–3; *United States vs. Samuel Matthews*, U.S. District Court, District of Kansas, 1855–1945, September 6, 1886, Court Record 122, p. 5, Federal Record Center, Kansas City, RG 21, NA; "Stilwell, Hunting Stray Cattle," Arnold Archives, El Reno.

14. Barnard, *Rider of the Cherokee Strip*, 103.

15. Capt. Jesse M. Lee, Acting Agent of the Cheyenne-Arapaho Agency, Reports of Agents in Indian Territory, August 31, 1886, p. 122, *Annual Report of the Secretary of the Interior*, vol. 1, 1888, 332, RG 48, NA.

16. "Sheriff's Report of Prisoners in County Jail, Sedgwick County Jail Calendar, 1886–1907," August 4, 1886, p. 155, Archives, Wichita Public Library, Wichita, Kans.

17. "Stilwell, Hunting Stray Cattle," Arnold Archives, El Reno.

18. Indian Agent G. D. Williams to S. E. Stilwell, September 27, 1886, letters sent from Cheyenne and Arapaho Agency, Volumes C&A-16, p. 345, no. 881, Oklahoma Historical Society, Oklahoma City. For the characterization of Williams, see Berthrong, *Cheyenne and Arapaho Ordeal*, 131.

19. "S. E. Stilwell called in yesterday," *Wichita* (Kans.) *Eagle*, November 30, 1886. In 1881 there was a Mr. Snyder, supposedly a prospector from Colorado, who promoted what was said to be a "silver strike" in the Wichita Mountains near Fort Sill. In the end the Great Silver Strike, as it was called, proved to be only in the mind of the promoter. It was a failure; see Nye, *Carbine and Lance*, 294–96.

20. "S. E. Stilwell, Issue Clerk, at Cantonment," Records of Employees, Irregular White Labor, Cheyenne and Arapaho Agency, I.T., 1886–87, December 7, 1886, p. 37, Edna May Arnold Archives, Carnegie Library, El Reno, Okla. See also Berthrong, *Cheyenne and Arapaho Ordeal*, 244–45; Wallace and Hoebel, *The Comanches*, 338–39.

21. "J. E. Cooley, An Old Citizen Passes Away," *Purcell* (Okla.) *Register*, January 24, 1924.

22. "S. E. Stilwell, preventing and detecting liquor traffic," Records of Employees, Irregular White Labor, Cheyenne and Arapaho Agency, I.T., 1886–87, February 1–28, April 6–30, May 2–31, June 1–10, 1887, p. 50–52, 54, Edna May Arnold Archives, Carnegie Library, El Reno, Okla.

23. Ibid.

24. "Sheriff's Report of Prisoners in County Jail, Sedgwick County, Kansas, Calendar, 1886–1907," 6306-A, May 31–September 8, 1887, p. 157, Archives, Wichita Public Library; "Jack Stilwell came up from territory," *Wichita Eagle*, September 8, 1887.

25. "Sheriff's Report of Prisoners in County Jail, Sedgwick County, Kansas, Calendar, 1886–1907," 6303-A, May 31–September 8, 1887, p. 157, Archives, Wichita Public Library.

26. *United States vs. Mexican Joe, who's* [sic] *full Christian name is unknown*, U.S. District Court, District of Kansas, 1855–1945, September 5, 1887, Court Record 287, Federal Record Center, Kansas City, RG 21, NA.

27. "The Indians," *Wichita Eagle*, September 10, 1886.

28. "The United States District Court," *Wichita Eagle*, September 8 and 11, 1887. The 1888 Sheriff's Report of Prisoners in the County Jail showed that Barney Cooper was discharged from the jail to the penitentiary on September 17, 1888.

29. The 1887 Sheriff's Report of Prisoners in the County Jail, Sedgwick County Jail Calendar, 1886–1907, 6306-A, 1887, p. 157, Archives, Wichita City Library.

30. Barnard, *Rider of the Cherokee Strip*, 92–94.

31. "The old scout and frontiersman, S. E. Stilwell's visit," *Canadian* (Tex.) *Free Press*, February 8, 1888.

32. *United States vs. Kias Williams*, U.S. District Court, District of Kansas, 1855–1945, September Term 1888, Court Record-290, Federal Record Center, Kansas City, RG 21, NA.

33. Ibid.; "U.S. District Court," *Wichita Daily Eagle*, September 14, 1888.

34. *United States vs. James Jones alias Whiskey Jim*, U.S. District Court, District of Kansas, 1852–1945, September Term 1888, Court Record, 490, 491, Federal Record Center, Kansas City, RG 21, NA.

35. "U.S. District Court," *Wichita Daily Eagle*, September 13, 1888.

36. "Trap Sprung," *Wichita Daily Eagle*, November 22, 1888.

37. Louise Barry, "Legal Hangings in Kansas," *Kansas Historical Collections* 35 (August 1950): 300–301.

38. *Eddy* (N.Mex.) *Argus*, June 9, 1893.

39. "Comanche Jack's Record," a December 1888 Wichita letter to the *Saint Louis Post-Dispatch*, undated newspaper clipping from Ed Bartholomew's scrapbook. Bartholomew authored *The Biographical Album of Western Gunfighters* (Houston: Frontier Press of Texas, 1958). See also *Wichita Daily Eagle*, March 7, 1889.

40. "Comanche Jack's Record" appeared in the *Chicago Daily Tribune*, February 24, 1889; *Atchison* (Kans.) *Daily Champion*, March 6, 1889; *Wichita Daily Eagle*, March 7, 1889; *Herald and Torch* (Hagerstown, Md.), March 28, 1889.

41. See, for example, *Wichita Daily Eagle*, March 7, 1889.

42. Capt. Daniel Frasor Stiles to W. H. H. Miller, Attorney General, April 12, 1890, "Compensation of United States Marshals for Services in Indian Territory," House Exec. Doc. 431, 51st Cong, 1st Sess., 4.

43. "Special Detective," Record of the Employees, Irregular white labor, at the Cheyenne and Arapaho Agency, Darlington, I.T., April 1889, p. 92, Edna May Arnold Archives, Carnegie Library, El Reno, Okla.

44. "Report from United States Marshal Jones Regarding the Conduct of his Deputies in Oklahoma, Washington, May 14, 1889," *Galveston Daily News*, May 15, 1889; Stan Hoig, *The Oklahoma Land Rush of 1889* (Oklahoma City: Oklahoma Historical Society, 1989), 102.

45. "Into Oklahoma at Last: Held on the Line," *Chicago Daily Tribune*, April 23, 1889.

46. Hoig, *Oklahoma Land Rush*, 180–181; "Reno City, OK: The Town Site laid out And the Officers Elected," *Wichita Daily Eagle*, May 10, 1889; "Reno City, O.K.," *Oklahoma Capital* (Guthrie), May 11,1898.

47. "Down in Oklahoma," *Wichita Daily Eagle*, Friday, July 12, 1889.

48. Clyde Musgrove, "Word Picture of Evolution from Reno City in the Mud," *El Reno Daily Tribune*, April 22, 1934: Hoig, *Oklahoma Land Rush*, 180–81.

49. "Claims for services as Deputy Marshals in Oklahoma," Exhibit L, *The United States of America to S. E. Stilwell*, p. 13, House Exec. Doc. 144, 52nd Cong. 1st Sess., 2955–144.

50. Ibid.; George Alexander Lambe Interview 10265, Indian Pioneer History, Forman Collection, vol. 107, p. 63, Western History Collection, University of Oklahoma, Norman (hereafter Lambe Interview 10265).

51. Lambe Interview 10265.

52. E. E. Brown Interview 8195, Indian Pioneer History, Forman Collection, vol. 12, p. 39, Western History Collection, University of Oklahoma, Norman. Under the Compromise of 1850, Texas surrendered its lands north of 36 degrees, 30 minutes latitude. The 170-mile stretch of land, a "neutral strip," was left with no state or territorial ownership from 1850 to 1890. It was officially called the "Public Land Strip" but was commonly referred to as "No Man's Land."

53. Ancestry.com, U.S. City Directories, 1822–1995; "J. E. Cooley, An Old Citizen Passes Away," *Purcell Register*, January 24, 1924.

54. "Democratic Convention," *Frisco* (O.T.) *Herald*, June 5, 1890.

55. Irving Geffs (Bunky), *The First Eight Months of Oklahoma City* (1890; reprint, Oklahoma City: Quantum Forms, 1988), 27–29.

56. "Democratic Convention," *Frisco Herald*, July 17, 1890.

57. "Sheriff's Report of Prisoners in County Jail, Sedgwick County, Kansas," Calendar 1886–1907, May 8, 1890, p. 172, Archives, Wichita Public Library; *Minco* (I.T.) *Minstrel*, October 24, 1890.

58. *Minco Minstrel*, January 30, 1891, and February 6, 1891.

59. "Sheriff's Report of Prisoners in County Jail, Sedgwick County, Kansas," 6806-A, Calendar 1886–1907, p. 186, Archives, Wichita City Public Library.

60. *Minco Minstrel*, August 21, 1891.

61. "Mysterious assault," *Minco Minstrel*, February 5, 1892.

62. Oklahoma Town site Case Files, El Reno, O.T., *William Redder and Jorgen Paterson vs. Isaac Jalonick*, Testimony of S. E. Stilwell, November 18, 1892, Case 254, Contest no. 118, Oklahoma Collection, University of Central Oklahoma Libraries, Edmond.

63. Oklahoma Town site Case Files, El Reno, O.T., *D. D. Davisson vs. Henry P Shimer*, Testimony of S. E. Stilwell, December 13, 1892, Case 274, Contest no. 172, Oklahoma Collection, University of Central Oklahoma Libraries, Edmond.

64. Oklahoma Town site Case Files, El Reno, O.T., *D.D. Davisson vs. A.C. McComb*, Testimony of S. E. Stilwell, December 16, 1892, Case 299, Contest no. 171, Oklahoma Collection, University of Central Oklahoma Libraries, Edmond.

Chapter 13. El Reno Police Judge and Friend of Buffalo Bill

1. U.S. Department of Interior, Bureau of Indian Affairs, Deposition of D. P. Brown, 26, Investigation of the Purchase of Cattle for the Indians by Frank D. Baldwin, U.S.A., Acting Indian Agent on the Kiowa and Comanche Reservation, from John W. Light under Contract, Letters Received, 1881–1907, File no. 26006, 1896, RG 75, NA (hereafter Deposition of D. P. Brown).

2. According to D. P. Brown the "genteel element" in El Reno consisted of saloonkeepers and gamblers. Deposition of D. P. Brown; El Reno City Council Minutes, December 16, 1892, p. 232, Edna May Arnold Archives, Carnegie Library, El Reno, Okla. For Stilwell's nickname, see the *Frisco Herald*, June 5, 1890.

3. "Jack Stilwell elected police judge of El Reno," *Minco Minstrel*, December 23, 1892.

4. Police Judge Docket No 2, City of El Reno, December 20, 1892–February 9, 1893; Reports of Police Judge, S. E. Stilwell, to El Reno City Council (monthly) December 1892–March 1893, both Edna May Arnold Archives, Carnegie Library, El Reno.

5. *Oklahoma Herald* (El Reno), January 6, 1893.

6. *Minco Minstrel*, January 27 and February 17, 1893.

7. Ibid., February 24, 1893.

8. *Oklahoma Herald*, March 16, 1893.

9. William T. Hagan, *Indian Police and Judges* (Hartford, Conn.: Yale University Press, 1966; reprint, Lincoln: University of Nebraska Press, 1980), 130; *Oklahoma Herald*, March 23, 1893.

10. El Reno City Council Minutes, April 7, 1893, p. 273, Edna May Arnold Archives, Carnegie Library, El Reno.

11. "Jack Stilwell comes to the Fair," *Chicago Tribune*, May 25, 1893.

12. Richard J. Walsh and Milton S. Salsbury, *The Making of Buffalo Bill, A Study in Heroics* (1928; reprint, Kissimmee, Fla.: International Cody Family Association, 1978), 298–300; QGR, Index to Scouts, S. E. Stilwell and William F. Cody, Fort Hays, Kans., Capt. A. S. Kimball, 1868, RG 92, NA.

13. See Al Jennings, *Through the Shadows with O. Henry* (1921; reprint, Lubbock: Texas Tech University Press, 2000). Jennings and William Sydney Porter (O. Henry) served time together in a Columbus, Ohio, prison.

14. "Hensley-Jennings Feud Ends in a Scrap," *El Reno* (O.T.) *Herald*, June 26, 1893.

15. "Hensley-Jennings, the Disgraceful Affair Still the Theme of Public Comment," *El Reno Herald*, June 27, 1893.

16. "Jennings-Hensley Trial," *El Reno Herald*, June 28, 1893.

17. El Reno City Council Minutes, June 28, 1893, pp. 13–14, Edna May Arnold Archives, Carnegie Library, El Reno.

18. *El Reno* (O.T.) *Eagle*, September 22, 1893.

19. Ibid., September 29, 1893.

20. Ibid. See also the *Dallas Morning News*, November 24, 1893, for a longer version of the article.

21. Joy S. Kasson, *Buffalo Bill's Wild West: Celebrity, Memory, and Popular History* (New York: Hill and Wang, 2000), 101.

22. *El Reno Eagle*, October 13, 1893.

23. Ibid., October 20, 1893.

24. Ibid.

25. Ibid., November 3, 1893.

26. *El Reno* (O.T.) *Democrat*, November 16, 1893, p. 4; interview with J. E. Penner, pioneer businessman, El Reno, Okla., May 13, 1937, by Anna R. Barry, Indian Pioneer History, Foreman Collections, vol. 70, p.154, Oklahoma Historical Society, Oklahoma City.

27. *El Reno Democrat*, November 16, 1893.

28. Dan W. Peery, "General Hugh L. Scott," *Chronicles of Oklahoma* 8, no. 3 (Fall 1930): 355–56.

29. Hugh Lenox Scott, *Some Memories of a Soldier* (New York: Century Co., 1928), 179–80; Virginia W. Johnson, *The Unregimented General: A Biography of Nelson A. Miles* (Boston: Houghton Mifflin, 1962), 352–53.

30. "The Hunters Return," *El Reno Democrat*, November 30, 1893.

31. "Famous Hunting Parties of the Plains by 'Buffalo Bill,'" *The Cosmopolitan* 17, no. 2 (June 1894): 142–43.

32. *Norman* (O.T.) *Transcript*, December 15, 1893; *Blackwell* (O.T.) *Record*, December 21, 1893.

33. "Deaths," *Kansas City Star*, December 5, 1893.

34. Disposition of S. E. Stilwell, August 19, 1897, Pension Request of Mariah Stilwell, RG 15, NA.

35. Index to Illinois Marriage Records, Marriage Index, 1860–1920, Millard Stilwell m. Emma A. Lathaw, September 10, 1884, Jefferson, Ill., State Public Records, Springfield.

36. *El Reno Democrat*, February 15, 1894.

37. Ibid., March 29, 1894.

38. *Wichita Daily Eagle*, March 17, 1894.

39. "United States vs. Texas," *El Reno Democrat*, April 5, 1894; Emma Estill-Harbour, "Greer County," *Chronicles of Oklahoma* 12 (June 1934): 161–62.

40. *El Reno Democrat*, April 5, 1894; Estill-Harbour, "Greer County," 161–63. While Stilwell did not mention them, there probably were old Comanchero trails along the North Fork of the Red River.

41. "The Official List," *El Reno Democrat*, June 7, 1894. Travis F. Hensley, the editor of the *Democrat*, wrote an article that also named his old enemies Al, Ed, and John Jennings as part of the scheme. At the end of the article, Hensley called on all the farmers to vote in the fall. On Stilwell's salary, see El Reno City Council Minutes, May 23, 1894, Edna May Arnold Archives, Carnegie Library, El Reno.

42. *El Reno Democrat*, June 14, 1894.

43. Russell, *Life and Legends of Buffalo Bill*, 378; Stella Adelyne Foote, *Letters from Buffalo Bill* (Billings, Mont.: Foote Publishing Co., 1954), 41–42.

44. "Caught the Indians at War Dance Given before an Edison Kinetoscope," *Dallas Morning News*, September 26, 1894.

45. "Famous Scout in Quincy," *Quincy* (Ill.) *Daily Journal*, October 9, 1894; *El Reno Eagle*, December 13, 1894.

46. *Minco Minstrel*, March 15, 1894.

47. Ibid., April 12, 1895.

48. "Cody bought property in El Reno for Jack Stilwell to Manage," *Perry* (Okla.) *Journal*, June 28, 1904.

49. Ibid.

Chapter 14. Federal Court Commissioner in Anadarko

1. "From the *El Reno Democrat*," *Chickasha* (O.T.) *Express*, January 31, 1895. The position of U.S. commissioner was the precursor to what is now a federal magistrate judge. Commissioners were used to try petty offenses committed on federal property, to issue search warrants and arrest warrants, to determine bail for federal defendants, and to conduct other initial proceedings in federal criminal cases.

2. "Circular Letter to United States Commissioners by Horace Speed, U.S. Attorney," Court Relations, ca. 1890, KA-36, Oklahoma Historical Society, Oklahoma City.

3. *Minco Minstrel*, April 26, 1895.

4. See *El Reno Democrat*, February 15, 1894, and March 29, 1984; see also *Wichita Daily Eagle*, March 17, 1894.

5. John W. Jordan, *Genealogical and Personal History of Western Pennsylvania* (New York: Lewis Historical Publishing Co., 1915), 2:613–14.

6. "Wedded Today; Judge Stilwell Claims His Bride and They Go West at Once," *Braddock* (Pa.) *Daily News*, May 6, 1895.

7. "Jack Stillwell a married man," *Minco Minstrel*, May 17, 1895.

8. *Minco Minstrel*, May 24, 1895.

9. "Personal Column," *Chickasha Express*, July 4, 1895.

10. Fred L. Wenner Collection, Jack Stilwell Manuscript, November 1895, Box 1, F-20, Western History Collections, University of Oklahoma Library, Norman.

11. Robert H. Steinbach, *A Long March: The Lives of Frank and Alice Baldwin* (Austin: University of Texas Press, 1989) 162–63.

12. See Nye, *Carbine and Lance*, 212–14.

13. Kiowa, Comanche and Wichita Agency, Frank B. Farwell, Chief of Police, Kiowa Agency Files, vol. K-42, July 26, 1894, p. 132, Oklahoma Historical Society, Oklahoma City.

14. Hagan, *Indian Police and Judges*, 194; David LaVere, *Contrary Neighbors: Southern Plains and Removed Indians in Indian Territory* (Norman: University of Oklahoma Press, 2000), opposite 137.

15. Paul Nesbitt, "Daniel William Peery, 1864–1940," *Chronicles of Oklahoma* 20, no. 1 (March 1942): 6–7.

16. Dan W. Peery, "The Kiowa's Defiance," *Chronicles of Oklahoma* 13, no. 1 (March 1935): 31.

17. *Minco Minstrel*, August 9, 1895.

18. Ibid.

19. Kiowa, Comanche and Wichita Agency, Marshal E. D. Nix, Guthrie, O.T., to Frank Baldwin, Indian Agent, Anadarko, O.T., August 13, 1895, KA Roll 36, Court Relations,

1865–1906, Oklahoma Historical Society, Oklahoma City; Nix to Baldwin, October 17, 1895, in ibid.

20. "Mr. J. L. Stilwell Dead," *Baldwin* (Kans.) *Republican*, August 16, 1895. See also "Letter from Jacob Stilwell," *Arizona Daily Star* (Tucson), April 9, 1882.

21. Sigmund Schlesinger Collection (1868–1975), S. E. Stilwell, Anadarko, O.T., to Schlesinger, Cleveland, Ohio, August 7, 1895, MS #130, American Jewish Archives, Hebrew Union College, Cincinnati.

22. Clint Chambers, "Dear Sam. . . . The Letters of an Old Army Scout, Jack Stilwell, to Sigmund Schlesinger," *West Texas Historical Association Year Book* 74 (1998): 78.

23. Sigmund Schlesinger Collection (1868–1975), S. E. Stilwell, Anadarko, O.T., to Schlesinger, Cleveland, Ohio, September 5, 1895, MS #130, American Jewish Archives, Hebrew Union College, Cincinnati.

24. Lewis Hornbeck, "Jack Stilwell tamed down to domestic life," *Minco Minstrel*, January 31, 1896.

25. Stilwell Pension Testimony, May 22, 1896.

26. Ibid.

27. William T. Hagan, *United States–Comanche Relations: The Reservation Years* (New Haven, Conn.: Yale University Press, 1976; reprint, Norman: University of Oklahoma Press, 1990), 240–46; William T. Hagan, "Squaw Men on the Kiowa, Comanche, and Apache Reservation," in *The Frontier Challenge*, ed. John G. Clark (Lawrence: University Press of Kansas, 1971), 187–94.

28. Steinbach, *A Long March*, 164.

29. See Jimmy M. Skaggs, *The Cattle-Trailing Industry: Between Supply and Demand, 1866–1890* (Norman: University of Oklahoma Press, 1973), 13, 16–17.

30. U.S. Department of the Interior, Bureau of Indian Affairs, Investigation of Purchase of Cattle for Indians by Frank D. Baldwin, U.S.A., Acting Indian Agent of Kiowa and Comanche Reservation, from John W. Light under Contract, Letters Received, 1881–1907, File no. 26006, 1896, RG 75, NA.

31. Senate Exec. Doc. 34, 55th Cong. 1st Sess., Investigation of Affairs at the Kiowa, Comanche, and Apache Indian Reservation, Testimony of William F. Dietrich, December 16, 1896, pp. 66–78; ibid., Testimony of S. E. Stilwell, December 29, 1896, pp. 237–42, RG 46, NA.

32. Ibid.

33. "United States Court House, Chickasha, Indian Territory," *Chickasha* (I.T.) *Record*, vol. 1, no. 25 (February 6, 1896), 1.

34. Alvin Rucker Collection, "John Samuel Stilwell better known as 'Jack' Stilwell," p. 13, Manuscript Division, Oklahoma Historical Society, Oklahoma City.

35. Del Snaw, "Daring Jack Stilwell, His Larks Were as Audacious as His Exploits Were Courageous," *Daily Oklahoma State Capital* (Guthrie), June 14, 1897. A similar story appeared in the *San Antonio Daily Light*, August 23, 1897.

36. Franklin G. Adams, Letters Sent and Received, Adams to S. E. Stilwell, Anadarko, O.T., September 18, 1897; and S. E. Stilwell, Anadarko, to F. G. Adams, Topeka, September 21, 1897, relating to Arickaree fight (Battle of Beecher Island), History of

Arickaree, T.L.I.S., Kansas Historical Society, Topeka, Kansas; "Survivors to Meet," *Kansas Semi-Weekly Capital* (Topeka), October 8, 1897.

37. Sigmund Schlesinger Collection (1868–1975), S. E. Stilwell, Anadarko, O.T., to Schlesinger, Cleveland, Ohio, MS #130, American Jewish Archives, Hebrew Union College, Cincinnati.

38. W. A. Jones, Commissioner of Indian Affairs, Washington, D.C., to Capt. F. D. Baldwin, Acting Indian agent, Kiowa Agency, O.T., January 3, 1898, Indian Archive, KA-29, vol. K-60, 26, Oklahoma Historical Society, Oklahoma City.

39. "Judge S. E. Stilwell received word that his pension bill passed," *El Reno Globe*, May 27, 1898.

40. Claude Hensley Collection, "Army Scouts and Guides," Box N8, File 5, Western History Collection, Oklahoma University, Norman.

41. "U.S. Commissioner Stillwell Resigned" *El Reno Globe*, October 14, 1898.

42. Criminal Docket of the United States, Cases brought before S. E. Stilwell, U.S. Commissioner, at the Kiowa-Comanche Reservation, 1–91, October 19, 1896–September 28, 1898, Edna May Arnold Archives, Carnegie Library, El Reno.

Chapter 15. In Cody, Wyoming

1. Will Frackelton and Herman Seely, *Sagebrush Dentist* (Chicago: A. C. McClung & Co., 1941; Pasadena, Calif.: Trail's End Publishing, 1947), 168–69.

2. U.S. District Courts, District of Wyoming, Charles F. Manderson, General Solicitor for Burlington & Missouri River Railroad, Omaha, Neb., to Timothy F. Burks, U.S. Attorney, District of Wyoming, Cheyenne, January 9, 1899, RG 21, Federal Records Center, Denver (hereafter Wyoming District Court Records, FRC, Denver); "Notice of Publication that final proof of land claim to be made before S. E. Stilwell, U.S. Commissioner, Cody, Wyoming," *Cody Enterprise*, May 2, 1901.

3. "The Proposed Military Post," *Sheridan* (Wyo.) *Post*, November 3, 1898.

4. "Col. W. F Cody and Judge S. E. Stilwell were in the City Friday night," *Billings* (Mont.) *Gazette*, November 1, 1898.

5. Wyoming District Court Records, Letter of recommendation for S. E. Stilwell, John H. Burford, Chief Justice of the Supreme Court, O.T., to John A, Riner, District Judge for the District of Wyoming, December 17, 1898, RG 21, FRC, Denver.

6. Wyoming District Court Records, Letter of recommendation of S. E. Stilwell, Charles F. Manderson, Solicitor, Burlington & Missouri River Railroad, Omaha, Neb., to T. F. Burk, Esq., Cheyenne, Wyo., January 9, 1899, RG 21, FRC, Denver.

7. Wyoming District Court Records, Letter of recommendation of S. E. Stilwell, Timothy F. Burke, U.S. Attorney, to District Judge John A. Riner, January 14, 1899, RG 21, FRC, Denver.

8. Wyoming District Court Records, Order appointing S. E. Stilwell U.S. Commissioner at Cody, Big Horn County, Wyo., by District Judge John R. Riner, January 14, 1899, RG 21, FRC, Denver.

9. Wyoming District Court Records, Oath of office taken and signed by Simpson E. Stilwell before the Clerk of the District Court, January 14, 1899, RG 21, FRC, Denver.

10. "Judge S.E. Stilwell was in city on this way back to Cody," *Billings Gazette*, January 20, 1899.
11. Twelfth U.S. Census, 1900, Marquette Pct., Big Horn County, Wyo., NA, 1900, T623, 1854 rolls.
12. "Personals," *Billings Gazette*, March 10, 1899.
13. Sigmund Schlesinger Collection (1868–1975), S. E. Stilwell, U.S. Commissioner, Cody, Wyo., to Schlesinger, Cleveland, Ohio, August 13, 1899, MS #130, American Jewish Archives, Hebrew Union College, Cincinnati; Robert E. Bonner, *William F. Cody's Wyoming Empire: The Buffalo Bill Nobody Knows* (Norman: University of Oklahoma Press, 2007), 112–13.
14. Peggy Samuels and Harold Samuels, eds., *The Collected Writings of Frederic Remington* (Garden City, N.Y.: Doubleday, 1979), 397–400; Frederic Remington, "How Stilwell Sold Out," *Collier's Weekly* 24, no. 11 (December 16, 1899): 10–12.
15. Remington, "How Stilwell Sold Out," 10–12.
16. State Court Records, State of Wyoming, Supreme Court, Office of the Clerk, Application of S. E. Stilwell for admission to the Wyoming Bar, February 28, 1900, admitted to the Bar on October 1, 1900, Bar Applications and Actions Record Book, 115, Cheyenne.
17. Bonner, *Cody's Wyoming Empire*, 108–9.
18. Ibid., 120–21.
19. "Local Short Stories," *Cody* (Wyo.) *Enterprise*, November 1, 1900.
20. "Notice for Publication," ibid., May 2, 1901.
21. "Jack Stilwell had died," *El Reno Globe*, November 23, 1900.
22. "Stilwell death Report," *Cody Enterprise*, December 13, 1900.
23. "Jack Stillwell, Noted Scout, Denies That He Is Dead or Intends to Die," *Oklahoma State Capital* (Guthrie), December 26, 1900.
24. "Judge Stilwell at Clark's Fork on legal business," *Cody Enterprise*, May 23, 1901.
25. "Jack Stilwell's strawberry farm," ibid., June 6, 1901.
26. Agnes Chamberlin, Jeannie Cook, and Joanita Monteith, eds., *The Cody Club: A History of the Cody Country Chamber of Commerce* (New York: J. J. Little & Ives Co., 1940; reprint, Cody, Wyo.: Yellow Stone Printing & Design, 1999), 2–3.
27. "Annual Meeting of the Cody Club," *Cody Enterprise*, September 5, 1901.
28. "Judge Stilwell holding court in Cody," ibid., September 15, 1901.
29. "Judge Stilwell very ill," ibid., December 12, 1901.
30. "The condition of Judge Stilwell remains about the same," ibid., January 2, 1902.
31. "Stilwell is slightly better," *Cody Enterprise*, January 16, 1902. A railroad line had reached Cody by November 1901, thus erasing the necessity of a jarring, two-day stagecoach ride to the nearest train station; see "Cody, Wyoming," Wyoming State Historical Society, www.wyohistory.org/encyclopedia/cody-wyoming.
32. "Stilwell to Kansas City," ibid., January 24, 1902; *Wyoming Dispatch* (Cody), January 24, 1902.
33. "Stilwell showing rapid improvement after treatment," ibid., February 7, 1902.
34. "S. E. Stilwell, a cousin of Mrs. J. C. Bare of Media, is visiting here this week," *Baldwin* (Kans.) *Republican*, February 21, 1902.

35. "Jack Stilwell is improving," ibid., March 7, 1902.

36. "Judge Stilwell to return home," *Cody Enterprise*, April 17, 1902.

37. "Stilwell is negotiating for property in Cody," ibid., May 1, 1902.

38. "Judge and Mrs. Stilwell move to Cody," ibid., May 29, 1902.

39. Sigmund Schlesinger Collection (1868–1975), S. E. Stilwell to Schlesinger, Cleveland, Ohio, July 1, 1902, MS #130, American Jewish Archives, Hebrew Union College, Cincinnati.

40. Ibid.

41. "Judge Stilwell up to Marquette," *Wyoming Dispatch*, August 1, 1902.

42. "Judge Stilwell is fast recovering his health," ibid., September 5, 1902.

43. Nelson A. Miles, "Famous Indian Scout Dying," *New York Herald-Sun*, September 21, 1902.

44. "Death of Judge S. E. Stilwell," *Cody Enterprise*, February 19, 1903; Lucille Nichols Patrick, *The Best Little Town by a Dam Site: Cody's First 20 Years* (Cheyenne, Wyo.: Flintlock Publishing, 1968), 59.

45. Patrick, *Best Little Town*, 59.

46. "A Noted Scout Dead," *Baldwin* (Kans.) *Ledger*, February 20, 1903.

47. "Jack Stilwell Crosses the River," *Guthrie* (O.T.) *Daily Leader*, March 9, 1903.

48. "Decided in Favor of Mrs. Stilwell," *Cody Enterprise*, September 24, 1904.

49. Quit Claim Deed, No. 19745, Cody Trading Company to Esther Stilwell, November 17, 1905, Recorded in Book 7 of Deeds, p. 604, Cody, County of Big Horn, State of Wyoming.

50. "Married, Esther Stilwell and Carl Hammitt," *Cody Enterprise*, May 24, 1906.

51. "Ladies of the Episcopal church organize a Guild," ibid., June 28, 1906.

52. William F. Cody, *True Tales of the Plains* (New York: Cupples & Leon Co., 1908), 128–35.

53. Ibid.

54. Malone, *Dictionary of American Biography*, vol. 9, Sewell-Trowbridge, 30.

55. Alvin Rucker Collection, Box 12, File 23, Manuscript Division, Oklahoma Historical Society, Oklahoma City.

56. J. K. Rollinson, Altadena, Calif., to Mary A. McGrath, State Librarian, April 24, 1947, Wyoming Historical Department, Wyoming State Library, Cheyenne.

57. "Disinterment and reburial of Jack Stilwell," Minutes of the Board of Trustees, Riverside Cemetery District, Cody, Wyo., March 12, 1984.

58. *Cody Enterprise*, April 21, 1984.

59. Ibid., May 9 and May 14, 1984.

BIBLIOGRAPHY

Archive and Manuscript Sources

Adams, Franklin G., Letters Sent and Received, 1897. History of Arickaree, T.I.L.S, Kansas Historical Society, Topeka.

Archives of the Wichita Public Library, Wichita, Kans.

Arnold, Edna May, Archives. Carnegie Library, El Reno, Okla.

Arnott, James, Collection. Highlands University Library, Las Vegas, N.Mex.

Brown, George W. "Recollections." Manuscript No. 4, Boot Hill Museum, Dodge City, Kans.

Camp, Walter M., Papers. "An Interview with Scout John Hurst." Manuscript 57, Box 4, Interview Notes, September 11, 1916. Special Collections and Manuscripts, Harold B. Lee Library, Brigham Young University, Provo, Utah.

Cheyenne and Arapaho Agents and Agency File, 1881. Indian Archives, Oklahoma Historical Society, Oklahoma City.

Clark, Ben, Papers. Western History Collection, University of Oklahoma Library, Norman.

Depue, Monette. "Descendants of Joseph E. Stilwell." Personal Communication, May 6, 1998.

Elm Springs Lodge No. 7 Archives. Grand Lodge of Oklahoma, Guthrie, Okla.

Farwell, Frank B. Kiowa Agency Files, vol. K-42, 1894. Oklahoma Historical Society, Oklahoma City.

Forman, Grant, Collection. Western History Collection, University of Oklahoma Library, Norman.

Fort Sill. Special Orders, 1869–74, vols.1 and 2; and Letters Sent and Received, 1875, U.S. Army Field Artillery and Fort Sill Museum, Fort Sill, Okla.

Gabel, Susan Cooley. "Genealogy of the Stilwell-Cooley Family." Personal Communication, April 16, 1998.

Grahame, James W. Tales of the Texas Border manuscript. Manuscript Collections, Texas State Library and Archives, Austin.

Grierson, Benjamin H., Papers. Southwest Collection/Special Collections Library, Texas Tech University, Lubbock.

Hensley, Claude, Collection. Box N8, File 5, Army Scouts and Guides. Western History Collection, University of Oklahoma Library, Norman.

Jones, W. A. Letters Sent. Indian Archive, KA-29, vol. K-60. Oklahoma Historical Society, Oklahoma City.

Kiowa, Comanche and Wichita Agency. Miscellaneous Letters Sent and Received, 1885–86, Microfilm KA-15, vol. 22. Oklahoma Historical Society, Oklahoma City.

Lewis, Anna, Collection, 1803–2005. Nash Library, University of Science and Arts of Oklahoma, Chickasha.

Mead, J. R. Letters Sent, 1908. Manuscript Division, Kansas Historical Society, Topeka.

Nix, Marshal E. D. Letters Sent, 1895, Kiowa Agency Roll 35, Court Relations, 1865–1906, Oklahoma Historical Society, Oklahoma City.

Oklahoma Collection. Oklahoma Town Site Case Files, University of Central Oklahoma Libraries, Edmond.

Reynolds, Andrew J., Collection, 1880–88. Archives, Oklahoma Historical Society, Oklahoma City.

Rogers, Joseph Phelps, Manuscript Collection. Miscellaneous Manuscript Division, Kansas Historical Society, Topeka.

Rollinson, J. K. Letters Sent, 1947. Wyoming Historical Department, Wyoming State Library, Cheyenne.

Rucker, Alvin, Collection. Box 12, File 23. Manuscript Division, Oklahoma Historical Society, Oklahoma City.

Schlesinger, Sigmund, Collection (1868–1975). MS #130. American Jewish Archives, Hebrew Union University, Cincinnati, Ohio.

Speed, Horace. Circular Letter to United States Commissioners. Court Relations, ca. 1890, KA-36, Oklahoma Historical Society, Oklahoma City.

State Court Records, State of Indiana. Jackson County Circuit Court, *William Henry Stilwell vs. Simpson E. Stilwell et al.*, 1879. Brownstown, Ind.

State Court Records, State of Oregon. Union County Circuit Court, *Sarah J. Stilwell vs. William Henry Stilwell*, 1884.

State Court Records, State of Texas. Clay County District Court, Henrietta: *State of Texas vs. Henry H. Whaley and Lena Baker*, 1874; *State of Texas vs. John Kilmartin, J. Jones and Jack Stilwell*, 1875.

State Court Records, State of Wyoming. Bar Applications and Actions Record Book, 1900, Cheyenne.

Stilwell, Frank. Kiowa Agency Passes, Microfilm KA-40. Oklahoma Historical Society, Oklahoma City.

Stilwell, Simpson Everett "Jack." Reference File. Southwest Collection/Special Collections Library, Texas Tech University, Lubbock.

U.S. Department of the Interior. Office of Special Examiner, Bureau of Pensions, Case of Mariah Stilwell, no. 587090, widow of William H. Stilwell, Pvt., Company B, 18th Missouri Infantry, Kansas City, Mo., July 3, 1896, Record Group 15, National Archives.
———. Records of the Bureau of Indian Affairs, National Archives:
Letters Received, 1881–1907, Record Group 75;
Reports of Agents in Indian Territory, 1886, Record Group 48.
U.S. Department of War. Judge Advocate Office, Record Group 153, National Archives:
Court-Martial of William H. Beck, Department of Texas, San Antonio, 1879, File QQ-1107;
Proceedings of General Court-Martial, William Umbles, Department of Texas, Fort McKavett, 1877.
———. Quartermaster General Reports, Record Group 92, National Archives:
Index to Scouts, Service Record, Stilwell, S. E., or Simpson E., In the Field, Fort Hays, Kans., 1870;
Index to Scouts, S. E. Stilwell and William F. Cody, Fort Hays, Kans., 1868;
Reports of Persons and Articles Employed or Hired:
Fort Dodge, Kans., 1867;
Fort Hays, Kans., 1868;
Fort Sill, Indian Territory, 1871–76;
Fort Stockton, Tex., 1878;
Fort Reno, Indian Territory, 1880–81;
Medicine Bluff Creek, Kans., 1869;
Whipple Depot, Ariz., 1877.
———. Organizational Returns, Tenth Cavalry, 1868–69.
———. Returns from United States Military Posts, 1800–1916, Adjutant General's Office, Record Group 94, National Archives:
Fort Davis, Tex., May 1871–May 1882;
Fort Dodge, Kans., June–August 1867;
Fort Reno, Indian Territory, December 1880–January 1881;
Fort Sill, Indian Territory, August 1871–April 1875;
Fort Stockton, Tex., October–December 1878.
———. Records of United States Army Commands. Department of Missouri, Letters Received and Letters Sent, Adjutant General's Office, Record Group 393, National Archives.
———. Records of United States Army Commands, Department of Texas, Selected Letters Received. Record Group 393, National Archives.
———. Records of United States Army Commands, Department of Upper Arkansas, Letters Sent, Record Group 393, National Archives.
———. Records of United States Army Continental Commands, 1821–1920, Record Group 393, National Archives:
Fort Dodge, Kans., 1867;
Fort Hays, Kans., 1867;

Fort Sill, Indian Territory, 1875–76;
Letters Received, Assistant Adjutant General, Department of Texas, 1878;
Letters Received and Letters Sent, Assistant Adjutant General, District of the
    Pecos, 1878.
U.S. District Courts. Records of the District of Kansas, Wichita. Federal Records Center,
    Kansas City, Record Group 21, National Archives:
    United States vs. Jim Jones alias Whiskey Jim, 1888;
    United States vs. Kias Williams, 1888;
    United States vs. Mexican Joe, who's full Christian name is unknown, 1887;
    United States vs. Samuel Matthews, 1886.
———. Records of the District of Wyoming, Cheyenne. Record Group 21, Federal Records
    Center, Denver.
———. Records of the Western District of Arkansas, Fort Smith. Court Records, Southwest
    Branch of the National Archives, Fort Worth, Tex.:
    United States vs. Charles and David McGee, 1876;
    United States vs. Jack Kilmartin and one Stillwell, 1875;
    United States vs. James Henry, 1875;
    United States vs. James Jones, 1875–76;
    United States vs. James Jones and John Kilmartin, 1875;
    United States vs. Simpson E. Stilwell, 1876.
U.S. Supreme Court. *United States vs. State of Texas*, 1894. Deposition of S. E. Stilwell,
    March 31, 1894. Record Group 267, National Archives.
Wenner, Fred L., Collection. Box 1, F-20, Western History Collections, University of
    Oklahoma Library, Norman.
Wichita City Records, 1871–81. Microfilm No. 09-1876 XLS, 60906. Kansas State Historical
    Society, Topeka.
Williams, Gilbert D. Letters Sent, vol. C & A 16, no. 881. Oklahoma Historical Society,
    Oklahoma City.

Government Documents

City Records

"Disinterment and Reburial of Jack Stilwell." *Minutes of the Board of Trustees,* March
    12, 1984, Riverside Cemetery District, Cody, Wyo.
Extracts from Chancery Court Books, 1826–35. Madison County, Ala.
General Index to Deeds and Register of Deeds, 1854–64. Douglas County, Kans., Land
    Records: Book A, 1858; Book C, 1859; Books D and E, 1860; Book E, 1861; and Book
    F, 1864.
Index to Illinois Marriage Records, Marriage Index, 1860–1920, State Public Records,
    Springfield.
Marriage Book. Jackson County, Ind., Book G, 1874, 1876; Book H, 1879.
Marriage Book. Lawrence County, Ind., 1844–51, License No. 907.
Record Book 7. Quit Claim Deed No. 19745, 1905, Cody, Big Horn County, Wyo.
Register of Marriages. Henrietta, Clay County, Tex., 1875.

Territorial Censuses

Kansas State Census, 1875. Brown County, Irving Township.
———, 1885. Sumner County, Caldwell.
———, 1885. Shawnee County, Topeka.
Kansas Territorial Census, 1857. Douglas County, Calhoun Township (later Palmyra Township).
———, 1859. Douglas County, Palmyra Township.

United States Censuses

Fifth Census, 1830. Index to 1830 Census of Alabama.
Sixth Census, 1840. Jackson County, Ind.
Seventh Census, 1850. Pleasant Run Township, Lawrence County, Ind.; Redding Township, Jackson County, Ind.; and District No. 9, Iowa City, Johnson County, Iowa.
Eighth, Census, 1860. Palmyra Township, Douglas County, Kans.; Dallas County, Tex.
Ninth Census, 1870. Palmyra Township, Douglas County, Kans.; Owen Township, Jackson County, Ind.; Ward 1, Saint Joseph, Buchanan County, Mo.
Tenth Census, 1880. Charleston Village, Pima County, Ariz.
Twelfth Census, 1900. Marquette Pct., Big Horn County, Wyo.

U.S. Congressional Records

Department of Interior. *Annual Report of the Secretary of the Interior,* 1875, 1886.
House Exec. Doc. 58, 47th Cong., 1st Sess., Committee on Territories, Lawlessness in Parts of Arizona, February 2, 1882.
House Exec. Doc. 431, 51th Cong. 1st Sess., 1889–90, Compensation of United States Marshals for Service in Indian Territory.
House Exec. Doc. 144, 52nd Cong. 1st Sess., 1889–90, Claims of Deputy Marshals in Oklahoma.
House Exec. Doc. 1060, 54th Cong., 1st Sess., 1896, Committee on Pensions.
Sen. Bill 2728 and Senate Report 667, 54th Cong., 1st Sess., 1896, Senate Committee on Pensions. "A Bill Granting a Pension to Simpson Everett Stilwell."
Sen. Exec. Doc. 54, 48th Cong., 1st Sess., 1884, Leases of Lands for Cattle Grazing.
Sen. Exec. Docs. 16 and 17, 48th Cong. 2nd Sess., 1885, Leases of Lands in Indian Territory.
Sen. Exec. Doc. 1278, 49th. Cong., 1st Sess., 1885, Leases of Lands in Indian Territory.
Sen. Exec. Doc. 34, 55th Cong., 1st Sess., 1896. Investigation of the Affairs at the Kiowa, Comanche and Apache Indian Reservation, RG 46, NA.
Sen. Report 1278, 49th Cong., 1st. Sess., 1885, Condition of Indians in Indian Territory.

Newspapers

Arizona Daily Star (Tucson), 1882
Arizona Weekly Star (Tombstone), 1882
Atchison (Kans.) *Daily Champion,* 1889
Baldwin (Kans.) *Ledger,* 1903
Baldwin (Kans.) *Republican,* 1895, 1902

Billings (Mont.) *Gazette*, 1898–99
Blackwell (O.T.) *Record*, 1893
Braddock (Pa.) *Daily News*, 1895
Caldwell (Kans.) *Journal*, 1884
Caldwell Post, 1881
Canadian Free Press (Tex.), 1888
Cheyenne Transporter (Darlington, I.T.) 1880–85
Chicago Tribune, 1889, 1893
Chickasha (Okla.) *Daily Express*, 1937
Chickasha Express, 1895
Chickasha Record, 1896
Cody (Wyo.) *Enterprise*, 1900–1902, 1904, 1906, 1984
Daily Oklahoma State Capital, (Guthrie), 1897, 1901
Dallas Morning News, 1885, 1894
Eddy (N.Mex.) *Argus*, 1893
El Reno (Okla.) *Daily Tribune*, 1934
El Reno Democrat, 1893, 1894
El Reno Eagle, 1893
El Reno Globe, 1898, 1900
El Reno Herald, 1893
Frisco (O.T.) *Herald*, 1890
Galveston Daily News, 1889
Guthrie (O.T.) *Daily Leader*, 1903
Herald and Torch (Hagerstown, Md.), 1889
Kansas Semi-Weekly Capital (Topeka), 1897
Kansas City Star, 1893, 1909
Los Angeles Times, 1882
Minco (I.T.) *Minstrel*, 1891–96
New York Herald-Sun, 1902
Norman (Okla.) *Transcript*, 1893
Oklahoma Capital (Guthrie) 1889
Oklahoma Herald (El Reno), 1893
Oklahoma Star (Caddo), 1877
Perry (Okla.) *Journal*, 1904
Purcell (Okla.) *Register*, 1924
Quincy (Ill.) *Daily Journal*, 1894
San Antonio Daily Light, 1897
San Diego Union, 1882
Sheridan (Wyo.) *Post*, 1898
Weekly Arizona Miner (Prescott) 1877
Wichita (Kans.) *Daily Eagle*, 1888–89, 1894
Wichita (Kans.) *Eagle*, 1886–87, 1889
Wyoming Dispatch (Cody), 1902

Books and Articles

Adjutant General, U.S. Army. *Chronological List: Actions, &c with Indians from January 15, 1837, to January 1891.* Fort Collins, Colo.: Old Army Press, 1979.

Altshuler, Constance Wynn. *Chains of Command: Arizona and the Army 1856–1875.* Tucson: Arizona Historical Society, 1981.

Ashton, Sharon Standifer. "Law Enforcement in the Twin Territories: Marshals Deputies and the Indian Police." *Oklahoma Genealogical Society Quarterly* 36, no. 1 (1991): 13–16.

Andrist, Ralph K. *The Long Death: The Last Days of the Plains Indians.* New York: Collier Books, 1964.

Armes, George A. *Ups and Downs of an Army Officer.* Washington, D.C.: Deposited in Library of Congress, 1900.

Bailey, Lynn R. *The Bosque Redondo: The Navajo Internment at Fort Sumner, New Mexico, 1863–1868.* Albuquerque, N.Mex.: Westernlore Press, 1998.

Bailey, Mahlon. "Medical Sketch of the Nineteenth Regiment of Kansas Cavalry Volunteers." *Kansas Historical Quarterly* 6 (November 1937): 378–86.

Baker, T. Lindsay, and Billy R. Harrison. *Adobe Walls: The History and Archeology of the 1874 Trading Post.* College Station: Texas A&M University Press, 1986.

Barde, Fred S. "Edmund Gasseau Choteau Guerrier: French Trader." *Chronicles of Oklahoma* 47, no. 4 (Winter 1969–70): 360–76.

Barnard, Evan G. *A Rider of the Cherokee Strip.* Boston: Houghton Mifflin, 1936.

Barry, Louise. "The Ranch at Cimarron Crossing." *Kansas Historical Quarterly* 39, no. 3 (Autumn 1973): 353–61.

———. "Legal Hangings in Kansas." *Kansas Historical Collections* 15 (August 1950): 279–83.

Bartholomew, Ed. *The Biographical Album of Western Gunfighters.* Houston: Frontier Press of Texas, 1958.

Battery, Thomas C. *The Life and Adventures of a Quaker among the Indians.* 1875; reprint, Norman: University of Oklahoma Press, 1990.

Bergem, Teunis G. *Register of the Early Settlers of Kings County, Long Island, N.Y.* Cottonport, N.Y.: Polyanthus, 1973.

Berthrong, Donald J. "Cattlemen on the Cheyenne-Arapaho Reservation, 1881–1885." *Arizona and the West* 13 (1971): 5–32.

———. *The Cheyenne and Arapaho Ordeal: Reservation and Agency Life in Indian Territory, 1875–1907.* Norman: University of Oklahoma Press, 1976, 1992.

Biddle, Ellen McGowan. *Reminiscences of a Soldier's Wife.* 1907; reprint, Mechanicsburg, Pa.: Stackpole Books, 2002.

Billington, Ray Allen. *The Far Western Frontier, 1830–1860.* New York: Harper & Row, 1956.

Blackburn, Forest B. "The 18th Kansas Cavalry and the Indian War." *The Trail Guide* 9, no. 1 (March 1994): 1–15.

Bonner, Robert E. *William F. Cody's Wyoming Empire: The Buffalo Bill Nobody Knows.* Norman: University of Oklahoma Press, 2007.

Brady, Cyrus Townsend. *Indian Fights and Fighters.* 1904; reprint, Lincoln: University of Nebraska Press, 1971.

Brandes, Ray. "A Guide to the History of U.S. Army Installations in Arizona, 1849–1886." *Arizona and the West* 1 (1949): 42–55.

Brigham, Lalla Malog. *The Story of Council Grove on the Santa Fe Trail.* 4th ed. Council Grove, Kans.: Morris County Historical Society, 1989.

Brown, George W. "The Life and Adventures of George W. Brown: Soldier, Pioneer, Scout, Plainsman, and Buffalo Hunter." Edited by William E. Connelley. *Collections of the Kansas State Historical Society* 17 (1926–28): 98–134.

Brune, Gunnar. *Springs of Texas.* Fort Worth: Branch Smith, 1981.

Bryant, Keith L. Jr. *History of the Atchison, Topeka & Santa Fe Railway.* New York: McMillan, 1974; reprint, Lincoln: University of Nebraska Press, 1982.

Burgess, Henderson Lafayette. "The Eighteenth Kansas Volunteer Cavalry and Some Incidents Connected with Its Service on the Plains." *Collections of the Kansas State Historical Society* 13 (1913–14): 534–38.

Burley, Blaine. *Custer, Come at Once! The Fort Hays Years of George and Elizabeth Custer, 1867–1868.* Hays, Kans.: Thomas Moore Prep., 1976.

Butler, Josiah, and J. B. Thoburn, eds. "Pioneer School Teaching at the Comanche Kiowa Agency, 1870–1873." *Chronicles of Oklahoma* 6, no. 4 (December 1928): 483–528.

Cabeza de Baca, Fabiola. *We Fed Them Cactus.* Albuquerque: University of New Mexico Press, 1954.

Campbell, Charles E. "Down among the Red Men." *Kanas State Historical Society Collections* 17 (1926–28): 623–91.

Capps, Benjamin. *The Warren Wagon Train Raid.* New York: Dial, 1974.

Carlson, Paul H. *The Buffalo Soldier Tragedy of 1877.* College Station: Texas A&M University Press, 2003.

——. *The Plains Indians.* College Station: Texas A&M University Press, 1998.

Carriker, Robert C. *Fort Supply, Indian Territory: Frontier Outpost on the Plains.* Norman: University of Oklahoma Press, 1970.

Carter, Robert G. *The Old Sergeant Story: Fighting Indians and Bad Men in Texas, 1870–1876.* Bryan, Tex.: J. M. Carroll & Co., 1982.

——. *On the Border with Mackenzie: Or, Winning West Texas from the Comanches.* 1935; reprint, Austin: Texas State Historical Association, 2003.

Cassal, Hillary. "Missionary Tour of the Chickasaw Nation and Western Indian Territory." *Chronicles of Oklahoma* 34 (Winter 1956): 397–416.

Castel, Albert. *Civil War Kansas: Reaping the Whirlwind.* Lawrence: University Press of Kansas, 1997.

Chalfant, William Y. *Hancock's War: Conflict on the Southern Plains.* Norman, Okla.: Arthur H. Clark, 2010.

Chamberlin, Agnes, Jeannie Cook, and Joanita Monteith, eds. *The Cody Club: A History of the Cody County Chamber of Commerce.* New York: Little & Ives, 1940; reprint, Cody, Wyo.: Yellow Stone Printing & Design, 1999.

Chambers, Clint E. "Dear Sam. . . . The Letters of an Old Army Scout, Jack Stilwell, to Sigmund Schlesinger." *West Texas Historical Association Yearbook* 74 (1998): 75–80.

———. "Fort Sill's Emissaries to the Quahada Comanches on the Staked Plains." *West Texas Historical Association Yearbook* 72 (1996): 58–68.

———. "Jack Stilwell: A Teenager on the Santa Fe Trail, 1863–1866." *West Texas Historical Association Yearbook* 84 (2008): 20–30.

———. "S. E. (Jack) Stilwell and the Court-Martial of William H. Beck." *West Texas Historical Association Yearbook* 68 (1992): 76–92.

———. "Simpson Everett (Jack) Stilwell: Teamster, Hunter, Scout, Cowboy, Lawman, and Judge." *West Texas Historical Association Yearbook* 87 (2011): 84–97.

———. "Surviving Disease on the Plains." *Wagon Tracks, Santa Fe Trail Association Quarterly* 20, no. 3 (May 2006): 10–13.

———. "Texas Panhandle Branches of the Old Santa Fe Trail in the 1860s." *Wagon Tracks, Santa Fe Trail Association Quarterly* 28, no. 1 (November 2013): 10–13.

———. "Using the Deposition of S. E. Stilwell in *The United States vs. State of Texas* to Scout the Life of 'Jack' Stilwell." *West Texas Historical Association Yearbook* 67 (1991): 111–21.

Clapsaddle, David J., and Leo Oliva, eds. *The Fort Riley–Fort Larned Road: A Phenomenon in the Shift from Trail to Rail.* Woodson, Kans.: Santa Fe Trail Association Publication, 1996.

Clark, John G., ed. *The Frontier Challenge.* Lawrence: University of Kansas Press, 1989.

Clendenen, Clarence C. *Blood on the Border: The United States Army and Mexican Irregulars.* New York: Macmillan, 1969.

Cody, William F. "Famous Hunting Parties of the Plains." *Cosmopolitan* 17 (June 1894): 131–43.

———. *True Tales of the Plains.* New York: Cupples & Leon Co., 1908.

Colcord, Charles F. "Reminiscences of Charles F. Colcord, Address at Pioneer Reunion at Medicine Lodge, Kansas, February 9, 1934." *Chronicles of Oklahoma* 12, no.1 (March 1934): 5–18.

Connelley, William E., ed. "John McBee's Account of the Expedition of the Nineteenth Kansas." *Collections of the Kansas State Historical Society* 17 (1926–28): 361–74.

Conover, George W. *Sixty Years in Southwest Oklahoma: Autobiography of George W. Conover.* Anadarko, Okla.: N.T. Plummer Book and Job Printer, 1927.

Cook, John R. *The Border and the Buffalo: An Untold Story of the Southwest Plains.* Austin, Tex.: State House Press, 1989.

Corwin, Hugh D. *Comanche and Kiowa Captives in Oklahoma and Texas.* Guthrie, Okla.: Cooperative Publishing Co., 1959.

Cox, James. *Historical and Biographical Record of the Cattle Industry of Texas and Adjacent Territories.* 2 vols. 1895; reprint, New York: Antiquarian Press, 1959.

Cozzens, Peter, ed. *Eyewitness to the Indian Wars, 1865–1890.* Vol. 3, *Conquering the Southern Plains.* Mechanicsburg, Pa.: Stackpole Books, 2003.

Crawford, Samuel J. *Kansas in the Sixties.* 1911; reprint, Ottawa: Kansas Heritage Press, 1994.

Criqui, Orvel A. *Fifty Fearless Men: The Forsyth Scouts and Beecher Island.* Marceline, Mo.: Walsworth Publishing, 1993.

Custer, Elizabeth Bacon. *Boots and Saddles or, Life in Dakota with General Custer.* Norman: University of Oklahoma Press, 1961.

———. *Following the Guidon.* 1890; reprint, Lincoln: University of Nebraska Press, 1994.

Custer, George Armstrong. *My Life on the Plains or Personal Experiences with Indians.* Norman: University of Oklahoma Press, 1962.

Dale, Edward Everett. "The Cheyenne-Arapaho Country." *Chronicles of Oklahoma* 20 (December 1942): 360–71.

———. "Ranching on the Cheyenne-Arapaho Reservation, 1880–1885." *Chronicles of Oklahoma* 6 (March 1928): 35–59.

Dary, David. *Cowboy Culture: A Saga of Five Centuries.* New York: Avon, 1981.

Davidson, Homer K. *Black Jack Davidson, a Cavalry Commander on the Western Frontier: The Life of General John W. Davidson.* Glendale, Calif.: Arthur H. Clark, 1974.

Debo, Angie, ed. *The Cowman's Southwest: Being the Reminiscences of Oliver Nelson.* Glendale, Calif.: Arthur H. Clark, 1953; reprint, Lincoln: University of Nebraska Press, 1986.

Dietrich, Jim A. *Tomasa: The Tie That Binds: A Story of Three Families.* Owasso, Okla.: private printing, 1993.

Dimock, A. W. *Wall Street and the Wilds.* New York: Outing Publishing, 1915.

Dixon, David. *Hero of Beecher Island: The Life and Military Career of George A. Forsyth.* Lincoln: University of Nebraska Press, 1994.

Dixon, David, and Orvel Criqui. "Forsyth's Scouts: Unit History." *Military Images* 14, no. 6 (May–June 1993): 22–27.

Dixon, Olive K. *The Life of "Billy" Dixon: Plainsman, Scout and Pioneer.* Austin, Tex.: State House Press, 1987.

Earp, Josephine Sarah Marcus. *I Married Wyatt Earp: The Recollections of Josephine Sarah Marcus Earp.* Edited by Glenn G. Boyer. Tucson, Ariz.: University of Arizona Press, 1976.

Ebright, John Kingsley. *The History of Baker University.* Baldwin City, Kans.: Baker University, 1951.

Estill-Harbour, Emma. "Greer County." *Chronicles of Oklahoma* 12, no. 2 (June 1934): 145–62.

Ely, Glen Sample. *The Texas Frontier and the Butterfield Overland Mail, 1858–1861.* Norman: University of Oklahoma Press, 2016.

Field, Ron. *Buffalo Soldiers, 1866–1891.* Oxford, U.K.: Osprey Publishing, 2004.

———. *U.S. Army Frontier Scouts, 1840–1921.* Oxford, U.K.: Osprey Publishing, 2003.

Finney, Frank F. "The Osages and Their Agency during the Term of Isaac T. Gibson, Quaker Agent." *Chronicles of Oklahoma* 36, no. 4 (Winter 1958–59): 416–28.

Foote, Adelyne. *Letters from Buffalo Bill.* Billings, Mont.: Foote Publishing, 1954.

Forman, Grant. "Historical Background of the Kiowa-Comanche Reservation." *Chronicles of Oklahoma* 19, no. 2 (June 1941): 120–40.

Forsyth, George A. *The Story of the Soldier.* New York: D. Appleton, 1900.

———. *Thrilling Days in Army Life.* 1900; reprint, Lincoln: University of Nebraska Press, 1994.

Frackelton, Will, and Herman Seely. *Sagebrush Dentist*. Chicago: A. C. McClung & Co., 1941; reprint, Pasadena, Calif.: Trail's End Publishing, 1947.

Freeman, Winfield. "The Battle of Arickaree." *Collections of the Kansas State Historical Society* 6 (1900): 346–57.

Fulton, Richard W. "Millville-Charleston, Cochise County, 1878–1889." *Journal of Arizona History* 7 (1966): 9–22.

Gard, Wayne. *The Chisholm Trail*. Norman: University of Oklahoma Press, 1954.

Gardner, Mark L. "Malcom Conn: Merchant of the Trail." *Wagon Tracks: Santa Fe Trail Council Newsletter* 1, no. 2 (February 1987): 7–8.

Geffs, Irving "Bunky." *The First Eight Months of Oklahoma City*. 1890; reprint, Oklahoma City: Quantum Corporation, 1988.

Gent, William J. "Simpson Everett Stilwell." In *Dictionary of American Biography*. 20 vols. in 10. American Council of Learned Societies. New York: Charles Scribner & Sons, 1946.

Glass, E. L. N., Maj., comp. and ed. *The History of the Tenth Cavalry, 1866–1921*. Fort Collins, Colo.: Old Army Press, 1972.

Goetzmann, William H. *Army Exploration in the American West, 1803–1863*. New Haven, Conn.: Yale University Press, 1959, 1965.

Greene, Jerome A. *Washita: The U.S. Army and the Southern Cheyenne, 1867–1869*. Norman: University of Oklahoma Press, 2004.

Grey, Annette. *Journey of the Heart: A True Story of Mamie Aguirre (1844–1907), a Southern Belle in the "Wild West."* Markerville, Alberta, Can.: Greywest Books, 2001.

Griswold, Gillett. "Old Fort Sill: The First Seven Years." *Chronicles of Oklahoma* 36 (Spring 1958): 2–14.

Guild, Thelma S., and Harvey L. Carter. *Kit Carson: A Pattern for Heroes*. Lincoln: University of Nebraska Press, 1984.

Hadley, James A. "The Nineteenth Kansas Cavalry and the Conquest of the Plains Indians." *Collections of the Kansas State Historical Society* 10 (1907–8): 428–46.

Hagan, William T. *Indian Police and Judges*. New Haven, Conn.: Yale University Press, 1966; reprint, Lincoln: University of Nebraska Press, 1980.

———. "Squaw Men on the Kiowa, Comanche, and Apache Reservation." In *The Frontier Challenge*, edited by John G. Clark, 187–94. Lawrence: University Press of Kansas, 1971.

———. *United States-Comanche Relations: The Reservation Years*. New Haven, Conn.: Yale University Press, 1976; reprint, Norman: University of Oklahoma Press, 1990.

Hale, Donald R. "The Old Plainsmen's Association." Edited by Mark L. Gardner. *Wagon Tracks: Quarterly Journal of the Santa Fe Trail Association* 14, no. 3 (May 2000): 17–18.

Haley, James L. *The Buffalo War: The History of the Red River Indian Uprising of 1874*. Garden City, N.Y.: Doubleday, 1976.

Hämäläinen, Pekka. *The Comanche Empire*. New Haven, Conn.: Yale University Press, 2008.

Hamner, Laura V. *Short Grass and Longhorns*. Norman: University of Oklahoma Press, 1943.

Harman, S. W. *Hell on the Border: He Hanged Eighty-Eight Men.* Lincoln: University of Nebraska Press, 1992.

Harrel, Melvin. "Oklahoma's Million-Acre Ranch." *Chronicles of Oklahoma* 29 (Spring 1951): 70–78.

Haywood, C. Robert. *Trails South: The Wagon Road Economy in the Dodge City–Panhandle Region.* Norman: University of Oklahoma Press, 1996.

Heitman, Francis H. *Historical Register and Dictionary of the United States Army, 1789–1903.* 2 vols. 1903; reprint, Urbana: University of Illinois Press, 1965.

History of Jackson County Indiana. Evansville, Ind.: Unigraphic, 1972.

Hoig, Stan. *The Oklahoma Land Rush of 1889.* Oklahoma City: Oklahoma Historical Society, 1989.

———. *Tribal Wars of the Southern Plains.* Norman: University of Oklahoma Press, 1993.

———. *White Man's Paper Trail: Grand Councils and Treaty-Making on the Central Plains.* Boulder: University Press of Colorado, 2006.

Hooker, Forrestine C. *Child of the Fighting Tenth: On the Frontier with the Buffalo Soldiers.* Edited by Steve Wilson. New York: Oxford University Press, 2003.

Hume, C. Ross, ed. "Statistical Report of the First Ten Years of the Grand Lodge of Indian Territory, 1874–1884." *Chronicles of Oklahoma* 23, no. 2 (Summer 1945): 171–73.

Huning, Franz. *Trader on the Santa Fe Trail: The Memoirs of Franz Huning.* Albuquerque, N.Mex.: Calvin Horn Publisher, 1972.

Hurst, John. "The Beecher Island Fight: Battle of the Arikaree." *Collections of the Kansas State Historical Society* 15 (1919–22): 530–47.

———. "Scout John Hurst's Story of the Fight." In *The Beecher Island Annual, Sixty-Second Anniversary of the Battle of Beecher Island, September 17–18, 1868,* edited by Robert Lyman, 68–73. Wray, Colo.: Beecher Island Battle Memorial Association, 1930.

Hutton, Paul Andrew. *Phil Sheridan and His Army.* Lincoln: University of Nebraska Press, 1985.

Hyde, George E. *Life of George Bent Written from His Letters.* Edited by Savoie Lottinville. Norman: University of Oklahoma Press, 1968.

Jackson County Genealogical Society. *Jackson County, Indiana, Brownstown Township Cemeteries.* Seymour, Ind.: Rainbow-Miller Printing, 1993.

Jenness, George B. "The Battle of Beaver Creek." *Kansas Historical Collections* 9 (1905–6): 443–52.

Jennings, Al. *Through the Shadows with O. Henry.* 1921; reprint, Lubbock: Texas Tech University Press, 2000.

Johnson, David D. *John Ringo, King of Cowboys: His Life and Times from the Hoo Doo War to Tombstone.* 2nd ed. Denton: University of North Texas Press, 2008.

Johnson, Virginia W. *The Unregimented General: A Biography of Nelson A. Miles.* Boston: Houghton Mifflin, 1962.

Jones, Douglas C. *The Treaty of Medicine Lodge: The Story of the Great Council as Told by Eyewitnesses.* Norman: University of Oklahoma Press, 1966.

Jordan, John W. *Personal History of Western Pennsylvania.* 3 vols. New York: Lewis Historical Publishing Co., 1915.

Kasson, Joy S. *Buffalo Bill's Wild West: Celebrity, Memory, and Popular History.* New York: Hill and Wang, 2000.

Kavanagh, Thomas W. *Comanche Political History: An Ethnohistorical Perspective, 1706–1875.* Lincoln: University of Nebraska Press, 1996.

Kehoe, Mary Urban. "The Educational Activities of Distinguished Catholic Missionaries among the Five Civilized Tribes." *Chronicles of Oklahoma* 24 (Summer 1946): 166–82.

Keim, De Benneville Randolph. *Sheridan's Troopers on the Borders: A Winter Campaign on the Plains.* 1885; reprint, Lincoln: University of Nebraska Press, 1985.

Kelly, Katharine B. *Along the Santa Fe Trail in Douglas County, Kansas: A Brief History of the Seven D.A.R. Marker Sites and Town Sites.* Baldwin City, Kans.: n.p., 1987.

Kenner, Charles L. *The Comanchero Frontier: A History of New Mexican-Plains Indian Relations.* Norman: University of Oklahoma Press, 1994.

Keyes, Sarah. "Western Adventurers and Male Nurses: Indians, Cholera, and Masculinity in Overland Trail Narratives." *Western Historical Quarterly* 43, no. 1 (Spring 2018): 43–64.

Kinevan, Marcus. *Frontier Cavalryman: Lieutenant John Bigelow with Buffalo Soldiers in Texas.* El Paso: Texas Western Press, 1998.

LaVere, David. *Contrary Neighbors: Southern Plains and Removed Indians in Indian Territory.* Norman: University of Oklahoma Press, 2000.

Leckie, Shirley A. *The Colonel's Lady on the Western Frontier: The Correspondence of Alice Kirk Grierson.* Lincoln: University of Nebraska Press, 1989.

———. *Elizabeth Bacon Custer and the Making of a Myth.* Norman: University of Oklahoma Press, 1993.

Leckie, William H. *The Military Conquest of the Southern Plains.* Norman: University of Oklahoma Press, 1963.

Leckie, William H., and Shirley A. Leckie. *The Buffalo Soldiers: A Narrative of the Black Cavalry in the West.* Rev. ed. Norman: University of Oklahoma Press, 2003.

———. *Unlikely Warriors: General Benjamin H. Grierson and His Family.* Norman: University of Oklahoma Press, 1984.

Lee, Wayne C., and Howard C. Raynesfort. *Trails of the Smoky Hill from Coronado to Cow Towns.* Caldwell, Idaho: Caxton Press, 1980.

Lynn, Alvin R. *Kit Carson and the First Battle of Adobe Walls: A Tale of Two Journeys.* Lubbock: Texas Tech University Press, 2014.

Malone, Dumas, ed. *Dictionary of American Biography.* New York: Charles Scriber's Sons, 1934.

Markham, Virginia Gatch. *John Baldwin and Son Milton Come to Kansas: An Early History of Baldwin City, Baker University, and Methodism in Kansas.* Baldwin City, Kans.: Baker University, 1982.

Marks, Paula Mitchell. *And Die in the West: The Story of the O.K. Corral Gunfight.* New York: Morrow, 1989; reprint, Norman: University of Oklahoma Press, 1996.

Marriott, Alice. *The Ten Grandmothers.* Norman: University of Oklahoma Press, 1945.

Martin, Jack. *Border Boss: Captain John R. Hughes-Texas Ranger.* Austin, Tex.: State House Press, 1990.

McCoy, Sondra Van Meter. "Central Kansas Trading Ranches on the Santa Fe Trail." In *Adventures on the Santa Fe Trail*, edited by Leo E. Oliva, 107–22. Topeka: Kansas State Historical Society, 1988.

Mead, James R. *Hunting and Trading on the Great Plains, 1859–1875.* Edited by Schuyler Jones and Ignace Mead Jones. Norman: University of Oklahoma Press, 1986.

Merrill, James M. "General Sherman's Letter to His Son: A Visit to Fort Sill." *Chronicles of Oklahoma* 47 (Summer 1969): 126–31.

Michalicka, John. "First Catholic Church in Indian Territory, 1872: St. Patrick's Church in Atoka." *Chronicles of Oklahoma* 50 (Winter 1972–73): 479–85.

Miller, Dorlis A. "Freighting for Uncle Sam." *Wagon Tracks, Quarterly Journal of the Santa Fe Trail Association* 5 (November 1990): 11–15.

Moore, Horace L. "The Nineteenth Kansas Cavalry." *Collections of the Kansas State Historical Society* 6 (1897–98): 35–51.

Monett, John H. *The Battle of Beecher Island and the Indian War of 1867–1869.* Niwot: University Press of Colorado, 1992.

Murphy, John. "Reminiscence of the Washita Campaign and the Darlington Indian Agency." *Chronicles of Oklahoma* 1 (1921–23): 259–78.

Murphy, Joseph F. *Tenacious Monks: The Oklahoma Benedictine, 1875–1876, Indian Missionaries, Catholic Founders, Educators, Agriculturists.* Shawnee, Okla.: Benedictine Color Press, St. Gregory Abbey, 1974.

Nankivell, John H. *The History of the Twenty-Fifth Regiment United States Infantry, 1869–1926.* Fort Collins, Colo.: Old Army Press, 1927, 1972.

Neeley, Bill. *The Last Comanche Chief: The Life and Times of Quanah Parker.* New York: John Wiley and Sons, 1995.

Nelson, Kitty Jo Parker. "Prescott: Sketch of a Frontier Capital, 1862–1900." *Arizoniana, Journal of Arizona History* 4, no. 4 (Winter 1963): 17–26.

Nesbitt, Paul. "Daniel William Peery, 1864–1940." *Chronicles of Oklahoma* 20, no. 1 (Spring 1942): 3–8.

Nye, Col. W. S. *Carbine and Lance: The Story of Old Fort Sill.* Rev. ed. Norman: University of Oklahoma Press, 1974.

———. *Plains Indian Raiders: The Final Phases of Warfare from the Arkansas to the Red River, with Original Photos by William S. Soule.* Norman: University of Oklahoma Press, 1968.

Oaks, George Washington. *Man of the West: Reminiscences of George Washington Oaks, 1840–1917.* Edited by Ben Jaastad and Arthur Woodward. Tucson: Arizona Pioneers Historical Society, 1956.

Officer, Helen Bugbee. "A Sketch of the Life of Thomas Sherman Bugbee, 1841–1925." *Panhandle-Plains Historical Review* 5 (1932): 8–22.

Oliva, Leo E., ed. *Adventure on the Santa Fe Trail.* Topeka: Kansas State Historical Society, 1988.

———. *Confrontation on the Santa Fe Trail.* Woodston, Kans.: Santa Fe Trail Publications, 1996.

———. *Fort Dodge: Sentry of the Western Plains.* Topeka: Kansas State Historical Society, 1998.

———. *Soldiers on the Santa Fe Trail.* Norman: University of Oklahoma Press, 1967.

Otero, Miguel Antonio. *My Life on the Frontier, 1864–1882.* 1935; reprint, Albuquerque: University of New Mexico Press, 1987.

Parsons, Chuck. *Captain John R. Hughes: Lone Star Ranger.* Denton: University of North Texas Press, 2011.

Patrick, Lucille Nichols. *The Best Little Town by a Dam Site: Cody's First 20 Years.* Cheyenne, Wyo.: Flintlock Publishing, 1968.

Pearson, Henry. "Campaign against Indians in Oklahoma, Kansas, Colorado, New Mexico, and Indian Territory." *Winners of the West* 7, no. 1 (December 1926): 5.

Peery, Dan W. "General Hugh L. Scott." *Chronicles of Oklahoma* 8, no. 3 (Fall 1930): 355–56.

———. "The Kiowa's Defiance." *Chronicles of Oklahoma* 13, no. 1 (March 1935): 30–36.

Pettis, George H. "Kit Carson's Fight with the Comanche and Kiowa Indians." *Order of the Indian Wars* 1, no. 4 (Summer 1980): 1–14.

Pohanka, Brian C., ed. *A Summer on the Plains with Custer's 7th Cavalry: The 1870 Diary of Annie Gibson Roberts.* Lynchburg, Va.: Schroeder Publications, 2004.

Powers, Ramon, and Gene Younger. "Cholera on the Plains: The Epidemic of 1867 in Kansas." *Kansas Historical Quarterly* 37, no. 4 (Winter 1971): 351–93.

Pratt, Richard Henry. *Battlefield and Classroom: Four Decades with the American Indian, 1867–1904.* Edited by Robert M. Utley. New Haven, Conn.: Yale University Press, 1964.

Raber, Charles. "Personal Recollections of Life on the Plains from 1860 to 1866." *Kansas Historical Collections* 16 (1923–25): 316–41.

Rathjen, Frederick W. *The Texas Panhandle Frontier.* Rev. ed. Lubbock: Texas Tech University Press, 1998.

Rattenbury, Richard C. *Hunting the American West: The Pursuit of Big Game for Life, Profit, and Sport, 1800–1900.* Missoula, Mont.: Boone and Crockett Club, 2008.

Remington, Frederic. "How Stilwell Sold Out." *Collier's Weekly* 24, no. 11 (December 16, 1899): 10–12.

Remley, David. *Kit Carson: The Life of an American Border Man.* Norman: University of Oklahoma Press, 2012.

Rister, Carl Coke. "Colonel A. W. Evan's Christmas Day Indian Fight, 1868." *Chronicles of Oklahoma* 16, no. 3 (September 1938): 275–301.

Robinson, Charles M. III. *Bad Hand: A Biography of General Ranald S. Mackenzie.* Austin, Tex.: State House Press, 1993.

———. *The Indian Trial: The Complete Story of the Warren Wagon Massacre and the Fall of the Kiowa Nation.* Spokane, Wash.: Arthur H. Clark, 1997.

———. *Satanta: Life and Death of a War Chief.* Austin, Tex.: State House Press, 1997.

Robinson, Pauline Durrett, and R. L. Robinson. *Cowman's Country: Fifty Frontier Ranches in the Texas Panhandle, 1876–1887.* Amarillo, Tex.: Paramount Publishing, 1981.

Roenigh, Adolph. *Pioneer History of Kansas.* 1933; reprint, Salina, Kans.: Lincoln County Historical Society, 1973.

Rollins, Philip Ashton. *The Cowboy: An Unconventional History of Civilization on the Old-Time Cattle Range.* Rev. ed. Norman: University of Oklahoma Press, 1997.

Russell, Don. *The Lives and Legends of Buffalo Bill.* Norman: University of Oklahoma Press, 1960.

Ryan, John, and Sandy Barnard, eds. *Ten Years with Custer: A 7th Cavalryman's Memoirs.* Fort Collins, Colo.: Citizen Printing, 2001.

Samuels, Peggy, and Harold Samuels, eds. *The Collected Writings of Frederic Remington.* Garden City, N.Y.: Doubleday, 1979.

Schlesinger, Sigmund. "The Beecher Island Fight: Battle of the Arikaree." *Collections of the Kansas State Historical Society* 15 (1919–22): 520–47.

———. "Scout Schlesinger's Story." In *The Beecher Island Annual: Sixty-Second Anniversary of the Battle of Beecher Island, September 17–18, 1868,* edited by Robert Lyman, 75–82. Wray, Colo.: Beecher Island Battle Memorial Association, 1930.

Schubert, Frank N. *Voices of the Buffalo Soldiers: Records, Reports, and Recollection of Military Life and Service in the West.* Albuquerque: University of New Mexico Press, 2003.

Scott, Hugh Lenox. *Some Memories of a Soldier.* New York: The Century, 1928.

Seger, John H. *Early Days among the Cheyenne and Arapahoe Indians.* Edited by Stanley Vestal. Norman: University of Oklahoma Press, 1934.

Sheridan, Philip Henry. *Personal Memoirs of P. H. Sheridan, General United States Army.* 2 vols. 1888; reprint, New York: Da Capo Press, 1992.

Shillingberg, William B. *Dodge City: The Early Years, 1872–1886.* Norman, Okla.: Arthur H. Clark, 2009.

———. *Tombstone, A.T.: A History of Early Mining, Milling, and Mayhem.* Spokane, Wash.: Arthur H. Clark, 1999.

Shrik, George H. "Military Duty on the Western Frontier." *Chronicles of Oklahoma* 47, no. 2 (Summer 1969): 118–25.

Simmons, Marc. *Coronado's Land: Essays on Daily Life in Colonial New Mexico.* Albuquerque: University of New Mexico Press, 1991.

———. *The Old Trail to Santa Fe: Collected Essays.* Albuquerque: University of New Mexico Press, 1996.

———. "The Santa Fe Trail as High Adventure." In *Adventure on the Santa Fe Trail,* edited by Leo E. Oliva, 1–10. Topeka: Kansas State Historical Society, 1988.

Skaggs, Jimmy M. *The Cattle Trailing Industry: Between Supply and Demand, 1886–1890.* Norman: University of Oklahoma Press, 1973.

Smith, Todd. *The Caddos, the Wichitas, and the United States.* College Station: Texas A&M Press, 1996.

Snell, Joseph W., ed. "Diary of a Dodge City Buffalo Hunter, 1872–1873." *Kansas Historical Quarterly* 31 (Winter 1965): 345–95.

Spotts, David L. *Campaigning with Custer.* Edited by E. A. Brininstool. 1928; reprint, Lincoln: University of Nebraska Press, 1988.

Stanley, F. (Francis Louis Crocchiolia). *Fort Bascom: Comanche-Kiowa Barrier.* Pampa, Tex.: Pampa Print Shop, 1961.

Stanley, Henry M. *My Early Travels and Adventures in America.* 1895; reprint, Lincoln: University of Nebraska Press, 1982.

Steinbach, Robert H. *A Long March: The Lives of Frank and Alice Baldwin.* Austin: University of Texas Press, 1989.

Stillwell, John E. *The History of Lieutenant Nicholas Stillwell: Progenitor of the Stilwell Family in America.* New York: n.p., 1929–31.

Strate, David J., ed. *West by Southwest: Letters of Joseph Pratt Allyn, a Traveler along the Santa Fe Trail in 1863.* Dodge City: Kansas Heritage Center, 1984; reprint, Dodge City: Village Press, 1999.

Strom, Charles R. *Charles G. Parker: Wagonmaster on the Santa Fe Trail.* White City, Kans.: Village Press, 1999.

Tatum, Lawrie. *Our Red Brothers and the Peace Policy of President Ulysses S. Grant.* 1899; reprint, Lincoln: University of Nebraska Press, 1970.

Taylor, Joe F., ed. "The Indian Campaign on the Staked Plains, 1874–1875." *Panhandle-Plains Historical Review* 34 (1961): 1–216.

Taylor, William Charles. "Henry A. Whaley, First Permanent White Settler of Clay County, Texas." *West Texas Historical Association Yearbook* 45 (1969): 127–37.

Tefertiller, Casey. *Wyatt Earp: The Life behind the Legend.* New York: John Wiley & Sons, 1997.

Thompson, Gerald. *The Army and the Navajo: The Bosque Redondo Reservation Experiment, 1863–1868.* Tucson: University of Arizona Press, 1976.

Thrasher, Luther A. "Diary of Luther A. Thrasher, Quartermaster Nineteenth Kansas Cavalry, October 15 to December 31, 1868." *Collections of the Kansas State Historical Society* 10 (1907–8): 660–63.

Trafzer, Clifford E. *The Kit Carson Campaign: The Last Great Navajo War.* Norman: University of Oklahoma Press, 1982.

Uglow, Lloyd M. *Standing in the Gap: Army Outposts, Picket Stations, and the Pacification of the Texas Frontier, 1866–1886.* Fort Worth: Texas Christian University Press, 2001.

Utley, Robert M. *Frontier Regulars: The United States Army and the Indian, 1866–1890.* New York: Macmillan, 1973.

———. *The Indian Frontier of the American West, 1846–1890.* Albuquerque: University of New Mexico Press, 1984.

Vance, Randy. "Comancheros." In *Hidden History of the Llano Estacado,* edited by Paul H. Carlson and David J. Murrah, 33–36. Charleston, S.C.: History Press, 2017.

Vilott, Fletcher, as told to A. Bailey. "Withstood the Siege: The Story of Col. George A. Forsythe's Brave Defense at Arickaree Fork." *National Tribune* 26, nos. 4 and 5 (November 5 and 12, 1896): 1–4, 1–8.

Wallace, Ernest, ed. "The Journal of Ranald S. Mackenzie's Messenger to the Kwahadi Comanches." *Red River Valley Historical Review* 3, no. 2 (Spring 1978): 227–46.

———. *Ranald S. Mackenzie on the Texas Frontier.* College Station: Texas A&M University Press, 1993.

Wallace, Ernest, and E. Adamson Hoebel. *The Comanches: Lords of the South Plains.* Norman: University of Oklahoma, 1952.

Walsh, Richard, and Milton S. Salisbury. *The Making of Buffalo Bill: A Study in Heroics.* 1928; reprint, Kissimmee, Fla.: Cody Publications, 1978.

Weeks, Philip. *Farewell, My Nation: The American Indian and the United States, 1820–1890.* Arlington Heights, Ill.: Harlan Davidson, 1990.

Weigley, Russell F. *History of the United States Army.* New York: Macmillan, 1967.

West, Anson. *History of Methodism in Alabama.* Spartanburg, S.C.: Reprint Company, 1983.

West, Elliott. *The Contested Plains: Indians, Goldseekers, and the Rush to Colorado.* Lawrence: University Press of Kansas, 1998.

Wheeler, Homer W. *The Frontier Trail, or From Cowboy to Colonel.* Los Angeles: Times Mirror Press, 1933.

White, Lonnie J., ed. "The Battle of Beecher Island: The Scouts Hold Fast on the Arickaree." *Journal of the West* 5, no. 1 (January 1966): 1–24.

———. *Hostiles and Horse Soldiers: Indian Battles and Campaigns in the West.* Boulder, Colo.: Pruett Publishing, 1972.

———. "The Nineteenth Kansas Cavalry in Indian Territory, 1868–1869: Eyewitness Accounts of Sheridan's Winter Campaign." *Red River Valley Historical Review* 3 (1978): 164–85.

———, comp. and ed. "Texas Panhandle News Items, 1877–1885, from the *Dodge City Times.*" *Panhandle-Plains Historical Review* 40 (1967): 1–162.

Whitlock, V. H. ("Ol' Waddy"). *Cowboy Life on the Llano Estacado.* Norman: University of Oklahoma Press, 1970.

Williams, Harry T. *The History of American Wars: From Colonial Times to World War I.* New York: Alfred A. Knopf, 1981.

Wooster, Robert. *The Military and United States Indian Policy, 1865–1903.* New Haven, Conn.: Yale University Press, 1988.

Young, Roy B. "The Assassination of Frank Stilwell." *Journal, Wild West History Association* 1, no. 4 (August 2008): 16–33.

———. *Cochise County Cowboy War: A Cast of Characters.* Apache, Okla.: Young and Sons Enterprises, 1999.

Zimmerman, Jean L. "Ranald S. Mackenzie at Fort Sill." *Chronicles of Oklahoma* 44 (Spring 1966): 12–21.

INDEX

References to illustrations appear in italic type.

Gent, W. T., 198
Georgia, Civil War, 20
Gibson, George, 69
Gibson, Isaac T., 105–6
gold hunting, 17, 115, 155, 233n19
Gonnigle, A. J., 63
Goodykountz, A. P., 159
Goose Creek, Beecher Island conflict, 50
Gordon, Michael, 88
Gordon, William, 113
Gosper, John, 135
Grace, Jane, 12
Graham, Texas (court case), 153
Graham, William, 9–10
Grahame, James W., 85
Grant, Ulysses S., 32, 71–72
Gravesend village, New Netherlands
  (Stillwell family), 4
Greeley, Horace, 10
Green, L. F. (Prairie City founder), 9–10
Green, Louis (farmer), 11
Greer County conflict, 176
Grey Beard, 87
Grierson, Benjamin H., 72, 73–74, 76, 93,
  117, 118, 123, 126
Griffin, Burt, 154
Griffin, G. Watson, 74
Grimes, William C., 163
Grinnell Station, Indian conflict, 69
Grover, Abner T. "Sharp," 46, 47
Guadalupe Mountains, Indian pursuit
  route, 118
Guerrier, Edmund, 59
guerrilla raids, Civil War, 18
Guthrie, Oklahoma, 163, 164, 183
Guthrie Daily Leader, 198

Habbewithcut (Habby wake), 89–90
Hackberry Point, Sheridan's winter
  campaign, 57–58, 59
Haddon, J. W., 163
Hadley, James A., 64–65

Haile, Pink, 182
Hale, Donald R., 17
Hall, Banks, 10
Hall, Bathney, 10
Hall, Jesse L., 149, 152
Hammitt, Carl D., 192, 195, 198
Hammitt, Esther Hannah (earlier White,
  later Stilwell), 102, 180–81, 186, 190–91,
  192, 196, 198–99, 200
Hancock, Winfield Scott, 31, 34–35
Hannahan, August, 123
Harney, William S., 39–40
Harper's New Monthly Magazine, 183
Hatch, John Porter, 112
Hauser, Herman, 131–32, 227n25
Hauser, Mollie, 131–32, 227n25
Haworth, James, 78, 90, 107, 109–10
hay camp murder, 105
Hayden, C. E., 195
Hays, Rutherford, 125
Hazen, William B., 61–62
health issues, Stilwell's, 116, 117, 138–39,
  145, 151, 165, 183–84, 185, 195–98
Heber Institute, 10
Heck, Harry, 113
Heffner, William, 115
Hennessy, Patrick, 82
Henrietta, Texas (Christmas arrest), 88
Henry, James, 86
Henry, O., 170
Hensley, Travis F., 170, 177, 237n41
Herald and Torch, 160
Herd Creek, cattle grazing, 87
Hickory, 138
Hillsborough, Alabama (Stillwell family),
  5, 6
Hobart, C. H., 166
Hornbeck, Letitia, 164
Hornbeck, Lewis N., 99, 164, 167, 168, 180,
  181, 182, 184–85
Horseback, 84
Horsehead Crossing, Indian pursuit, 119

CPSIA information can be obtained
at www.ICGtesting.com
Printed in the USA
LVHW032033250119
605299LV00002B/280/P